The Hidden Power of Flash Components

The Hidden Power™ of Flash™ Components

J. SCOTT HAMLIN

WITH JARED TARBELL | BRANDON WILLIAMS

SAN FRANCISCO | LONDON

Associate Publisher: DAN BRODNITZ
Acquisitions Editor: MARIANN BARSOLO
Developmental Editor: PETE GAUGHAN
Production Editor: LESLIE E.H. LIGHT
Technical Editor: DANIEL GRAY
Copyeditor: ANAMARY EHLEN
Compositor: KATE KAMINSKI, HAPPENSTANCE TYPE-O-RAMA
CD Coordinator: DAN MUMMERT
CD Technician: KEVIN LY
Proofreaders: EMILY HSUAN AND SARAH TANNEHILL
Indexer: TED LAUX
Interior Designer: CARYL GORSKA
Cover Designer: INGALLS + ASSOCIATES
Cover Illustrator/Photographer: ØIVIND SANDUM

LIBRARY OF CONGRESS CARD NUMBER: 2003101648

ISBN: 0-7821-4210-9

MANUFACTURED IN THE UNITED STATES OF AMERICA

10 9 8 7 6 5 4 3 2 1

Dear Reader,

Thank you for choosing *The Hidden Power of Flash Components*. This book is part of a new wave of Sybex graphics books, all written by outstanding authors—artists and professional teachers who really know their stuff, and have a clear vision of the audience they're writing for.

At Sybex, we're committed to producing a full line of quality digital imaging books. With each title, we're working hard to set a new standard for the industry. From the paper we print on, to the designers we work with, to the visual examples our authors provide, our goal is to bring you the best graphics and digital photography books available.

I hope you see all that reflected in these pages. I'd be very interested in hearing your feedback on how we're doing. To let us know what you think about this, or any other Sybex book, please visit us at `www.sybex.com`. Once there, go to the product page, click on Submit a Review, and fill out the questionnaire. Your input is greatly appreciated.

Best regards,

Daniel A. Brodnitz
Associate Publisher—Graphics
Sybex Inc.

Software License Agreement: Terms and Conditions

The media and/or any online materials accompanying this book that are available now or in the future contain programs and/or text files (the "Software") to be used in connection with the book. SYBEX hereby grants to you a license to use the Software, subject to the terms that follow. Your purchase, acceptance, or use of the Software will constitute your acceptance of such terms. ■ The Software compilation is the property of SYBEX unless otherwise indicated and is protected by copyright to SYBEX or other copyright owner(s) as indicated in the media files (the "Owner(s)"). You are hereby granted a single-user license to use the Software for your personal, noncommercial use only. You may not reproduce, sell, distribute, publish, circulate, or commercially exploit the Software, or any portion thereof, without the written consent of SYBEX and the specific copyright owner(s) of any component software included on this media. ■ In the event that the Software or components include specific license requirements or end-user agreements, statements of condition, disclaimers, limitations or warranties ("End-User License"), those End-User Licenses supersede the terms and conditions herein as to that particular Software component. Your purchase, acceptance, or use of the Software will constitute your acceptance of such End-User Licenses. ■ By purchase, use or acceptance of the Software you further agree to comply with all export laws and regulations of the United States as such laws and regulations may exist from time to time.

Reusable Code in This Book The author(s) created reusable code in this publication expressly for reuse by readers. Sybex grants readers limited permission to reuse the code found in this publication, its accompanying CD-ROM or available for download from our website so long as the author(s) are attributed in any application containing the reusable code and the code itself is never distributed, posted online by electronic transmission, sold, or commercially exploited as a stand-alone product.

Software Support Components of the supplemental Software and any offers associated with them may be supported by the specific Owner(s) of that material, but they are not supported by SYBEX. Information regarding any available support may be obtained from the Owner(s) using the information provided in the appropriate read.me files or listed elsewhere on the media. ■ Should the manufacturer(s) or other Owner(s) cease to offer support or decline to honor any offer, SYBEX bears no responsibility. This notice concerning support for the Software is provided for your information only. SYBEX is not the agent or principal of the Owner(s), and SYBEX is in no way responsible for providing any support for the Software, nor is it liable or responsible for any support provided, or not provided, by the Owner(s).

Warranty SYBEX warrants the enclosed media to be free of physical defects for a period of ninety (90) days after purchase. The Software is not available from SYBEX in any other form or media than that enclosed herein or posted to www.sybex.com. If you discover a defect in the media during this warranty period, you may obtain a replacement of identical format at no charge by sending the defective media, postage prepaid, with proof of purchase to:

SYBEX Inc.
Product Support Department
1151 Marina Village Parkway
Alameda, CA 94501
Web: http://www.sybex.com

After the 90-day period, you can obtain replacement media of identical format by sending us the defective disk, proof of purchase, and a check or money order for $10, payable to SYBEX.

Disclaimer SYBEX makes no warranty or representation, either expressed or implied, with respect to the Software or its contents, quality, performance, merchantability, or fitness for a particular purpose. In no event will SYBEX, its distributors, or dealers be liable to you or any other party for direct, indirect, special, incidental, consequential, or other damages arising out of the use of or inability to use the Software or its contents even if advised of the possibility of such damage. In the event that the Software includes an online update feature, SYBEX further disclaims any obligation to provide this feature for any specific duration other than the initial posting. ■ The exclusion of implied warranties is not permitted by some states. Therefore, the above exclusion may not apply to you. This warranty provides you with specific legal rights; there may be other rights that you may have that vary from state to state. The pricing of the book with the Software by SYBEX reflects the allocation of risk and limitations on liability contained in this agreement of Terms and Conditions.

Shareware Distribution This Software may contain various programs that are distributed as shareware. Copyright laws apply to both shareware and ordinary commercial software, and the copyright Owner(s) retains all rights. If you try a shareware program and continue using it, you are expected to register it. Individual programs differ on details of trial periods, registration, and payment. Please observe the requirements stated in appropriate files.

Copy Protection The Software in whole or in part may or may not be copy-protected or encrypted. However, in all cases, reselling or redistributing these files without authorization is expressly forbidden except as specifically provided for by the Owner(s) therein.

Acknowledgments

Thanks to the team at Sybex, particularly Mariann Barsolo and Pete Gaughan for going beyond being top-notch professionals, but also being a real pleasure to work with. ■ I'd also like to thank Brandon Williams and Jared Tarbell for bringing their impressive skills to this book, both with many of the components and several of the chapters in this book. Thanks also to Brian Finlay for his fun cartoon images in Chapter 1. Also, I'd like to thank Scott Balay for developing some of the components featured in this book. Thanks also to Daniel Gray for his technical editing. ■ I'm also thankful for my son Aidan and my daughter Audrey, who help me keep my perspective with playful breaks. Thank you isn't enough for the support my wife, Staci, has given me as I worked on this book and throughout my so-called career. ■ Finally, out of sheer humble recognition of the raw facts, I am, as always, compelled to acknowledge the source. It is fully by the grace of God that I came to be capable of producing this book. For my part, it is He who should be given all credit—not me.

About the Author

Scott Hamlin is the director of Eyeland Studio, Inc. (`www.eyeland.com`). Eyeland Studio is a web-content design studio specializing in Flash game production and original content design. Eyeland Studio's client list includes Wrigley, Scholastic, Basic Fun, Nokia, Procter & Gamble, Sun Microsystems, MTV Europe, and Nabisco. Eyeland Studio produces several products sold over the Web and on CD. Eyewire.com, one of the world's largest stock imagery companies, carries Eyeland Studio's products.

Scott is also the author/coauthor of numerous books, including *Flash MX ActionScript: The Designer's Edge* with Jennifer Hall.

CONTENTS AT A GLANCE

Introduction ■ **xiii**

Chapter 1 ■ What Are Components and Why Should I Care? **1**

Chapter 2 ■ Using Components 101 **15**

Chapter 3 ■ Using Components with Custom User Interfaces **33**

Chapter 4 ■ Button Components **55**

Chapter 5 ■ Interface Components **73**

Chapter 6 ■ Animation Components **107**

Chapter 7 ■ Text Effect Components **133**

Chapter 8 ■ Video and Audio Components **145**

Chapter 9 ■ Game Components **163**

Chapter 10 ■ Creating Components **179**

Chapter 11 ■ Component Extras **209**

Chapter 12 ■ Troubleshooting Components **223**

Index ■ **241**

Contents

Introduction xiii

Chapter 1 ■ What Are Components and Why Should I Care? 1

The Power of Components 2

All Right, Already!! So What Is a Component Exactly? 3

What Can I Do with Components? 5

Where Can I Find Components? 11

Conclusion 13

Chapter 2 ■ Using Components 101 15

Parameters and the Default Component User Interface 16

Exploring the Component Parameters Panel 18

Exploring the Component Definition Dialog Box and Value Types 21

Experimenting with Values 27

Conclusion 32

Chapter 3 ■ Using Components with Custom User Interfaces 33

The Feel of a Custom UI 34

Using Components with Custom Interfaces 37

Conclusion 52

Chapter 4 ■ Button Components 55

Editing Color and Font Parameters 56

Adjusting the Dimensions of Components with Live Preview 65

Working with MXP Files 68

Conclusion 72

Chapter 5 ■ Interface Components 73

Using Basic ActionScript with Components 74

Editing Click Actions in Components 79

Loading a URL 83

Loading a Movie 86

Using Simple Scripts for Basic Navigation 91

Using the Advanced Script to Call Custom Functions 95

Conclusion 105

Chapter 6 ■ Animation Components 107

The Animation Component Set 108

Customizing the Artwork Used by Animation Components 122

Understanding the Limits of Flash Animation 126

Using Multiple Animation Components 128

Conclusion 132

Chapter 7 ■ Text Effect Components 133

Why Use Component Text Effects? 134

The Text Effect Component Set 134

The FlushTextEffect Component 135

Shared Fonts in Flash MX 138

The ScrambleTextEffect Component 140

The SpinTextEffect Component 142

The FlushTextEffect Component and Shared Fonts 144

Conclusion 144

Chapter 8 ■ Video and Audio Components 145

The Audio Player 146

The Video Player 155

ActionScript Control of the Players 159

Conclusion 162

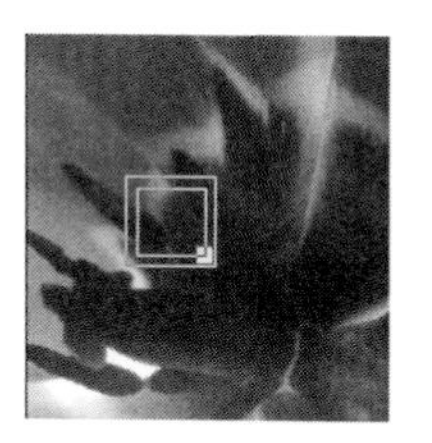

Chapter 9 ■ Game Components 163

Editing a Quiz Component 164

Customizing the Images 168

Editing a Concentration Component 170

Replacing the Images 174

Conclusion 178

Chapter 10 ■ Creating Components 179

The Process of Component Creation 180

Basic Component Creation: The RandomSquares Component 183

Advanced Component Creation: The Particles Component 189

Conclusion 207

Chapter 11 ■ Component Extras 209

Understanding the Role of a Custom UI 210

Designing a Custom UI 210

Creating a Custom Icon 215

Component Live Previews 217

Packaging Components for Mass Release 218

Conclusion 221

Chapter 12 ■ Troubleshooting Components 223

Preloading Components 224

Building Conscientious Components 227

Reducing Errors in Component Creation 233

Common Mistakes with MXP Files 234

Flash 5–Compatible Components 235

Conclusion 240

Index 241

Introduction

Macromedia Flash has progressed far beyond its humble roots. When Flash was initially released, the appeal was based on little more than the advantage of having resolution-independent interfaces and animations download quickly over the Internet. Early users were wowed merely by the ability to implement interactive buttons without the need to program.

In the context of the Web at the time, that was hot stuff, and it started something of a revolution. Now Flash is all but the de facto Internet multimedia standard. As such, people of just about every discipline, from former print graphic designers and HTML programmers to teachers and lawyers, are getting interested in using Flash to bring their visions of Internet paradise to life.

Many of those new to Flash are in for a rude awakening because in order to be competitive on the increasingly sophisticated realm of the Web, Flash files frequently require significant Flash programming (ActionScript). Although ActionScript's genesis was also relatively humble, the scripting language for Flash has evolved into something that is often beyond the means of many beginners to learn in a short amount of time.

Components are the answer to this dilemma. Components allow Flash users to implement functionality that is based on advanced ActionScript without the need to actually work with the ActionScript. While components are not always a comprehensive solution to every conceivable requirement, they can, at the very least, provide significant shortcuts toward the required ends.

Components can also be very useful for advanced Flash users as well as beginners. For advanced programmers, components offer the ability to implement necessary functionality quickly and easily—allowing the programmers to focus on something else.

Who Should Read This Book?

Anyone who is even half serious about working with Flash should learn to utilize components. This book is for anyone who wants to learn how to leverage components to work more effectively and efficiently. The book introduces you to using various types of components. It also shows you how to create components. If you are completely new to components, I recommend that you read the first few chapters before moving to more advanced chapters.

If you are familiar with components and you are interested in some of the specific components featured in this book, there is no reason why you cannot skip ahead to those chapters.

Each chapter features one or more components that you'll find on the accompanying CD. I recommend that you copy these files to your local computer so that you can save any changes and so that you can test any changes that you make.

How Is This Book Organized?

This book begins by assuming that you have little or no experience with components and moves you from relatively basic material through to more advanced topics:

Chapter 1: What Are Components and Why Should I Care? This chapter explains the incredible value of using components and discusses common misconceptions concerning components. Specifically, you'll see that the components that come with Flash MX are not indicative of the real raw potential that components truly embody.

Chapter 2: Using Components 101 We jump right into the basics of using components, especially the difference between the default interface for editing component parameters and a custom interface for editing clip parameters.

Chapter 3: Using Components with Custom User Interfaces Find out how to customize components and how you work with components in general. In particular you will learn the advantages of working with components that utilize a custom user interface.

Chapter 4: Button Components This chapter leads you through using and customizing various button components that come on the companion CD. You'll learn how to use a single component to create several different animated button effects, and also learn about components that utilize Live Preview and how to install an MXP file.

Chapter 5: Interface Components See how to utilize components to create popular interface elements using the example of a drop-down menu. You will learn how to implement navigational elements with components that use `goto` commands, Load Movie, and function calls.

Chapter 6: Animation Components You will see how to generate an array of animation effects. Explore the value of combining duplicates of components that have slightly different parameter settings—or even completely different art or audio resources—to enrich their effects.

Chapter 7: Text Effect Components Chapter 7 looks at components that deal with text and text-related issues. In particular, this chapter shows you how to work with shared fonts and embedded fonts.

Chapter 8: Video and Audio Components This chapter steps you through using and customizing various video and audio components provided on the book's CD. You will learn how to utilize the components to generate controls for video and audio assets, such as volume controls and fast-forward/rewind controls.

Chapter 9: Game Components You'll learn how to utilize the components to generate Flash-based games such as a concentration game and a quiz game. The components featured in this chapter contain more parameters than those featured in previous chapters; they demonstrate that components can be used to create elements that go well beyond the scope of the components that ship with Flash MX.

Chapter 10: Creating Components Move beyond just using, or customizing, premade components, and start building your own. We turn our attention to ActionScript, so you can understand all aspects of how a sample component is created.

Chapter 11: Component Extras Using a component from Chapter 10, I show you how to generate a professional-looking custom user interface for your component. You will also learn how to utilize Live Preview and how to create MXP files.

Chapter 12: Troubleshooting Components In this chapter you will learn how to deal with common troubleshooting issues related to building and testing components. You'll learn how to embed the user interface in your Flash MX components and how to make components compatible with Flash 5.

The "Hidden Power" Components

One of the most important parts of this book are the Flash components provided free on the CD. Not only does the CD carry two dozen components that are explained in detail in the text, but it includes many more components from several Flash developers—over 75 components in all, any one of which will save you time and make your web pages more interesting and effective.

The components featured in this book are not just simple ones used to create radio buttons. They generate rich Flash content such as dynamic animations, navigational systems, and games. However, even components that would be considered "basic" can prove to be very valuable, so, I recommend that you start with the earlier chapters and read the book from beginning to end.

These components are meant for readers of this book only and should not be shared except as described in the CD README file. They must be installed into Flash to be accessible.

Practice Image Files

All images, movies, sound files, or animations used as practice files in the book are provided on the CD so you can work along with the exercises. They are Mac- and Windows-compatible and in common formats supported by Flash. These files are for educational purposes only and should not be used elsewhere except as described in the CD README file.

Compatible with Windows and Macintosh

Just as Macromedia Flash works on both Macintosh and Windows operating systems, the book always gives shortcuts for both so that users on either platform can successfully use the book and techniques. The standard notation for shortcuts gives Mac and Windows keys at the same time: Mac/Windows + (whatever). For example, Command/Ctrl+O will open an image, that is, use Command+O on a Mac, and Ctrl+O on a PC. The following table of keyboard equivalents will cover almost any situation.

MACINTOSH	WINDOWS	EXAMPLE
Shift	Shift	Shift+X
Option	Alt	Option/Alt+X
Command	Ctrl	Command/Ctrl+X
Control+click	right-click	Control/right-click

How to Contact the Authors

Scott Hamlin is the director of Eyeland Studio, Inc. and can be reached at `jshamlin@eyeland.com` or by visiting `www.eyeland.com`, `www.flashfoundry.com`, or `www.gamesinaflash.com`. Brandon Williams can be reached at `mbw234@nyu.edu`, and Jared Tarbell can be reached at `jt@levitated.net`.

Chapter 1: What Are Components and Why Should I Care?

Components are valuable resources for Macromedia Flash designers, whether you are a beginner or an advanced user. There is no reason to be intimidated by components. Most components are very accessible, easy-to-use resources. In fact, typically you can leverage the value of many components with little or no Flash experience.

Dive into this chapter. I'll show you what a component is, what it can do, and how to recognize one.

- **The power of components**
- **What components are, in detail**
- **What to do with components**
- **Where to find components**

The Power of Components

Probably the quickest and easiest way to understand what components are and why they are valuable is to compare them with a product you already know. In many ways, Flash components are similar to plug-ins for programs such as Adobe Photoshop or Discreet 3ds max. Components also have similarities to macros used by popular word processors like Microsoft Word. But to call components "plug-ins" or "macros" would be a disservice. They are much more powerful than that, as suggested by Figure 1.1.

Components are resources that have the Flash programming (ActionScript) encapsulated with any other required resources (graphics, text, audio, etc.). If you can use ActionScript to program something in Flash, you can turn that something into a component.

Components are particularly useful for automating any kind of repetitive or complex task that requires ActionScript. While we'll be looking at the value of components more from a user's perspective in this book, let's look at an example on the programming side to illustrate the usefulness of components.

Let's say you need a bunch of slick drop-down menus for a variety of Flash interfaces. You are a very good ActionScript programmer and can easily program the drop-down menu. Once you program the drop-down menu, you have useful code that you can use again and again.

While most programmers are in the practice of using their code repeatedly, it still takes a lot of time for even the quickest and most incredibly talented programmers to make modifications to their code. Often programmers only need to modify variables in their code. However, those variables might be buried in hundreds of lines of code, or the programmer might need to modify multiple references to the variables or to modify a large array of variables.

Figure 1.1
Would it be immodest of me to tell you that I was the model for this illustration?

In fact, it's not uncommon for programmers to spend more time modifying their existing code than they did when they originally programmed the code. If a programmer comes back to their code six months after they originally coded it, they might easily forget a variable reference or something else important that could lead to hours and hours of bug hunting.

This often leads programmers to simply recode the item. Whether you're a programmer or not, you can probably appreciate the fact that it is very inefficient to continually recode something from scratch.

Components help you avoid such a fate. Developers can create components so that the variables for the code can be more easily modified through a much more accessible interface. This, in turn, allows programmers and nonprogrammers alike to leverage that code repeatedly without tediously rooting through the actual code to make modifications.

As mentioned earlier, if you can generate something with Flash and ActionScript, then you can make a component out of it. You can make components generate any sort of effect that can be created using Flash and ActionScript, including dynamic menus, programmatic animation effects, and audio or video controls. You can even use components to generate entire games.

Your Flash projects can even contain multiple components. You could, for example, create a Flash site that contains a component that generates the navigation system along with a component that controls what audio is playing in the background.

If you are relatively new to Flash, components let you add advanced functionality into your projects without requiring that you learn programming. If you are an advanced Flash designer or programmer, components save you time by automating repetitive tasks. You can then put that time towards making your projects all the more compelling.

Components do not increase the download time of a Flash movie. Flash components are made from the same resources you would use if you didn't use a component. A drop-down menu made with a component usually uses the same resources as a drop-down menu created without a component. The only difference is that the component is easier to use and modify.

This book is about showing you how to leverage the incredible value of components. In the following chapters, you will learn how to use, manage, and even create components. The book's companion CD gives you all of the components featured in this book as well as many additional sample components.

When you are finished with this book, you will be able to "save the world before bedtime" and leap tall deadlines with a single bound. You'll feel compelled to think of a cool super hero name for yourself, and you'll soon be making sketches for your new costume, all the while wondering how good you'll look in spandex and tights.

Well okay, you may not find yourself hiding your secret identity with a pair of cheap glasses while fighting off a sudden crush for anyone named Lana Lang, but learning to utilize components will certainly empower you to do more things in much less time with Flash.

All Right, Already!! So What Is a Component Exactly?

A *component* is a movie clip in Flash that has been prewired to generate some sort of functionality. As you will see later in the book, you begin generating a component by creating a standard movie clip. You then transform the movie clip into a component with a few relatively simple steps.

Components were introduced in Flash version 5 as *smart clips*. The name indicated a movie clip with smarts added to it. Macromedia changed the name from smart clips to components in Flash MX. If you see something referred to as a smart clip, you can treat it exactly as you would treat a component.

Figure 1.2

You can tell components apart from movie clips, buttons, graphic symbols, bitmap symbols, and audio symbols by their icons.

Smart clips developed in Flash 5 work perfectly well in Flash MX. Components that are programmed in Flash MX can be made to work in Flash 5. However, if you use code that was introduced in Flash MX in your components, they will not work in Flash 5.

So if a component is like a movie clip, how can you tell a component apart from a movie clip? The easiest way is by looking at its icon in the Flash Library. Figure 1.2 shows the library of a component called Link Scroller from Eyeland Studio's Flash Foundry (`www.eyeland.com`). The item highlighted, named "link scroller," is a component. Several other elements are visible in the library, all of which are actually used by the component and contained within the component.

> Many of the components featured in this book are from Eyeland Studio's Flash Foundry product. Similar components can be found at `www.eyeland.com` or `www.flashcomponents.com`.

The default component icon is this: . The standard movie clip icon is this: . If you see the default component icon, then you know you're dealing with a component.

However, Macromedia has provided several icons that you can use for components and has introduced the capability to create custom component icons. Any resource that displays one of the following icons will also be a component. Fortunately, both the alternative icons and custom icons are not used very frequently. Most components simply utilize the default component icon.

> See Chapter 11 for information on how to create a custom icon for your components.

Identifying a Component on the Stage

When you see an item on the stage, it can be difficult to determine if it is a component or some other type of Flash resource (movie clip, button, graphic symbol, etc.). As with any Flash resource, if you are in doubt about what kind it is, you can always select it and look at the Properties panel. For example, Figure 1.3 shows the Properties panel for a movie clip. You can tell at a glance that the object is a movie clip because of its icon and its Movie Clip label.

Figure 1.3

The Properties panel clearly indicates what type of object you have selected—in this case, a movie clip.

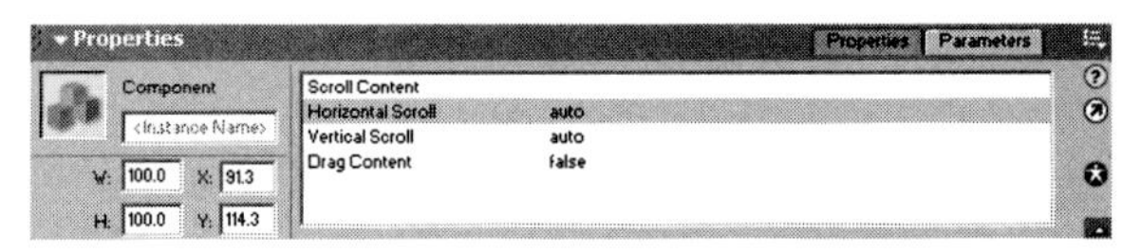

Figure 1.4

The Properties panel displays several indicators when you have selected a component.

When a component is selected, the Properties panel can take on several appearances. Figure 1.4 shows the Properties panel for a component that comes with Flash MX. On the top left, you can see the default component icon and the Component label—both of which, of course, indicate that a component is selected. Notice the two tabs on the top right: Parameters and Properties.

Figure 1.5

The component user interface is like a control panel on a machine.

The Parameters tab is displayed in Figure 1.4; this tab is only visible when a component is selected. Also, notice the area within the Properties panel that looks like a small database field. This is probably the most noticeable indication that a component is selected: these are the parameters for the component.

This area is referred to as the *component user interface (UI)*. In Figure 1.4, this is the default user interface. Component parameters allow you to customize a component. If you think of a component as a sort of machine or engine that can be used to create something, then the component's user interface is like the machine's control panel (see Figure 1.5). The UI allows you to adjust specific characteristics for whatever the component is making.

So if a component is like a machine that makes a doohickey, then the component UI is like the machine's control panel that lets you tell the machine to make a red doohickey rather than a blue doohickey.

Figure 1.6 shows the Properties panel for a selected component with a different type of parameter user interface—in this case, a custom user interface. We will look at component UIs and parameters, including custom UIs, in detail in Chapter 2 (and, really, throughout this book).

What Can I Do with Components?

You can use components to generate almost anything you can imagine (anything that Flash is capable of creating, that is)—games, dynamic menu systems, interactive buttons, audio controls, video controls, transition effects, database systems, interactive mouse effects, animation effects, and much, much more. This might be a little bit of a surprise if you have noticed the components that come with Flash MX.

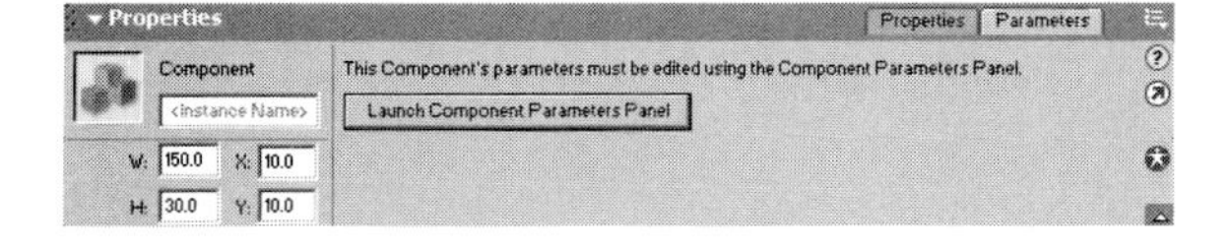

Figure 1.6

The Properties panel for a component with a custom user interface. You must click the Launch Component Parameters Panel button to view the custom UI.

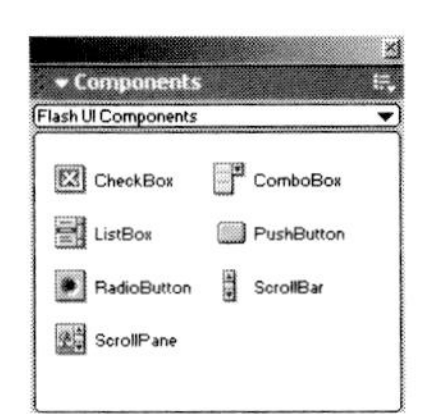

Figure 1.7

The components that come with Flash MX

Figure 1.7 shows the included components. You can open this panel by selecting Components from the Windows menu. If you drag a few of these onto the stage and then publish your movie, you won't exactly receive the thrill of a lifetime. The components that come with Flash generate relatively humble things like radio buttons.

If you care to inspect the code of some of these components, such as the ComboBox component, you'll see that the ActionScript used to create the component is actually somewhat complex. Nevertheless, these standard Flash MX components merely scratch the surface of what is possible with components.

To begin to appreciate the real value of components, we need to look at a few examples of components in action. Figure 1.8 shows an interface that uses two different components. One component generates the navigation system on the left, and the other controls the scrollable text field.

The navigation is controlled by a component called Springy Thingy. It looks like a standard, vertically oriented navigation system. You can roll over the buttons, and each button changes color as you do. However, you can also drag a button, and the other buttons will move along with it in a fun bouncy or springy motion (see Figure 1.9). The scrollable text component controls the functionality that lets you click the up or down arrows or drag the bar to view all of the text in the field.

Figure 1.8

The interactive elements in this Flash interface are generated using components.

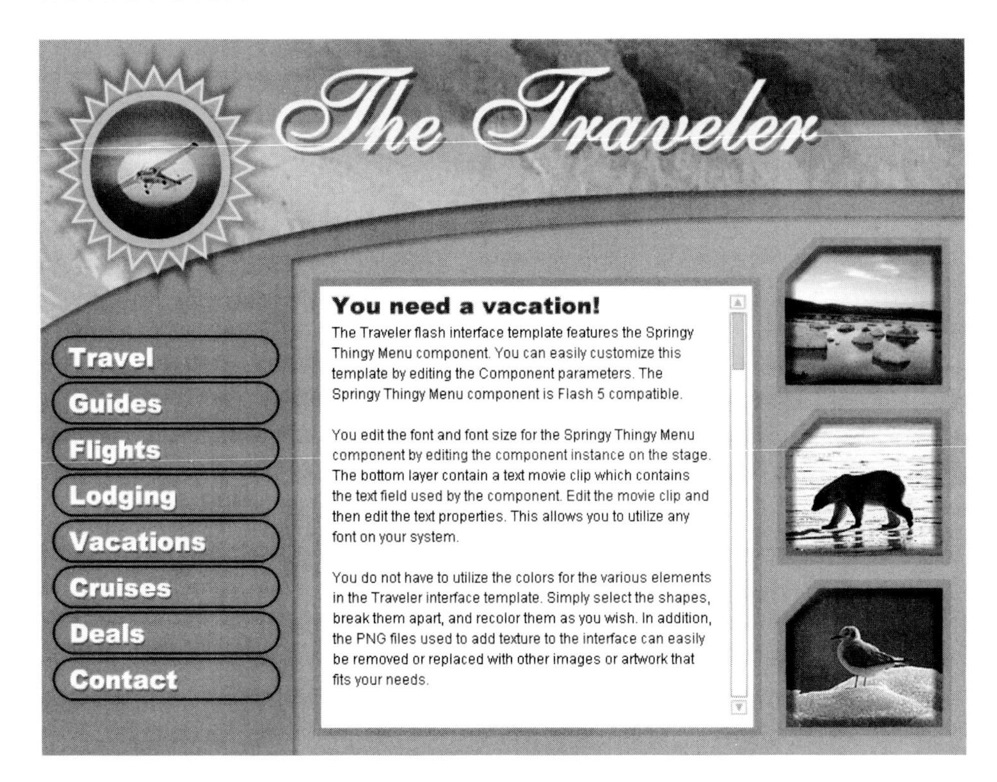

Figure 1.10 shows the interface within Flash MX. The gray box with the Springy Thingy label is the component used to create the navigation system. Since components are created from standard movie clips, they can look like just about anything when you are working with them in Flash. In Figure 1.10, the gray box with the component icon to the left is Eyeland Studio's standardized look for our components. This visual treatment helps to set it apart from other resources on the stage, but it is not representative of what all components will look like.

The scroll bar to the right of the "You Need a Vacation!" field is also a component. The scroll bar component is more indicative of the kind of component you are likely to find on the Web.

> Components that you find on the Internet are commonly hard to identify as components when you are working with them in Flash. There is no standard for how components look when they are on the stage. See later in this chapter for some sites that distribute components.

Figure 1.11 shows the component user interface for the Springy Thingy component. The controls in the interface let you adjust various parameters in the component. In the case of Springy Thingy, different parameters allow you to specify the text for each button, the colors for the text, the colors for the various states of the buttons, the shape of the buttons, the size of the buttons, and much more.

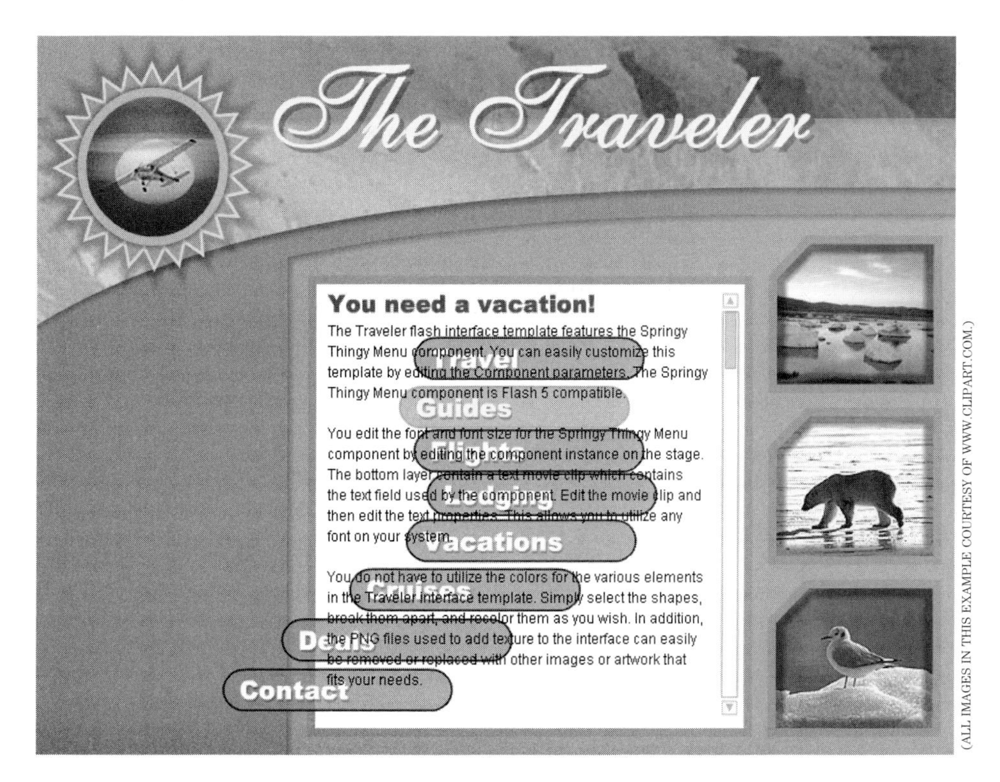

(ALL IMAGES IN THIS EXAMPLE COURTESY OF WWW.CLIPART.COM.)

Figure 1.9

Dragging the navigation bar around produces a bouncy or springy animation effect.

Figure 1.10

One of the components is easier to pick out than the other.

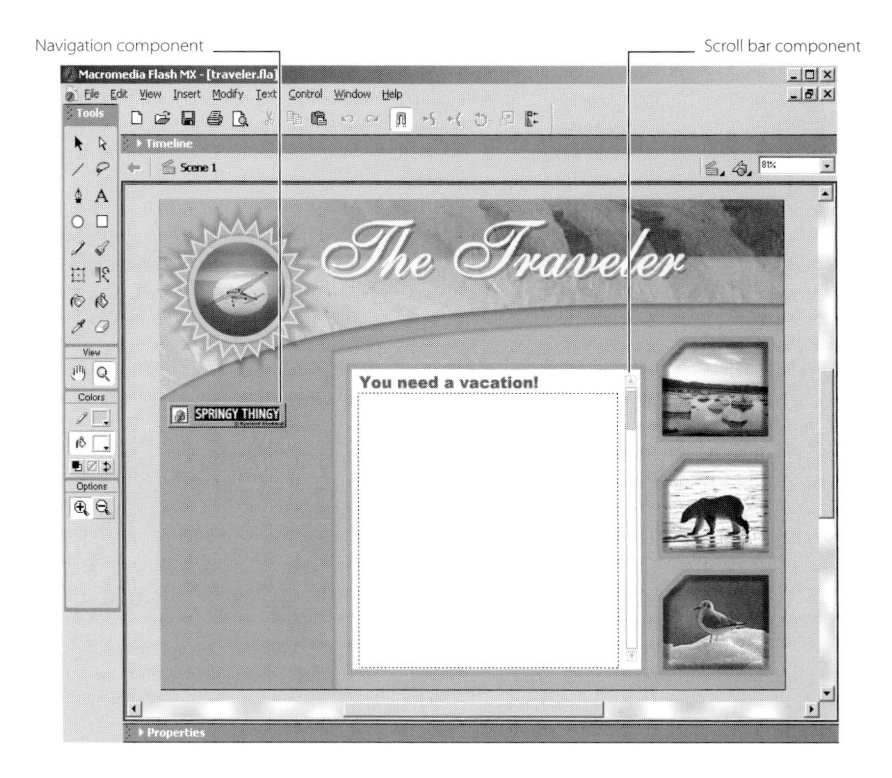

Figure 1.11

The user interface for Springy Thingy provides a quick and easy way for customizing the characteristics of the component.

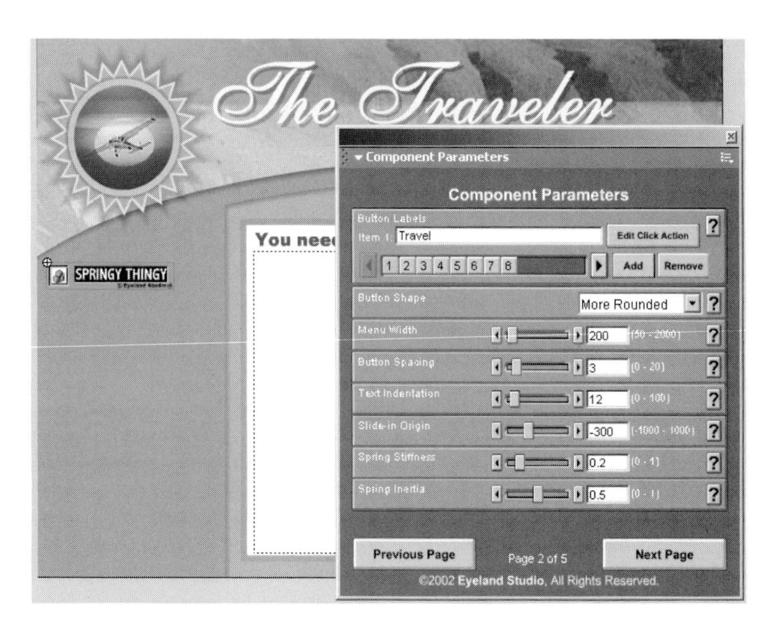

While the user interface might look a little intimidating at first, it's actually not that much harder to use than any dialog box or panel in Flash. If you are familiar with how to adjust font characteristics for text in Flash, then you should have very little trouble using a component UI like this. You will get plenty of hands-on experience using component UIs similar to this one, in later chapters.

The advantage of using components becomes clear when you consider what it would take to generate the same functionality by coding from scratch. Scott Balay from Eyeland Studio coded the Springy Thingy component. Scott has over 10 years professional programming experience and has been programming with ActionScript ever since it was introduced in Flash 5.

Programming the essential elements of the Springy Thingy navigation system took Scott about six hours, including testing and troubleshooting. This does not include time spent creating the actual Springy Thingy component or the component user interface. Scott readily admits that some programmers might be able to work faster; however, it would still take most Flash programmers several hours to program the overall navigation system from scratch.

When I created this Flash interface template for Eyeland Studio's Flash Foundry, it took me only 15 or 20 minutes to set the parameters for the Springy Thingy component so that it looked good in context with the rest of the artwork in the template. Much of this time was actually taken up by making an adjustment, testing to view the results, and then going back to make a few more adjustments.

Obviously, 15 to 20 minutes is better than six hours. Relatively inexperienced programmers might take days to program similar functionality. However, by using a component to generate the functionality, I was able to use those hours and days for other things (such as sleep, having a life, and other previously inconceivable things).

Let's look at one more example. Figure 1.12 shows a concentration game for the Musco Family Olive Company (`www.olives.com`). The Olives site design and the artwork for the game was done by the Tesser agency (`www.tesser.com`). The game is a classic concentration or match game with four levels. Each level increases in difficulty and in the points earned for completion.

Brandon Williams did the programming for this game. Brandon is also an advanced programmer who has been published in several books. It took Brandon approximately 12 hours to program this game. Once again, it took me about 15 to 20 minutes to change the parameters for this game using the component.

This component, however, is a little different than the Springy Thingy example. The concentration game component works with art resources extracted from the library. The art that works with the component is used for the game pieces as well as the pictures that are revealed when the player makes matches. Although setting up these game pieces to work with the component takes some time, it is not nearly as cumbersome as it would be without the component.

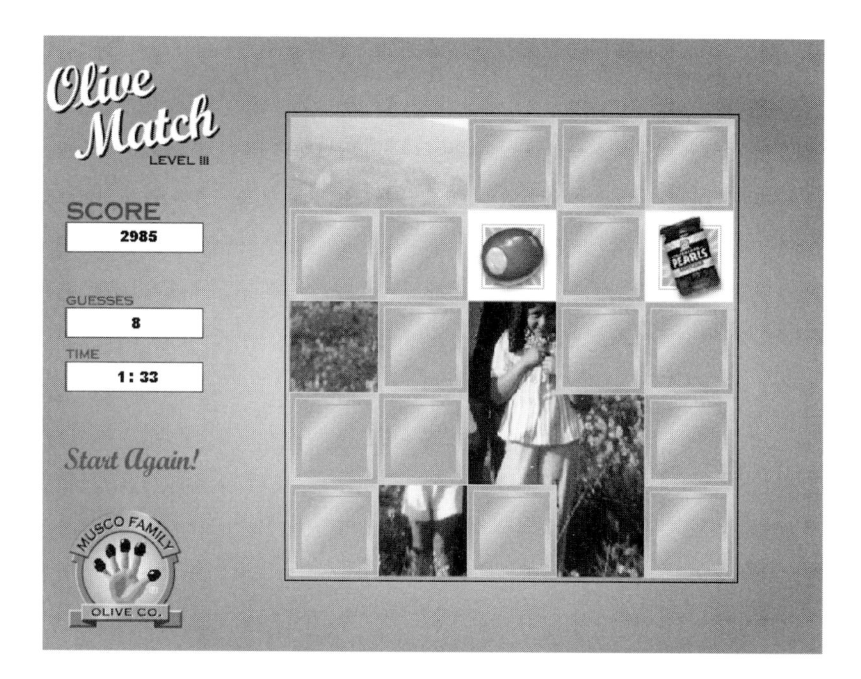

Figure 1.12

This concentration game for the Musco Family Olive Company was created using components.

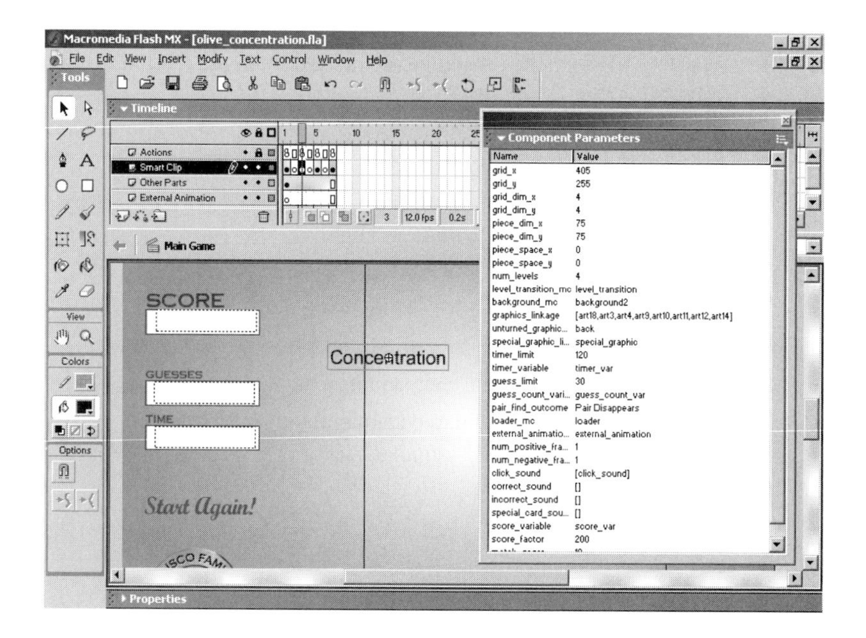

Figure 1.13

There is an instance of the concentration for each level of the game. Each instance has the parameters set differently.

Figure 1.13 shows the concentration game component in Flash with its user interface open. Notice that there are no game pieces on the stage for the game. The artwork for the game is not on the stage. This is because the component actually extracts the art resources from the library. Since there are several levels to the game, this helped keep the game nice, neat, and tidy during production. In other words, using the component, in this case, made this game easier to generate because I didn't have to go to the trouble of programming it and because it was more manageable.

Where Can I Find Components?

At the time of this writing, there aren't too many sites devoted to components, yet more and more sites are popping up on the Internet. Some developers create components and distribute them for free to help promote themselves. An increasing number of sites are beginning to sell components. Components can range from doing very small tasks such as powering a radio button to generating highly elaborate navigational systems of customizable games. The following is a list of places where you can find components:

Macromedia Macromedia's site hosts Flash Exchange. The link is dynamic. The easiest way to find Flash Exchange is to go the Products section at macromedia.com. Select Flash and then click on the Flash Exchange link. Flash Exchange features free components and a rating system so that you can get some idea of what other people think of the component. Since they are free, most of the components in Flash Exchange are modest in scope. You won't find previews for the components, but you can join a public forum for Flash Exchange where you can benefit from the knowledge of other component developers and component users.

`www.macromedia.com`

Flash Foundry, Eyeland Studio Flash Foundry is a membership-based product. Members purchase access to components and other Flash resources. The components in Flash Foundry utilize a highly developed custom UI. You can preview the components and enter a public forum for support and information exchange. Flash Foundry also features very detailed interactive Flash tutorials that cover topics ranging from specific components to general tutorials that apply to any number of components. Flash Foundry is updated frequently with more components. Most of the components featured in this book are modified versions of components found at flashfoundry.com.

`www.flashfoundry.com`

FlashComponents.com, Art Today FlashComponents.com is based on the same components and flash resources as the previously mentioned site. However, FlashComponents.com is operated by Art Today, the company behind clipart.com, photos.com, and rebelartists.com. FlashComponents.com has most of the same benefits mentioned above; however, from time to time members can also benefit from special offers for Art Today's other membership products.

`www.flashcomponents.com`

Flashkit.com Flashkit offers several free components and smart clips in their free movies section. Flashkit does only rudimentary screening of the resources placed on their site, which means the quality of the resources can be somewhat unimpressive. However, free is free, and you usually get what you pay for.

`www.flashkit.com`

Flashcomponents.net Flashcomponents.net is one of the first sites devoted to components on the Internet. The components are free, although some might have usage restrictions. Flashcomponents.com has previews, and the quality of the components are above average—particularly for a free site.

`www.flashcomponents.net`

Games in a Flash Games in a Flash offers a growing collection of component-based Flash game engines for licensing. The games are customizable via the components, and the graphics and audio in the games can be edited to customize the look of the games. The game engines come with interactive Flash tutorials that demonstrate how to customize the games.

`www.gamesinsaflash.com`

Methinks Methinks offers a small collection of components for Flash that generate special effects such as rotation, zoom, and fading.

`www.methinks.com`

Not listed above are personal sites that offer free components (although many of those same components are available at flashcomponents.net or Flash Exchange). There is no shortage of free components on the Internet, but the trade-off is that they usually do not utilize user-friendly, custom user interfaces, and there is usually no guarantee of any kind of support. Components that you pay for are typically held to a higher standard, and they almost always come with at least some level, if not multiple levels, of support (such as tutorials, built-in help information, FAQs, forums, e-mail support, and even phone support).

Conclusion

Components free you from concern with how you are going to implement the advanced functionality for a project. Furthermore, using components allows you to keep your projects from getting out of hand. These in turn free you up to do things like focus more on generating effective designs, creating compelling content, and maybe even meeting your deadlines with time to spare (cue laugh track).

While we will be looking at how to *create* components later, in Chapters 10 and 11, the majority of this book is about how to *use* components. We go step-by-step through the process of using many different types of components. Whether you are a beginner or an advanced Flash user, learning how to grab the power of components can be very worthwhile. If there is a component available that performs the functionality you need, then—as the saying goes—there's usually no point in reinventing the wheel.

In the next chapter, we will look at the basics of using components. While components have some similarities to plug-ins or macros, components have their own set of characteristics—some of them are even a bit on the quirky side. However, a little hands-on experience with components will help you to see their incredible potential.

Chapter 2: Using Components 101

Macromedia has constructed Flash MX with a few little features that can easily trip up the uninitiated. In addition, many of the same aspects that make components versatile and powerful can also make them slightly confusing to work. If you know what to look for and what to watch out for, components can be extremely valuable resources.

The best way of overcoming these minor hurdles is to simply start working with components. In this chapter, you will work with a relatively simple component that utilizes the default component user interface for the Component Parameters panel, exploring some of the advantages and disadvantages (mostly disadvantages) of the default UI. I'll also explain the parameters you'll encounter and their types.

Most of this book's components use custom user interfaces. However, components available for free frequently utilize the default UI. In addition to learning the basics of components, working with the default UI will help you appreciate the value of good custom UIs.

- **The default component UI**
- **Understanding parameter types and value types**
- **Experimenting with values**

Parameters and the Default Component User Interface

Fundamentally, a component allows you to manipulate variables within ActionScript without having to delve into the actual ActionScript. For instance, let's say you had some ActionScript that utilizes Flash MX's ability to draw a rectangle with code. Even something as simple as a rectangle has several potential variables. How high is the rectangle? How wide? Where is the rectangle on the stage? What color is it? What is its alpha?

All of these variables can be "hard-coded" within the ActionScript, meaning that the variables are part of the code. The problem with this is that if you want to change these variables, you must go into the code. Finding and editing the code required to generate a rectangle would not be particularly hard. However, components that perform more complex actions like creating a collapsible menu or a game contain code that can be hundreds of lines long.

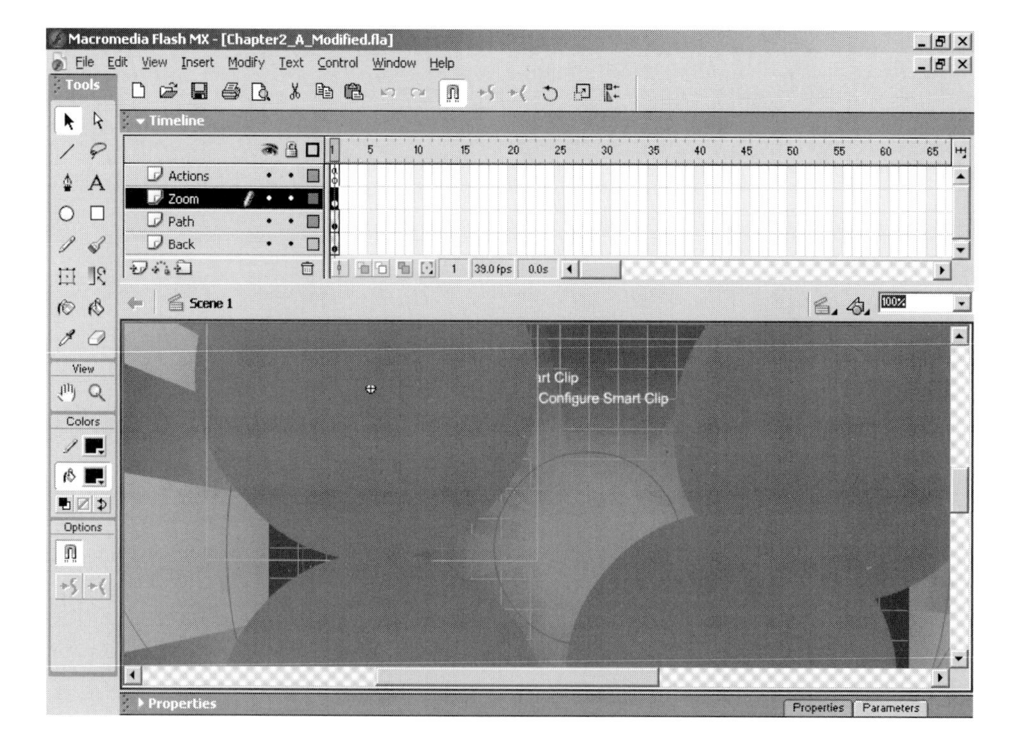

Figure 2.1

The `Chapter2_A_Modified.fla` **sample file is dotted with multiple instances of two separate components.**

Furthermore, the code might not all be in one place. For complex resources, finding and editing the variables can be difficult and time-consuming even for experienced programmers—even for the person who wrote the code, particularly if they need to change the variables a long time after they originally wrote it. Components provide a solution to this problem and, in the process, make the code easier to customize, for the programmer and nonprogrammer alike.

In components, each variable is called a *parameter*. Components make it easier to customize or change the parameters by placing them in a more accessible location: the Component Parameters panel. As you will see in the following example, the Component Parameters panel can take on a wide range of different appearances.

Open `Chapter2_A_Start.fla` in the Chapter 2 folder on this book's CD. Save the file to your local hard drive as `Chapter2_A_Modified.fla`.

In this Flash file, the stage is peppered with components. Actually, there are only two components, but there are multiple instances of each of the two components. An *instance* refers to a particular copy of a symbol in Flash. For example, if you create a movie clip and then drag three copies of that movie clip onto the stage in Flash, you have three instances of that movie clip.

You can manipulate components in much the same way you can manipulate any other symbol in Flash. You can generate multiple instances of a component, and you can duplicate and/or copy a component. If you use multiple instances of a component, you gain the same file-size-saving advantages that other symbols provide.

Go ahead and test the movie to observe what it does (see Figure 2.2). What you will see is a rich animation. If you look carefully, you'll notice two types of animations, both of which utilize simple circles. A series of circles marches end to end, and lines of circles march up, down, left, and right in all different sizes and varied opacities. Each line of marching circles is controlled by a component. Notice, also, the series of circles that zoom in and out of view. Some zoom in, some zoom out. Each zooming circle is also controlled by a component. Close the test movie.

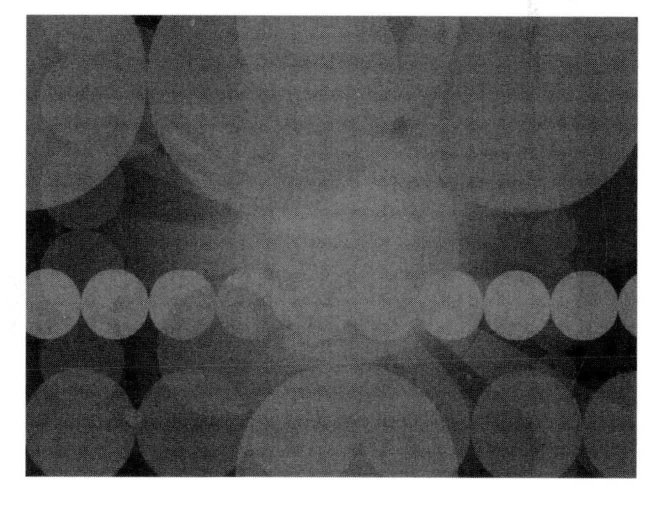

Figure 2.2

Multiple copies of two components are used in this example to generate a rich, textured, animated background.

Exploring the Component Parameters Panel

Go to the Zoom layer, select one of the large red circles, and open the Component Parameters panel. You can open the panel in several different ways, but each requires that you first select the component on the stage. Once you have selected the component, you can choose Windows → Component Parameters (see Figure 2.3). You can also right-click or Control+click a component and then select Component Parameters from the Panels submenu (see Figure 2.4). Probably the easiest method for opening the Component Parameters panel, however, is to use the shortcut key: Option/Alt+F7.

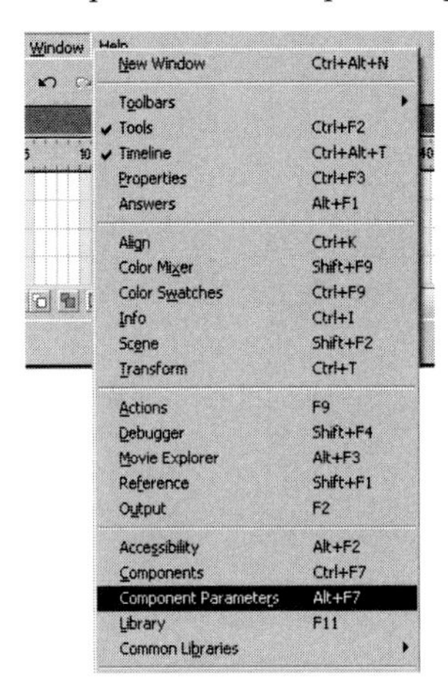

Figure 2.3

You can open the panel by selecting Component Parameters from the Windows menu.

The Properties panel also provides access to a component's parameters when you have the component selected (see Figure 2.5). The Properties panel will actually display different things depending on how the component is set up. (Some people use the Properties panel because they find that it doesn't obstruct the stage as much as the Component Parameters panel.) We will talk more about this later when we discuss custom user interfaces for Component Parameters.

Each of the large red circles is a component. The Component Parameters panel for the Zoom component is shown in Figure 2.6. Flash allows you to create a custom look for the Component Parameters interface, but this is what the default UI looks like.

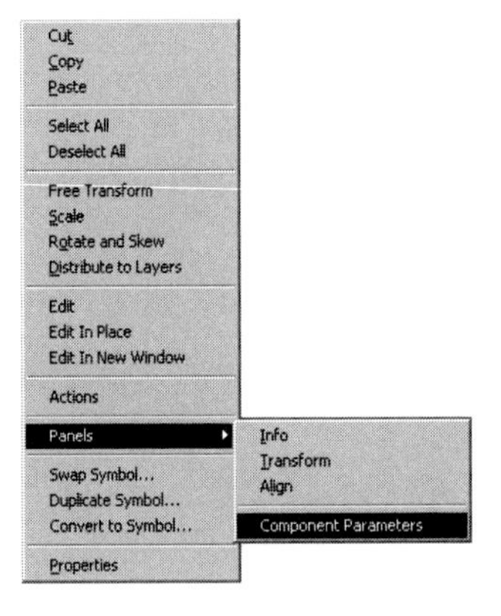

Figure 2.4

You can right-click or Control+click to produce a pop-up menu from which you can select Component Parameters.

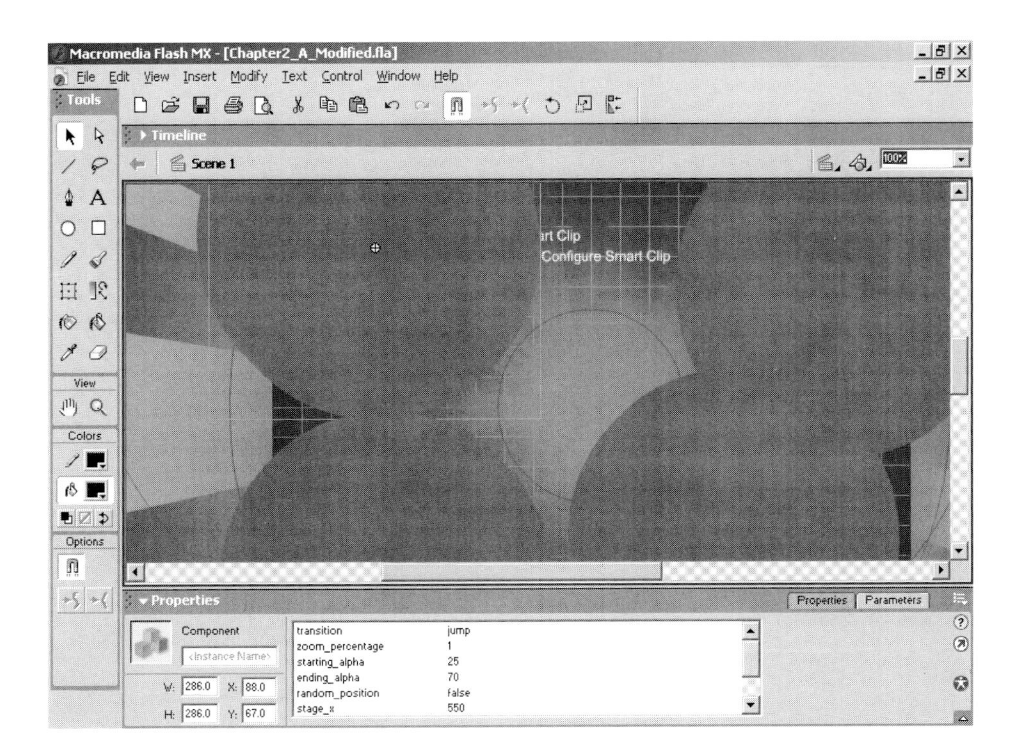

Figure 2.5

The Properties panel also offers access to a component's parameters.

When a component utilizes the default user interface for the Component Parameters panel, the panel will open much larger than it needs to be, as shown in Figure 2.7. The opposite problem commonly occurs when a custom UI is used. Like all panels in Flash, you can resize the Component Parameters panel by dragging corners or edges of the panel window.

You can work in Flash with the Component Parameters panel open. However, most changes that you make within the panel will not be visible until you actually test or publish the movie. This can cause a problem because the panel must be closed before you test or publish your movie. When you have the Component Parameters panel open, the variables that can be edited in the various parameters are in flux. Closing the panel fixes those variables with the values that you have entered.

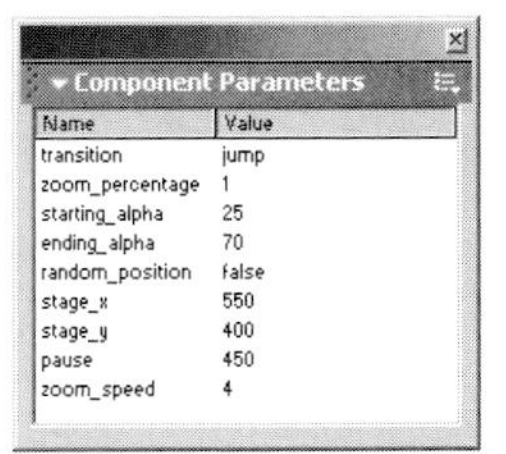

Figure 2.6

The default user interface for the Component Parameters panel

If you publish or test a movie when the Component Parameters panel is open, Flash will often crash, or your movie may not work properly. So it is very important to get into the habit of always closing the panel before you publish or test.

In the default user interface in Figure 2.7, notice that there are two columns. The left column is the name of the parameter, and the right column is its value. It should immediately become apparent why the default Component Parameters user interface is not ideal.

First of all, the name of the parameter is typically the only indication as to what any given parameter is for. Often, the name gives you a good idea of the parameter's purpose. However, sometimes you are forced to experiment with some values and then observe the results to ascertain the purpose of the parameter.

Another problem with the default UI is that there are actually several different types of values. For some values, you can simply double-click the value and edit it. However, some parameters that may appear to be simple alphanumerical values may actually be a different value type. Component parameters can be many different types. Let's take a look at them now.

Figure 2.7

The Component Parameters panel often opens up too large.

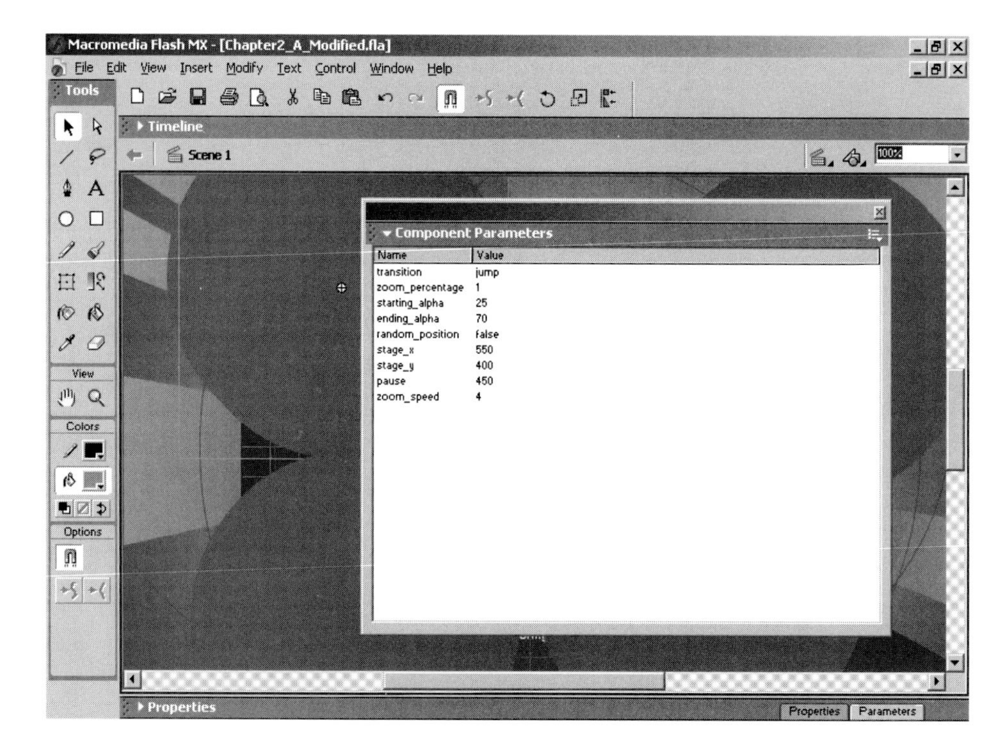

Exploring the Component Definition Dialog Box and Value Types

Open the library and right-click or Control+click the Zoom component. Select Component Definition from the pop-up menu (see Figure 2.8). As we will discuss in Chapter 10, you use the Component Definition dialog box (shown in Figure 2.9) to create a component. Right now we just want to poke around a bit and look at the different value types that there can be for component parameters.

Notice that the Component Definition dialog box looks somewhat similar to the Component Parameters panel. There is a column for names and a column for values. However, there is another column named Type. Click the top field in the Type column. You will see a gray button with a down-arrow on it. Click this button to open a list of value types (see Figure 2.10). As you can see, nine different types can be used for component parameter values: Default, Array, Object, List, String, Number, Boolean, Font Name, and Color.

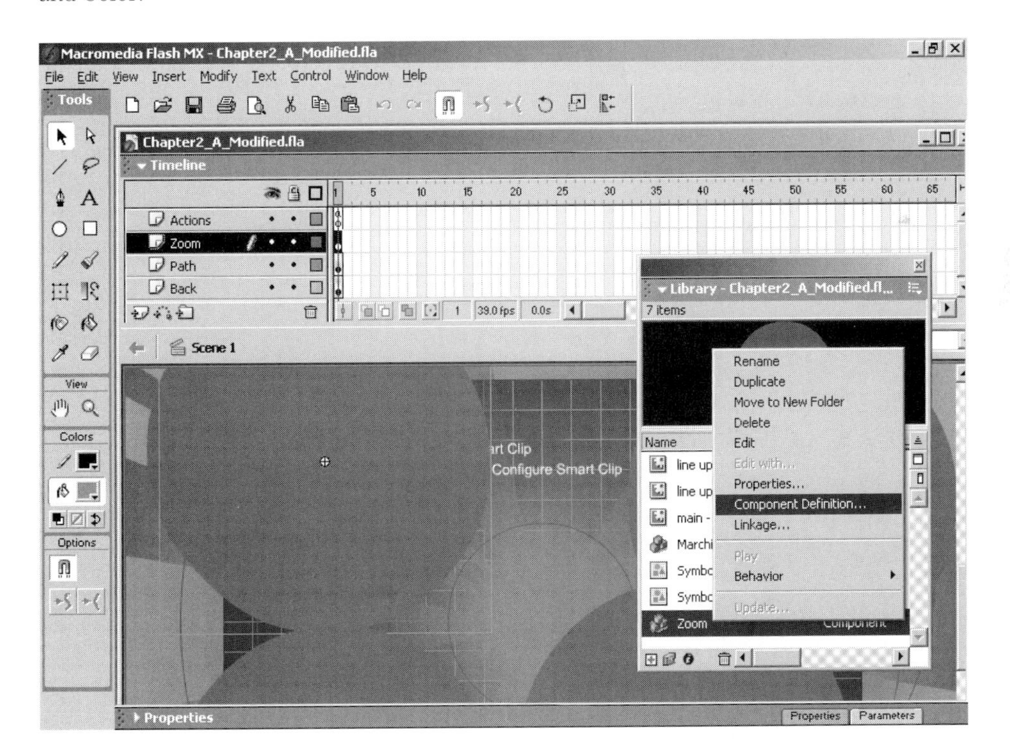

Figure 2.8

Open the Component Definition dialog box for the Zoom component.

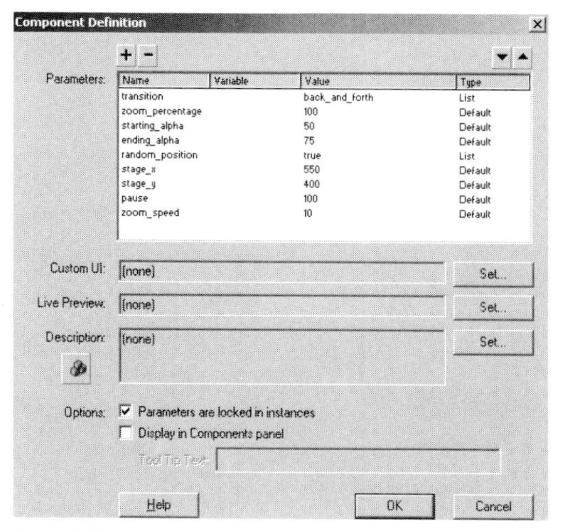

Figure 2.9

You use the Component Definition dialog box to create components.

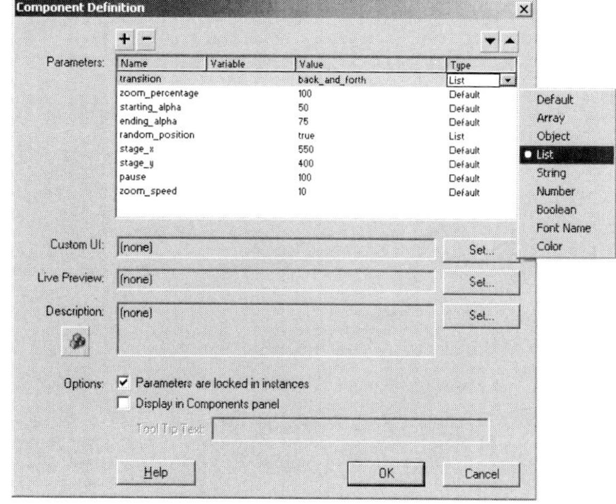

Figure 2.10

There are nine value types for component parameters.

In the Zoom component, select one of the circles on the Zoom layer. Open the Component Parameters panel again. Some value types for component parameters make things a little easier on you. For instance, click once on the value for Transition (the top parameter), which is a List value type. A small gray button will appear on the right side of the value field. Click the button, and you will be presented with two options, Back_And_Forth and Jump, as shown in Figure 2.11.

Selecting the Back_And_Forth value will cause the zooming to start from the smaller size, zoom to the larger size, and then reverse the motion. The Jump value, on the other hand, will cause the component to zoom the shape from the starting size up to the larger size, and then it will jump back to the smaller size and begin the process again.

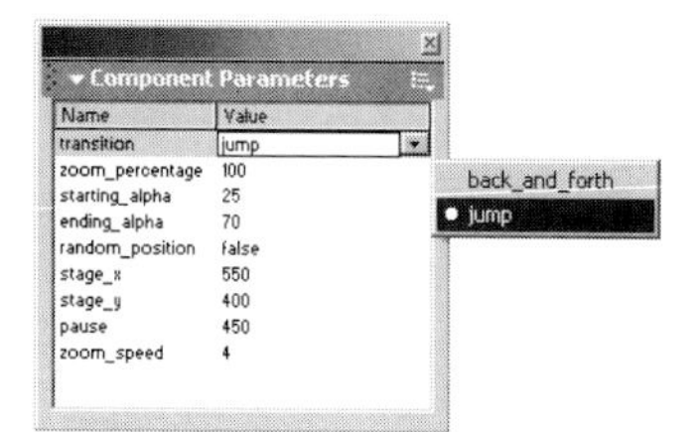

Figure 2.11

The Transition parameter has a List value type.

Let's take a look at the various value types for parameters. It's helpful to be at least aware of the value types, so you can understand how to edit and use them better and also so you can better understand the capabilities and limitations of components.

The Zoom component contains only two value types—Default and List.

The Default Value Type

As you would expect, the most frequently used value type is the Default value type, which is essentially a literal. You can use it to specify strings or numbers or any type of value for a simple variable. When you are working with a component that is utilizing the default user interface for the component parameters, editing a value that is set to default value type is obviously very simple: simply click in the value field and enter whatever value you want to specify. Clicking a default value field automatically selects the entire value so you can more easily replace it with a new value. You can even copy and paste values into default value fields.

Unfortunately, there is a potential problem. Since default value fields can be letters or numbers, users may have difficulty determining what kind of value to enter for a Default value type. For instance, the value for the first Zoom_Percentage parameter in the Zoom component is set to 1 by default. For some users, it may not take very much deduction to figure out that this parameter specifies the zoom percentage of the object.

Values below 100 will make the component start at the original size of the object and then zoom down. Therefore, if you enter a value of 5, the component will begin at its original size and then zoom down to 5 percent of the original size. A value of 300 will tell the component to zoom the object to 300 percent of its original size. If you enter a value of 100, nothing will appear to happen, because you will be directing the object to zoom to 100 percent of its original size.

Thus, for the Zoom_Percentage parameter, you pretty much can't mess anything up as long as you enter a numeric value. However, you can enter a value such as "False" for the Zoom_Percentage parameter and cause the component to no longer work. You can easily make a mistake like this if you don't have a clear idea of what values are acceptable for a given parameter.

> The Default value type is commonly used, rather than the more specific Number or String value types, in order to make the component backwards-compatible with Flash 5. In the Zoom component, it would have been better to have set the values that take numerical values to a Number value type so that users couldn't inadvertently specify a string as a value for any parameter that requires a number. However, Flash 5 only supports Default, List, and Array value types. In general, if you are writing a component that is to be compatible only with Flash MX, don't use the Default value type. Flash MX provides more specific value types, such as the Color or Font value type.

The next two parameters in the Zoom component's Component Parameters panel, for example, are named Starting_Alpha and Ending_Alpha. These parameters are used to specify the alpha transparency for the shape when it begins zooming and when it ends zooming. The default values are 25 for Starting_Alpha and 75 for Ending_Alpha. This means that the shape will be set to 25% alpha or 25% opaque when it begins zooming, and it will gradually change to 75% alpha or 75% opaque when it zooms to the maximum size.

Unlike the Zoom_Percentage parameter, however, the Starting_Alpha and Ending_Alpha parameters will not work with just any number. The alpha setting for an object can only be set from 0 to 100. In this case, the code is written so that if you enter a value over 100, the code will automatically round it down to 100. Without this safety net code, users could inadvertently set a value that wouldn't work for the Starting_Alpha and Ending_Alpha parameters.

The Default value type for a component parameter is easy enough to edit, and if you know the purpose of the parameter, then you will likely have little difficulty using it. However, if you download a component from the Internet that utilizes the default component parameters interface, you might be in for a little frustration and experimentation figuring out what the parameters are for and what values they can take.

The Number and String Value Types

The Number and String value types operate similarly to the Default value type, except they accept only numeric or string values, respectively.

Click the Cancel button in the Component Definition dialog box for now.

The List Value Type

Refer back to Figure 2.10 and notice that the Transition parameter's value type is List. The List value type allows you to specify specific options that component users can select from. The advantage of the List value type is that users can select only those options. There is no possibility for entering a value that will not work for a List value type (assuming all the relevant coding works properly in the component).

> The only minor problem with the List value type is that it is not readily apparent that the value is a list value. That is, when you initially look at a parameter with a List value type, you cannot immediately see that it is any different from the Default value type. A single click rectifies this problem, but it is not ideal having to click around to figure out what the value type is for each value.

The Array Value Type

The Array value type allows you to specify an array of values. Like the List value type, it requires a different interface. Figure 2.12 shows an example of a parameter that uses the Array value type.

When you click a value that is set as an Array value type, you will see a small gray button at the right side of the value field with a magnifying glass icon. Clicking this button opens the Values dialog box. You can enter the values for the array in the Values dialog box.

Unlike the List value type, there are a few small indications that an Array value type is different from other types. Values in array are enclosed with brackets (see Figure 2.13). Also, Array value types frequently have multiple values separated by commas rather than a single value.

The Font Name and Color Value Types

The Font Name and Color Value types also provide slightly different interface options. The Font Name value type allows you to select from the available fonts on the system, and the Color value type adds a color picker to the Components panel so you can select colors from within the Component Parameters default user interface.

The Font Name value type, shown in Figure 2.14, is similar to the List value type. When you click the value field, you are presented with a small gray button with a down-arrow (the middle image in the figure). Clicking the button produces a list of all the fonts on the user's local system.

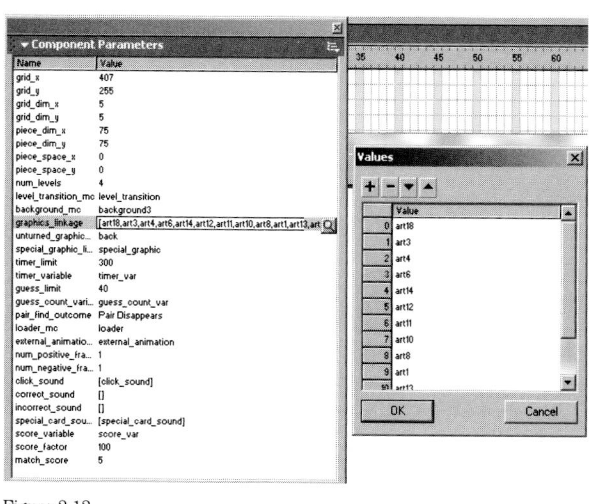

Figure 2.12

The Array value type requires a separate dialog box so that you can enter multiple values.

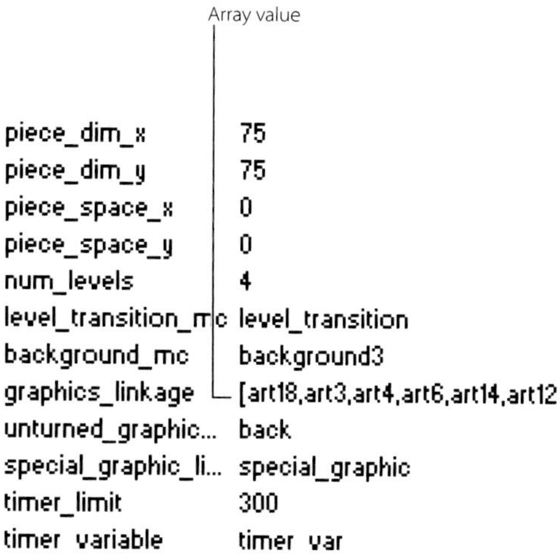

Array value

piece_dim_x 75
piece_dim_y 75
piece_space_x 0
piece_space_y 0
num_levels 4
level_transition_mc level_transition
background_mc background3
graphics_linkage [art18,art3,art4,art6,art14,art12
unturned_graphic... back
special_graphic_li... special_graphic
timer_limit 300
timer_variable timer_var

Figure 2.13

Brackets in a value field help to identify that the field is an Array value type.

The Color value type offers a little more. A value set to be a Color value type will include a small color bar on it. When you click the value field, it produces a color picker that allows you to either select from one of the color swatches or enter a Hex value (see Figure 2.15). You can further click a button in the upper-right corner of the color picker to open the standard Color dialog box, which allows you to specify colors according to RGB or HSB values (see Figure 2.16).

> If you open the Color dialog box from the color picker for a Color value type in the Component Parameters panel, you must enter a value. If you do not enter a value while you are in the Color dialog box and you press the Cancel button instead, the corresponding value in the Component Parameters panel will be emptied of any color value information. You can click it again and reenter the information.

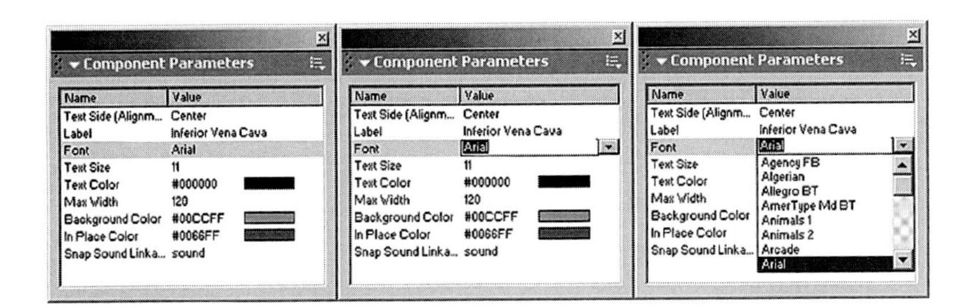

Figure 2.14

The Font Name value type provides a means for the user to specify any font that is on the user's local system.

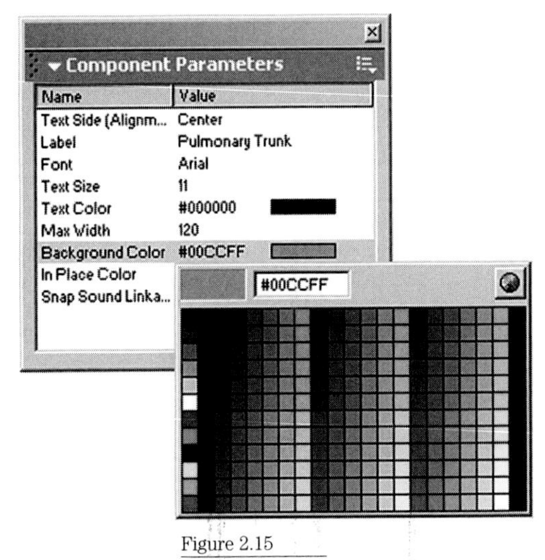

Figure 2.15

The Color value type provides a means for the user to specify a color for an object or text.

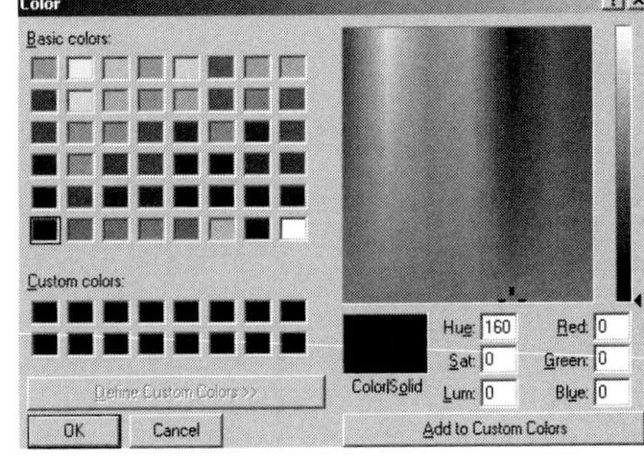

Figure 2.16

You can open the standard (for your given OS) color picker from the pop-up color picker for the Color value type.

Experimenting with Values

First let's review the parameters we've already looked at in this Zoom component sample by looking at its Component Parameters panel, shown in Figure 2.17.

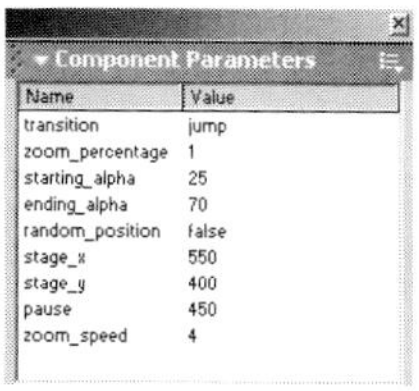

Transition Allows you to specify either Back_And_Forth or Jump. The Back_And_Forth value tells the component to zoom the object back and forth between the minimum and maximum sizes for the object; the Jump setting tells the component to zoom the object from the minimum size to the maximum size and then back to the minimum size to start the process over again.

Component Parameters

Name	Value
transition	jump
zoom_percentage	1
starting_alpha	25
ending_alpha	70
random_position	false
stage_x	550
stage_y	400
pause	450
zoom_speed	4

Figure 2.17

The Component Parameters panel for the Zoom component

Zoom_Percentage Determines how the object within the component will zoom. Values below 100 will make the component start at the original size of the object and then zoom down. So if you enter a value of 1, the component will begin at its original size and then zoom down to 1 percent of the original size. A value of 200 will tell the component to zoom the object to 200 percent of its original size. If you enter a value of 100, nothing will appear to happen, because you will be telling the object to zoom to 100 percent of its original size.

Starting_Alpha and Ending_Alpha Specify the beginning and ending transparency of the object.

Random_Position Specifies whether the object will be randomly positioned on the stage.

Stage_X and Stage_Y Work with Random_Position to tell the component the dimensions of the stage. Stage_X is the width and Stage_Y is the height.

Pause Sets a time in milliseconds that the zooming process will pause. The component will only utilize Pause if the Transition parameter is set to Jump.

Zoom_Speed Specifies how fast the zooming animation will go. This value is used to increment the zoom percentage. So, if you enter a value of 5, then 5 will be added to the zoom percentage on every frame. Therefore, small numbers for Zoom_Speed cause the zoom animation to progress slowly, while larger numbers cause the zoom animation to progress very fast.

Now let's try entering a few values for these parameters and see what happens.

Start entering different values for the various parameters to get a feel for how they work. Select any instance of the Zoom component on the stage, open the Component Parameters panel, and experiment with editing the parameters. For instance, try setting the Zoom_Percentage to a large number, and then close the Component Parameters window and test the movie. Edit the component's parameters again and set the Zoom_Percentage parameter to a small number.

> It's very important to close the Component Parameters panel each time before you test the movie. Closing the panel sets the values for the variables in the component's code. When you have the panel open, the variables are essentially in flux. When you close the Component Parameters panel, Flash populates the variables in the code with the values that you specified. If you do not close the panel, Flash may crash, or the component may not work properly.

Remember, there are actually multiple instances of the two components. Therefore, when you test the movie, you will see lots of motion, and the majority of the motion will not be from any given component that you are editing. When you test the movie, it should look similar to Figure 2.18. Let's create a new file so see you can see the results of your changes more easily. Follow these steps:

1. Before opening a new file, open the library for the `Chapter2_A_Modified.fla` file. Copy an instance of the Zoom component. Now open a blank file (File → New). Paste the component instance into the new file. Save the new file with the name `Component Test`. Notice that the library for the `Component Test` file now contains an instance of the Zoom component. Notice also that all of the resources that are linked to or used by the Zoom component are also included in the `Component Test` file's library (see Figure 2.19).

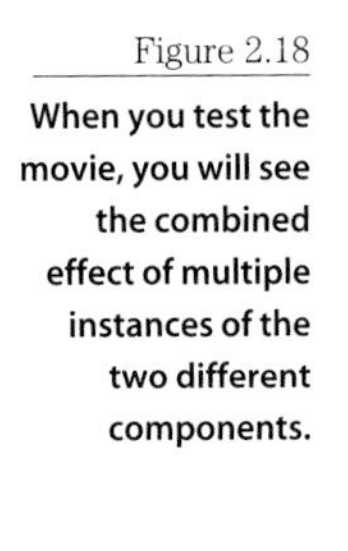

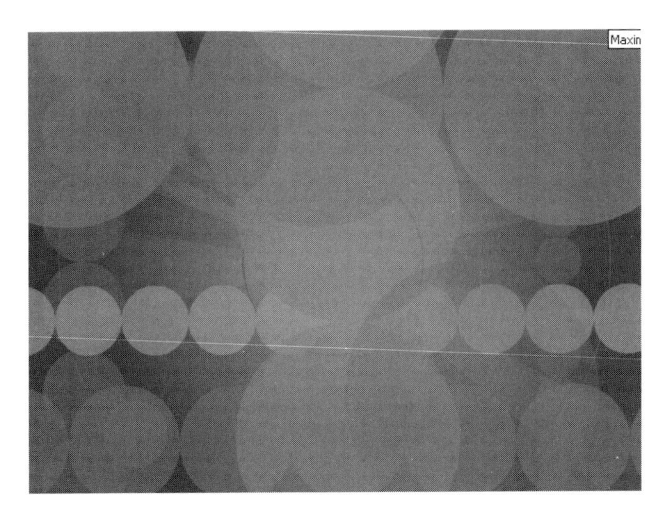

Figure 2.18

When you test the movie, you will see the combined effect of multiple instances of the two different components.

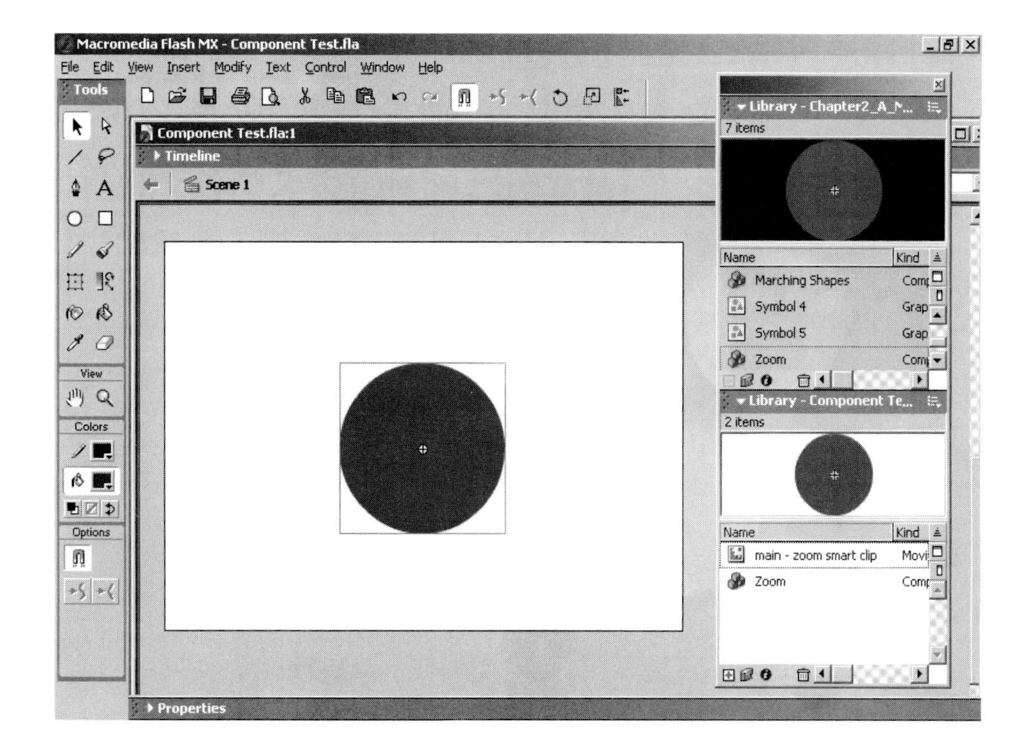

Figure 2.19

The Zoom Component and its related resources are now in the `Component Test` file's library.

2. Now when you test the movie, you can more clearly see the results of any changes you make in the Component Parameters panel. Try entering different values for the parameters. Remember to close the panel each time and test to view the results. Although it's easier to see the results, one instance of the Zoom component, by itself, doesn't make for a very interesting animation. After you've had an opportunity to view the results of various changes to the Zoom components parameters, let's add a few more instances of the component so that we have a more interesting animation effect.
3. Select the red circle on the stage (which is the Zoom component). Hold down the Ctrl key or Command key and press the D key three times to make three duplicates. Drag the duplicates around the stage so that they are each in different locations, similar to the example shown in Figure 2.20.

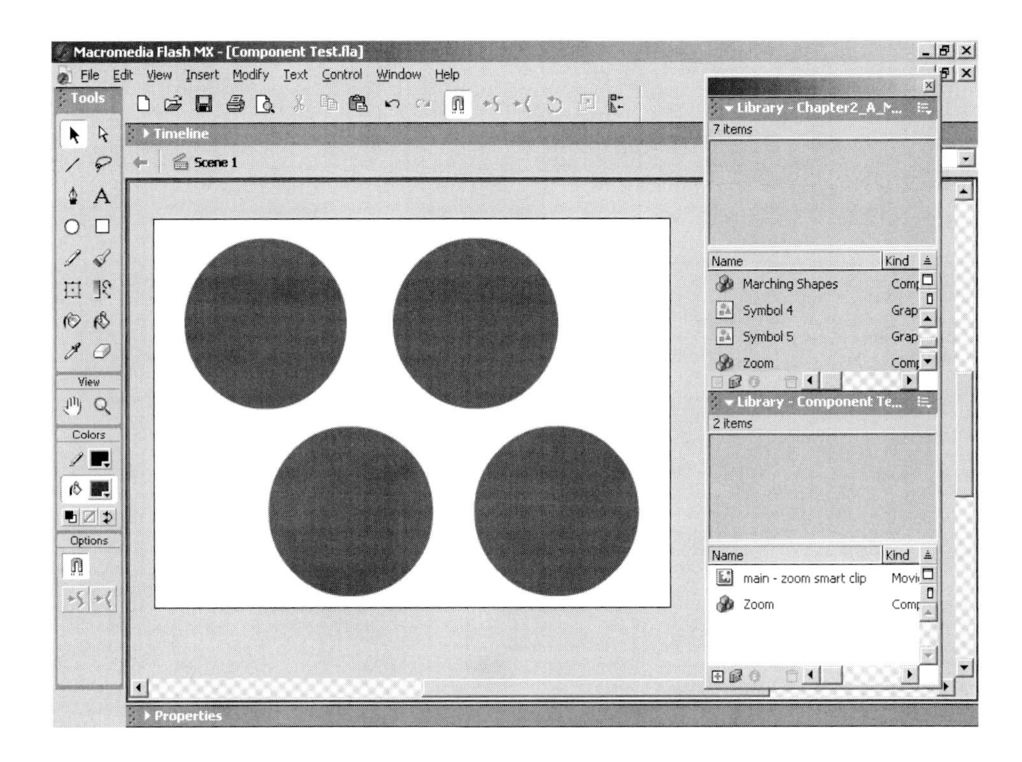

Figure 2.20

Duplicates of the Zoom component instance are positioned on the stage so that they are some distance apart from each other.

4. Now edit the Component Parameters panel of each instance of the Zoom component. Give each component different values. For example, set the Transition parameter of one instance of the Zoom component to Jump and set another to Back_And_Forth. Try setting the Zoom_Percentage parameter of one instance of the Zoom component to a small number and the Zoom_Percentage of a different instance to a large number. After you have edited the parameters of each component, test the movie to view the results.

You don't need to close the Component Parameters panel when going from component to component. When you've finished editing the parameters for one component, simply click another one, and the Component Parameters panel will automatically reflect the values of the selected component.

5. Test the movie and notice that each instance of the component acts independently according to the values you specified for their respective component parameters. Flash remembers the values for each component. If you save the file, close it, and reopen it, Flash will still remember the component parameter values for each instance of each component.

This example demonstrates that components work similarly to other resources you should already be familiar with in Flash—namely movie clips. Like movie clips, components can be copied and duplicated. You drag them from the library and create multiple instances of them. You can adjust the effects of each instance of a movie clip (such as the alpha or tint) without affecting the other instances of the same movie clip. Similarly, you can edit the parameters of each instance of a component without affecting the other instances of the same component.

Editing a Movie Clip to Make Global Changes

This particular component is also similar to movie clips (as well as other Flash symbols) in that we can easily make global changes to the imagery used by the Zoom component. Let's try a few examples:

1. Click any one of the Zoom component instances on the stage and then choose Edit → Edit Selected.
2. Select the red shape on the stage again and then choose Edit → Edit Selected once more.
3. Now select the red circle on the stage and change its color to blue (see Figure 2.21). Return to scene 1 and notice that all instances of the Zoom component have been changed to blue .
4. Test the movie.

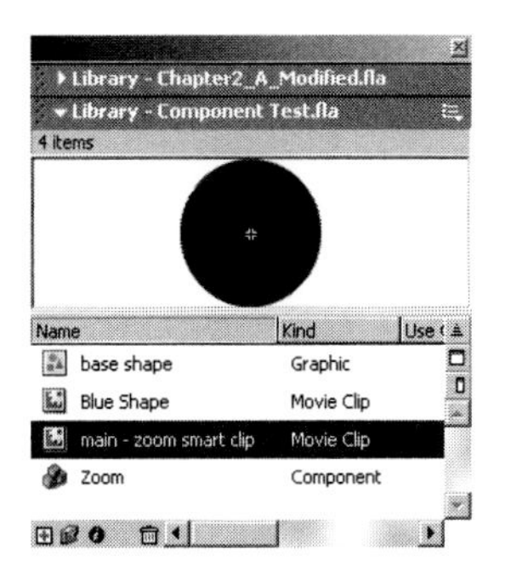

Figure 2.21

Editing the movie clip within any instance of the Zoom component changes all of the other Zoom component instances.

All of the zooming circles are now blue. Like any other Flash symbol, we edited the movie clip that the Zoom component utilizes, and those changes were reflected in all of the instances of the Zoom component. This means that the Zoom component can actually work with any kind of Flash resource. In fact, you can even place a movie clip within the component. Follow these steps:

1. Open the `loop.fla` file from the Chapter 2 folder on the CD and copy the movie clip on the stage from that file.

2. Return to the `Component Test` file. Click any one of the Zoom component instances on the stage and choose Edit → Edit Selected.
3. Select the blue shape on the stage again and choose Edit → Edit Selected once more.
4. Delete the blue circle; then paste in the movie clip that you copied from the `loop.fla` file.
5. Now return to scene 1 and test the movie. Notice that the Zoom component works in the same way with an animated movie clip as it did with a movie clip containing a static image (see Figure 2.22).

This example begins to demonstrate the power and versatility of components. This relatively simple component can be set to operate in many ways. Further, you can duplicate the component and vary the parameters to create a more interesting combined effect. Finally, you can use the component with any graphic or movie clip. You can do all of this without having to know a single line of ActionScript and without doing loads of tedious tweens.

Conclusion

Components can be incredibly valuable resources. While Macromedia hasn't set up components to be absolutely intuitive, you will likely find them easy enough to work with once you get in the practice of using them. When you get familiar with a few unique characteristics of components, you will see that they are like many of the other resources in Flash that you already work with. For example, you can drag and drop them from the library like any other symbol. You can also copy, paste, and duplicate the components easily. To adjust how they operate, you simply edit the parameters. However, the default interface for the Component Parameters panel leaves much to be desired. In the next chapter, we will look at components that utilize custom user interfaces for the panel. We will also look at several other features provided by Macromedia that can make it even easier to work with components.

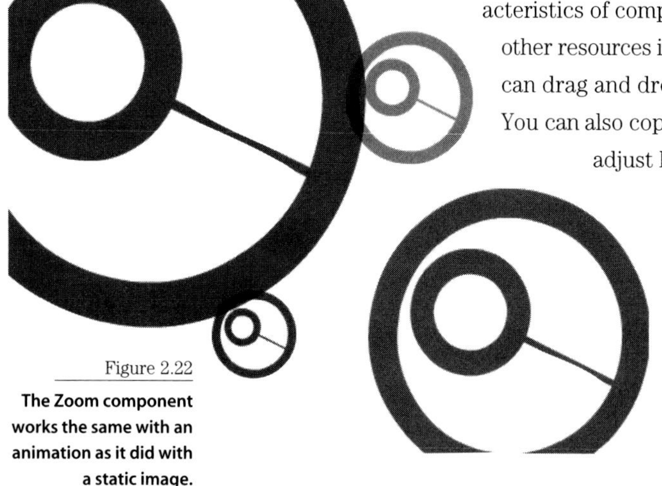

Figure 2.22

The Zoom component works the same with an animation as it did with a static image.

Chapter 3: Using Components with Custom User Interfaces

In the previous chapters, you got a glimpse of how easy components can be to use. However, you also saw that a few things can cause problems when using components—particularly with the default Component Parameters user interface.

While the default Component Parameters UI is perfectly functional, it is not very user-friendly. The default UI looks somewhat similar to a database application, which can be intimidating to some people. Also, as I pointed out in the last chapter, the default UI's values can be confusing, and there is no way to keep users from entering values for some parameters that may not work properly with the component.

Fortunately, Macromedia provides a means for component designers to design a more intuitive user interface for editing component parameters. In this chapter, we'll look at several examples of components that utilize custom interfaces for their parameters. I will discuss the advantages of custom interfaces as well as the few things that you need to watch out for when using components with custom interfaces. You will also experience, first hand, the advantages that custom UIs provide over the default UI for editing parameters.

- **Understanding custom UIs**
- **Good and bad characteristics of UIs**
- **Working with custom UIs**

The Feel of a Custom UI

A custom user interface for a component's parameters is essentially a separate Flash file that has been constructed to make it easier to adjust the component's parameters. While there are some fairly stringent requirements for setting up a custom interface to work with a component, the actual appearance of a component can look like just about anything.

Presumably, the key goal for creating a custom user interface for a component's parameters is to make it easier and more intuitive for the user to edit those parameters. However, it's up to the designer of the custom interface to actually accomplish this goal. In reality, designers can easily create custom interfaces that are even more confusing or difficult to use than the default user interface for component parameters.

Figure 3.1
The plug-in interface for Xaos Tools' Terrazzo

If you are familiar with plug-ins for programs such as Adobe Photoshop, this may not be as problematic or intimidating as you might think. Like plug-ins, components are essentially custom-built features. Since anyone can create these features, the interfaces used to control them can have wildly different looks and feels.

Figures 3.1 and 3.2 show the interfaces for two popular plug-ins for Photoshop (and Photoshop-compatible applications): Xaos Tools' Terrazzo and Procreate's KPT Effects. These plug-in interfaces have very little in common. Photoshop users, however, are used to adapting to or figuring out such plug-ins. Part of their appeal, in fact, is that they are fun to look at and play with.

Figure 3.2
The plug-in interface for Procreate's KPT Effects

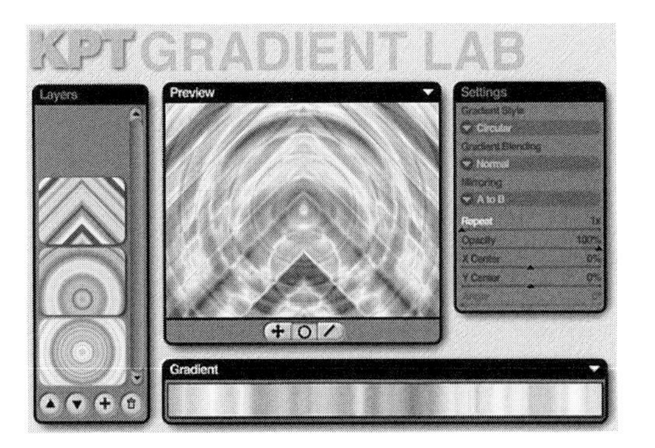

Even wild Photoshop plug-in interfaces, however, take advantage of interface elements that most people are familiar with. For example, look carefully at Figures 3.1 and 3.2. Notice that each plug-in interface features an Opacity setting that is controlled with a slider. This is because host applications like Photoshop also use sliders for their opacity settings (see Figure 3.3). Although there are slight stylistic differences between the plug-in sliders and the slider in Photoshop, the fundamental functionality is the same.

It's worth noting that a custom user interface isn't necessarily any better than the default user interface. Whether or not the custom interface is an improvement over the default one is up to the custom interface's designer. The default interface is small, which can make it hard to read. The size makes it difficult for the designer to provide information about each parameter. Also, in the default interface it is easy to inadvertently place a value that is unusable. If a custom interface does not improve on shortcomings like these, then it might be more of a hindrance than a help.

Most of the components featured in this book use a custom interface for the component parameters. In this chapter, you'll get hands-on experience working with custom user interfaces for component parameters. We'll also discuss the advantages and disadvantages of using custom interfaces. First, let's look at some custom interfaces for the parameters of several Flash components.

Good and Bad Custom UIs

Figures 3.4 through 3.7 show several examples of custom interfaces for the component parameters of various components. All of these custom interfaces are by Eyeland Studio and show somewhat of a progression. Each new UI reflects improvements we added to our custom UIs based on lessons learned.

For example, notice that all of the fields in the custom UI shown in Figure 3.4 are standard text fields. These fields are similar to the default value fields in the default user interface for the Component Parameters panel. Several of the parameters in Figure 3.4 allow for only true or false as the available values. Because this was one of our first custom UIs, we didn't utilize the List value type. Consequently, this custom UI has little value over the default UI.

A few additional features are provided by the custom UI shown in Figure 3.4. Notice the circular icons to the left of each parameter. When the user rolls over these icons, a short description of the parameter is shown at the bottom. This provides the user with

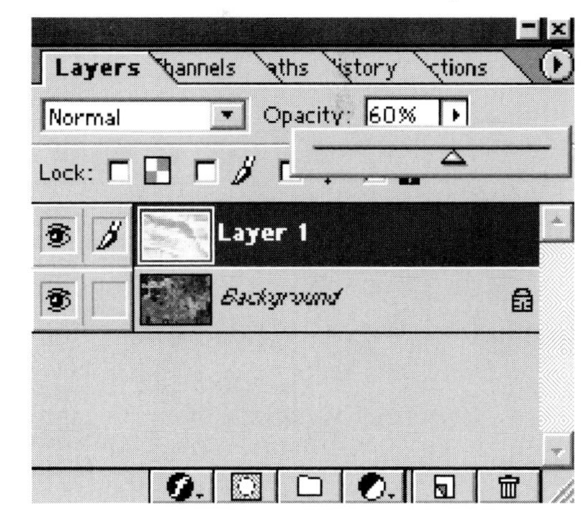

Figure 3.3

The opacity sliders in the third-party plug-in interfaces are similar to the opacity slider in Photoshop.

information that the default UI could not provide. Also notice the Check button at the bottom right; it allows the user to check if the values they set for the parameters will work with the component. The Check button is a small, added benefit that frees users from the trouble of testing the movies to determine if their chosen parameters will work properly.

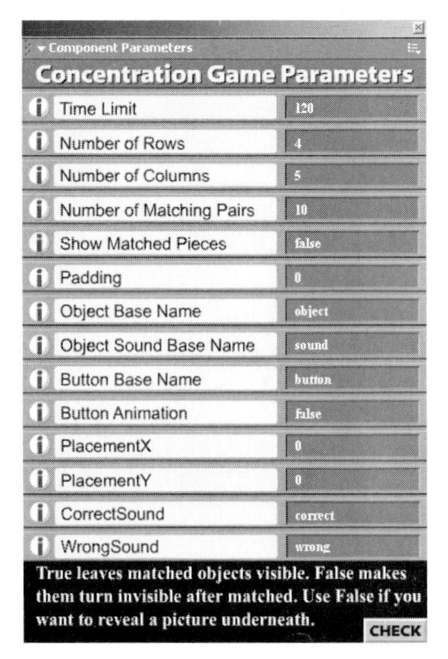

Figure 3.4

A custom UI that creates a concentration game

Another problem with the custom UI shown in Figure 3.4 is that it's a little crowded. There are so many parameters that the UI's dimensions are too tall. When we created this custom UI, we kept adding features, and at some point we started to run out of room to add more parameters. The custom UI shown in Figure 3.5 solves this problem by placing parameters on different tabs.

Although the custom UI shown in Figure 3.5 provides the freedom to add more parameters, it still does not offer many advantages over the default UI. Once again, we built in help information, placing it below the RGB color entry fields, but the RGB value entry fields don't even provide as many options as the default user interface.

The custom UIs shown in Figures 3.6 and 3.7 provide a much better solution. In Figure 3.7, you can enter RGB values or use standard HSB sliders and view the results in real time. Both of these custom UIs also provide standard sliders for specifying the values of some parameters. The sliders provide a benefit over the default UI because they show the user clear limits for the values of a parameter.

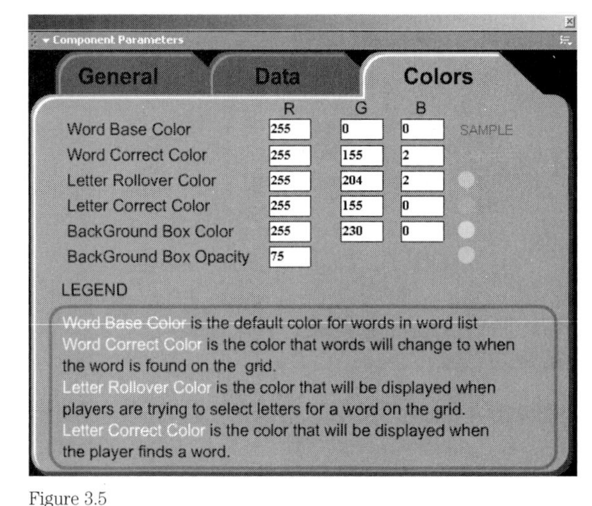

Figure 3.5

A word-search game

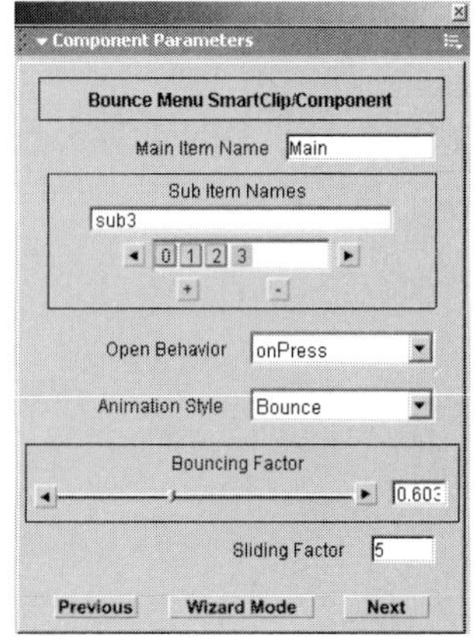

Figure 3.6

A dynamic drop-down menu

For example, let's say you have a parameter for which users need to specify a value between 0 and 255. If you use the default UI, you would probably use either the Default or Number value type fields. Either of these value types allows users to enter any value. If users aren't clear on what the parameter is for, they could easily enter a value of 500, which could potentially cause problems.

If you use a slider in a custom UI, then you can establish a range for that parameter. One end of the slider (usually the left end) would be the low value, and the other end would be the high value. Therefore, users could not specify values that won't work with the component.

The custom UI in Figure 3.6 shows the *advanced mode*, in which the parameters are grouped together with no explanations. This custom UI also features a *wizard mode*, which allows users to enter values for one or two parameters at a time. In wizard mode, each parameter is accompanied with a description of the parameter. Users can jump back and forth between advanced mode and wizard mode.

The custom UI shown in Figure 3.7 features pop-up help fields. At any time, users can roll over the buttons with question marks to receive information about the associated parameter. Therefore, users don't have to bother with going back and forth between advanced and wizard modes as they do in Figure 3.6.

Figure 3.7

A collapsible menu

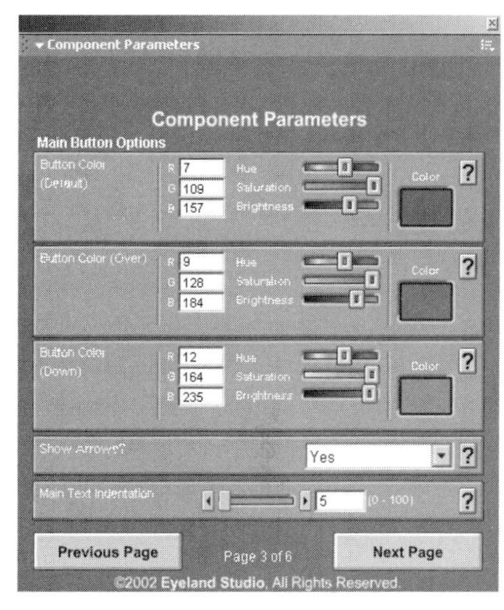

Both Figures 3.6 and 3.7 are examples of custom UIs that offer users clear improvements over the default UI. Each of these custom UIs provides information on each component parameter. They also offer improved methods for entering values for the parameters.

In addition, both custom UI examples look and operate similarly to dialog boxes and panels found in Flash (for the most part). Notice that Figure 3.7 displays the name of the parameter in a very consistent place. Each parameter is also clearly sectioned off from the other, which helps to minimize confusion. These subtle, stylistic features help to make the custom UI less intimidating and more intuitive to use. Most of the examples featured in this book use custom user interfaces similar to those shown in Figures 3.6 and 3.7.

Using Components with Custom Interfaces

Here's your chance to get some hands-on experience working with components that utilize custom interfaces for their component parameters.

Open the `Chapter3_A_Start.fla`. Save the file to your local hard drive as `Chapter3_A_Modified.fla` (see Figure 3.8). Zoom in on the gray rectangle labeled Spikes Background (as shown in Figure 3.9).

Figure 3.8

Save the `Chapter3_A_Start.fla` **file to your local hard drive.**

Figure 3.9

The Spikes Background component

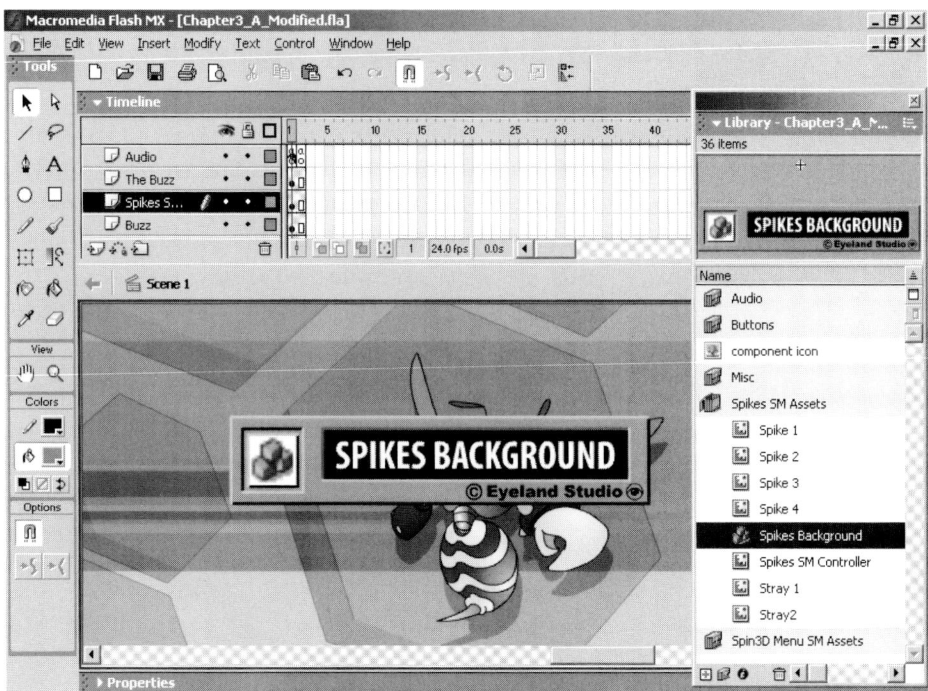

The gray rectangle is an instance of a component that generates a background pattern on a series of movie clips pulled from the library. In Chapter 2, we looked at the Zoom component. When that component was on the stage, it was represented by a big red circle. There was nothing about the Zoom component that distinguished it on the stage from another Flash symbol, such as a movie clip symbol or graphic symbol.

Notice that the gray rectangle has the same icon as a component in the library. We, at Eyeland Studio, use this same visual treatment for component instances to help users visually distinguish between components and other Flash resources (such as movie clips, graphic symbols, buttons, etc.). When the movie is published, the gray rectangle disappears and the component generates whatever effect it is programmed to create.

Many of the components featured throughout the rest of the book are represented by the same visual treatment. However, this is not a very common practice with component developers in general.

Now let's try to edit the parameters for the Spikes Background component (let's just call it Spikes). Select the instance of the component on the stage and open the Component Parameters panel by pressing Option/Alt+F7.

When you attempt to open the Component Parameters panel for Spikes, you should see the panel, but it will be grayed out except for the message, "There was an error opening the Custom UI for this Component," as shown in Figure 3.10. This problem occurs because the Spikes component was set up to look for an `.swf` file named `spikes_sc_UI.swf`, which is the Flash file that is the custom UI for the Spikes component.

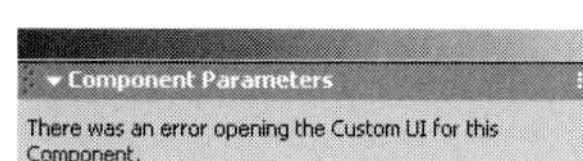

Figure 3.10

The Component Parameters panel displays an error message because it cannot access a necessary `.swf` file.

The Spikes component in the `Chapter3_A_Modified.fla` file that you are working with expects the `spikes_sc_UI.swf` file to be in the same directory on your hard drive where the `.fla` file is saved. However, when you saved the modified file to your hard drive, `spikes_sc_UI.swf` was not saved along with it. So, when you tried to open the Component Parameters panel, Flash couldn't oblige because the file was not where it was expected to be.

We will look at how to create a custom UI for a component's parameters in Chapter 11. For now, it's useful to know that custom UIs for component parameters are actually just Flash `.swf` files. If you see the "error opening" message in the Component Parameters panel, you know that the `.swf` the component needs is not in the right place.

Macromedia actually introduced a very valuable new capability in Flash MX to deal with this problem. Components developed in Flash MX can have their custom UIs embedded into them. If the custom UI is embedded into the file, then you don't have to worry about keeping track of any external `.swf` files.

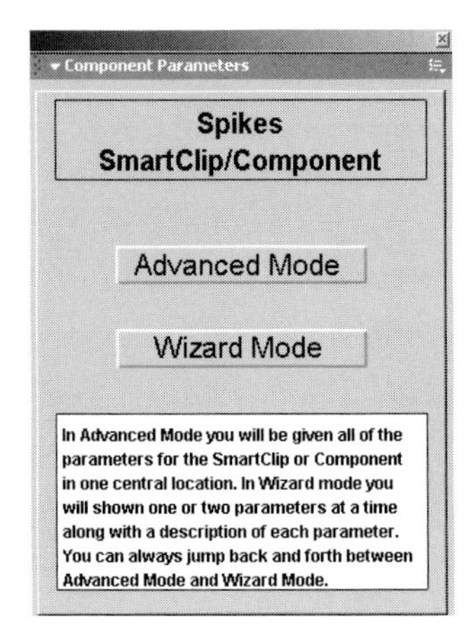

Figure 3.11

The Component Parameters panel displays the custom user interface.

Copy the `spikes_sc_UI.swf` and `3D_menu_UI.swf` files to the same directory on your local hard drive where you saved `Chapter3_A_Modified.fla`.

Select the instance of Spikes on the stage and open the Component Parameters panel (see Figure 3.11) by pressing Option/Alt+F7.

The first screen of the custom UI for the Spikes component presents two buttons that navigate to either advanced mode or wizard mode. The wizard mode allows you to enter parameters one or two at a time. Each screen in wizard mode provides a description of the parameter or parameters. Because we are discussing what each parameter does here, let's go right to advanced mode. Click the Advanced Mode button in the Component Parameters panel to see the window shown in Figure 3.12.

Parameters of the Spikes Component

There are two screenfuls of parameters in the advanced mode section of the Spikes custom UI. You can view and/or edit the second screen by clicking the Next button. Here are explanations of the parameters:

Number of Graphics The number specified in this field determines the number of graphics from Graphic Array that will be dynamically positioned on the stage.

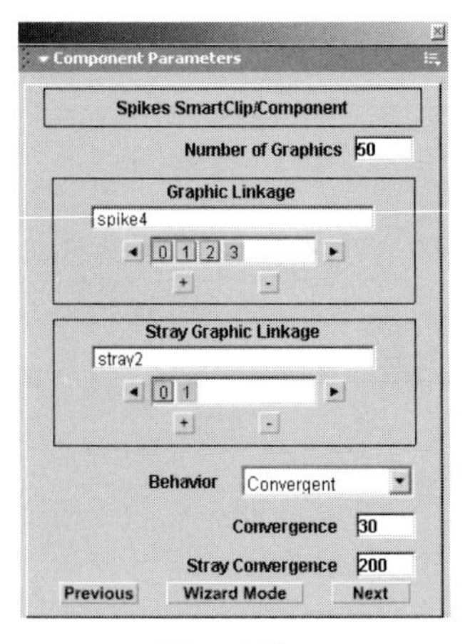

Figure 3.12

The first screen of the custom UI for the Spikes component in advanced mode

Graphic Linkage Each entry in this array handler is the linkage name for a movie clip that the component will dynamically position on the stage. You can use any movie clips you want by setting their Linkage names and then entering the value in this array. Hit the plus button to add Linkage name references to the array and the minus button to remove items from the array. The yellow button designates the item in the array that is currently selected.

Stray Graphic Linkage This is the array of graphic names. Stray graphics are also contained in movie clips. Strays add variance to the overall effect. Generally, you would use shapes that are slightly different, but complementary, to the main graphics.

Behavior This parameter specifies how the graphics will be positioned on the stage. Convergent means that the items in the Graphic and Stray Graphic Linkage arrays will be dynamically positioned around one spot. Divergent means that all of the graphics will be randomly positioned on the stage. The next two parameters, Convergence and Stray Convergence, are only utilized if you choose the Convergent option for the Behavior parameter.

Convergence This parameter specifies the distance in pixels that the graphics will be positioned around the Converge X and Converge Y positions (specified in later parameters).

Stray Convergence This does the same thing as the Converge parameters except for the stray graphics (also based on the Converge X and Converge Y values).

Stray Probability This parameter determines how many strays are likely to appear. Values closer to 1 increase the probability; values closer to 0 decrease the probability.

Stray Angle This specifies an angle that the strays will be positioned at. Enter values from 0 to 360.

Converge X and Converge Y These parameters specify where the graphics and strays will be positioned around if you select the Convergent option in the Behavior parameter.

Low Alpha and High Alpha These specify a range of variable transparency for the graphic objects (both graphics and strays). Enter values from 0 to 100.

Screen Width and Screen Height Enter the width and height of the stage, respectively.

The Graphic Linkage Parameters

Most of the parameters in the custom UI for the Spikes component require little additional explanation beyond the information already provided. However, the Graphic Linkage and Stray Graphic Linkage parameters need a little explanation.

Both the Graphic Linkage and Stray Graphic Linkage parameters are array handlers. They operate differently than the array value fields in the default UI. In addition, the values for the Graphic Linkage and Stray Graphic Linkage parameters are Identifiers for movie clips that the components pull from directly from the Flash Library.

We will be seeing array handlers similar to these in custom UIs featured in later chapters. In addition, many of the components featured in later chapters use resources from the library by referencing their "linkage" names or identifiers. So let's look at how array handlers in the Spikes custom UI work and then at how the component utilizes the linkage names or identifiers to pull resources from the library.

Click the small box labeled *0* in the Graphic Linkage parameter, as shown in Figure 3.13.

Notice that the box turns yellow when you click it, and the text field has the value *spike1* in it. The yellow box indicates which box is currently selected, and the text field reflects what text is associated with the selected box. If you click the box

Figure 3.13

Adjusting the Graphic Linkage parameter

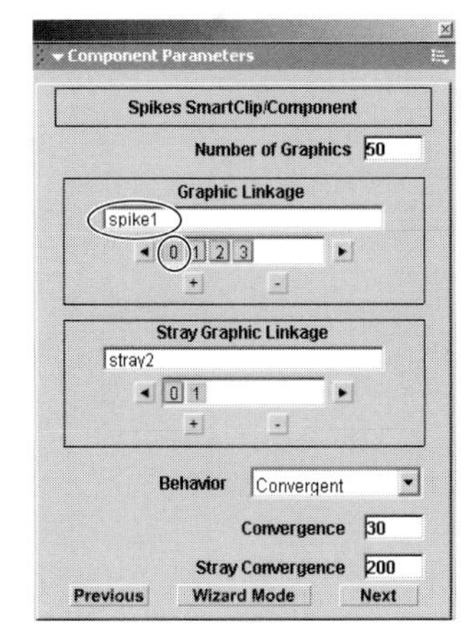

labeled *1*, the box will turn yellow and the value will change to *spike2*. In fact, each box has a value assigned to it. Therefore, to edit the values for the Graphic Linkage array handler, you simply need to click the boxes and edit their associated values. Adding or removing values to the array is very easy.

Click the box labeled *3* and then click the small button with the + symbol on it. Enter the text **spike5** in the field, as shown in Figure 3.14.

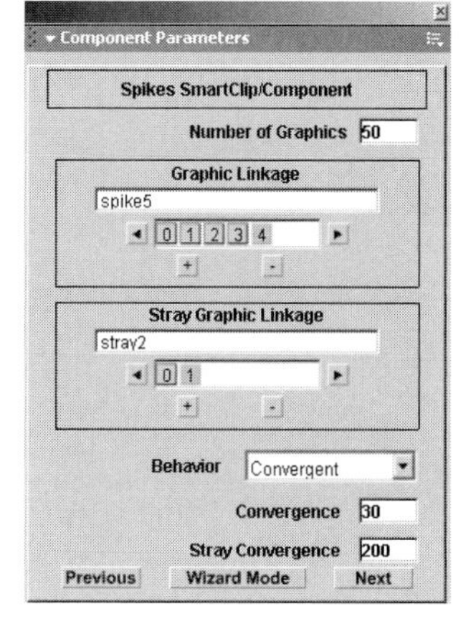

Figure 3.14

Click the add button (the plus sign) to add another item in the Graphic Linkage parameter array.

When you add an item to the array, the item is added after the currently selected item. So, for example, if you select the *2* box and click the plus button, the new item in the array will be inserted after the *2* box. If you click the minus button, the item that is currently selected will be removed. You will be using the item you just added to the array, so do not delete it.

Close the Component Parameters panel (Command/Alt+F4) and open the library (Command/Ctrl+L). Double-click the folder named `Spikes SM Assets`. Click the first movie clip named Spike 1, as shown in Figure 3.15.

Notice the shape that appears in the library preview. This is one of the shapes that the Spikes component utilizes. If you click the movie clips named Spike 2, Spike 3, and Spike 4, you will see the other shapes that the component uses. The component also uses the shapes in the Stray 1 and Stray 2 movie clips.

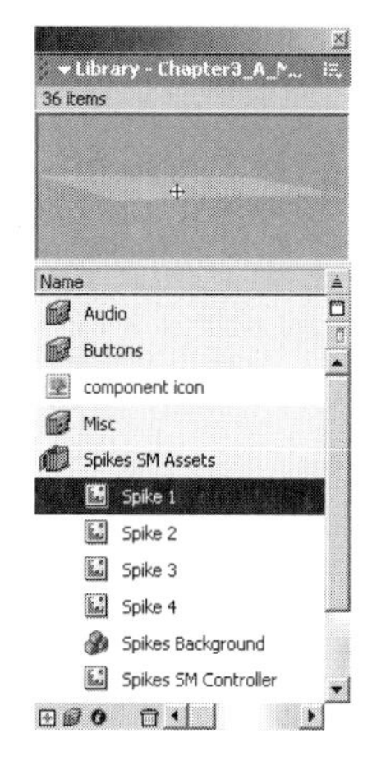

Figure 3.15

Open the `Spikes SM Assets` folder and select the Spikes 1 movie clip.

You might have noticed that the boxes in the Graphic Linkage array parameter start with the number *0* and the values start with the number *1*. That is, the box labeled *0* has the value *spike1*, the box labeled *1* has the value *spike2*, and so on. This is due to how arrays work in Flash's ActionScript. As far as the ActionScript is concerned, the first item in the array is numbered zero, the second item is numbered one, and so forth. This is known as *zero-based counting*. Arrays in Flash's ActionScript employ zero-based counting.

If you zoom out and inspect the stage, you will see that none of these shapes are on the stage. They are not hidden off the stage, and they are not on another scene. These movie clips are only in the library. However, when the movie plays, they appear on the stage because they are pulled from the library when the movie is exported. Let's see how this is accomplished.

Right-click or Option+click the Spike 1 movie clip. Select Linkage from the pop-up menu (see Figure 3.16) to open the Linkage Properties dialog box (shown in Figure 3.17).

Notice the contents of the Identifier field; the text in it is *spike1*. This is the same name as the first item in the Graphic Linkage parameter array. In fact, the Identifier is what the component uses to access the Spike 1 movie clip. Each entry in the Graphic Linkage parameter array is an Identifier for a movie clip. The value for the Identifier for any given movie clip must be entered exactly the same in the Graphic Linkage parameter array; otherwise, the component will not be able to access the movie clip.

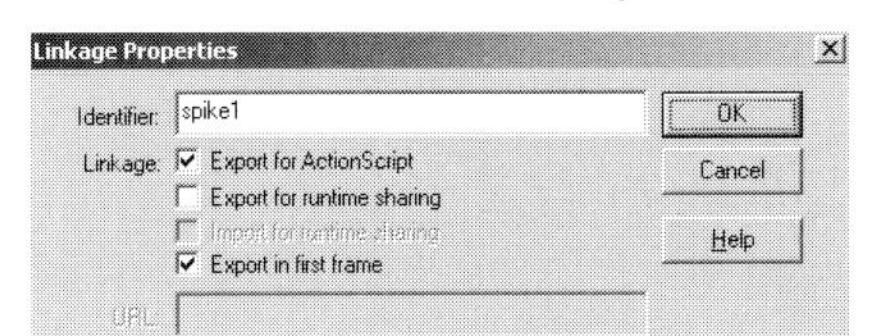

Figure 3.17

The Linkage Properties dialog box for the Spike 1 movie clip

Earlier we added an item to the Graphic Linkage array. Now let's create another movie clip and assign the Identifier name to it that we entered in the Graphic Linkage parameter array (*spike5*).

Click the Cancel button in the Linkage Properties dialog box. Right-click or Option+click the Spike 4 movie clip and choose Duplicate from the pop-up menu (see Figure 3.18). Enter the text **Spike 5** in the Name box in the Duplicate Symbol dialog box (see Figure 3.19).

Now click the Advanced button. Click the Export For ActionScript option. Then enter **spike5** in the Identifier field (see Figure 3.20). Click OK when you are done.

The Advanced button in the Duplicate Symbol dialog box is a nice little shortcut. We could have hit the OK button in the Duplicate Symbol dialog box without using the Advanced button. Then we could have opened the Linkage Properties dialog box as we did before to set the Identifier for the Spike 5 movie clip. Flash saves us an extra step by letting us set the Identifier within the Duplicate Symbol dialog box.

Notice that you must select the Export For ActionScript option before the Identifier field will become available. When you select this option, the Export In First Frame option is also selected automatically. The Export In First Frame option has to do with how the movie clip is loaded. It can substantially affect how the component loads over the Internet—particularly if preload code is built into the movie. We will look at this issue in detail in Chapter 5.

When you click the Export For ActionScript option, the Identifier field is automatically filled with the movie clip's name, Spike 5. If you leave the Identifier field with that name, the component will not be able to access the Spike 5 movie clip because there is an added space in the name. Earlier you entered *spike5* in the Graphic Linkage parameter array, not *Spike 5*. Linkage names are not case-sensitive, so you can enter *spike5* or *Spike5* or even *SPIKE5* and it will work, but the added space in *Spike 5* will not work.

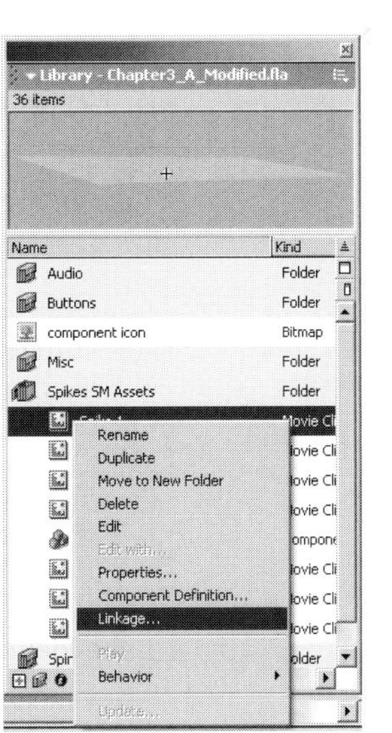

Figure 3.16

Selecting Linkage from the pop-up menu

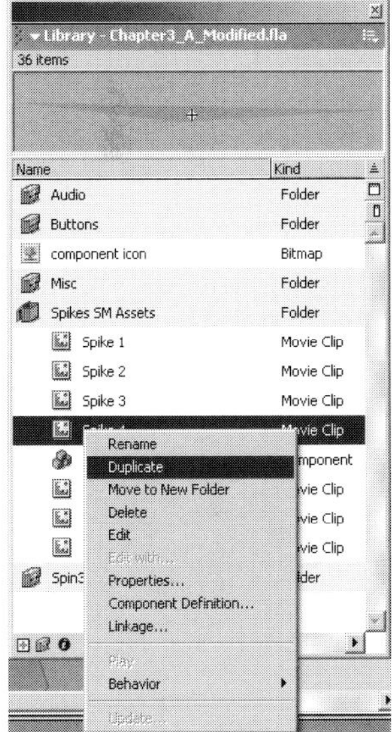

Figure 3.18

Creating another movie clip

Editing Component Assets

Now edit the Spike 5 movie clip. Delete the polygonal shape within it and use the Line tool to draw a simple lightning-bolt line. To help the line blend in better with the other shapes, color the line burgundy and use the Color Mixer panel to set the opacity to 50%, as in Figure 3.21.

Right now the Spikes Background is on a layer that's above most of the elements in the movie so that you could see it when you began working with the movie. Drag the Spike Smart Clip layer down below the Bottom Elements layer and above the Back layer. When you are finished, return to the main scene and press Command/Ctrl+Enter to test the movie (see Figure 3.22).

Figure 3.19

Changing the name to Spike 5

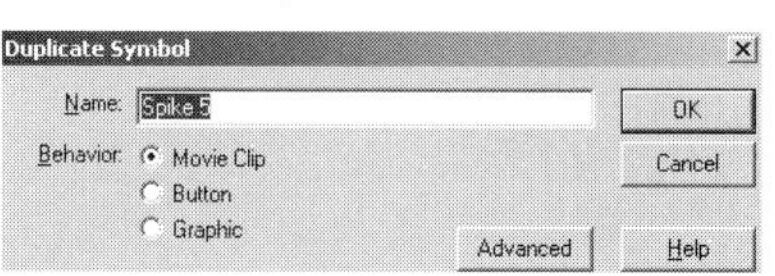

Figure 3.20

The Advanced button in the Duplicate Symbol dialog box provides access to Linkage property settings.

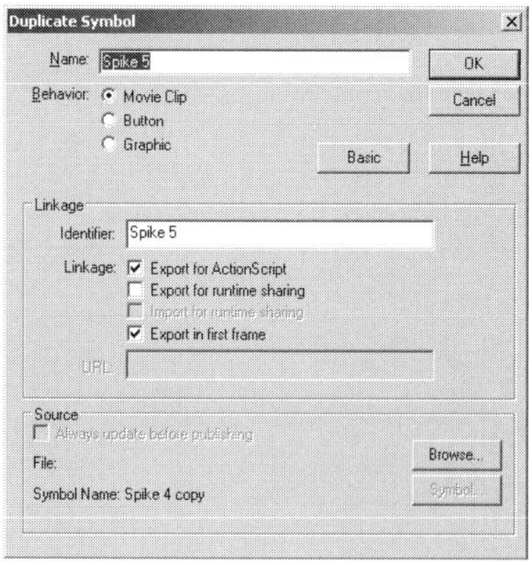

Look at the upper-left corner region of the movie and notice the texture created by a random array of spike graphics. You should also see several instances of the line you created in the previous step. The effect is random, so if you do not see the lines, close the test movie and retest. If you do not see any lines, then your spelling for the Identifier for the Spike 5 movie clip probably does not match what you entered in the Graphic Linkage parameter array.

In Chapter 2, we looked at the default UI for an array. The array handler in Spikes' custom UI is an improvement over the default UI because it does not require that you open a separate dialog box to add or remove items to the array. Also, in the custom UI, it is much more readily apparent that the Graphic Linkage parameter is an array handler. While you do need to learn how the custom UI handles arrays, once you know how it works, it is very easy to see at a glance which parameters in the custom UI are array parameters and which are not.

This example demonstrates how easy it is to add graphics to the array of graphics used by the Spikes Background component. In spite of the name of the component, however, you can actually use it to generate backgrounds with any shapes simply by editing all of the movie clips that the component uses. Of course, you can also get more out of the Spikes Background component by leveraging some of the other options in the parameters.

Other Custom UI Improvements

Of course, the fact that there is additional information about each parameter (in the wizard mode) is also an advantage over the default UI. Now let's edit a few more parameters.

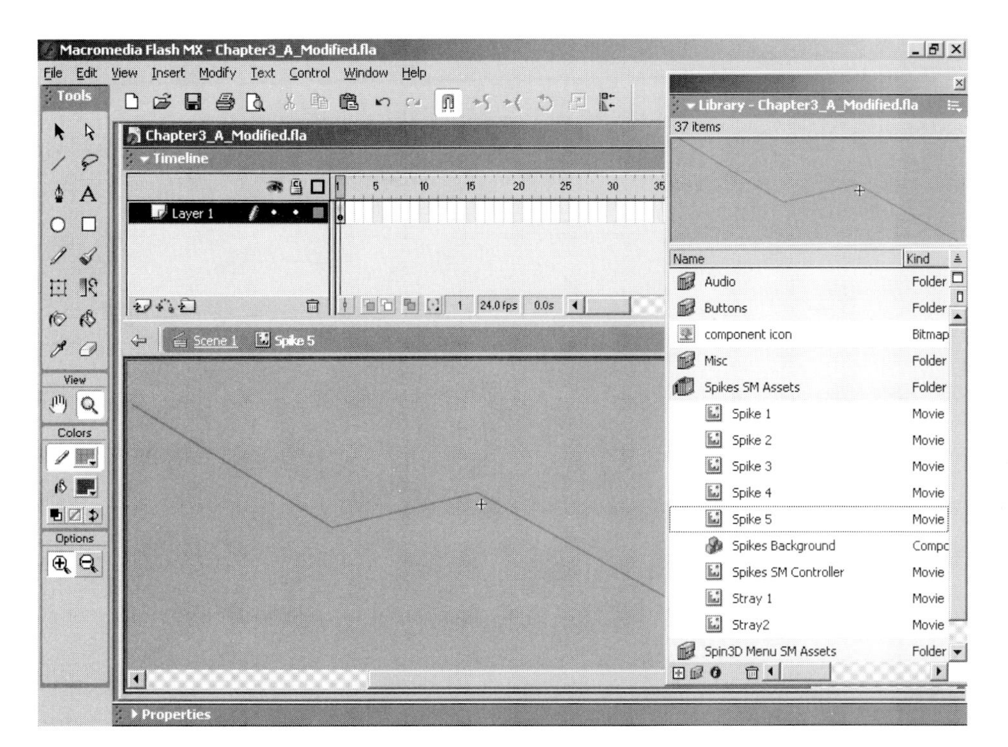

Figure 3.21

Editing the Spike 5 movie clip

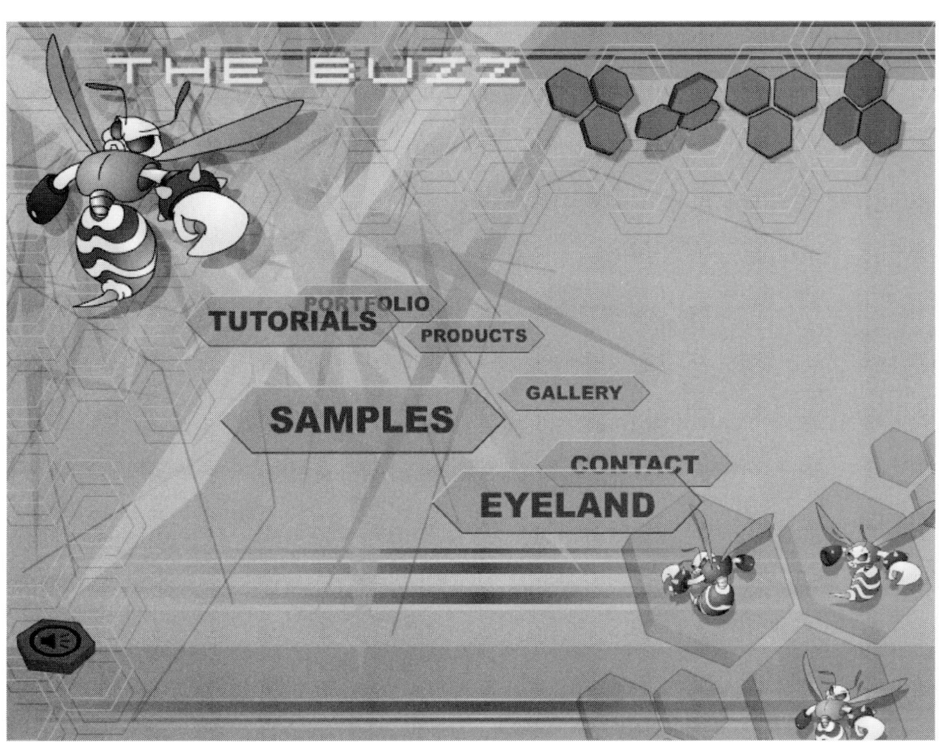

Figure 3.22

Notice that the component has used the movie clip with the lightning bolt line you added.

Close the test movie and close the library. Make all the layers above the Spikes Smart Clip layer invisible. Select the instance of the Spikes Background component on the stage again and open the Component Parameters panel. Click the Advanced Mode button. Change the value for the Number Of Graphics parameter to 75. Now click the down-arrow next to the Behavior parameter and select Divergent, as shown in Figure 3.23.

Notice that the drop-down menu option for the Behavior parameter is a slight improvement over the default UI. The default UI requires that you first click the value field before you can see that it is a List value type. The custom UI for the Spikes component reveals the fact that the Behavior parameter is a List value type at a glance.

PARAMETER	VALUE
Low Alpha	35
High Alpha	80
Screen Width	800
Screen Height	600

Click the Next button and change the parameter values as indicated in the following list and shown in Figure 3.24. When you are finished, close the Component Parameters panel.

Now test the movie. Notice that all of the polygon shapes and the line you created earlier are distributed all over the stage, as in Figure 3.25. Some of the shapes are also more transparent, and none of the shapes are fully opaque. If you don't quite like the effect, you can close the Test Movie window, reedit the parameters, and test again. Although opening and closing the Component Parameters panel might seem a little tedious, it's not nearly as tedious as having to sift through ActionScript to adjust all of the relevant variables. The custom UI also makes things a little easier and more intuitive by providing a more user-friendly environment to adjust the parameters.

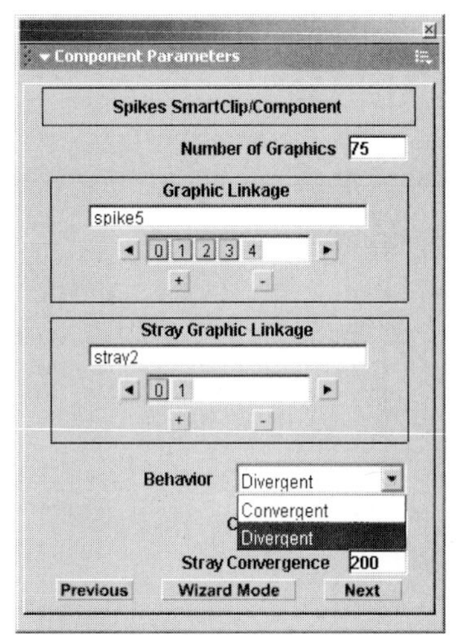

Figure 3.23

Editing the Number Of Graphics and Behavior parameters

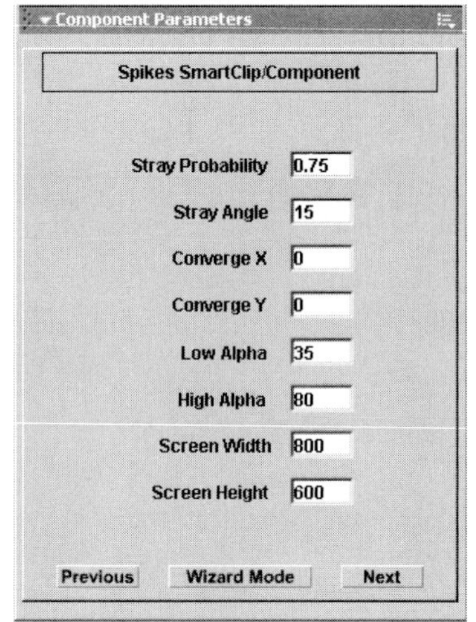

Figure 3.24

The second screen in Advanced mode

WHY YOU NEED TO CLOSE THE COMPONENT PARAMETERS PANEL

It is especially important to close the Component Parameters panel before you test a movie when you are working with a component that utilizes a custom UI. Critical communication between a custom UI and the Flash file that contains the component occurs when you close the panel: Flash collects the values for the respective variables from the parameters in the custom UI. If you test the movie before closing the panel, the variables may not have values. The result is that Flash will very often crash or the movie may not work properly. Therefore, it's a good idea to get in the practice of always closing the Component Parameters panel when you are finished editing the parameters. It may get a little tedious to always have to open the panel, edit the parameters, close the panel, test the movie, close the Test Movie window, and then start the process all over again if you see something that needs to be adjusted. However, it is much better than crashing Flash and potentially losing all your hard work.

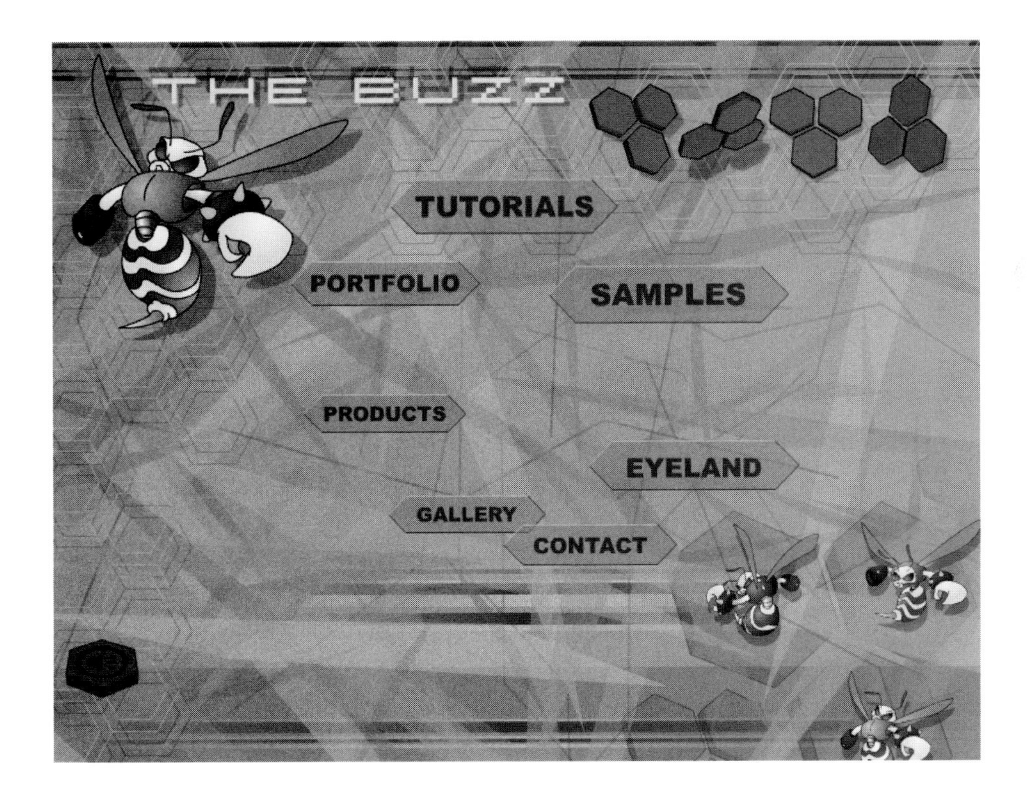

Figure 3.25

The Spikes Component now distributes the shapes all over the stage.

Resizing the Component Parameters Panel

Before I move on to another example component, let's look at a characteristic or a byproduct of working with custom UIs that is useful to be aware of. Select the Spikes Background component and open the Component Parameters panel. Drag the bottom-right corner of the panel and resize it so that it is much smaller. The exact size is not important; the panel should look something like Figure 3.26.

Custom component UIs can be created so that they resize when you resize the Component Parameters panel. Actually, it is more accurate to say that custom UIs can be programmed so that they *won't* resize when the panel is resized. That is the case with the custom UI for Spikes. When the panel is resized, the custom UI does not scale down or scale up. If a custom UI does scale, you might want to scale the Component Parameters panel up a little so that it is easier to see the parameters or built-in instructions.

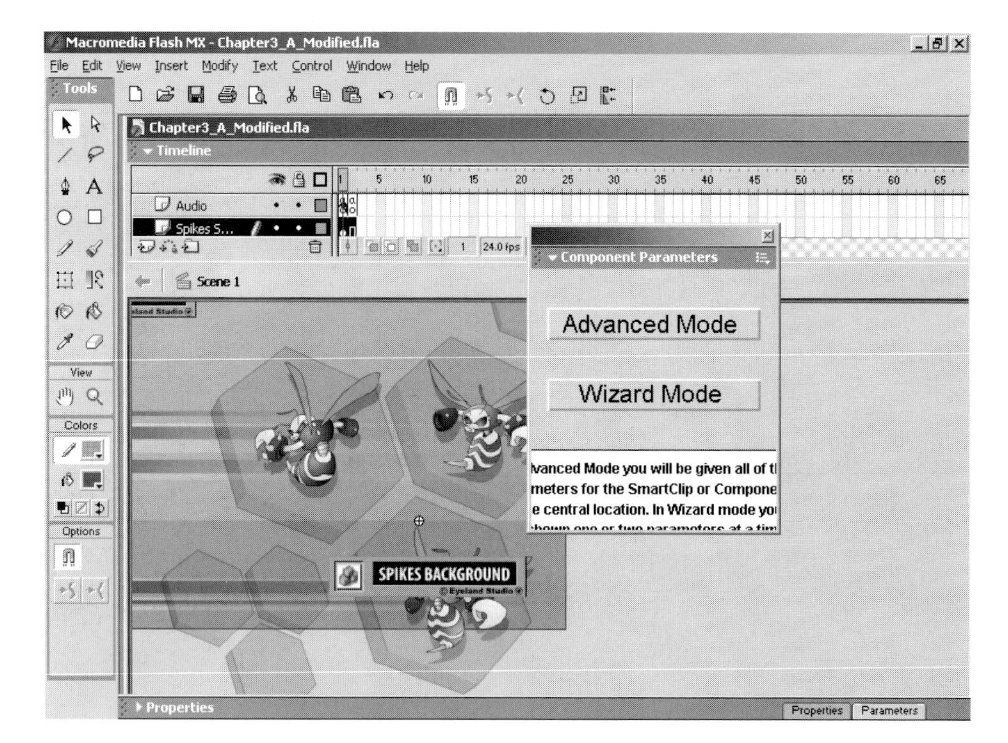

Figure 3.26

Resize the Component Parameters panel so that it is much smaller.

The fact that you can resize the Component Parameters panel can lead to some problems. If, for example, the panel has been resized so that it is very small, a component with a custom UI may open up so that the parameters are too small to read or manipulate. If you encounter this problem, you can resize the Component Parameters panel so that the custom UI within the panel is easier to read.

We'll emulate the problem in this example. We have just sized the Component Parameters panel down as if we had been working with a custom UI that was much smaller. Close the panel. Then select the 3D Spin Menu component instance and open the panel again (see Figure 3.27).

It might look as if you accidentally had selected the Spikes Background component instead of the 3D Spin Menu component; the two custom UIs look very similar.

Notice that the size of the Component Parameters panel is the same as when we left it in the previous step. When you open the panel, it will always open up at the same size that it was when you closed it. This is true even when you're working with components in different Flash files. If the custom UI is not coded so that it won't scale with the size of the Component Parameters panel, then the custom UI might appear to be very small.

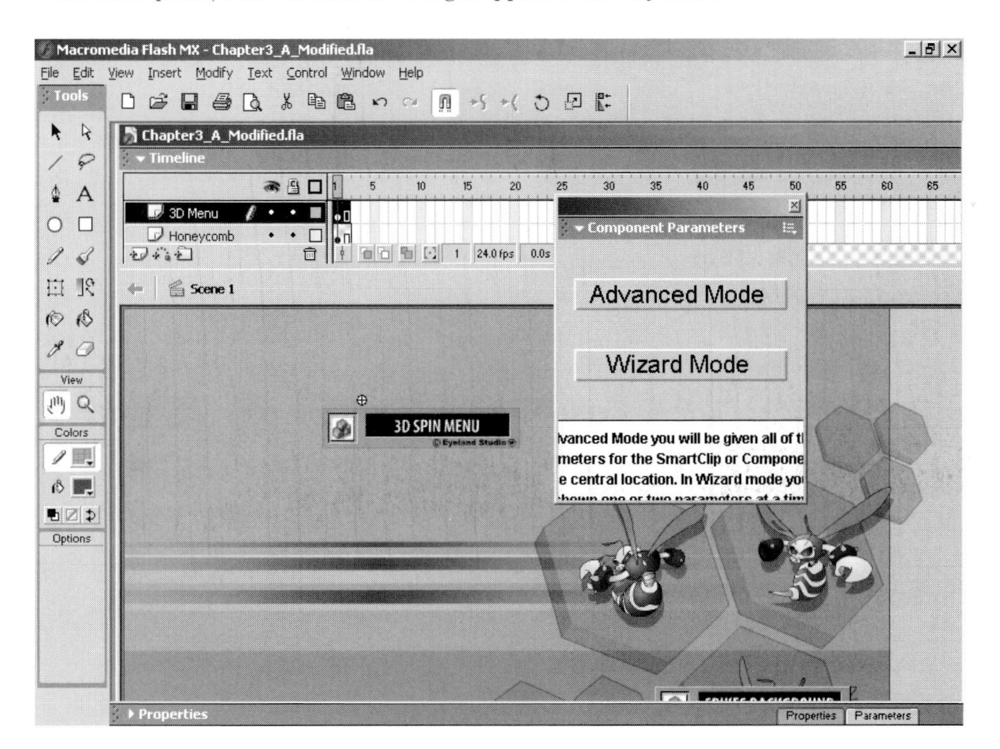

Figure 3.27

The Component Parameters panel opens to the size that it was when it was last closed.

Of course, the solution is to simply resize the Component Parameters panel. However, if you ever see a custom UI in the panel that's really small, don't assume that the designers intended it to be very small and illegible. It is far more likely that the panel is just not sized properly.

Parameters of the 3D Spin Menu Component

The 3D Spin Menu component instance is in the middle of the stage. You have probably already noticed the results of the 3D Spin Menu when you tested the movie: it generates the rotating menu. Let's take a look at this component.

Drag the bottom-right corner of the Component Parameters panel and resize it so that it displays the entire custom UI. The exact size is not important. Click the Advanced button when you have finished resizing; the panel should look something like Figure 3.28.

Here is a list of the parameters and their descriptions for the 3D Spin Menu component:

Center x-Position and Center y-Position These parameters specify the point that the menu rotates about. Each parameter takes stage coordinates.

Circle Radius This parameter specifies the radius for the items to animate around. The radius is the maximum distance any item will be from the center point.

Graphics Linkage Each entry in this array handler is the linkage name for a movie clip that the component will dynamically position on the stage for the 3D menu. You can add as many movie clips as you want, and they will all be placed at an equidistance around a circle. The movie clips can also contain buttons for rollover effects and additional actions.

Spin Behavior This list parameter specifies how the menu spins. Selecting Horizontal makes the items spin as if they were on a carousel, Vertical makes the items spin as if they were on a Ferris wheel, and All Directions makes the menu spin on all axes.

Spin Control This list parameter specifies what the user must do to spin the menu. The Mouse Position option spins the menu depending on how far the mouse is from the center, the Click And Drag option spins the menu according to how fast the user moves the mouse while it is being clicked, and the Click, Drag And Throw option does the same as Click And Drag except the menu will keep spinning after the user has let go of the mouse.

Menu Movement This list parameter specifies how the menu behaves when the mouse is over an item. The Freeze On Rollover option stops the menu when the mouse is over an item, and the Move On Rollover option allows the menu to continue in motion even when the mouse is over an item.

Actions On Press, Actions On Rollover, Actions On Rollout These are array handlers. They allow you to specify an action for each of the menu items that will be executed when the user clicks, rolls over, or rolls out of the item, respectively. You can provide a URL to another web page, the path to an SWF file that will be loaded, or a simple ActionScript command. You can use any of the following actions: `gotoAndPlay`, `gotoAndStop`, `nextFrame`, `play`, `prevFrame`, and `stop`. Use dot-syntax to define the Timeline that the action should be called in, for example, `_root.mc.gotoAndPlay(3)`. Each of these parameters can be left blank if you do not want any actions to occur for that particular event.

Load Movie Level This parameter allows you to specify a numeric value that defines what level to load any SWFs. This value is important only if you linked any of the menu items to load a movie. This parameter can be left blank.

URL Window If any of the menu items are linked to web pages, this parameters defines whether the page should be opened in a new browser window or the same.

Perspective Depth This parameter specifies a numeric value that controls the perspective appearance of the 3D menu. This value must be greater than the value for the menu's radius. If the menu items appear too big when you publish your file, increase this value.

Mouse Factor This determines how fast the menu spins with the user's input. The larger the value, the slower the menu spins.

Notice that the custom UI for the 3D Spin Menu component's parameters is very similar to the custom UI for Spikes. The nice thing about this is that now that you have learned how to use the Spikes component, you should have a good idea how to use many of the parameters for 3D Spin Menu.

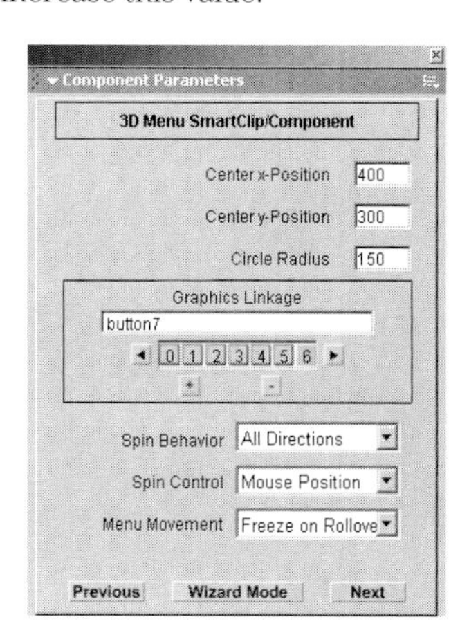

Figure 3.28

Resize the Component Parameters panel to view the entire custom UI.

For example, notice that there is a Graphics Linkage array parameter in the custom UI for 3D Spin Menu. The Graphics Linkage parameter in the 3D Spin Menu custom UI works exactly the same as the Graphic Linkage parameter in the Spikes custom UI. If you open the library and look in the `Buttons` folder, you will see a series of buttons. If you open the Linkage Properties for the movie clip named Button 1, you will see that its Identifier name matches the value for the first item in the Graphics Linkage array in the 3D Spin Menu custom UI (see Figure 3.29).

If you click the Next button, you'll notice several more array parameters (see Figure 3.30). All of these parameters are for actions that occur either on press, rollover, or rollout. These array parameters differ from the Graphics Linkage parameters in that they can have several different types of values. For instance, you can enter a URL, or you can enter a simple ActionScript command such as:

```
_root.instance_name.gotoAndStop(5);
```

The additional information in the wizard mode lets the user know the difference between acceptable values for the Graphics Linkage parameter and acceptable values for, say, the Actions On Press parameter. This is a good example of a case where the ability to include additional information in the custom UI is a strong advantage over the default UI.

We will be working with these Actions On Press and similar parameters in the next chapter. For now, let's look at one more example of a custom UI feature that is an improvement over the default UI.

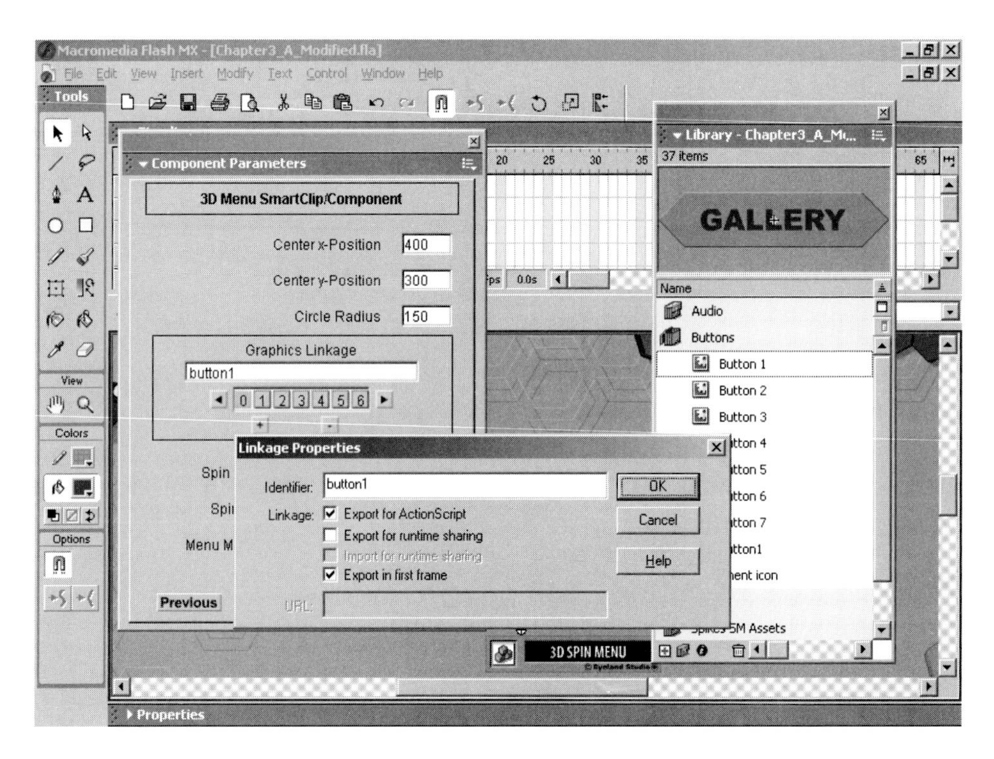

Figure 3.29

The Graphics Linkage parameter in the 3D Spin Menu works the same as the Graphic Linkage parameter in the Spikes custom UI.

Click the Next button again and notice the last parameter: the Mouse Factor parameter, shown in Figure 3.31. The Mouse Factor parameter controls how fast the menu items will rotate. If you click and slide the slider to the far right and far left, you will see that the range of values is from 250 to 3000. Many of the parameters we've looked at already had values that were far below 3000. In fact, many parameters have acceptable values that range from 0 to only 100.

If this parameter had only a simple field for the user to enter a number into, the user could mistakenly enter a value that wouldn't work very well. If the user looked at the other parameters and decided to try a value from 0 to 100, the component might not work properly. The custom UI, however, lets you use interfaces like the slider element. By incorporating the slider into the 3D Spin Menu, the component designer allows the user to edit the parameter with no opportunity to inadvertently enter a value that won't work properly. Also, without an interface like the slider, the user might never discover that a value as high as 3000 could work.

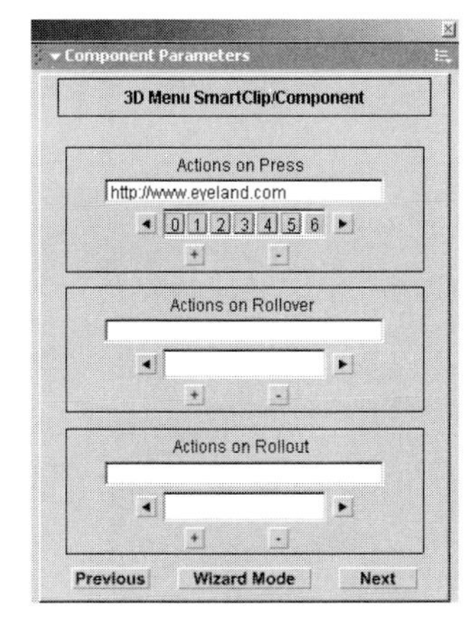

Figure 3.30

The arrays on the next page in advanced mode work the same as the Graphics Linkage parameter.

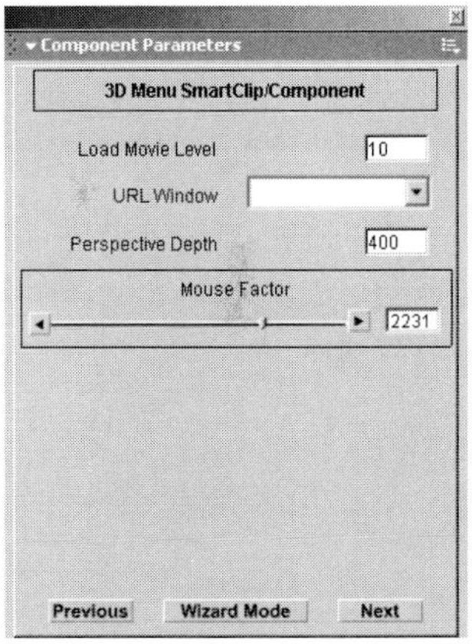

Conclusion

Custom user interfaces for editing component parameters can be very valuable. You do have to remember steps such as closing the Component Parameters panel before testing or publishing your movie. However, custom UIs give you the ability to create a more intuitive and less troublesome means for adjusting a component's parameters.

Like plug-ins for programs such as Adobe Photoshop, custom UIs can be very wild and fanciful or they can be very conservative and unimaginative. Whether a custom UI is actually an improvement over the default UI is entirely up to the component designer.

Most of the components that we have seen up to this point have been noninteractive. In the next chapter, we will start working with components for creating buttons and relatively basic navigation. Most of the components we will work with in the remainder of this book will feature custom UIs.

Figure 3.31

The Mouse Factor parameter utilizes a slider that keeps the user from entering a value that won't work with the component.

Chapter 4: Button Components

Buttons are one of the main resources in Flash that are used to facilitate interaction. It is very easy to create buttons in Flash, but even something as simple as this can be made easier by components. What if you need to create 10 buttons with a consistent look and feel? What if you're graphically challenged—wouldn't it be nice if you could get a component to draw the buttons for you?

In this chapter, you will look at several components used to create buttons. You will learn more about editing the component parameters for colors and fonts. You will also learn about components that use Live Preview, and you will learn some of the advantages and disadvantages of using Live Preview. You will begin working with the Components panel. You will learn what an MXP file is for, and you will also learn about the Macromedia Extension Manager.

In general, this chapter continues your journey to become more familiar and comfortable with components. The more practice you have working with components, the more you will see their incredible value and potential.

- **Editing color and font parameters**
- **Adjusting component dimensions**
- **Working with MXP files**

Editing Color and Font Parameters

Open the `PixelButton.fla` file in the Chapter 4 folder on the CD (see Figure 4.1). Save the file to your local computer so that you can save your edits as you follow along.

Test the movie and roll over the various buttons (see Figure 4.2). Notice that each of the buttons looks the same except that the default and rollover colors are different and the top center button is also wider than the other buttons. Each of these buttons is actually a different instance of the same component. Now go ahead and close the text movie window and return to the `PixelButton.fla` file.

Open the library and notice that the PixelButton component has a custom icon instead of the default component icon (see Figure 4.3). If you are not familiar with the default icons for Flash resources—such as movie clips, graphic symbols, bitmap symbols, audio symbols, and components—then it might not be very easy to spot a custom icon. Custom icons, however, cannot be created for anything other than components. Therefore, if you spot an icon that you haven't seen before, chances are it's a custom component icon.

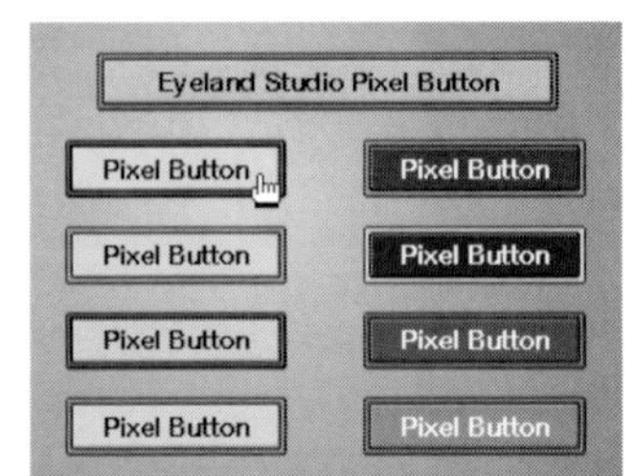

Figure 4.2

The movie shows nine buttons on the stage.

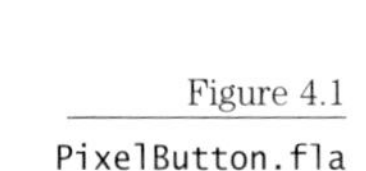

Figure 4.1

`PixelButton.fla`

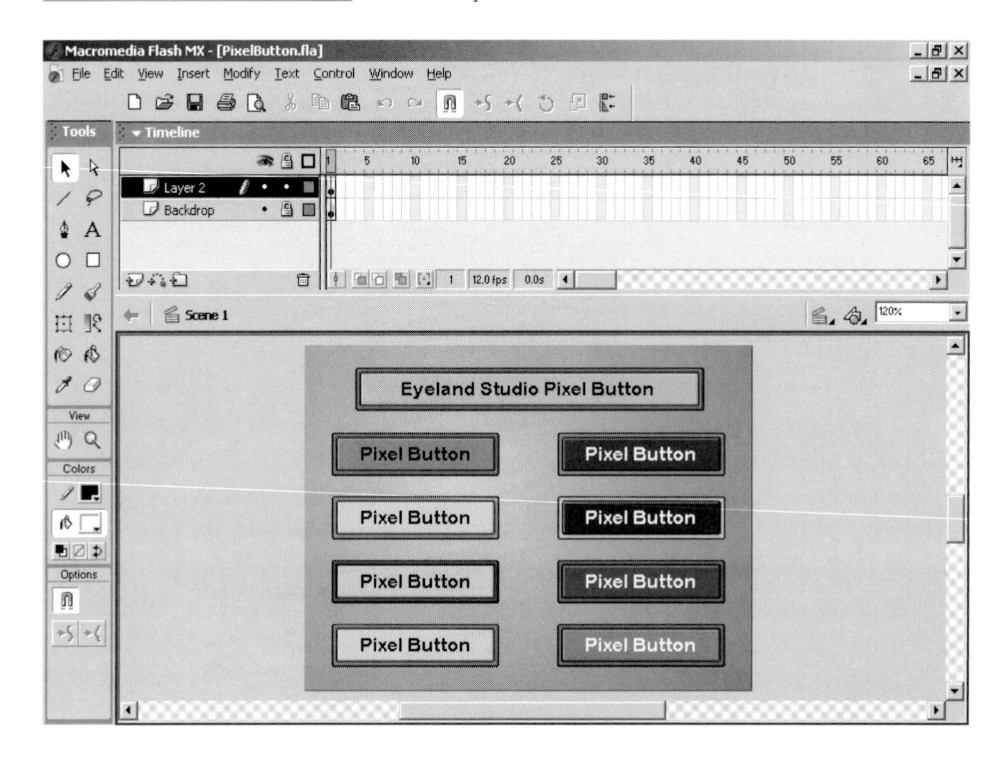

Custom component icons can help distinguish one component from another. They are particularly useful if you are using a series of components that have similar names and similar purposes. You will see an example of this later in this chapter when we look at using MXP files. Now let's look at the component parameters for the PixelButton component.

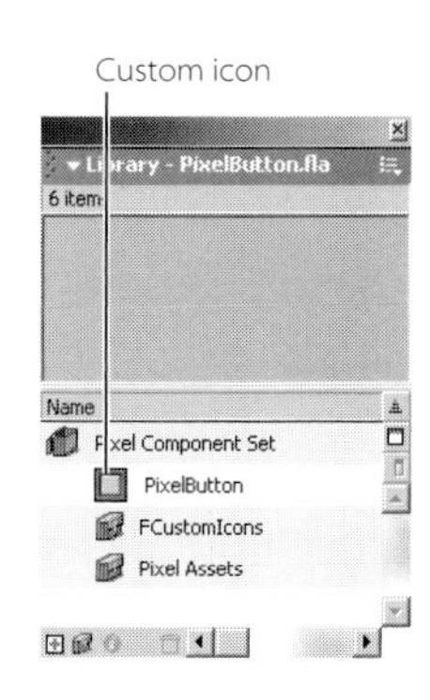

Figure 4.3

The PixelButton component features a custom icon in the library.

Select the top-left PixelButton component in the first column on the stage (the instance of the PixelButton that is green with a red outline) and press Option/Alt+F7 to open the Component Parameters panel. Read the Instructions if you like (see Figure 4.4) and then click the Next Page button to proceed to the editable parameters.

> Notice that you did not have to copy a `UI.swf` file to the local computer as discussed in Chapter 3. This is because the custom UI for the PixelButton component is embedded into the component. This means that an external `.swf` file is not needed for the custom UI. Embedding custom UIs will be covered in Chapter 11.

The PixelButton custom UI contains three pages of parameters. Here's description of each parameter:

Button Text Specifies text that will appear on the button. You can enter letters, numbers, and punctuation.

Text Size, Text Color, Text Font Specifies the size of the text in points (you can specify anything from 5 to 100 points), its color, and the font. You can only specify a font that is on your local system. It is important to enter the exact name of the font, or a default font will be displayed. Some fonts may not display perfectly centered on the button.

Figure 4.4

The first page of the Component Parameters panel for an instance of the PixelButton component

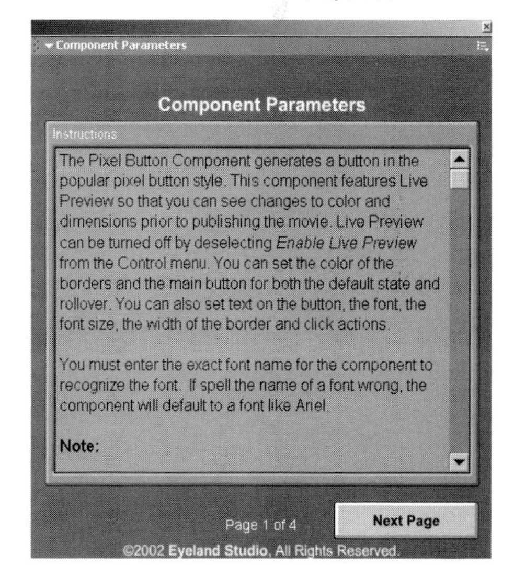

Inner Bevel Color, Outer Bevel Color Specifies the default colors of the button and its border. If the color of the first parameter is the same as the color specified for the Text Color parameter, the text may not be visible.

Rollover Inner Bevel Color, Rollover Outer Bevel Color Specifies the rollover colors of the button and its border. If the color of the Rollover Inner Bevel Color parameter is the same as the color specified for the Text Color parameter, the text may not be visible on rollover. If you specify the same for the Outer Bevel Color parameter as the Rollover Outer Bevel Color, then the border will not change color on rollover.

Button Width, Button Height Specifies the width and height of the button, in pixels.

Band Spacing Specifies the width of the border. The larger the value, the more the border will push into the button area. Very large values may make the main button area too small. This parameter accepts values from 2 to 50.

Action Type Specifies whether to load a URL, load a movie, or specify an action. Selecting any option will produce a related field. For instance, Get URL will produce a field to enter the URL in.

URL Allows you to specify a URL that will be opened if the user clicks on the button. For instance, enter `http://www.eyeland.com`. This parameter is only available if you specify URL in the Action Type parameter.

URL Window Specifies how you want the URL to load. The value _self will load the URL in the current browser window. Selecting _blank will load the URL in a new browser window. This parameter is only available if you specify URL in the Action Type parameter.

Load Movie SWF Specifies the movie to load. For example, enter `move.swf` to specify the movie to load. This parameter is only available if you specify Load Movie in the Action Type parameter.

Load Movie Level Specifies the level to load the movie in. If you enter 0 for the level, the movie you load will replace the current movie (which is not typically the desired effect). This parameter is only available if you specify Load Movie in the Action Type parameter.

Action Use this to specify an action that will be executed when the user clicks on the button. For example `_root.instance_name.gotoAndStop(10);`. This parameter is only available if you specify Action in the Action Type parameter.

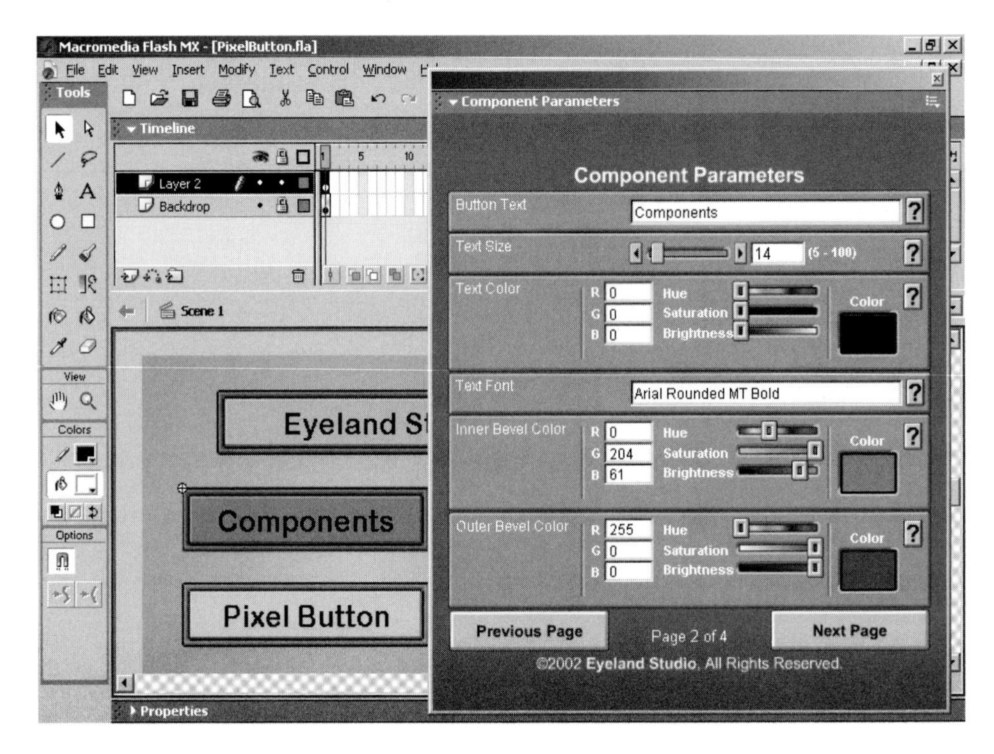

Figure 4.5

The change that you make to the Button Text parameter is reflected on the instance of the component.

Now change the text in the Button Text parameter to "Components". Move the Component Parameters panel so that you can see the instance of the PixelButton component that you are editing. Notice that the text has already been changed on the button (see Figure 4.5). You did not have to close the Component Parameters panel and you did not have to publish or test the movie in order to see the change that you made to the value of the Button Text parameter.

This behavior is made possible by a new feature in Flash MX called Live Preview. Components that take advantage of Live Preview let you see edits that you make to the component without forcing you to publish the movie. Obviously, this can help save time and frustration because you don't have to test and retest the movie as you make changes to the component's parameters. However, as you will see, there are some drawbacks to Live Preview.

THE FIRST DRAWBACK OF LIVE PREVIEW: CPU DRAIN

One of the key problems with Live Preview is that it can tend to slow things down while you are working in Flash. As you will learn in Chapter 11, Live Preview is implemented by creating a Flash movie that actually runs or displays within Flash. This should not be confused with Test Movie. When Live Preview is implemented for a component, a movie is actually running within the Flash working environment.

The trouble is, the movie that is running within Flash to facilitate the Live Preview functionality only runs at 1 frame per second. Any changes made in the Component Parameters panel for a component that utilizes Live Preview will only be reflected on the stage once every second. Obviously, this is not bad if Live Preview is displaying simple changes like text edits, color, height, width, position, and so on.

However, each instance of a component that uses Live Preview basically has a movie playing within Flash to show the updates. The Live Preview movie (or movies) is constantly running even if nothing is changing. If you have 20 instances of a component that utilizes Live Preview, then you have 20 movies playing at 1 frame per second within Flash.

This can pose a problem if a lot of code is being executed on a continual basis; the drain on your computer's resources could possibly cause your computer to crash. Live Preview can, in fact, be implemented to show live updates to components that perform animation or other dynamic effects. However, these sorts of things can be very distracting while you're working within Flash and can cause an excessive drain on your computer's resources.

Therefore, Live Preview is usually used in moderation to avoid these problems. In addition, if you need to use a large number of instances of a component that utilizes Live Preview, you might want to turn off Live Preview. You can turn off Live Preview by deselecting Enable Live Preview from the Control menu.

Now change the value of the Text Size parameter to 18. You can enter 18 in the value field by sliding the slider to the right until the value reads 18, or you can click the right arrow four times until the value reads 18. Notice that the changes you make to the Text Size parameter are also reflected on the instance of the PixelButton component on the stage (see Figure 4.6).

> Most custom UIs allow you to press the Tab key on your keyboard to navigate between fields. For instance, you can click the Text Button field in this example and then hit the Tab key five times to navigate to the Text Size field.

Now let's look at the Text Color parameter. Enter a value of 135 in the field with the *G* next to it. The R, G, and B fields are fields for Red, Green, and Blue values. The fields accept values between 0 and 255. Notice that when you change the value of the Green field, the values or slider positions for the Hue, Saturation, and Brightness fields automatically change (see Figure 4.7). Similarly, you can adjust the sliders for Hue, Saturation, and Brightness, and the values in the R, G, and B fields will automatically adjust to reflect the changes.

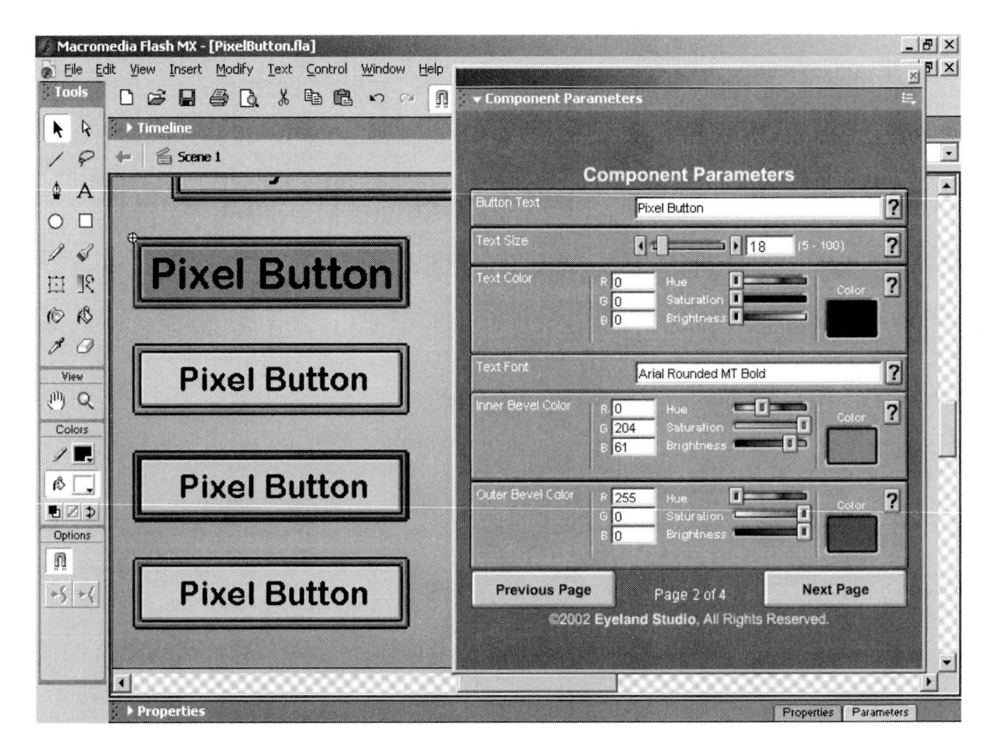

Figure 4.6

Changes to the Text Size parameter are reflected on the instance of the Pixel-Button component on the stage.

Once again, the changes that you made to the Text Color parameter are shown on the instance of the Pixel-Button component on the stage. As noted in the sidebar, Live Preview only updates once a second. It is a little easier to observe this if you try dragging one of the Hue, Saturation, or Brightness sliders while you watch the changes on the stage. You should be able to see that the changes will not be shown on the instance of the PixelButton component on the stage in real time. Go ahead and return each of the R, G, and B values for the Text Color parameter to 0 before we move on.

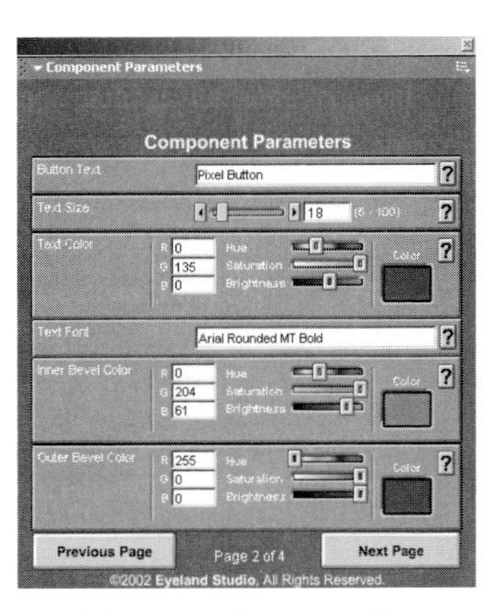

Figure 4.7

Edits to the R, G, and B fields are automatically reflected in the Hue, Saturation, and Brightness fields.

The next parameter is the Text Font parameter. As you might expect by now, edits to the Text Font parameter are, indeed, shown by Live Preview. This is particularly useful for letting you know if you've mistyped a font in the field. To see this, try to change the value for the Text Font parameter to a font that you have on your system. Stop before you've entered the entire name and notice that the font shown on the instance of the PixelButton component on the stage is a default font (see Figure 4.8).

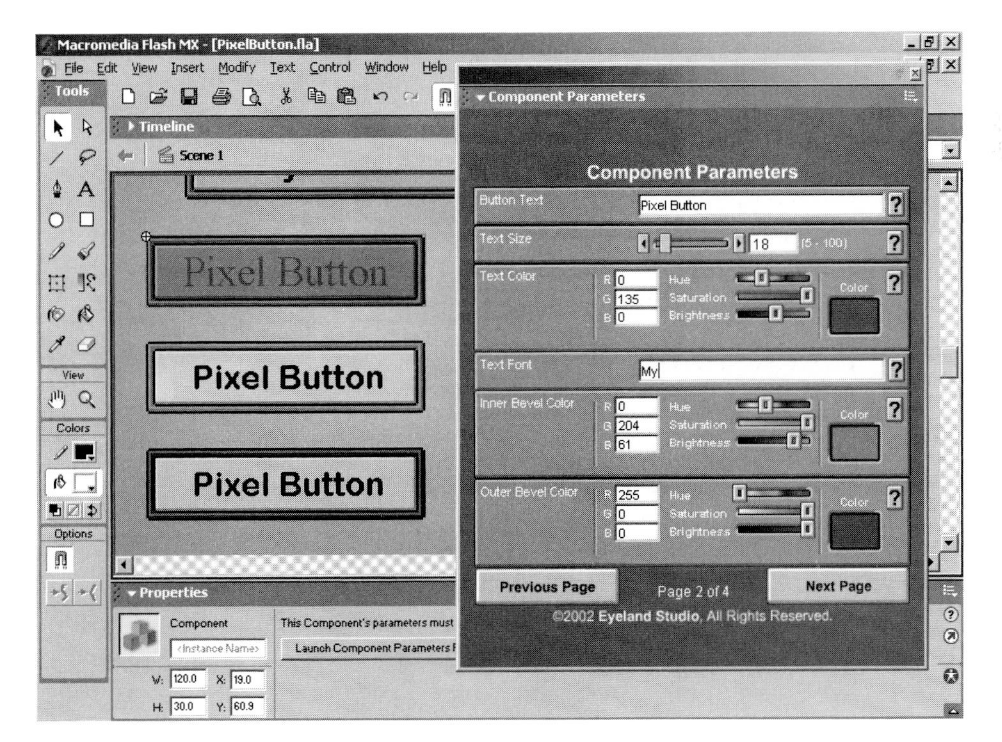

Figure 4.8

If the value for Text Font parameter is not a font name on your system, Flash will display a default font (or possibly no font).

Figure 4.9

If you enter the name of the font correctly, you will see the font displayed on the instance of the component.

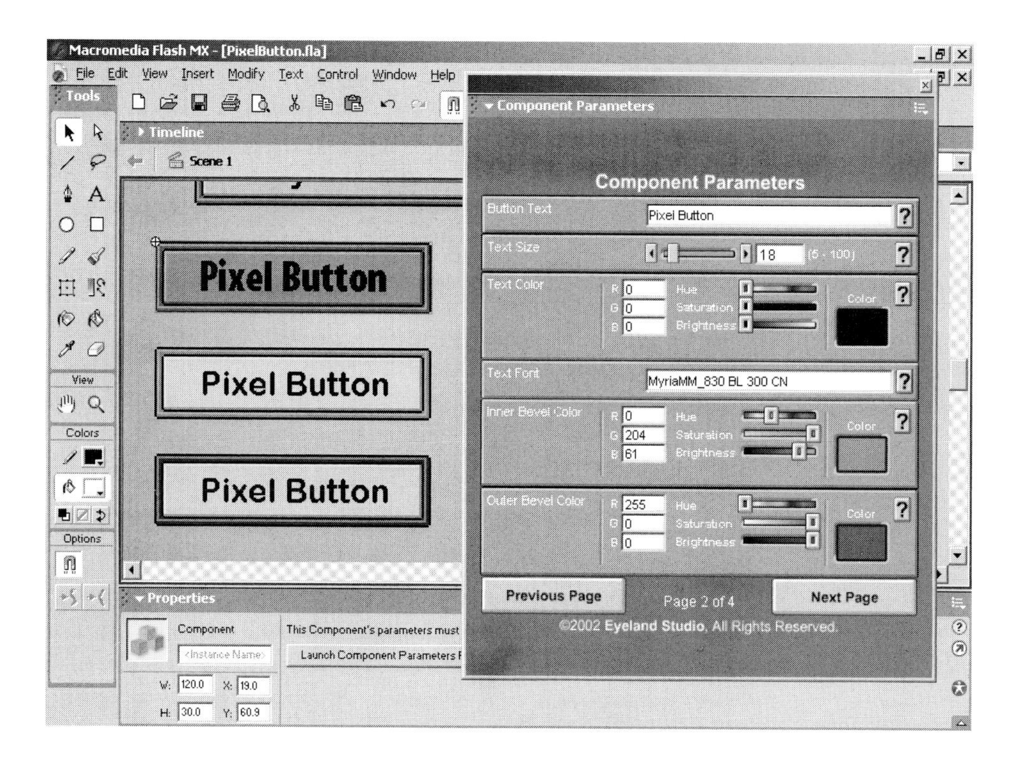

Figure 4.10

Even small errors will result in no font being displayed (the first letter is lowercase instead of uppercase in this example).

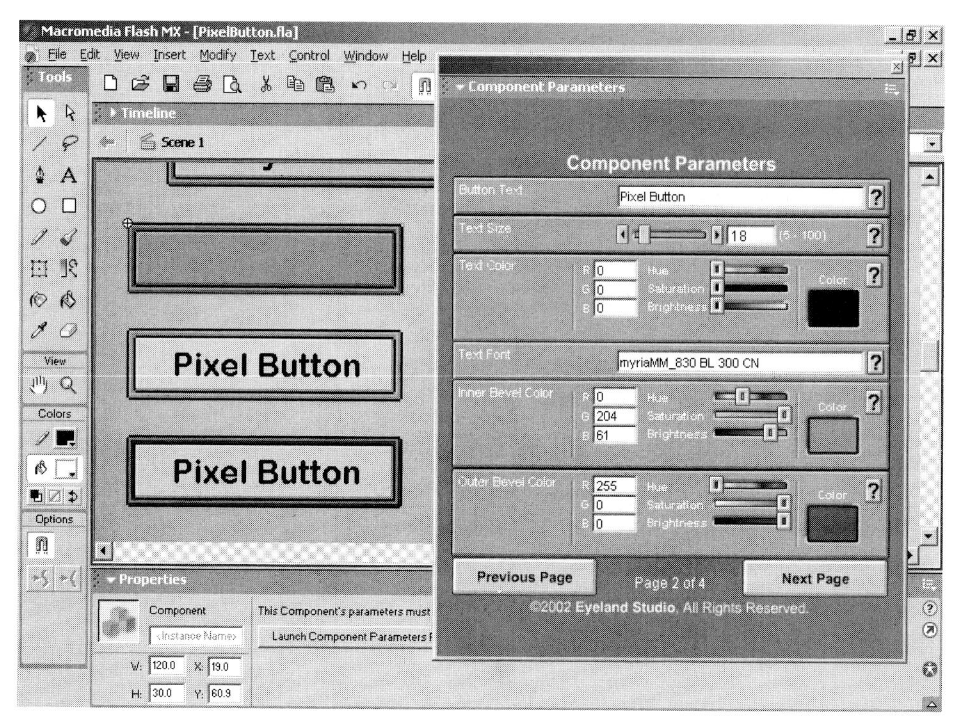

If you enter the Font name correctly, Flash will display that font on the instance of the PixelButton component on the stage (see Figure 4.9). However, note that the font names are case-sensitive, and you must enter even the spacing correctly. Small errors in the font name may result in no font being displayed (see Figure 4.10).

Now change the Inner Bevel Color parameter so that the R, G, and B values are 133, 255, and 177 respectively. Move on to the Outer Bevel Color parameter and change the R, G, and B values so that they are 0, 0, and 153 respectively (see Figure 4.11). These changes are reflected by Live Preview. The color controls for these two parameters work exactly the same as the controls for the Text Color parameter that we looked at earlier, so let's move on. Click the Next Page button to look at the third page of parameters for the PixelButton component.

Change the R, G, and B values for the Rollover Inner Bevel Color parameter to 212, 255, and 228 respectively. Notice that the edits you make to the Rollover Inner Bevel Color parameter are not reflected on the stage as shown in Figure 4.12 (changes to the Rollover Outer Bevel Color parameter will also not be displayed). The Rollover Inner Bevel Color parameter specifies the color that the button will change to when you roll over the button. However, even if you roll over the instance of the component on the stage, you will not be able to see the changes you enter in the Rollover Inner Bevel Color parameter.

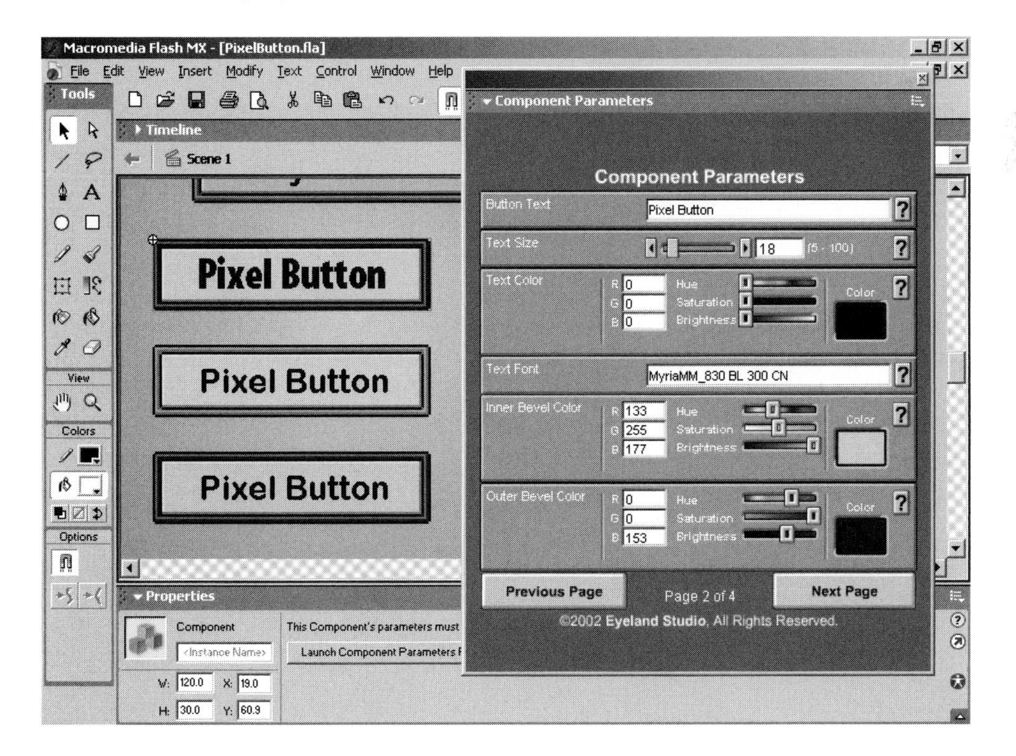

Figure 4.11

Changes to the Inner Bevel Color and Outer Bevel Color parameters are shown on the stage with Live Preview.

It won't even work if you turn on the Enable Simple Buttons and/or Enable Simple Frame Actions options in the Control menu. Live Preview doesn't display interactive functions. The only way to view the edits to these parameters is to close the Component Parameters panel and test the movie or publish and view the movie.

Notice that the value of the Rollover Outer Bevel Color parameter is already the same as the value that you entered for the Outer Bevel Color parameter. This means that when the movie is played, the border will not change when the user rolls over the button. If the values for the Outer Bevel Color and Rollover Outer Bevel Color parameters are different, then the border will change colors when you roll over the button.

Of course, you can also make the values for the Inner Bevel Color and Rollover Inner Bevel Color parameters the same and then make the values the Outer Bevel Color and Rollover Outer Bevel Color parameters different so that only the border colors change on rollover. These simple options may be obvious, but they nevertheless allow you to generate a range of rollover effects.

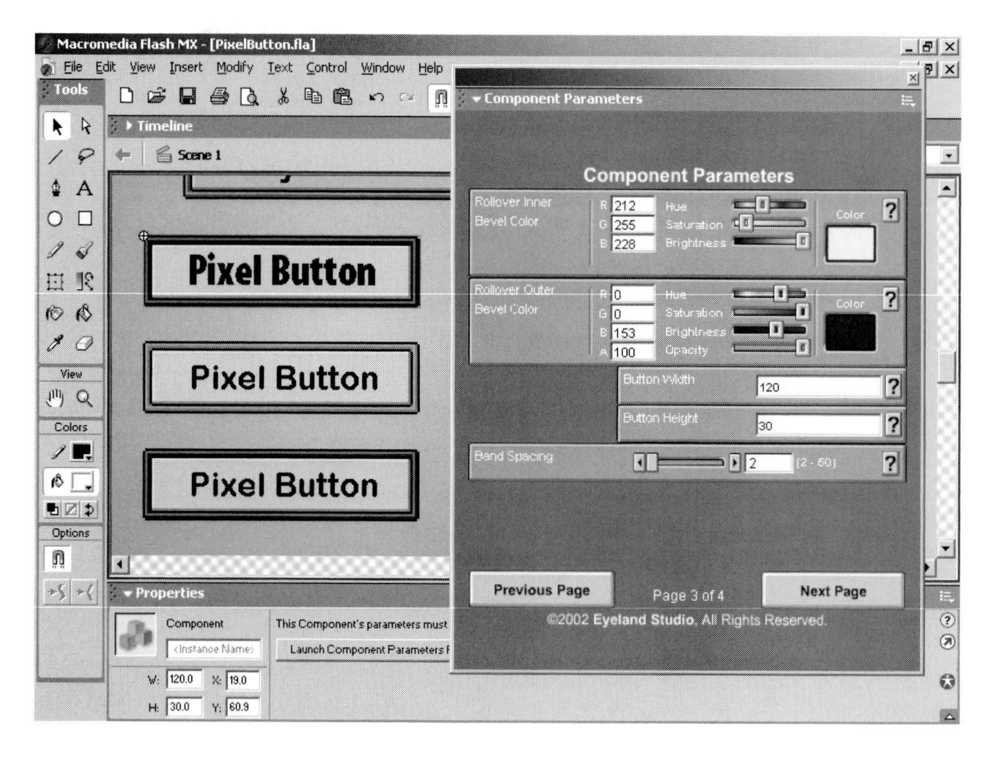

Figure 4.12

Adjustments made to the Rollover Inner Bevel Color and Rollover Outer Bevel Color parameters are not visible on the stage unless you publish or test the movie.

There is one more option on the Rollover Outer Bevel Color parameter: A, for Alpha. There is also a corresponding Opacity slider. This allows you to make, for example, the outer bevel invisible on rollover.

Adjusting the Dimensions of Components with Live Preview

Let's move on to the Button Width and Button Height parameters. Enter a value of 130 for the Button Width parameter and a value of 40 for the Button Height parameter. Now look very carefully at the button on the stage. Notice the blue outline Flash uses to indicate that an item on the stage is selected. Notice that the button has been resized so that there is a little bit of the button to the right of the blue outline and a little bit of the button below the blue outline (see Figure 4.13).

This is a slight shortcoming of Live Preview in Flash MX. The blue outline designates the selectable area for the instance of the PixelButton component on the stage. This is the

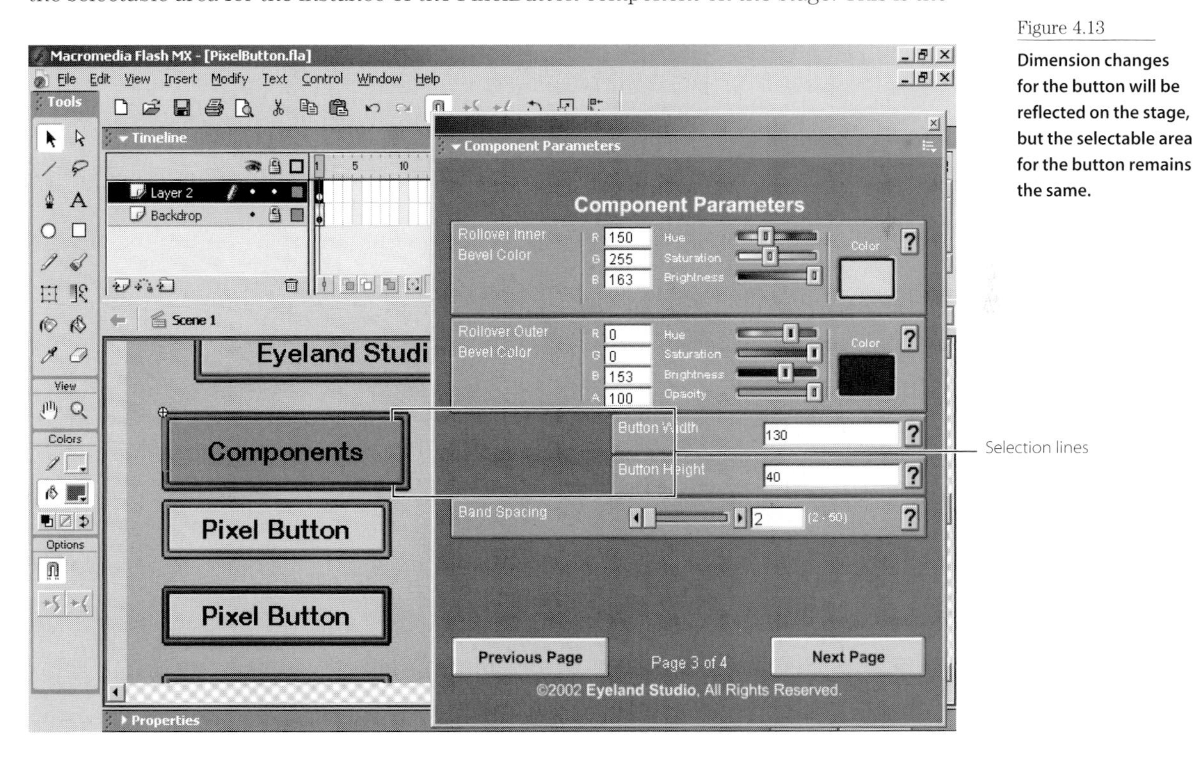

Figure 4.13

Dimension changes for the button will be reflected on the stage, but the selectable area for the button remains the same.

default size of the component instance. The selectable area is largely determined by the Flash movie used to generate the Live Preview in Flash. The selectable area of the component is the default size of the component in the Live Preview Flash file.

When the movie is published, the button works as it should. Every visible part of the button responds to interaction. However, when you're working within Flash, the instance of the component is only selectable within the original area, marked by the blue outline.

To see this, close the Component Parameters panel for a moment. Now try to click the instance of the PixelButton component that we've been working on. However, try to click only toward the right edge or the bottom. You shouldn't be able to select the instance of the PixelButton component along the right edge or the bottom. If you try to click it anywhere in the center or toward the top or to the left, you should have no problem.

This is just one little thing you will need to watch out for when you are working with components that utilize Live Preview. In the end, it's really only a minor, quirky behavior that you need to look out for when you change the dimensions of a component that uses Live Preview.

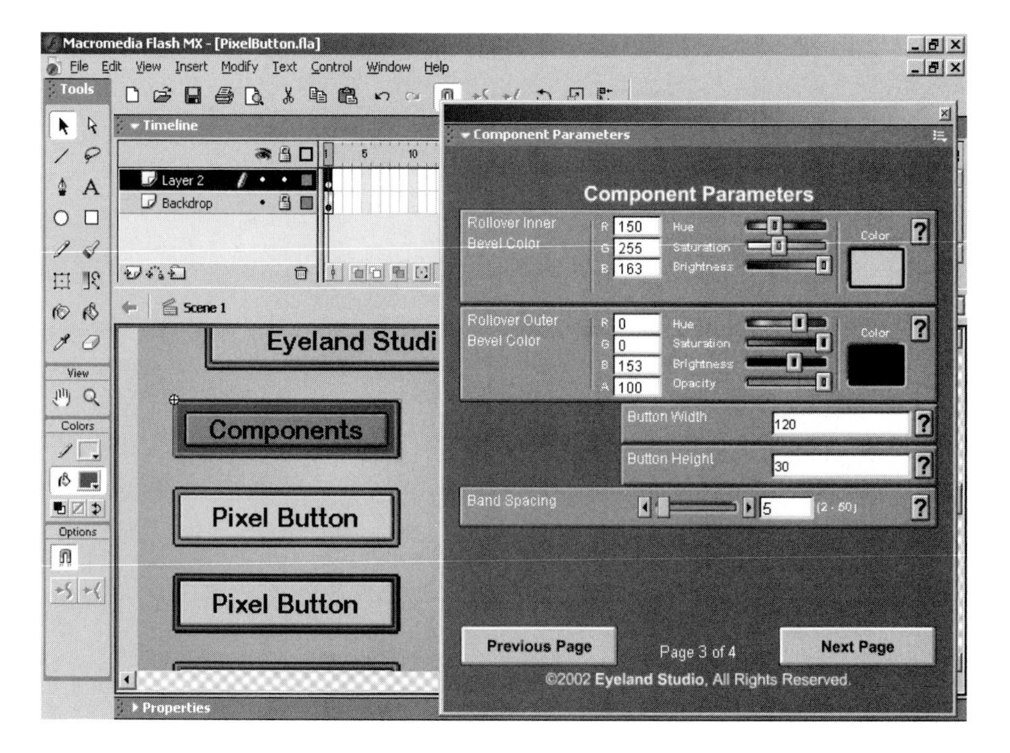

Figure 4.14

The Band Spacing parameter determines the width of the outer bevel.

Now select the instance of the PixelButton component that we have been editing and, on the Component Parameters panel, click the Next Page button twice. Return the values of the Button Width and Button Height parameters to 120 and 30 respectively. Now change the value of the Band Spacing parameter to 5 (see Figure 4.14).

Notice that when you increase the value of the Band Spacing parameter, it pushes into the button area. You can specify anything from 2 through 50 for the value of the Band Spacing parameter. However, large values may not look very good. For example, change the value of the Band Spacing parameter to 15. With a value of 15, there's almost no button left, which does not look very good (see Figure 4.15).

Change the value of the Band Spacing parameter back to 2. Now click the Next Page button. The first parameter on the last page of the custom UI for the PixelButton component is called Action Type. This parameter is a little different than any parameter we've covered so far. The value of the Action Type parameter determines what remaining parameters will appear. For example, select Load Movie from the drop-down menu on the Action Type parameter (see Figure 4.16).

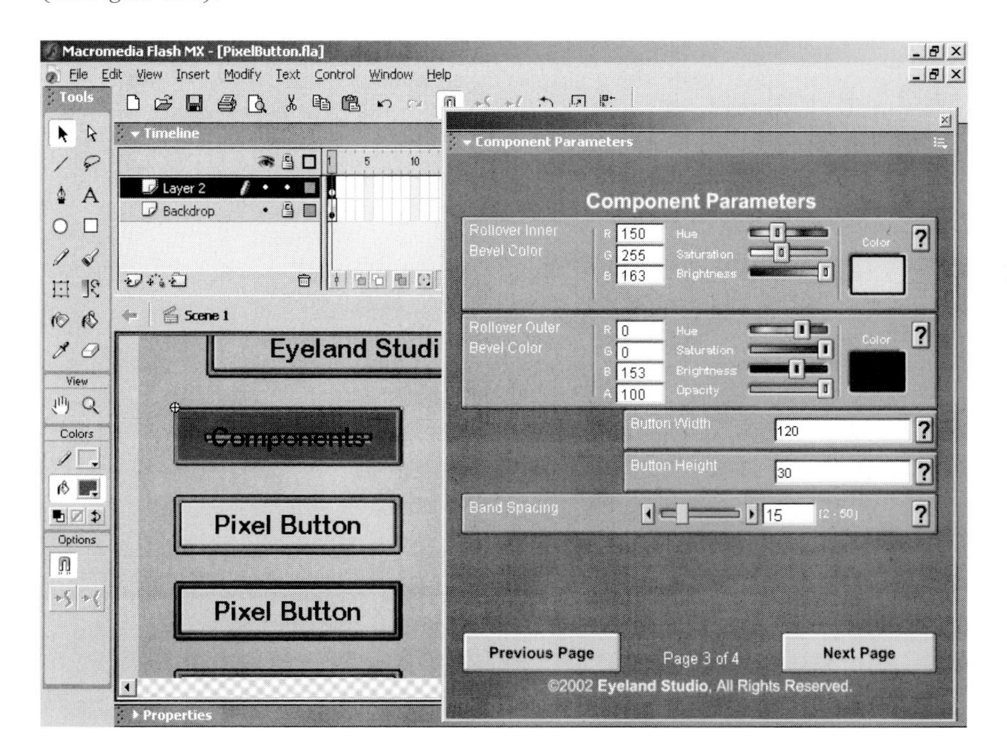

Figure 4.15

The outer bevel can push too far into the button if you specify higher values for the Band Spacing parameter.

Notice that the parameters below the Action Type parameter change when you select Load Movie, to Load Movie SWF and Load Movie Level.

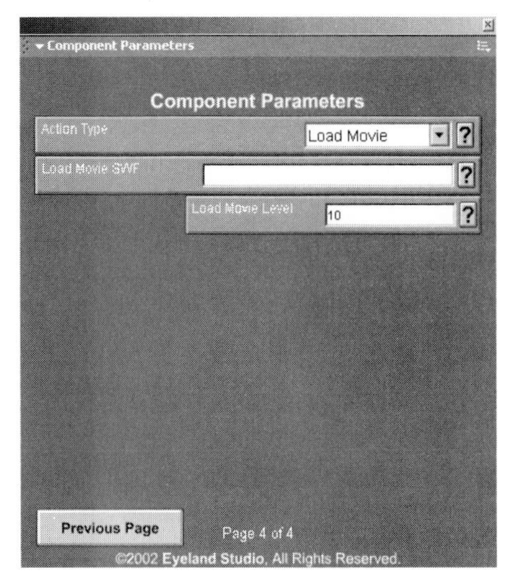

Figure 4.16

When you select Load Movie for the value of the Action Type parameter, the parameters related to Load Movie appear.

Now change the value of the Action Type parameter to URL. The parameters below the Action Type parameter should be URL and URL Window (see Figure 4.17).

As you might expect, the URL field allows you to enter a URL. Go ahead and enter a URL in the URL field, such as `http://www.flashfoundry.com`. Notice that it is important to include the full URL, including the `http://`.

The default value for the URL Window parameter is _self. This will cause the URL to load into the current browser window. If you want the URL to load into a new browser window, you can change the value of the URL Window parameter to _blank.

You will learn more about working with the Action Type parameter in the next chapter. In the next chapter you will learn how to use simple ActionScript commands for controlling basic navigation with components as well as how to use Load Movie with the components.

Now that you've worked through all of the parameters for the PixelButton component, go ahead and close the Component Parameters panel.

Working with MXP Files

Up to this point in the book, you have worked mostly with components that were already set on the stage. However, typically you'll want to create an instance of a component by dragging the component either from the library or from the Components panel.

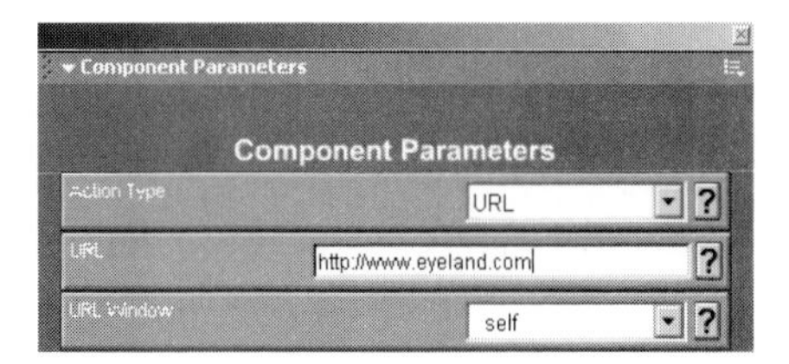

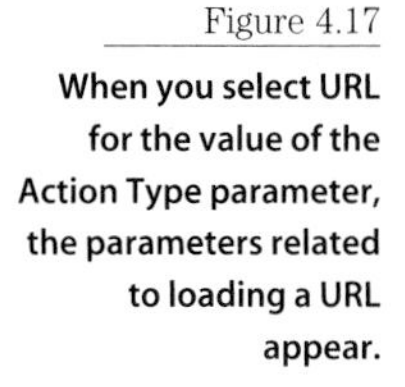

Figure 4.17

When you select URL for the value of the Action Type parameter, the parameters related to loading a URL appear.

Whenever you have components on the stage, Flash will automatically place them in the library just like any other symbol (such as movie clips, buttons, and the like). One obvious way to create a new instance of a component is to drag it from the library onto the stage.

To try this: select all of the instances of the PixelButton component and delete them. Now open the library and notice that the PixelButton component has a custom icon.

Click the PixelButton component in the library and look carefully at the preview window. Notice that nothing but a thin, rectangle outline appears in the preview window (see Figure 4.18). This is because the PixelButton component utilizes Flash MX's new ability to draw shapes programmatically. Drag an instance of the component onto the stage and notice that a button is immediately drawn on the stage.

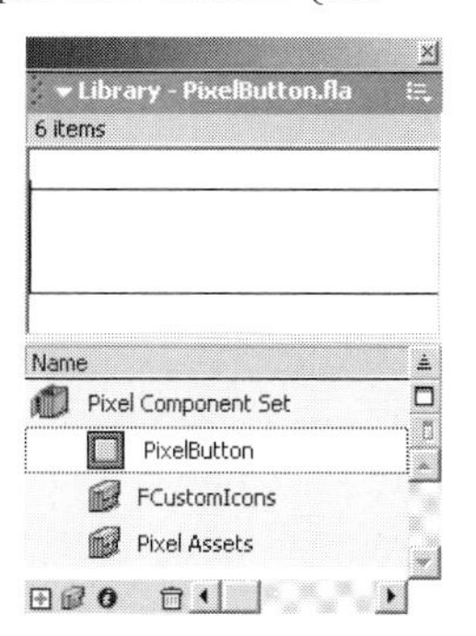

Figure 4.18

Flash MX can draw shapes programmatically.

Dragging a component from the library to the stage is obviously a very easy way of creating an instance of a component. However, if you are working on a project with a lot of resources in your library, it might be a little difficult to hunt down the component in the library. Also, you may not even have the component in your library to begin with. If you use a component frequently, you might want a more central location for your components.

You wouldn't be able to see this button on the stage without Live Preview. Typically, you would have to publish a movie to view the results of code used to draw shapes. However, Live Preview lets you see the button without publishing the movie.

For example, you may have a component, such as the PixelButton component, that you want to use in a series of projects. In this case, it would be nice to have the component in an easily accessible place rather than copy the component from project file to project file.

The Components panel allows you to essentially install components into Flash so that they are accessible to any Flash file you happen to be working on. While you can manually install components into the Components panel by dragging them into the `Flash MX/FirstRun/Components` folder (where you have Flash installed on your local system), this method has an important drawback. Specifically, it is hard to remove components that have been manually installed.

The best way to add and remove components to the Components panel is by using Macromedia Extension Manager (see Figure 4.19). This is a separate utility; it can be easily downloaded from a link on the companion CD.

The word *Extension* in Macromedia Extension Manager can be confusing. Macromedia has a little bit of an identity crisis where components are concerned. Although Macromedia has designated these resources as *components*, Macromedia also refers to them as *extensions*, and, of course, they were originally called *smart clips*. The word *extension* does, however, reflect the fact that Extension Manager can be used to manage extensions for many Macromedia applications, such as Dreamweaver, Director, and even Flash 5.

If you do not have Macromedia Extension Manager installed, take a few moments to install it and open it. Extension Manager will recognize any Macromedia program on your system that supports extensions it can manage. Therefore, the first thing you'll need to do is make sure that Flash MX is selected (see Figure 4.20).

Now select Install Extension from the File menu in Macromedia Extension Manager. Notice that the default file type in the Files Of Type field is the Macromedia Extension Packages or `.mxp` format. MXP files contain one or more components to be installed into Flash. You will learn how to create MXP files in Chapter 11.

Now let's install an MXP file. Go to the Chapter 4 directory on the CD and locate the `PixelComponentSet.mxp` file (see Figure 4.21). Double-click the file to install it. The first thing you will see is the standard Macromedia Extensions Disclaimer, shown in Figure 4.22, which is basically a means for Macromedia to say, "Install this component at your own risk."

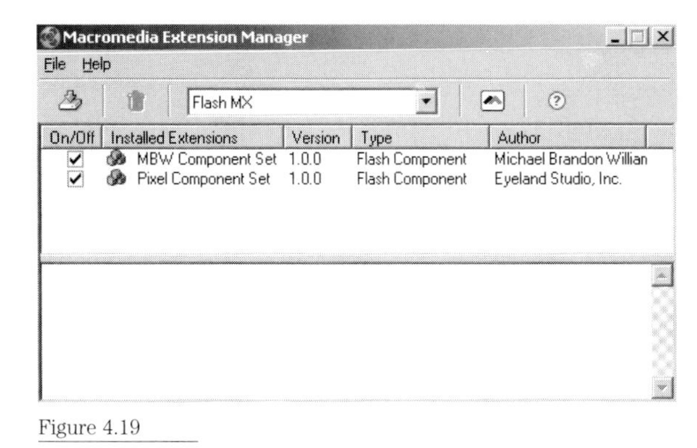

Figure 4.19

Macromedia Extension Manager provides an easy way to install and remove components to and from the Components panel.

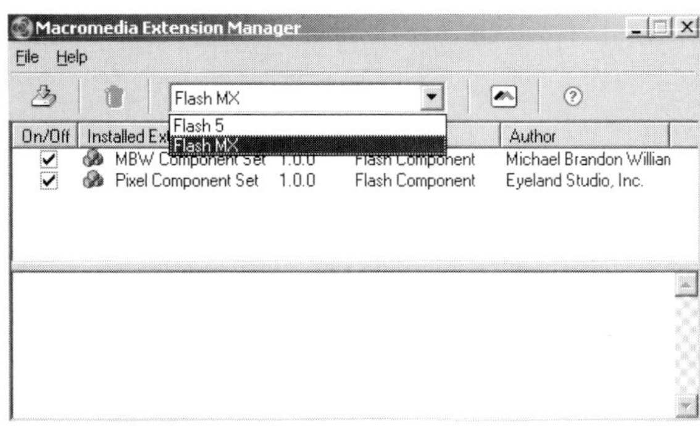

Figure 4.20

Select Flash MX from the drop-down list.

Click the Accept button. After you do, Extension Manager displays a dialog box letting you know the components have been installed. Click the OK button.

We will be installing more MXP files in later chapters, and we will take another look at Macromedia Extension Manager once we've installed a few more components. For now, close Extension Manager. If you have Flash MX open, save any files you have open, close Flash, and then reopen Flash to get the changes made by Extension Manager to take effect.

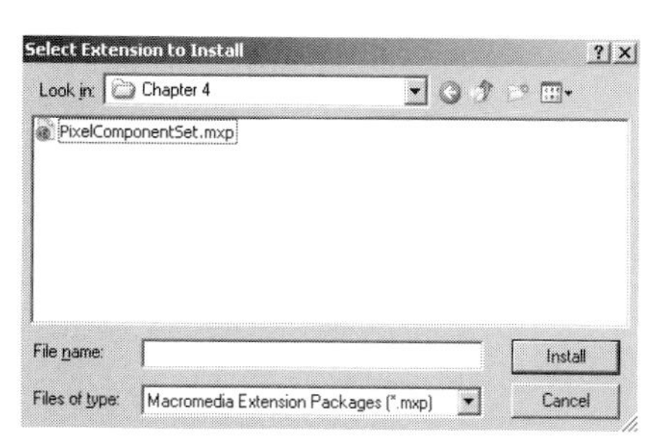

Figure 4.21

Open the `PixelComponentSet.mxp` **file from the Chapter 4 directory.**

Flash opens with an untitled document, and this will work just fine for our purposes. Open the Components panel either by selecting Components from the Windows menu or by pressing Command/Ctrl+F7.

> **Notice that the shortcut keys for opening the Components panel and the Component Parameters panel are similar. Command/Ctrl+F7 opens the Components panel, while Option/Alt+F7 opens the Component Parameters panel.**

Click the small, black, down-arrow in the top-right area of the Components panel and select PixelComponentSet from the pop-up menu (see Figure 4.23). You should now see three components in the Components panel. The first component is the PixelButton component (which is the same component we looked at earlier).

The other two components are called PixelFlatRadioButton and PixelRadioButton. These components are very similar to the PixelButton component. In fact, they were generated from the PixelButton component. After working through the parameters for the PixelButton, the parameters for these components will be very familiar.

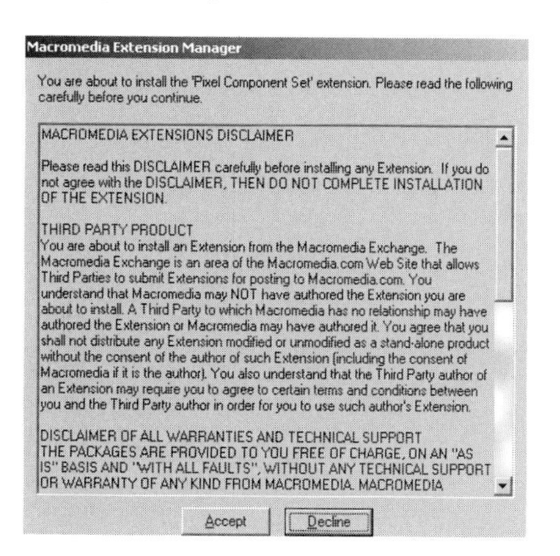

Figure 4.22

The Macromedia Extensions Disclaimer

The nice thing is that all three of these components are related and can be displayed together in the Components panel. Components in this panel are similar to plug-ins that have been installed in programs such as Adobe Photoshop. The components can be accessed by any file that you open in Flash much like any plug-in installed in Photoshop can be applied to any file you open in Photoshop.

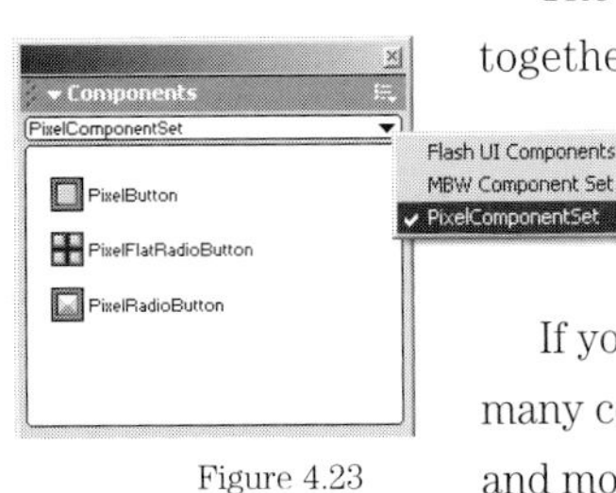

Figure 4.23
Selecting PixelComponentSet from the pop-up menu

If you have just installed Macromedia Extension Manager, then you probably don't have many components installed in the Components panel. However, as you begin to work more and more with components, you might find the list of components that are installed in the Components panel getting excessively long. In later chapters, we will install more MXP files, and then we will look at how you can manage your components with Extension Manager.

Finally, notice that each of the components in the PixelComponentSet have a unique custom icon. This helps to differentiate them. You will learn how to create custom icons for components in Chapter 11.

Conclusion

In this chapter, you've learned how to work with component parameters used for editing color, fonts, dimensions, and more. In addition, you've learned how to work with a component that utilizes Live Preview. Finally, you've learned how to install components into the Components panel with Macromedia Extension Manager. At this point, you should be getting fairly comfortable with components. In the next chapter, you will learn how to utilize basic ActionScript commands with components as well as how to work with components that utilize external resources. In upcoming chapters, you will work with components that begin to expose the real potential and value of components.

Chapter 5: Interface Components

When Flash, originally known as FutureSplash, was first introduced, one compelling aspect of the technology was that it was ideal for easily creating web interfaces with interactive buttons. Over the years, web interfaces created with Flash have become much more complex. Fortunately, this is one area where components come in particularly handy.

In this chapter, you will learn how to work with interface components. You will learn how to set components to perform common actions when a user clicks on a button. For example, you will learn how to set the component to load a URL, how to use basic navigational ActionScript with components, and how to use Load Movie with the component. You will also learn about using different graphic elements with the interface components.

This chapter represents a transition into more advanced components. If we've looked at similar parameters in previous chapters, we won't be spending much time with those parameters in the components featured here.

- **Using basic ActionScript with components**
- **Editing click actions in components**
- **Loading URLs and movies**
- **Using simple scripts for basic navigation**
- **Using advanced scripts to call functions**

Using Basic ActionScript with Components

Open the `take2.fla` file in the Chapter 5 folder on the CD (see Figure 5.1). Save the file to your local computer so that you can save your edits as you follow along.

> All photos in the `take2.fla` interface are from Art Today's www.clipart.com. To date, clipart.com offers over 2.5 million images including vector images, photos, sounds, fonts, and more. Their search engine is particularly useful because you can easily run a search to see if they have the art you need.

The `take2.fla` file is a sample Flash template from Eyeland Studio's Flash Foundry. This template features a component that generates a drop-down menu. Test the movie and notice that a drop-down menu is generated when the movie is published. Roll over the menus and click some of the options (see Figure 5.2).

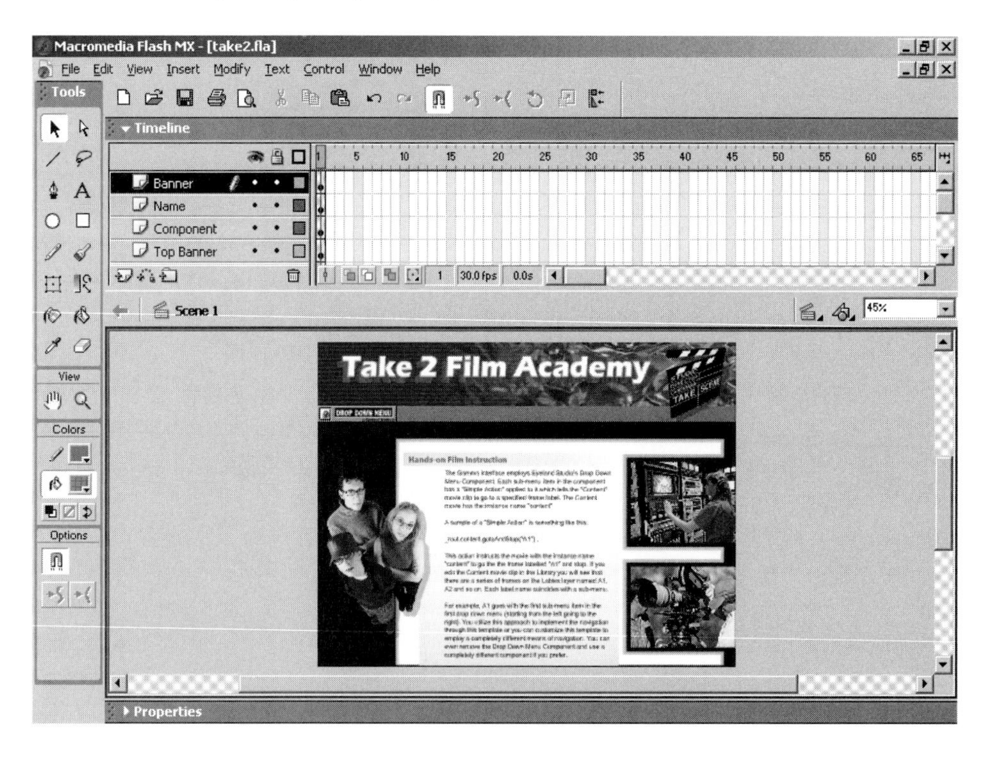

Figure 5.1
The `take2.fla` file

Notice that clicking an item within any of the drop-down menus navigates you to a different section of the overall template. In other words, when you click an item, you see text related to that section (only the Headline changes). As you can see, the drop-down menu is controlling the navigation within the template. You will soon see that the component allows you to specify several forms of navigation within its parameters. Close the test movie and return to the `take2.fla` file.

It might be a little difficult to see the component on the stage. Zoom in on the small gray bar labeled Drop Down Menu toward the top left of the stage. It is below the word *Take* in the heading Take 2 Film Academy, as shown in Figure 5.3. This component is similar to the components you worked with in Chapter 3. The gray bar is a place holder or temporary representation of the component on the stage. It helps you see the component while you are working with it in Flash, but the gray bar disappears and is replaced by the drop-down menu when you publish the movie.

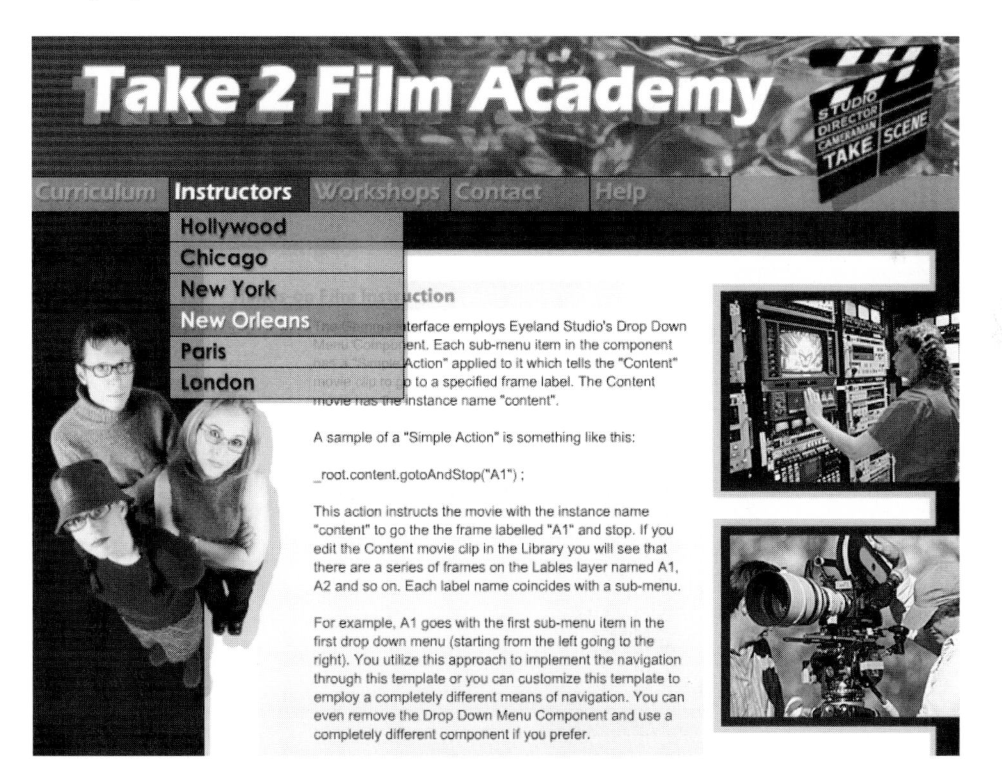

Figure 5.2

Test the movie and notice the drop-down menu.

Select the gray bar labeled Drop Down Menu and open the Component Parameters panel. The first screen in this custom UI, shown in Figure 5.4, contains a scrollable text field and a button to navigate to the next page.

The text field explains that the Drop Down Menu component helps you create menus similar to those used in typical applications. You can customize everything from the fonts, colors for on and off states, to complex actions via the component parameters. When you move the mouse cursor over one of the main buttons, the drop-down menu you've created will appear (using an "elastic" animation), showing the items in that menu. Moving the mouse off the menu will play another animation, collapsing the menus into their original shape. The text field also explains how to set up the component and how to adjust the fonts. We will be looking at setup and working with the fonts later in this chapter.

Click the Next Page button to view the first page of parameters for the Drop Down Menu component, shown in Figure 5.5. Notice that this is merely page 2 out of 6 pages. Below is a description of the parameters of the Drop Down Menu component.

Menu Items The Menu Items parameter specifies how many main menu items there will be and what the text will be on each. Each item you add to the Menu Items parameter has a label. This label will be the text that appears on the main menu. Each main menu item has an associated sub item or sub items. When you select an item in the Menu Items parameter, the associated sub items will be displayed.

Figure 5.3

The Drop Down Menu component is located toward the upper left of the stage.

Sub Item For Main Item #*n* This Sub Item For Main Item parameter is associated with the Menu Items parameter. The name of this parameter changes slightly depending on the Menu Items parameter you have selected. For example, if you have selected the second item in the Menu Items parameter, this parameter will be labeled "Sub Item For Main Item #2".

Each item you add to the Menu Items parameter has a label. This label will be the text that appears on the main menu. Each item in this parameter can also have a click action associated with it. For example, you can set each item so that a different URL loads when the viewer clicks on the sub item in the published movie.

Load Movie Level The Load Movie parameter specifies the level into which the movie will load. Level 0 is the level where the host movie is located. Therefore, if you specify 0 the movie being loaded will overwrite the host movie. Thus you usually want to specify a value other than 0. It is common to specify a level such as 10 or 100 to decrease the likelihood that another movie might inadvertently be loaded into the same level.

Main Button Width Specifies the width of the main items (specified in the Menu Items parameter). All of the main menu buttons will be set to the width specified in this parameter.

Menu Item Width Specifies the width of the sub items (specified in the Sub Item For Main Item parameter). All of the sub items will be set to the width specified in this parameter.

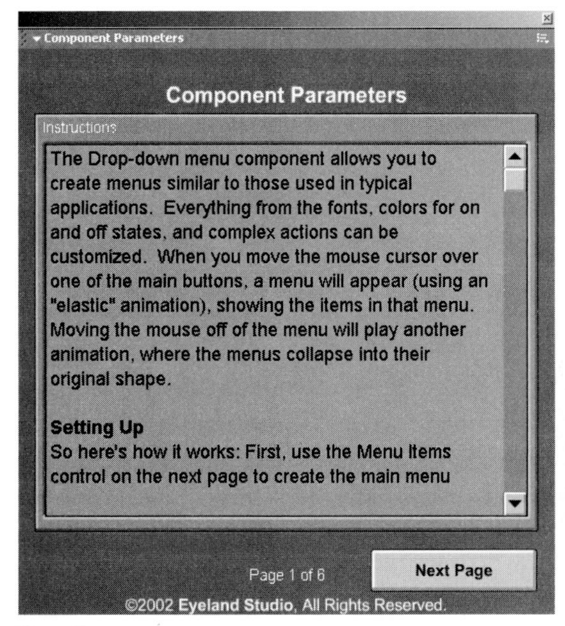

Figure 5.4

The first screen of the component parameters for the Drop Down Menu component

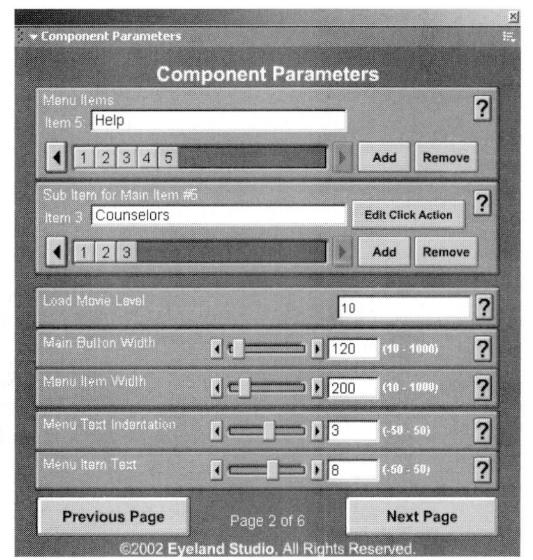

Figure 5.5

The parameters for the Drop Down Menu component begin on page 2 of the custom UI.

Menu Text Indentation Sets the distance, in pixels, that the text on the main menu buttons will be indented (to the right).

Menu Item Text Sets the distance, in pixels, that the text on the submenu buttons will be indented (to the right).

Main Button Border Color Sets the color for the 1-pixel border around each main menu button. You can set the Alpha for this parameter to 0 if you do not want a border for the main menu buttons.

Menu Item Border Color Sets the color for the 1-pixel border around each submenu button. You can set the Alpha for this parameter to 0 if you do not want a border for the submenu buttons.

Spring Stiffness Adjusts the stiffness (also known as the spring constant k) of the menu opening animation. The higher the value of the Spring Stiffness parameter, the more quickly the menu will open to its full size. If you set this to 0, the menu won't open at all. Note that the menu items will not appear until the menu stops moving.

Spring Inertia Adjusts the inertia of the menu opening animation, or its tendency to keep moving back and forth. In general, as you increase inertia, the menu's motion becomes more bouncy. Note that the menu items will not appear until the menu stops moving. A value of 1 will result in no bouncing effect which, in turn, means that menu items will not appear.

Menu Closing Speed Adjusts the speed that the menu will close when the mouse is moved off a button. Set this to the maximum value (20) to have the menus close instantly.

Main Button Color (Default) and Main Button Color (Over) Adjusts the color used for main menu buttons in their default state (when the mouse is not hovering over the button) and in their "over" state (when the mouse is hovering over the button).

Menu Item Color (Default) and Menu Item Color (Over) Adjusts the color used for the submenu buttons in their default state (when the mouse is not hovering over the button) and in their "over" state (when the mouse is hovering over the button).

Main Text Color (Default) and Main Text Color (Over) Specifies the text color for main buttons in their default state (when the mouse is not hovering over the button) and in their "over" state (when the mouse is hovering over the button).

Menu Item Text (Default) and Menu Item Text (Over) Specifies the text color for submenu buttons in their default state (when the mouse is not hovering over the button) and in their "over" state (when the mouse is hovering over the button).

Text Shadow Color Specifies the color for the text shadow on each button in the menu (both sublevel menu items and main buttons). Set the opacity to 0 if you don't want to display a shadow.

Text Shadow Offset X and Text Shadow Offset Y Adjusts the text shadow's position with relation to the text. For example, a Text Shadow Offset X setting of –2 will place the shadow 2 pixels left of the text; a Text Shadow Offset Y setting of 1 will place the shadow 1 pixel below the text.

Menu Shadow Color Specifies the color of the shadow for the menu. When the menu is open, a shadow will appear beneath it. Use this control to adjust the color and opacity of the shadow.

Menu Shadow Offset X and Menu Shadow Offset Y Adjusts the menu shadow's position with relation to the menu. For example, a Menu Shadow Offset X setting of –2 will place the shadow 2 pixels left of the menu; a Menu Shadow Offset Y setting of 10 will place the shadow 10 pixels below the menu.

Editing Click Actions in Components

Use the Drop Down Menu component's Previous Page button to return to page 2. Click Item 1 in the Menu Items parameter. (Item 1 is the small box with the number 1 on it.) The text field will display the text, Curriculum. Next click Item 1 in the Sub Item For Main Item #1 parameter. The text field should display the text General Film (see Figure 5.6).

The Menu Items parameter specifies the main headings for the drop-down menu. The first main heading is Curriculum. The Sub Item For Main Item #1 parameter specifies the submenu items for each main menu heading. Therefore, General Film is the first submenu item under the main heading Curriculum. If you click the second item in the Sub Item For Main Item #1 parameter, you will see that Post Production is the second submenu item. There are currently five submenu items under the main heading Curriculum.

When you hover your mouse over a main menu item in the published movie, all of the submenu items associated with that main menu item will appear. Clicking a main menu item does nothing. However, when you click a submenu item, something does occur. We will refer to this "something" as a click action. A *click action* is an action that occurs when you click a button—in this example, it is an action that occurs when you click a submenu item.

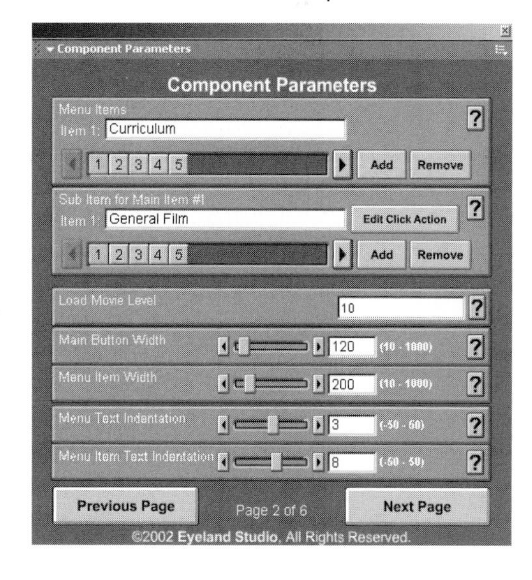

Figure 5.6

Select the first item in the Menu Items parameter and the Sub Item For Main Item #1 parameter.

Put another way, the submenus in this component are essentially buttons created by the component. Because the button is created by the component, you, the user, need another way to assign actions that you would usually assign to standard Flash buttons. In other words, if you were dealing with a normal Flash button, you could set the button to Load URL or assign it a `gotoAndPlay` command to control a movie clip. However, when you are dealing with buttons that are generated by a component, you can't use the normal methods for assigning such actions.

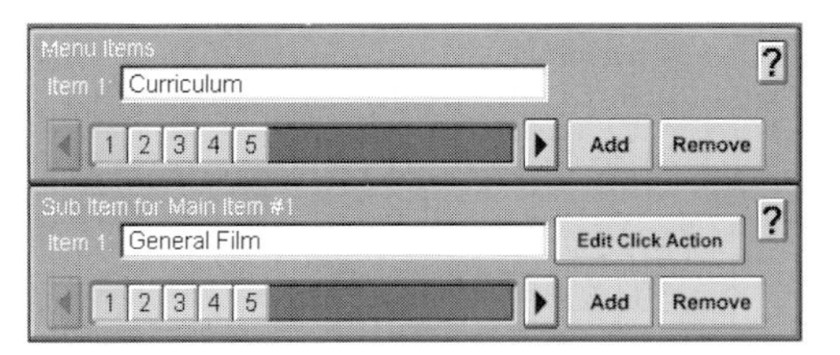

Figure 5.7
You can assign actions to your buttons using the Edit Click Action button.

If a component creates a button—in this case, a series of buttons—then the component needs to provide a means for entering these commands; otherwise, for all practical purposes, the component-generated button will be worthless. In the Drop Down Menu component, you can assign these actions via the Edit Click Action button, shown in Figure 5.7.

The Edit Click Action button is associated with each item in the Sub Menu For Main Item parameter. To see this, click Item 1 in the Sub Menu For Main Item #1 parameter and then click the Edit Click Action Button. You will see a screen labeled Click Action Parameters, which I will explain soon.

For now, notice that the text field toward the bottom contains the following ActionScript:

```
_root.content.gotoAndStop("A1") ;
```

Figure 5.8
The text field toward the bottom of the Click Action Parameters screen contains a simple ActionScript command that references a label named "A1."

This ActionScript (shown in Figure 5.8) is a simple `gotoAndStop` command. Notice that the command references the frame label, "A1." This ActionScript sends a `gotoAndStop` command to a movie clip with an instance name "content" on the main Timeline, and the command tells that movie clip to stop at the frame labeled "A1." Now click the Close button.

You can use the Edit Click Action button to specify the click actions for any submenu item. To see this, click Item 5 in the Menu Items parameter. The button labeled *5* should turn yellow, and the text field in the Menu Items parameter should display the text "Help." Notice that the Sub Item For Main Item parameter now reads Sub Item For Main Item #5. The parameter displays the submenu items for the main menu heading Help.

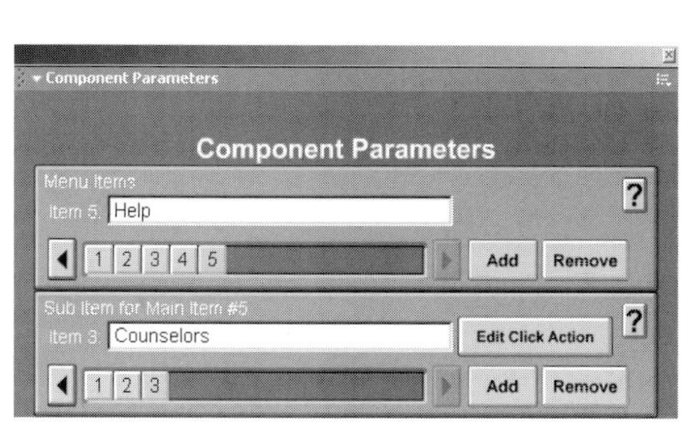

Figure 5.9

Select Item 5 in the Menu Items parameter, and the last item in the Sub Item For Main Item #5 parameter will automatically be selected.

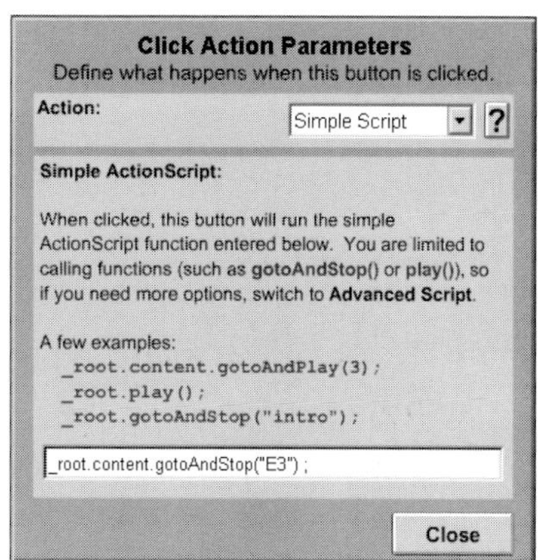

Figure 5.10

The `gotoAndStop` command references the frame labeled "E3".

Notice, also, that the last item in the Sub Item For Main Item #5 parameter is automatically selected. When you click any item in the Menu Items parameter, the last item in the associated Sub Item For Main Item parameter is automatically selected. In this case, Item 3 in the Sub Item For Main Item #5 parameter is already selected, and the text for Item 3 is "Counselors" (see Figure 5.9).

Now click the Edit Click Action button and notice that the last text field references a different frame label, "E3" (see Figure 5.10). So the Edit Click Action button is context-sensitive. You can use this button to edit the click actions for any submenu item under any main item or main heading.

The key is to make sure that you have the correct sub item selected when you click the Edit Click Action button. As noted earlier, the last item in the Sub Item For Main Item parameter is automatically selected when you select an item in the Menu Items parameter. So, for example, if you select an item in the Menu Items parameter and you want to edit its first sub item, you need to select the first item before you click the Edit Click Actions button.

When you click the Edit Click Action button, you are provided with several additional parameters on the next screen, which is named Click Action Parameters—as in a singular action. In this screen, you can only specify one action. For example, if you want to load a movie *and* load a URL, you cannot do that directly from the Click Action Parameters screen. We will, however, see how you can have two actions executed at once later in this chapter.

Now let's look at the parameters on the Click Action Parameters screen:

Action The Action parameter allows you to specify which type of action you would like to assign to the currently selected submenu button. The four options for the Action parameter—Load URL, Load Movie, Simple Script, and Advanced Script—are described below. Selecting any one of these options produces parameters related to the selected parameter. For example, if you select Load URL, you will be presented with parameters to specify which URL to load and a target for it to load in.

Load URL Allows you to set the submenu button to load a URL when it is clicked.

Load Movie Allows you to specify a movie that will be loaded into the movie that contains the Drop Down Menu component.

Simple Script Allows you to specify basic `goto`, `play`, or `stop` commands to control the main Timeline or the Timeline of a movie clip.

Advanced Script Provides a series of generic function calls that you can use to generate virtually any type of action you require, provided that you are proficient enough with ActionScript to write the required function.

URL To Load The URL To Load parameter is only visible when either the Load URL option or the Load Movie option is selected in the Actions parameter. This parameter allows you to enter the URL that you would like to load when the viewer clicks on the associated submenu button. You can enter either a relative URL or an absolute URL. For absolute URLs, enter the entire path starting with `http://`.

When you have selected the Load Movie option in the Action parameter, you use the URL To Load parameter to enter the name of the movie to load. You can enter a relative path to the `.swf` file (such as `movie1.swf`), or you can enter an absolute path (such as `http://www.flash-foundry.com/movies/movie1.swf`).

URL Target The URL Target parameter is only visible when the Load URL option is selected in the Actions parameter. The target specifies where you want the URL to load. The drop-down list offers four standard options: Self, New Window, Parent Frame, and Top Frame. Selecting Self loads the URL into the current browser window. The New Window option loads the URL into a new browser window. Parent Frame loads the URL into the parent frame if you are in an HTML frames environment. Similarly, Top Frame loads the URL into the top frame if you are in an HTML frames environment. To load the URL into a frame with a custom label, enter the label name in the Custom Target field.

Simple ActionScript The Simple ActionScript parameter is only visible if you have Simple Script selected in the Actions parameter. The Simple ActionScript parameter looks somewhat different from other parameters in the Drop Down Menu component's custom UI. This is due to the fact that ActionScript can be confusing for average users. Therefore, the explanation for the parameter has been added directly to the parameter itself.

The Simple ActionScript parameter allows you to enter simple `goto`, `play`, and `stop` commands. For example, you can enter something like `_root.intro.play();` to direct a movie clip with the instance name "intro" to play.

Advanced ActionScript The Advanced ActionScript "parameter" is only visible if you have Advanced Script selected in the Actions parameter. The Advanced ActionScript "parameter" is really not a parameter at all. Instead, it is an informational field telling you that when the Advanced Script option is selected in the Actions parameter, the component will automatically send out a series of function calls. The function calls will be sent out whether or not you have a function to take advantage of them.

Now that I've introduced the parameters for the Edit Click Action button, I'll teach you about each option in detail. First we will start with the Load URL option.

Loading a URL

Loading a URL when a user clicks on a button is a relatively easy click action to understand and implement. Even web designers who use a program such as Macromedia Dreamweaver or Microsoft FrontPage usually know how to enter a standard `href` HTML tag that sets a link to load a URL. Setting the Drop Down Menu component is, therefore, very intuitive. Let's look at a few examples.

If you have the Click Action Parameters screen still open, click Close and then follow these steps:

1. Select Item 5 in the Menu Items parameter, and once again Help should appear in the text field. Change the text to **Links**.
2. Select Item 1 in the Sub Item For Main Item #5 parameter. Change the text to **Flash Foundry**.
3. Click the Edit Click Action button. Notice that the action previously assigned to this button has remained the same even though we changed the text for the button.

4. Click the downward-pointing arrow to the right of the list field in the Action parameter and select Load URL from the list (see Figure 5.11).

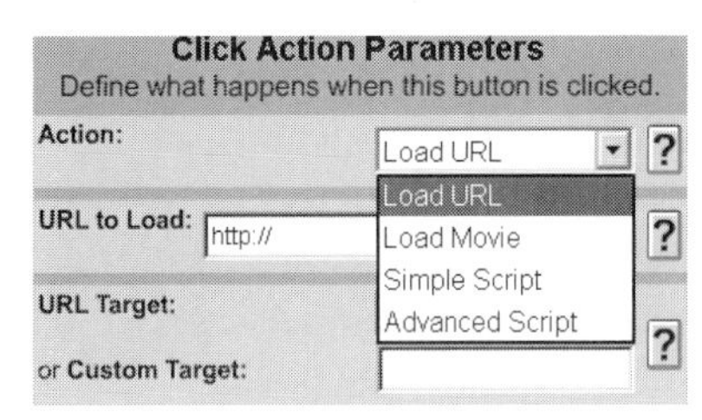

Figure 5.11

Selecting Load URL from the list field of the Action parameter

5. Type **`www.flashfoundry.com`** in the URL To Load parameter's text field after the `http://`. The default option for the URL Target parameter is Self. This will cause the `http://www.flashfoundry.com` URL to load into the current browser window (when this example is viewed on the Web).
6. To load the URL into a new browser window, click the down-arrow to the right of the list field in the URL Target parameter and select New Window from the list.
7. When you are finished, click the Close button.

Before we test or publish the movie to view the changes, let's enter a few more URLs.

8. Select Item 2 in the Sub Item For Main Item #5 parameter and change the text to **Eyeland Games**.
9. Click the Edit Click Action button and select Load URL from the Action list field.
10. In the URL To Load parameter text field, enter **`http://www.eyeland.com/games-all.php`**.
11. Select New Window for the URL Target parameter (see Figure 5.12).
12. Click the Close button.

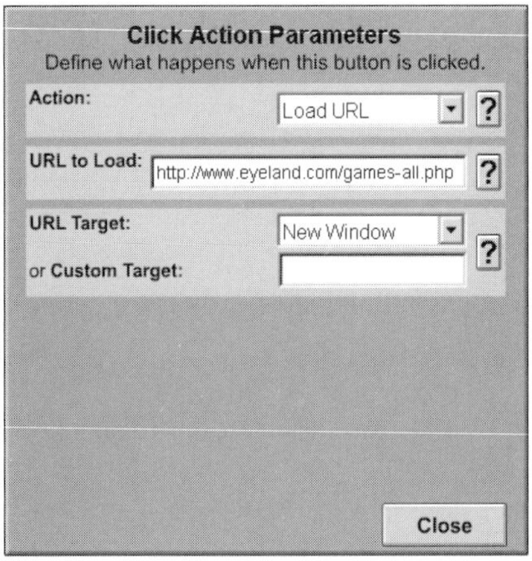

Figure 5.12

Entering a new URL for the second item in the Sub Item For Main Item #5 parameter

Here you see that you can enter URLs for scripts like PHP and ASP. You can also use long URLs and those with special characters—anything that's legal as an HTTP address.

13. Select Item 3 in the Sub Item For Main Item #5 parameter and change the text to **Flash Talk**.
14. Click the Edit Click Action button and select Load URL from the Action list field.

15. In the URL To Load parameter text field, enter the following URL:

    `http://www.graphics.com/modules.php?name=Sections&sop=viewarticle&artid=27`

16. Go ahead and leave the Self option as the value for the URL Target parameter (see Figure 5.13).

17. When you are finished, click Close and then close the Component Parameters panel.

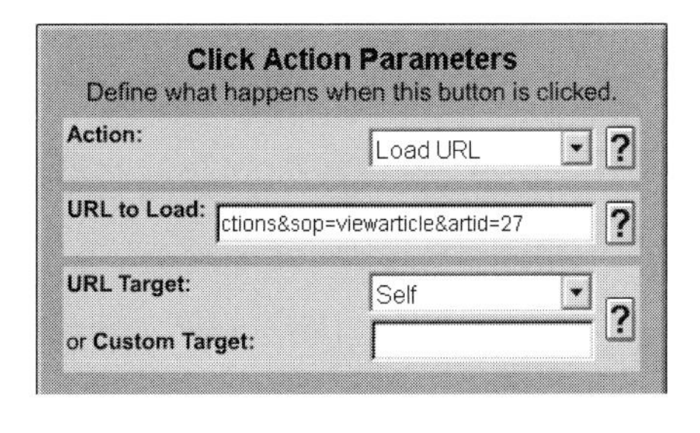

Figure 5.13

Entering a new URL for the third item in the Sub Item For Main Item #5 parameter

Now that you've edited several of the items, let's test the movie to see how it works. For this example, you need to view the overall movie in a browser so that you can observe if the target options you selected in the URL Target parameter are working properly.

To do this, choose File → Publish Settings to open the Publish Settings dialog box. Click the Formats tab and make sure that the Flash and HTML options are selected, as shown in Figure 5.14. Next, click the Publish button, and when the movie has finished publishing, click OK to close the dialog box.

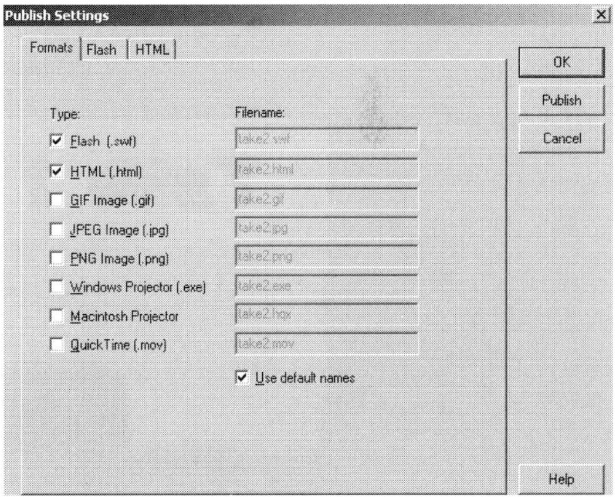

Figure 5.14

Turning on the Flash and HTML options

When you clicked the Publish button in the Publish Settings dialog box, Flash published both an `.swf` file and an `.html` file in the directory that you stored the `take2.fla` file on your local hard drive. Now go to that directory with Windows Explorer or your Mac's Finder and open the `take2.html` file in a browser (see Figure 5.15).

Now roll your mouse over the Links header on the drop-down menu and then click each of the submenu items in turn. Notice that the first two submenu items (Flash Foundry and Eyeland Games) launch a new browser. However, when you click the last submenu item (Flash Talk), the URL loads into the same browser window. Once you've tested the movie, close the browser window and return to the `take2.fla` file in Flash.

Now that you've learned how to set the Drop Down Menu component to load a URL, let's look at the next click action: loading a movie.

Loading a Movie

The ability to load a movie into another movie is particularly valuable if you are working with Flash movies that have high bandwidth content such as bitmap imagery, videos, or audio.

Let's say that you have five videos, each 500 KB. If you import them into your main movie, they would total at least 2.5 MB—which is usually far too much of a download. However, if you use Load Movie to load each movie, the main movie will load much faster, and the other movies will only load if the viewer clicks to view them. If the viewer decides to view only one movie, they need only wait for 500 KB of content to load versus waiting for 2.5 MB of content to load.

Setting the drop-down menu to load a movie is easy enough. The trouble is setting up that movie to behave the way you want it to. In particular, you need to set your movies to load in the positions that you want them. Let's look at an example.

Setting Up the Movies

One of the submenu items in the example instance of the Drop Down Menu component in the `take2.fla` file is labeled New York. In this next exercise, you will set that button to load a movie that contains a video of New York City.

Figure 5.15

View the `take2.html` file in a browser to test the movie.

The video's dimensions are 320 pixels wide by 240 pixels high. The stage size of the `take2.fla` file is 800 pixels wide by 600 pixels high. So, the first thing we need to do is determine where we want the video to be located on the stage. Follow these steps:

1. Start by adding a layer to the main Timeline of the `take2.fla` file. Find the top layer on the Timeline named Banner and add a new layer above that. Name the new layer "Video" (see Figure 5.16).
2. Now draw a rectangle that is 320 pixels wide by 240 pixels high on the stage.
3. Delete the outline and fill the rectangle with a bright green color so that it is easy to see.
4. Press Command/Ctrl+I to open the Info panel. Make sure the small black registration point is in the upper left and then enter **235** for the X position and **333** for the Y position. As you can see in Figure 5.17, this places the green rectangle over the bottom two-thirds of the area in the `take2.fla` file where the main text is displayed.
5. Now you need to create a movie with the video positioned in that same spot. Open the file named `newyork.fla` in the Chapter 5 directory on the CD.

6. Press Command/Ctrl+J to open the Document Properties dialog box.
7. Notice that the stage size for the `newyork.fla` Flash file is 320 pixels wide by 240 pixels high. Change the dimensions of `newyork.fla` to match the dimensions of the `take2.fla` file by entering **800** for the Width and **600** for the Height (see Figure 5.18).

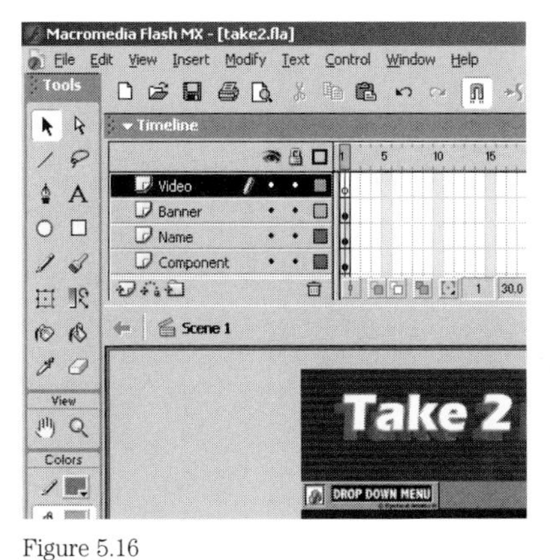

Figure 5.16

Add a new layer above the Banner layer named Video.

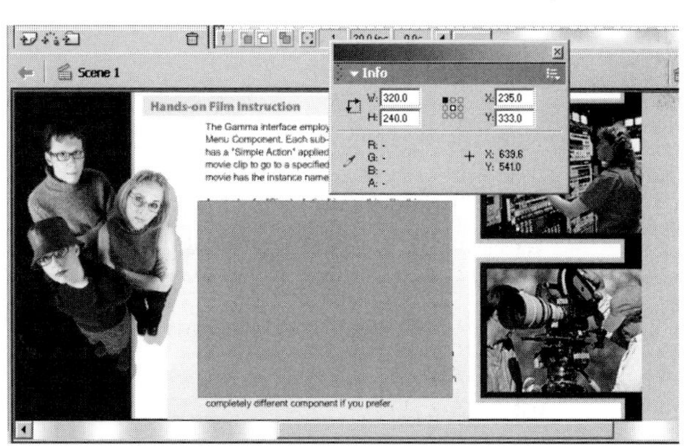

Figure 5.17

Creating a place for your video

8. Click OK to close the Document Properties dialog box.

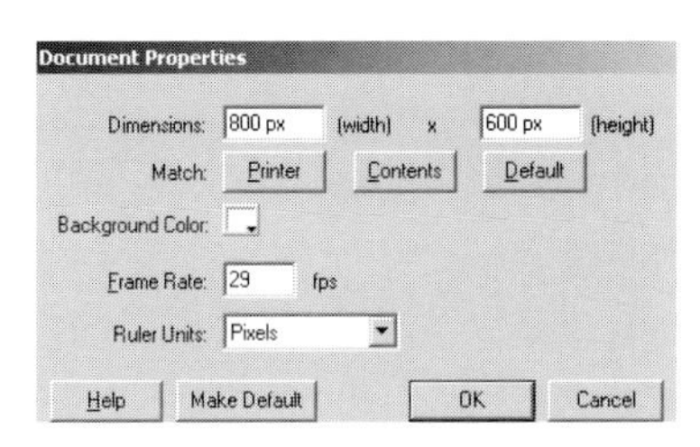

Figure 5.18

Changing the dimensions of the `newyork.fla` file

9. If the Info panel is not open, press Command/Ctrl+I to open the Info panel.
10. Make sure the small black registration point is in the upper left and then enter 235 for the X position and 333 for the Y position (see Figure 5.19). Now you have positioned the video in the same place that you positioned the green rectangle back in the `take2.fla` file.
11. Save the movie to your local hard drive. Be sure to save the movie in the same directory that you saved the `take2.fla` file.
12. Publish the movie, close the movie, and then return to the `take2.fla` movie.

Figure 5.19

Positioning the video at 235 X and 333 Y using the Info panel.

Setting Up the Load Action

Now let's load the movie into the Action parameter:

1. Delete the Video layer, which should delete the green rectangle.
2. Select the instance of the Drop Down Menu component and open the Component Parameters panel.
3. Click the Next Page button to go to the second page.
4. Select Item 2 in the Menu Items parameter and then select Item 3 in the Sub Item For Main Item #2 parameter. The label in the Menu Items parameter should be Instructors, and the label in the Sub Item For Main Item #2 parameter should be New York (see Figure 5.20).
5. Click the Edit Click Action button.
6. Set the Action parameter to Load Movie and enter **`newyork.swf`** in the URL To Load parameter, as shown in Figure 5.21.
7. Click the Close button; then close the Components Parameters panel.

Now you can publish the movie. Roll over the Instructors main heading and then click the New York submenu button. The `newyork.swf` file is loaded into the take2 movie in the correct position (see Figure 5.22).

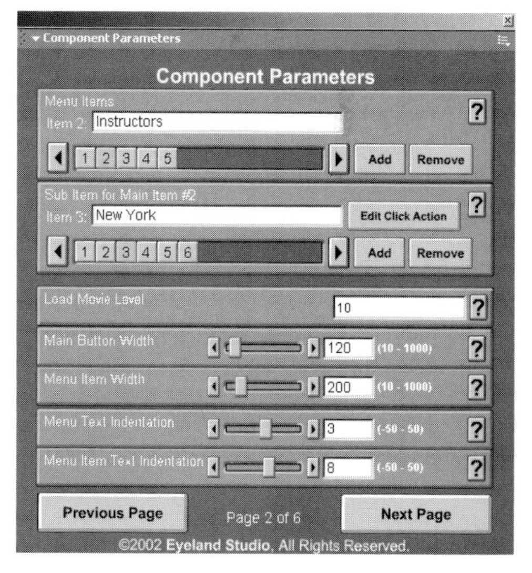

Figure 5.20

Selecting Item 2 in the Menu Items parameter and Item 3 in the Sub Item For Main Item#2 parameter

The `newyork.swf` movie loads into a predictable position because you set the `newyork.fla` file's stage size to the same size as the `take2.fla` stage size. Then you positioned the movie in the `newyork.fla` file in the same position that you wanted it to appear in the `take2.fla` file. When `newyork.swf` is loaded into `take2.swf`, the Flash player ignores the background and only displays the visible contents of the `newyork.swf` file, which is the video.

The Load Movie action works very well, and it's easy enough to implement. However, there are a few problems. First, notice that when you clicked the New York submenu option, the text associated with the submenu didn't appear. The only thing that happened was that the video loaded. So one problem with using the Load Movie option is that there is no support for navigating around the Flash movie and loading the movie at the same time.

You will notice another problem if you click any of the other submenu options when you're viewing the take2 movie. The problem is that the `newyork.swf` movie won't go away. Once you load the movie, it always stays visible until you unload the movie. Unfortunately, there's no "unload movie" option in the Drop Down Menu component's parameters.

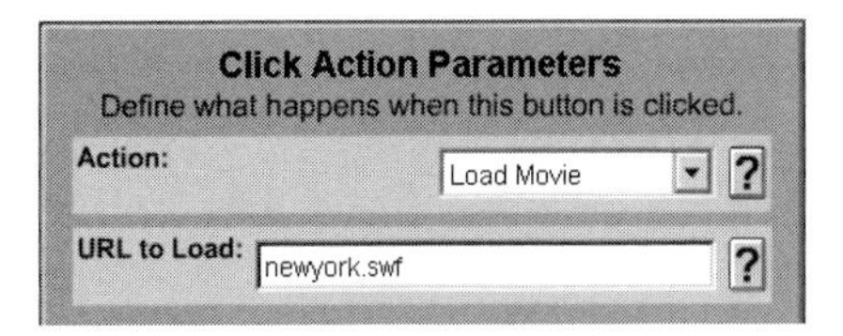

Figure 5.21
Loading a movie in the Action parameter

In the second page of the custom UI for the Drop Down Menu component is a parameter called Load Movie Level. The default value for this parameter is 10. If you change the value to 0, then you would replace the take2 movie with the newyork movie. Level 0 is the level that the host or main movie is on. Therefore, you need to set the Load Movie Level value to anything other than 0.

Figure 5.22
The `newyork.swf` movie loads into the proper position.

You could load another movie to replace the `newyork.swf` movie. So, for example, you could set every other submenu button to load a movie, and each time a new movie loads, it will replace the previously loaded movie. If you don't want another video to load when the viewer clicks a different submenu option, you could load a movie that has absolutely no visible contents.

These issues with the Load Movie option boil down to the fact that you'll probably want to use Load Movie only if you plan to use Load Movie with all of your button options. If you need to load a movie and perform one or more additional actions at the same time, you'll need to use the Advanced Script option. We will look at that option in a moment. First let's look at the Simple Script option.

Using Simple Scripts for Basic Navigation

All of the submenu items in the Drop Down Menu component that we've been looking at are already using the Simple Script option for the Action parameter. The Simple Script option allows you to specify basic ActionScript `goto`, `play`, and `stop` commands either to control the main Timeline of the overall Flash movie or to control a Timeline of a movie clip.

The ActionScript commands supported by the Simple Script Action are some of the most fundamental ActionScript commands in Flash. Commands like `gotoAndPlay` are the sort of commands you learn when you are starting to learn ActionScript. Most Flash designers who are not highly proficient with ActionScript usually are at least familiar with these commands. However, entering these simple commands into a component's parameters is a little different from entering these same commands in the Actions panel, so let's look at how these commands work with components.

Select the instance of the Drop Down Menu component and open the Component Parameters panel. Click the Next Page button to go to the second page. Select Item 1 in the Menu Items parameter and then select Item 1 in the Sub Item For Main Item #1 parameter. The text fields should contain the text Curriculum and General Film (see Figure 5.23).

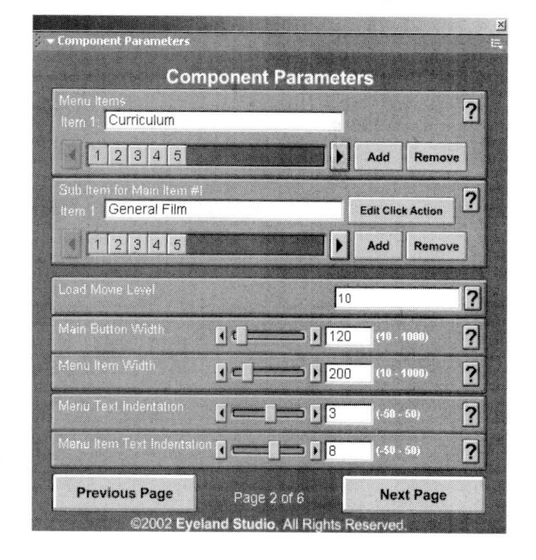

Figure 5.23

Item 1 is selected in both the Menu Items parameter and the Sub Item For Main Item #1 parameter.

Now click the Edit Click Action button. The Simple Script option is already selected in the Action parameter, and there is already a simple script in the Simple ActionScript parameter, as shown in Figure 5.24. As the text on the Simple ActionScript parameter explains, the code in the ActionScript parameter is executed when the user clicks the submenu button. However, the Simple ActionScript parameter supports a limited range of ActionScript commands.

Here are the commands that you can enter in the ActionScript parameter:

```
play();
stop();
gotoAndStop();
gotoAndPlay();
```

While these may not seem like very many commands, they can be adapted with a series of variations. For example, notice the command that's in the Simple ActionScript parameter in Figure 5.24:

```
_root.content.gotoAndStop("A1");
```

This code is essentially a `gotoandStop();` command. However, some additional elements have been added to the code. Let's evaluate how this code works.

The first part of the code is `_root`. The `_root` portion of this line of ActionScript code directs Flash to send the `gotoAndStop();` command to the main Timeline in Flash.

This makes sense if you recall that a component is essentially a movie clip that has been converted into a different type of a Flash resource. So the `gotoandStop();` command is being sent from inside of a movie clip. Therefore the `_root` portion of this line of ActionScript code sends the `gotoAndStop();` command outside of the component back up to the main Timeline.

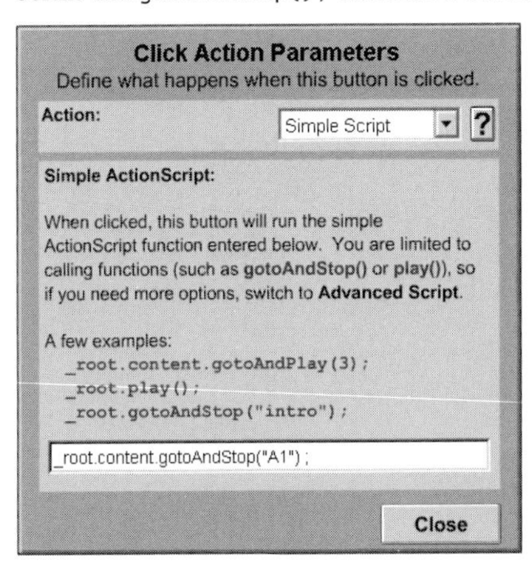

Figure 5.24

Simple Script is already selected, and a script is already in the Simple ActionScript parameter.

The next portion of the ActionScript is the word `content`. This is actually a reference to the instance name of a movie clip. To see this, close the Click Action Parameters screen and then close the Component Parameters panel. Now click the image of the three people to the left. Notice that when you click the picture, a blue outline appears around not only the image, but also the text and the two images on the right. All of these elements are surrounded by a blue line because they are all part of a movie clip.

Now press Command/Ctrl+F3 to open the Properties panel. Notice the instance name of the movie is "content," as shown in Figure 5.25. This instance name is the same "content" that is referenced by the ActionScript `_root.content`. In other words, `content` is a reference to the movie clip that has instance name "content."

So the `gotoAndStop` command is being sent up to the main Timeline with the `_root`, and then the `gotoAndStop` is sent down to the movie clip with the instance name "content."

Where is the "content" movie clip directed to go to and stop at? That is what the `"A1"` in the `gotoAndStop("A1");` portion of the ActionScript does. Whatever is in the parentheses is known as the "argument" of the `gotoAndStop` function. The argument qualifies the function. In this case, the argument tells the function where to go. When Flash sees something in quotations within the argument of a `gotoAndStop` or `gotoAndPlay` function, it knows that whatever is between the quotation marks is a frame label. Therefore the `"A1"` tells Flash to go to the frame labeled "A1" in the movie clip with the instance named "content."

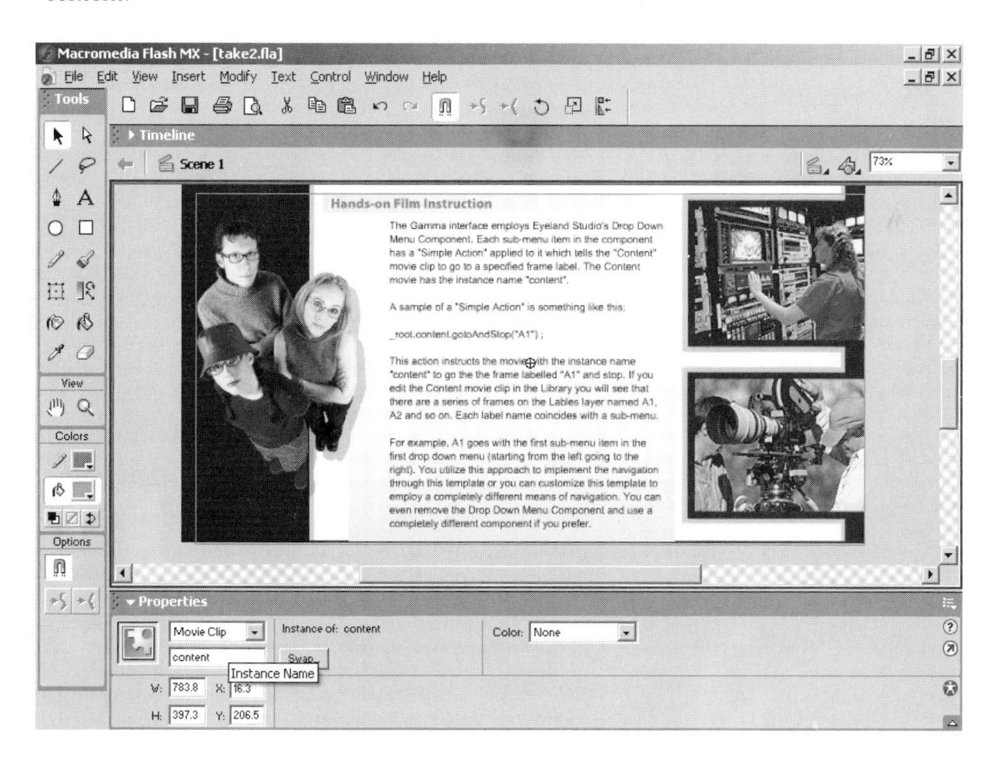

Figure 5.25

The instance name of the movie clip is "content."

The `_root` portion of the ActionScript tells Flash to look for the movie clip with the instance name "content" on the main Timeline. Without the `_root` portion of the ActionScript, the `gotoAndStop();` command would be sent to a movie clip with the instance name "content," but Flash wouldn't look for that movie clip on the main Timeline—it would look for that movie clip within the component. Of course, there is no movie clip with the instance name "content" in the component, so the `gotoandStop();` command would have no effect. Thus the `_root` portion of the code tells Flash to look in the right place for the movie clip with the instance name "content."

If you edit the movie clip with the instance name "content," you will see that the "A1" label is on frame 10 (see Figure 5.26).

Therefore the ActionScript:

```
_root.content.gotoAndStop("A1");
```

tells Flash to display frame 10 of the movie clip with the instance name "content." In fact, the same thing would happen if the command was written like this:

```
_root.content.gotoAndStop(10);
```

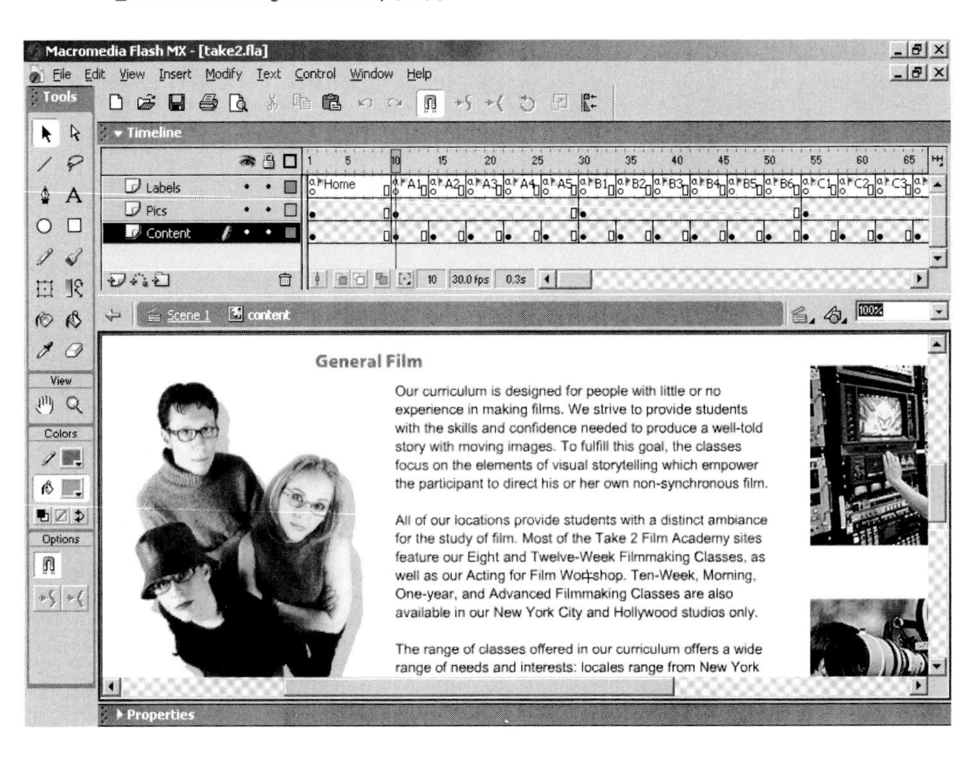

Figure 5.26

The "content" movie clip contains content associated with each submenu item. The content for each submenu item is located on keyframes, and each keyframe has a label that is referenced in the `gotoAndStop();` functions.

In this case, there are no quotation marks, and Flash knows that the number in the argument for the gotoAndStop function references a frame number. Therefore, this ActionScript would specifically direct Flash to display frame 10 of the movie clip named "content."

The gotoAndPlay, stop, or play commands can be used in the same way. The key is to send these commands to the place you want them. If, for instance, you only enter the command:

```
play();
```

then you will be telling the component movie clip to play. If you want to direct the main Timeline to play, you need to write the command like this:

```
_root.play();
```

If you want to play a movie clip with the instance name "mysillyanimation," then you need to be sure there is a movie clip with the instance name "mysillyanimation," and you need to direct the command to it properly. For example, if the "mysillyanimation" movie clip is within another movie clip with the instance name "allanimations," then the command would look like this:

```
_root.allanimations.mysillyanimation.play();
```

One final note before we move on. You can also use _parent, instead of _root. The _parent ActionScript directs the command up to the previous Timeline. In this example, _parent would accomplish the same thing because the main Timeline is up one Timeline from the movie clip that has been converted to the Drop Down Menu component. However, if the movie that contains the Drop Down Menu component is loaded into a separate movie, the _root command would route the command to the Timeline of that movie. In that case, you would need to use this command:

```
_parent.content.gotoAndStop("A1");
```

to send the gotoAndStop command to the proper place.

Now let's look at the last option in the Action parameter, the Advanced Script option.

Using the Advanced Script to Call Custom Functions

While the Load URL, Load Movie, and Simple Script options allow you to perform most of the more common actions that occur when clicking a button in Flash, there are some obvious limitations. The most obvious problem is that you can, for example, direct the component to send a simple script command at the same time it loads a movie or loads a URL. If you use the first three options in the Action parameter, you can only have one type of action occur at a time.

The Advanced Script option in the Action parameter provides a means to trigger more than one action at a time. However, as the designation "Advanced" suggests, you do need more advanced skills in coding ActionScript. In particular, you need to be able to write a function that performs.

While we don't have enough space in this book to teach you the ins and outs of writing a function, we can take a look at an example to see how it works. The following example will show you how to leverage the built-in function calls in the Advanced Script parameter.

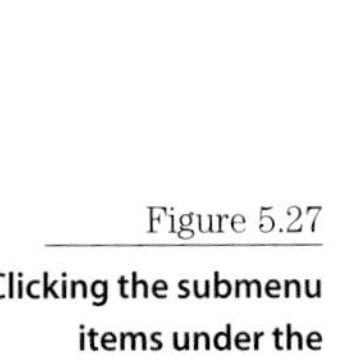

Locate the following files on the CD and copy them to the same directory on your hard drive:

```
video0.swf          video3.swf          empty.swf
video1.swf          video4.swf          take2_function.fla
video2.swf          video5.swf
```

Open the `take2_function.fla` file. Go ahead and test the movie. Roll over the Instructors header and click any of the submenu options. Notice that when you click the submenu items, the "content" movie clip goes to a new frame and a video loads (see Figure 5.27).

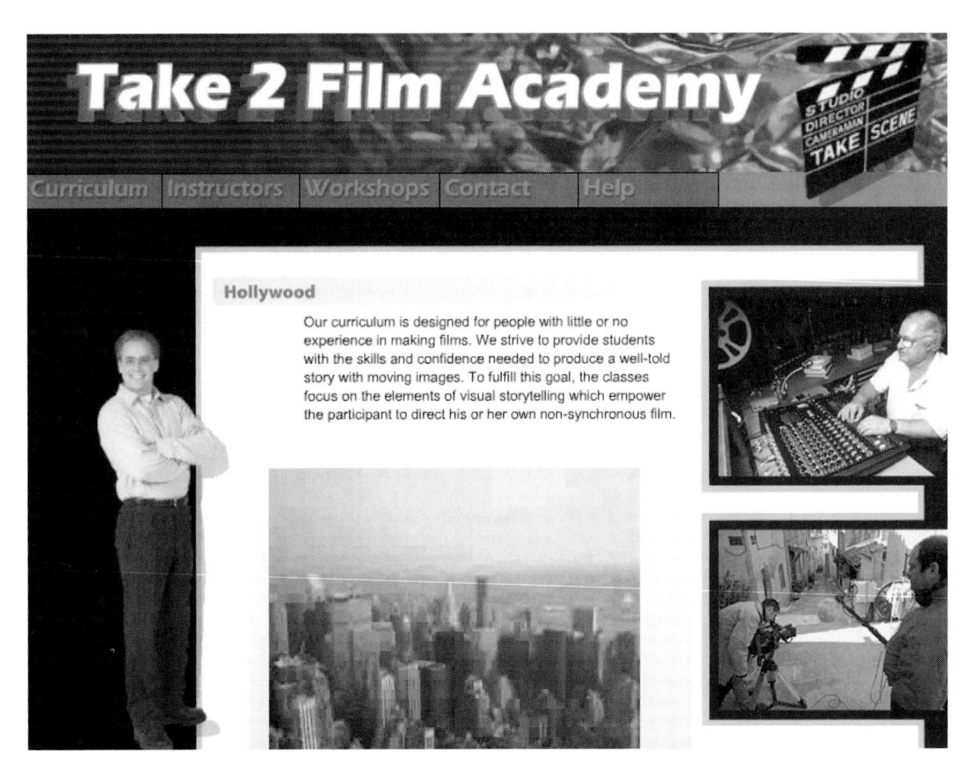

Figure 5.27

Clicking the submenu items under the Instructors heading both displays a different frame of the movie clip with the instance name "content" and loads a movie.

Also notice that clicking submenu items under different headings, such as Curriculum or Workshops, only shows a different frame of the "content" movie clip. Movies are only loaded when you click submenu items under the Instructors header. So, in this example, some submenu buttons trigger two actions, and some buttons only trigger one action. All of this is accomplished with a function that is called by the Advanced Script option in the Actions parameter of the Drop Down Menu component.

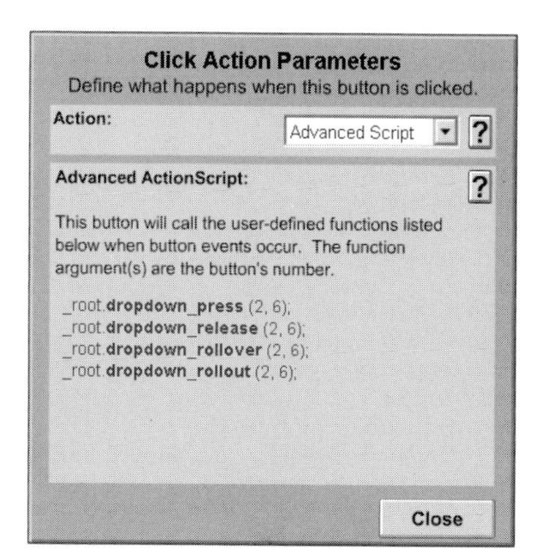

Figure 5.28

The Advanced Script option is selected.

Incidentally, you probably noticed that an Output box was generated when you clicked any of the submenu items. We'll touch on this in a moment. For now, just close the Output boxes as you preview the movie. I'll show you how to get rid of this annoyance soon. When you have finished previewing the movie, close the test movie and let's look at how it works. Follow these steps to access the Advanced ActionScript functions:

1. Select the instance of the Drop Down Menu component on the stage and open the Component Parameters panel.
2. Click the Next Page button to open the second page of the Component Parameters panel.
3. Select Item 2 in the Menu Items parameter. Item 6 in the Sub Item For Main Item #2 parameter is automatically selected, which is fine for our purpose. All of the items in the Sub Item For Main Item #2 have the same settings for their click actions, so Item 6 is as good as Item 1 for observing the settings.
4. Click the Edit Click Actions button. Notice that the Advanced Script option is selected in the Actions parameter, shown in Figure 5.28.
5. Notice the text box below the Actions parameter labeled Advanced ActionScript. It contains the following functions:

```
dropdown_press();
dropdown_release();
dropdown_rollover();
dropdown_rollout();
```

When the Advanced Script option is selected, the component will send out these four generic function calls to the main Timeline. Obviously, these function calls are for a press event, a release event, a rollover event, and a rollout event, respectively. In other words, the `dropdown_press()` function is called when you click the corresponding submenu button. These function calls are sent out whether or not you have a function written that captures these function calls. If you don't have a function, nothing will happen—that is, no error message will be generated.

Notice that each function has two arguments. For example, the `dropdown_press` function is listed in the Advanced ActionScript field as:

```
dropdown_press(2, 6);
```

The first argument represents the main menu item, and the second argument represents the submenu item. Therefore, when the sixth submenu item under the second main menu item is clicked, the function will send out a call to the `dropdown_press` function with the arguments `(2, 6)`. If the first submenu item under the first main menu is selected, then the arguments will be `(1, 1)`.

The trick, therefore, is to write a function that takes advantage of these function calls. Let's look at the function that the `take2_function.fla` file utilizes. Close the Component Parameters panel and look at the Timeline. Notice the new layer named Function above all the other layers on the main Timeline. Select the first frame on the Function layer and press F9 to open the Actions panel (see Figure 5.29).

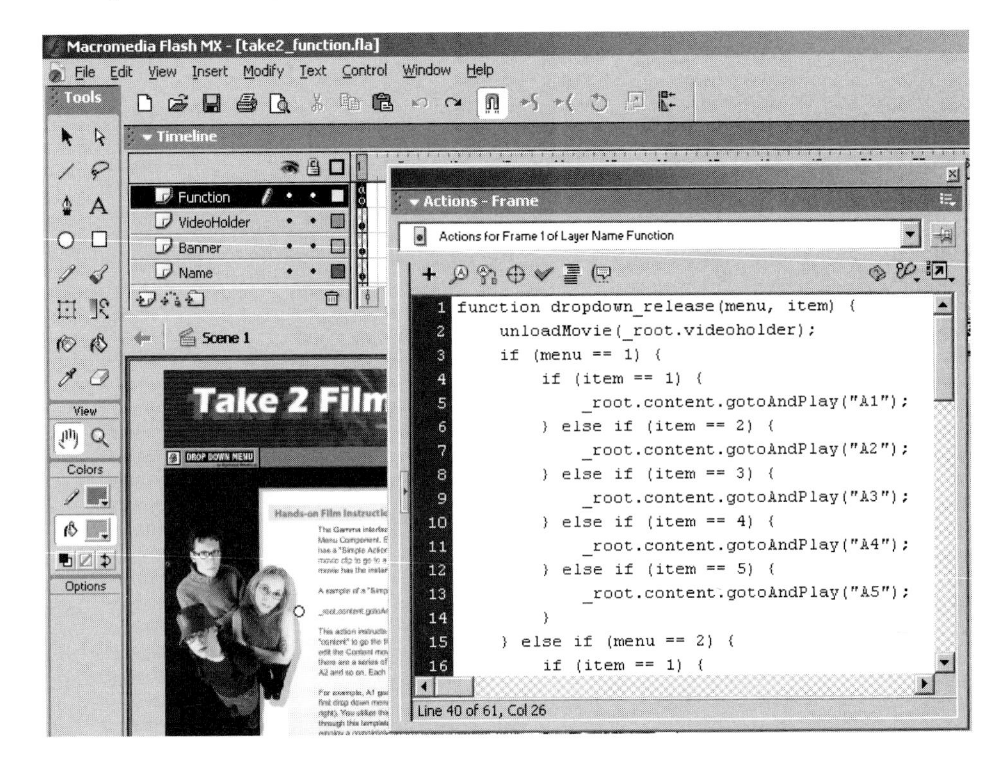

Figure 5.29

Open the Actions panel to view the ActionScript on the Function layer.

Listing 5.1 shows you the function located on the first frame of the Function layer. The function is on the first frame of the main Timeline to make it easy to access. Even though the code is on a keyframe, none of the code will be executed unless the function is called. Let's look at the code:

Listing 5.1

Leveraging the Function Call from the Drop Down Menu Component

```
function dropdown_release(menu, item) {
   unloadMovie(_root.videoholder);
   if (menu == 1) {
      if (item == 1) {
         _root.content.gotoAndPlay("A1");
      } else if (item == 2) {
         _root.content.gotoAndPlay("A2");
      } else if (item == 3) {
         _root.content.gotoAndPlay("A3");
      } else if (item == 4) {
         _root.content.gotoAndPlay("A4");
      } else if (item == 5) {
         _root.content.gotoAndPlay("A5");
      }
   } else if (menu == 2) {
      if (item == 1) {
         _root.content.gotoAndPlay("B1");
         loadMovie("video0.swf", _root.videoholder);
      } else if (item == 2) {
         _root.content.gotoAndPlay("B2");
         loadMovie("video1.swf", _root.videoholder);
      } else if (item == 3) {
         _root.content.gotoAndPlay("B3");
         loadMovie("video2.swf", _root.videoholder);
      } else if (item == 4) {
         _root.content.gotoAndPlay("B4");
         loadMovie("video3.swf", _root.videoholder);
      } else if (item == 5) {
         _root.content.gotoAndPlay("B5");
         loadMovie("video4.swf", _root.videoholder);
      } else if (item == 6) {
         _root.content.gotoAndPlay("B6");
         loadMovie("video5.swf", _root.videoholder);
```

continued

continues

```
        }
    } else if (menu == 3) {
        if (item == 1) {
            _root.content.gotoAndPlay("C1");
        } else if (item == 2) {
            _root.content.gotoAndPlay("C2");
        } else if (item == 3) {
            _root.content.gotoAndPlay("C3");
        } else if (item == 4) {
            _root.content.gotoAndPlay("C4");
        }
    } else if (menu == 4) {
        if (item == 1) {
            _root.content.gotoAndPlay("D1");
        } else if (item == 2) {
            _root.content.gotoAndPlay("D2");
        }
    } else if (menu == 5) {
        if (item == 1) {
            _root.content.gotoAndPlay("E1");
        } else if (item == 2) {
            _root.content.gotoAndPlay("E2");
        } else if (item == 3) {
            _root.content.gotoAndPlay("E3");
        }
    }
}
```

This function contains a lot of lines of code. However, the code is very repetitive. Let's examine its basic structure. If we simplify things, the essential function is structured like this:

```
function dropdown_release(menu, item) {
   unloadMovie(_root.videoholder);
   if menu = 1
      if item = 1
        else if item = 2
        else if item = 3
        else if item = 4
        else if item = 5
   else if (menu = 2) {
      if item = 1
        else if item = 2
```

```
            else if item = 3
            else if item = 4
            else if item = 5
            else if item = 6
      else if menu = 3
         if item = 1
            else if item = 2
            else if item = 3
            else if (item == 4) {
...
```

As you can see, the function is composed of a series of `if`, `else if` conditional statements. If you look carefully, you'll see that `if`, `else if` statements correspond to each of the submenu items. For example, the `if menu = 1` line corresponds to the first main menu in the Drop Down Menu component. The `if item = 1` statement corresponds to the first submenu item under the first main menu item. The `else if item = 2` line corresponds to the second submenu item under the first main menu item… and so on. Let's see how this works.

When a submenu item is pressed and released, the component sends out a call to the `dropdown_release` function. Included with this call to the `dropdown_release` function are the two arguments that correspond to the submenu that was clicked.

For example, let's say that you clicked the third submenu item under the second main menu item. The resulting function call would be:

```
_root.dropdown_release(2, 3);
```

Let's see how this would work with the function. Actually, the first thing the function does is execute the following code:

```
unloadMovie(_root.videoholder);
```

However, let's look at this in a moment. First we want to see how the arguments in the function call work. The second line with the `dropdown_release` function is:

```
if (menu == 1) {
```

This line checks to see if the first argument in the function call is equal to 1. Again, our example function call is:

```
_root.dropdown_release(2, 3);
```

so this first line of code would resolve to false because the menu argument is equal to 2, not 1. Therefore, the code would bypass everything within the `if (menu == 1) {` conditional statement. In other words, it would bypass all of the following:

```
if (menu == 1) {
      if (item == 1) {
         _root.content.gotoAndPlay("A1");
```

```
} else if (item == 2) {
   _root.content.gotoAndPlay("A2");
} else if (item == 3) {
   _root.content.gotoAndPlay("A3");
} else if (item == 4) {
   _root.content.gotoAndPlay("A4");
} else if (item == 5) {
   _root.content.gotoAndPlay("A5");
}
```

The code would continue executing to the following line:

```
else if (menu = 2) {
```

This line would resolve to true because the menu argument does equal 2. At this point, the code would start evaluating the second argument in the function call. The second argument is equal to 3. So the code would first execute through the `if` statement within the `else if (menu = 2)` statement. In other words the code would execute this line:

```
if (item == 1) {
```

This line of code would resolve to false since the item argument is equal to 3. So the next two lines of code would be skipped:

```
_root.content.gotoAndPlay("B1");
loadMovie("video0.swf", _root.videoholder);
```

and the following line of code would be executed:

```
} else if (item == 2) {
```

Once again, the item argument is equal to 3, so this line of code would resolve to false. The next two lines of code would be skipped, and the following line of code would be evaluated:

```
} else if (item == 3) {
```

Finally, this would resolve to true because the item argument is equal to 3. Therefore the two lines of code within the `else if` conditional statement would be executed:

```
_root.content.gotoAndPlay("B3");
loadMovie("video2.swf", _root.videoholder);
```

These two lines of code execute two actions. The first line should look familiar. It tells the "content" movie to go to the frame labeled "B3" and play. The second line of code executes a LoadMovie function.

The LoadMovie function contains two arguments. The first argument is the movie to be loaded, in this example, `"video2.swf"`. The second argument indicates where the movie should be loaded. In this example, the movie is loaded into a movie clip on the main Timeline that has an instance name "videoholder."

> The "video2.swf" is a relative path. It assumes that the video2.swf file is in the same directory as the main Flash movie (in this case, take2_function.swf). You can also use other relative URLs such as "movies/video2.swf", which means that the video2.swf file needs to be in a subdirectory named movies. You can also enter absolute URLs such as http://www.flashfoundry.com/movies/video2.swf.

There is now a white dot character on the stage (see Figure 5.30). Flash uses this white dot to represent a movie clip that has no visible contents. Movies can be loaded into a movie clip, or they can be loaded onto the main Timeline as demonstrated earlier. The upper-left corner of the "videoholder" movie clip designates where the loaded movies will be positioned at.

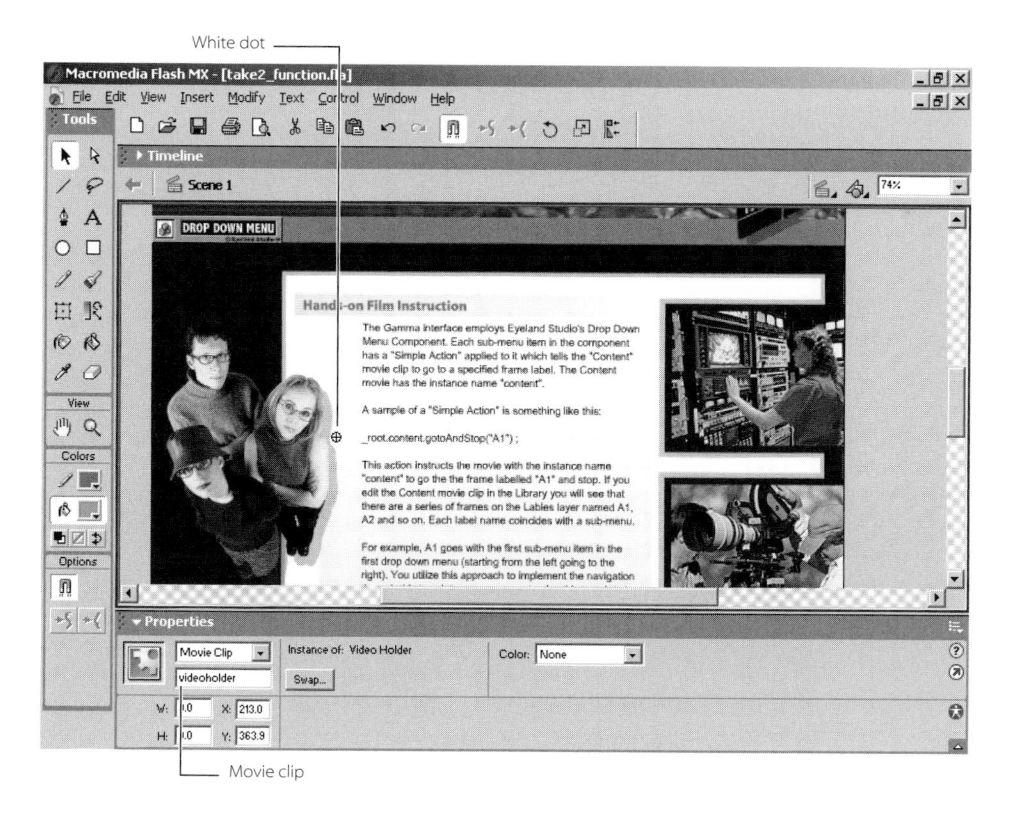

Figure 5.30

The white dot represents the "videoholder" movie clip that is used for loading the movies.

Resolving an Annoying Problem

Before we conclude this chapter, let's revisit the problem that we observed when we were testing the movie. When you test the movie and click a submenu, Flash produces an Output window with a message that begins, "Error opening URL...." The cause of this Output window is a known bug in Flash. It is not indicative of anything that is actually wrong. However, it is annoying.

The problem is the second line of code:

```
nloadMovie(_root.videoholder);
```

This code removes any movie that has been loaded into the videoholder movie clip. There is no syntax error in this line of code, and it is a perfectly valid way to use the `unloadMovie` function. Flash simply mishandles it in the Test Movie environment. If you open the SWF file outside of the Flash environment, or if you view the `take2_function.swf` file in a browser, the file will work just fine, and you will see no error messages. It is only an annoying problem when you are using Test Movie.

Using Test Movie is very convenient, so it is fortunate that there is a simple workaround to the problem. The workaround is to create an empty movie and then load the empty movie instead of executing the unload. Follow these steps:

1. Open Flash and export or publish the movie without putting anything on the stage—no graphics, no sound, no movie clips, nothing.
2. To load the empty movie into the videoholder movie, replace the following code:

   ```
   nloadMovie(_root.videoholder);
   ```

   with this:

   ```
   oadMovie("empty.swf", _root.videoholder);
   ```

3. Test the movie (you copied the `empty.swf` file to your local drive early on in the chapter, so it should work).

You will see that Flash no longer generates the error message.

It may occur to you that the code always loads the `empty.swf` file into the videoholder movie. If that is so, why, then, do the `video0.swf` through `video5.swf` movies load into the videoholder movie if you click any of the submenu buttons under the Instructors main menu heading? This is because the `empty.swf` movie is always loaded into the videoholder first, and *then* the other videos are loaded if the relevant buttons are clicked.

Now that you have an idea of how the function works to capture the built-in function calls from the Drop Down Menu component, you should be able to modify the code for your purposes. Fortunately, even if you are not an accomplished ActionScript programmer, there is no shortage of very good and very affordable (usually) Flash programmers available to help you with such a task. Of course, there is also no shortage of good books on ActionScript, such as my own *Flash MX ActionScript: The Designer's Edge* (Sybex, 2002), if you need more tutoring on ActionScript.

Conclusion

Once you understand the basics of all the available click actions, leveraging them is not very difficult. In fact, it can be almost trivial to enter a URL for the Load URL action. Using the Simple Script and even Advanced ActionScript options can be simply copying and pasting, more so than any amount of complex coding. Not all components implement click actions the same way the Drop Down Menu component does. However, due to how Flash and components work in general, most components will operate in fairly similar way. Once you take a few minutes to master the various click actions, you will be able be able to implement a wide range of interactive functionality very quickly and easily.

Chapter 6: Animation Components

Next, let's explore the reative potential of using animation components as both individuals and mixed together in unusual ways.

In almost every sense, this is an exploration. We might imagine ourselves at the frontier of some new computational universe, where our thoughts and the movements of our hands control the world that will unfold around us. It is unclear what exactly we may find during this exploration because of the sheer number of possibilities. We can rest assured, though, that our journey will be one that cannot be described, only observed.

In the following sections, we'll observe the landscape, learn of its dangers and pitfalls, and discover treasures of new knowledge. Now is the time to set our frames of mind as explorers, and set off.

- **The animation component set**
- **Customizing the artwork used by animation components**
- **Understanding the limits of Flash animation**
- **Using multiple animation components**

The Animation Component Set

Included in the Chapter 6 folder on the companion CD is a collection of five highly optimized Eyeland Studio animation components. They were created specially for this chapter as tools for explaining the concepts and methods we will be discussing. Beyond that, they are useful instruments in any designer's toolbox. I encourage you to modify and use them in exciting new ways.

You must install the animation component set before you can use them. Using the Macromedia Extension Manager (a link to which is provided on the companion CD), you can install, manage, and track all third-party expansions installed into any of Macromedia's suite of applications. This includes components and Flash MX.

Once you have installed Macromedia Extension Manager, open it. Choose File → Install Extension. Browse to the Chapter 6 folder on the companion CD and select the file `AnimationComponents.mxp`. Click OK. If all is successful, you will see a dialog box displaying the terms of the installation. Agree to the terms by clicking the Accept button. The animation components are now installed as part of your Flash MX development environment.

The best way to introduce these components is to give a brief explanation of each, one by one. We will observe the appearance and behavior of the component using its default configuration, and then I'll provide a brief explanation of how the component can be used, describe the parameters in the component definition, and most importantly, provide some inspirational implementations of the component.

When you have successfully installed the animation components, begin a new FLA file (see Figure 6.1); you will use this as a blank canvas on which to experiment. You can access the components through the Components panel. To use them, drag instances of them from the panel onto the stage where you would like them to appear. Each animation component has a unique set of properties that determines its appearance and general behavior. Modifying these properties allows you to create wild and new computationally generated animations.

General Parameters

The following parameters apply to more than one of the animation components:

Number Of <items> The total number of vertical bars, pebbles, or seeds to be displayed.

Color Points An array of hexadecimal color values from which shapes are assigned their colors.

Color Snap or Snap To Colors Setting this Boolean value to True causes each shape to be assigned one of the colors in the Color Points list. Setting it to False assigns shapes color values calculated from the gradients that form between colors in the Color Points list.

Alpha The amount of opacity for all the shapes, as a percentage. The lower this number is, the more transparent the shapes become. A value less than 5 is not recommended because the shapes will be practically invisible. A value of 100 keeps all shapes solid (no transparency).

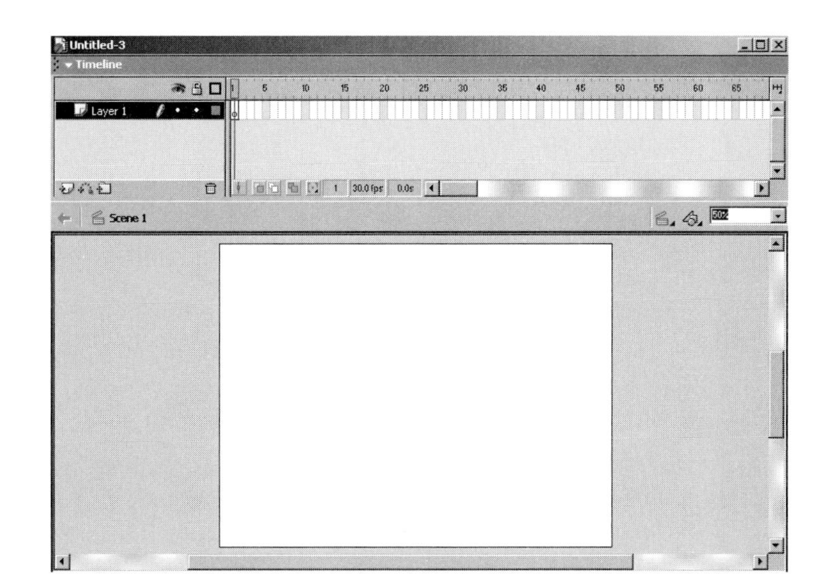

Figure 6.1

Begin a new FLA file to test this chapter's components.

The Parallel Bars Component

The Parallel Bars component fills a region of space with dynamic, animated vertical bars. The effect is commonly seen in both film and on the Web. What you cannot see in the pages of this book is the engaging visual effect created when these vertical bars are animated. Each bar slides and switches positions with the others in near continual, random fashion. With some tweaking of the component's settings, the Parallel Bars can even be a useful tool for displaying information.

Drag an instance of the Parallel Bars component onto the main stage. Then publish the movie and observe the results. The default configuration of the Parallel Bars is animated and looks something like a funny, gray-shaded square, shown in Figure 6.2.

Figure 6.2

The default appearance of the published Parallel Bars component

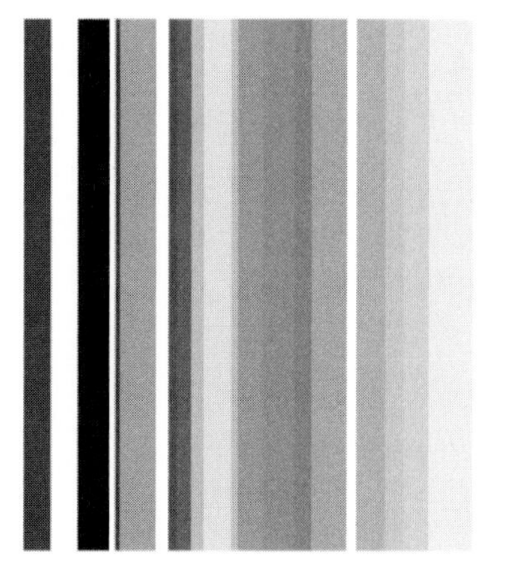

Looks pretty simple, right? Well, it really is. By default, a 100×100 pixel region of space is filled with vertical bars. Each of the bars operates independently from the rest unless collision detection is enabled, in which case they bounce off of each other. The side-to-side movement is random but controllable through three separate parameters. The number, color, and thickness of the bars are also fully customizable. As we will see later in this chapter, combining multiple Parallel Bars components can produce some astonishingly complex results.

Component Basics

Within the Component Parameters panel, shown in Figure 6.3, you will find the controls that allow you to customize the Parallel Bars component. Each of the animation components is accessible through a similar interface. This makes the customization and tweaking of the components very easy. (Notice that this user interface scrolls vertically, unlike the tabbed UIs shown in earlier chapters.)

In addition to the general parameters listed in the preceding section, the following parameters control the appearance and behavior of the Parallel Bars component.

Region Width, Region Height The width and height of the area to be filled with bars, measured in pixels.

Bar Thickness, Bar Thickness Variation Bar Thickness is the maximum width of each bar, measured in pixels. Bar Thickness Variation is the percentage of variation in that thickness; a value of 0 forces all bars to be the same width. A Bar Thickness Variation value of 100 randomizes each bar's thickness within the maximum set by Bar Thickness.

Movement Frequency The frequency with which the bars change position, measured in milliseconds. The lower this number is, the faster and more chaotic the bars' movement seems.

Movement Chaos A percentage that introduces randomness in almost every aspect of the bars' movement. A higher number causes more unpredictable, chaotic movement, while a lower number causes smooth, more rhythmic movement.

Movement Velocity The speed with which the bars actually move on the screen. A value of 1000 causes the bars to move so fast that they seem to blink into their next position. Low values cause gentle, sweeping movements.

Movement Variation A percentage that controls the differences in speeds between the individual bars. A high number produces bars that move at all kinds of different speeds, while a low number generally keeps the bars moving at the same rate.

Enable Collision Detection Setting this Boolean value to True causes the bars to bounce off of each other while moving. Setting it to False allows the bars to move freely, often over and under other bars.

Inspirational Examples

With a little experimentation using only the component's parameters, all of the following animation effects are possible.

This first example (shown in Figure 6.4) fills a region of 800 pixels by 200 pixels with 100 bars. The thickness of the bars is set to 30 pixels, but because the Bar Thickness Variation is set to 100%, many of the bars are actually much thinner. The shades of gray are the result of hand-entered color values that range over a subtle palette of Earth tones. There are 12 unique colors, each with a differing contrast.

To re-create this example, first select the Parallel Bars instance you dragged onto the stage earlier. Launch the Component Parameters panel. Move the Number Of Bars slider to

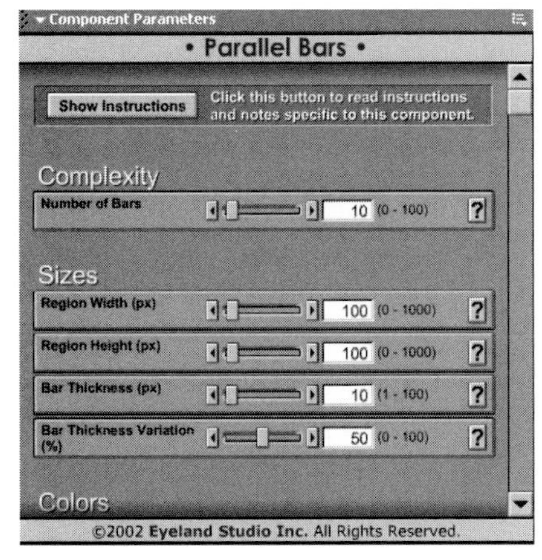

Figure 6.3

The component parameters for the Parallel Bars component

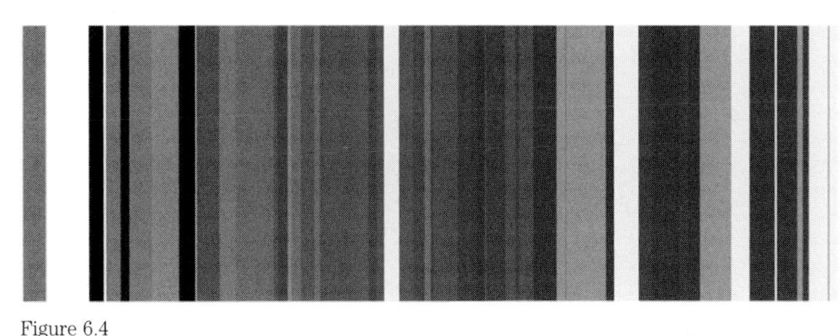

Figure 6.4

The Parallel Bars with custom settings

its maximum of 100—we want a lot of bars. Change the Region Width value to 800 pixels, to fill the horizontal stage of the same dimension, and change the Region Height value to 200 pixels, doubling the default value of 100. Next, change Bar Thickness to 30 pixels and move Bar Thickness Variation to 100%. This will give us a great range of thick and thin bars.

For the Color Points, I chose a favorite collection of 12 earthy tones using a scanned outdoor photograph and a paint program to pull hexadecimal values from it. For your own work, you will probably enter color values that best suit your project.

Entering color values is a two-step process. To enter colors into the list, first use the slider bars above the list to find the color you wish to enter. The hexadecimal value of the color will be shown and will look something like Hex#: FF0000. In this case, the color is bright red. Click the Add Color button in the Color Points list. In the dialog box that appears, type the hexadecimal number preceded by **0x**. Click OK, and the new color should show up in the Color Points list. Adjust the order of the colors in the list by selecting them and using the Move Up and Move Down buttons.

The second example (see Figure 6.5) combines two Parallel Bars components, juxtaposed on top of each other. You will notice right away the predominance of darker colors in the lower Parallel Bars. This is a great example of how individual instances of the same component can hold unique parameters. The component on the bottom is using the same color palette as the first example, while the component on top is using an entirely new set of mainly lighter colors. It is interesting to note that all other component parameters for these two instances are the same. The variations in spacing and sizing are a result of the ongoing chaotic animation. The easiest way to re-create this example is to duplicate the original component and then edit the colors of the duplication. In this fashion, all other component parameters will remain the same.

THE COLOR POINT LIST CONTROL AND THE HEXIDECIMAL COLOR SYSTEM

While it may seem somewhat complex, all the animation components use a color system based on numbers to allow the highest degree of color precision possible. This means that you enter colors into the Color Points list by their hexadecimal number. The hexadecimal color system allows 16.7 million possible unique colors. Each color is indicated by the amounts of red, blue, and green to mix together. The higher the number, the brighter the color. A hexadecimal number in Flash looks like 0xFFFFFF (bright white). Some other colors are 0x000000 (absolute black), 0xFF0000 (bright red), 0x00FF00 (bright green), 0x0000FF (bright blue), and 0xFF00FF (purple). The leading 0x tells the computer that the number is in hexadecimal format. The remaining six characters are broken into three separate groups of two digits each. They represent the red, green, and blue components respectively. Each digit is a value from 0 to F where the system counts by 0 1 2 3 4 5 6 7 8 9 A B C D E F, with 0 being null value, and F being highest value. Even the best mathematicians have a hard time calculating the hexadecimal equivalent of a particular shade or hue. This is why a color picker has been included as part of the Color Point list control. Simply choose a color visually using the picker and copy the computed hexadecimal value into the Color Point list.

For the final example with the Parallel Bars (see Figure 6.6), we have done something a little bit tricky. Although it appears to be some kind of grid component, the images in the figure were actually generated by placing two instances of the Parallel Bars component one on top of the other and rotating the uppermost instance by 90 degrees. The upper instance also has exactly one Color Point value, 0xFFFFFF (bright white). Keeping this in mind, take another look at the images. Their method of construction might now be a bit more obvious, although the effect is still intriguing.

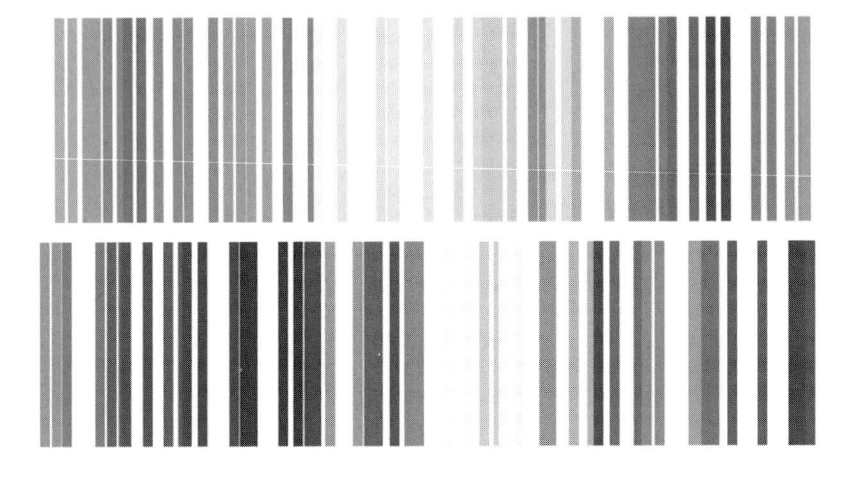

Figure 6.5

Two similar Parallel Bar components, each with different Color Points values

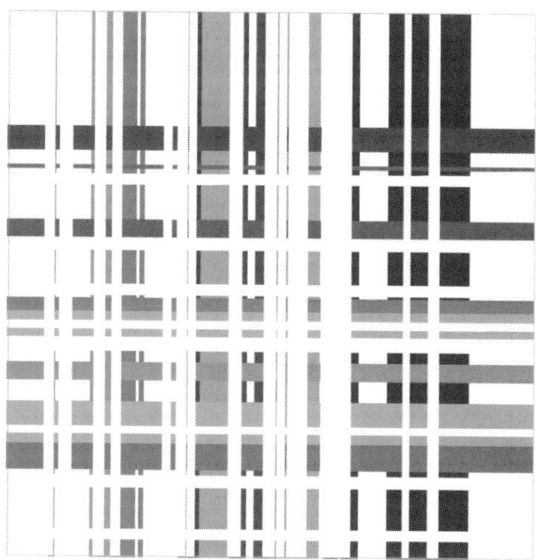

Figure 6.6

Abstract grid space illusions created using two Parallel Bars components

One great way to stack components on top of each other is to use separate layers. For each component to be stacked, create a new layer and place exactly one component within it. Keep in mind that the components on upper layers will block the components on lower layers. Use this to your advantage.

Using this technique of layering components will also speed the process of selecting and editing the components, since you can temporarily hide individual layers and select all objects on a layer by selecting the layer itself.

The Pond Ripples Component

The Pond Ripples component generates concentric, geometric structures of colored discs, shown in Figure 6.7. In many ways, this component is similar to the Parallel Bars component. One particularly interesting difference with this component, however, is the method in which the individual discs of the structure are animated. These discs breathe. The breathing cycle is a short animation loop that causes each disc's size to rise and fall, much like the chest of a breathing animal. When many discs are expanding and contracting in unison, the effect is sometimes, well, breathtaking.

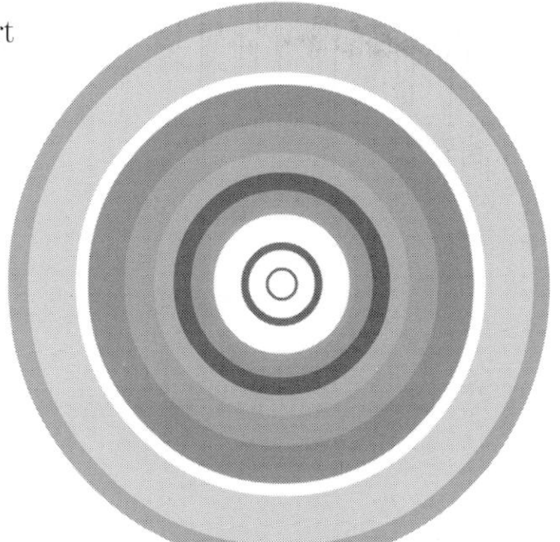

Figure 6.7

The default appearance of the Pond Ripples component

Component Basics

In addition to the Color and Alpha parameters listed in the first section of this chapter, the following parameters control the appearance and behavior of the Pond Ripples component.

Outer Radius This value determines the overall size of the component. To determine the actual size of the component in pixels, simply multiply the radius by 2.

Ring Thickness, Ring Thickness Variation The first of these determines the maximum thickness of each colored ring in the Pond Ripples in pixels. Experiment with this setting; if only a few colors are defined, several skinny rings of the same color will be created, giving the illusion of one fat ring, so you may want to add colors to see thin rings. Ring Thickness Variation allows ring thickness to be sized randomly; the higher the value, the more randomly sized the rings.

Centerpoint Offset, Centerpoint Offset Variation The Centerpoint Offset pixel number repositions individual rings some random amount from the center of the ripple. Higher numbers provide more room in which the rings might move around. The default value of 0 keeps all rings perfectly centered. The Variation value is a percentage that allows each ring's offset value to be randomized further. Higher values cause a more chaotic distribution of rings, while lower values generally keep rings within the same range.

Color Mixing Chaos This percentage determines to what extent the colors in the Color Points array will be mixed when applied to the rings. See the first example of this component for an illustration and further explanation on Color Mixing Chaos.

Breathing Intensity This number controls the depth of breath each ring takes. Larger values produce more exaggerated breaths. A value of 0 produces rings that do not breathe at all.

Breathing Variation This percentage is used to mix up the times that rings take their breaths. A value of 0 creates rings that breathe simultaneously (so the entire structure grows and contracts together), while higher values create with rings that breathe further and further out of sync.

Lifetime This setting imposes a specified time for the component to live. After the number of seconds entered has been reached, the Pond Ripples component begins to die. This is especially useful if many Pond Ripples are being created and some need to be destroyed to keep CPU resources plentiful. The Lifetime value is unique to the Pond Ripples component. A Lifetime value of 0 gives the Pond Ripples indefinite life.

Fade Out This Boolean value is used in conjunction with the Lifetime value. If set to True, the entire Pond Ripples effect fades away at the end of its lifetime.

Show Build Process This Boolean value controls the method in which the Pond Ripples effect is assembled. A setting of True shows the construction process of each ring being attached from the center outward. A value of False instantly displays the entire Pond Ripples. This component parameter is common to most of the other animation components.

Inspirational Examples

This first example of the Pond Ripples component (see Figure 6.8) is a demonstration of the power of the Color Mixing Chaos value. The instance on the left has a Color Mixing Chaos value of 0, and the instance on the right has a Color Mixing Chaos value of 100. All other component parameters are the same in the two instances. Clearly, setting a large value for the Color Mixing Chaos creates a Pond Ripples effect with severely mixed up colors. Try experimenting with this setting by creating a third instance with a Color Mixing Chaos value of 50. What will it look like?

The next example (see Figure 6.9) shows how changing just a couple of different settings can produce some beautiful results. The most striking feature of the images below is probably the strange alignment of rings. Setting a small number for the Centerpoint Offset value creates this effect. Also, the entire Pond Ripples component has some transparency because the Alpha value is set to 30.

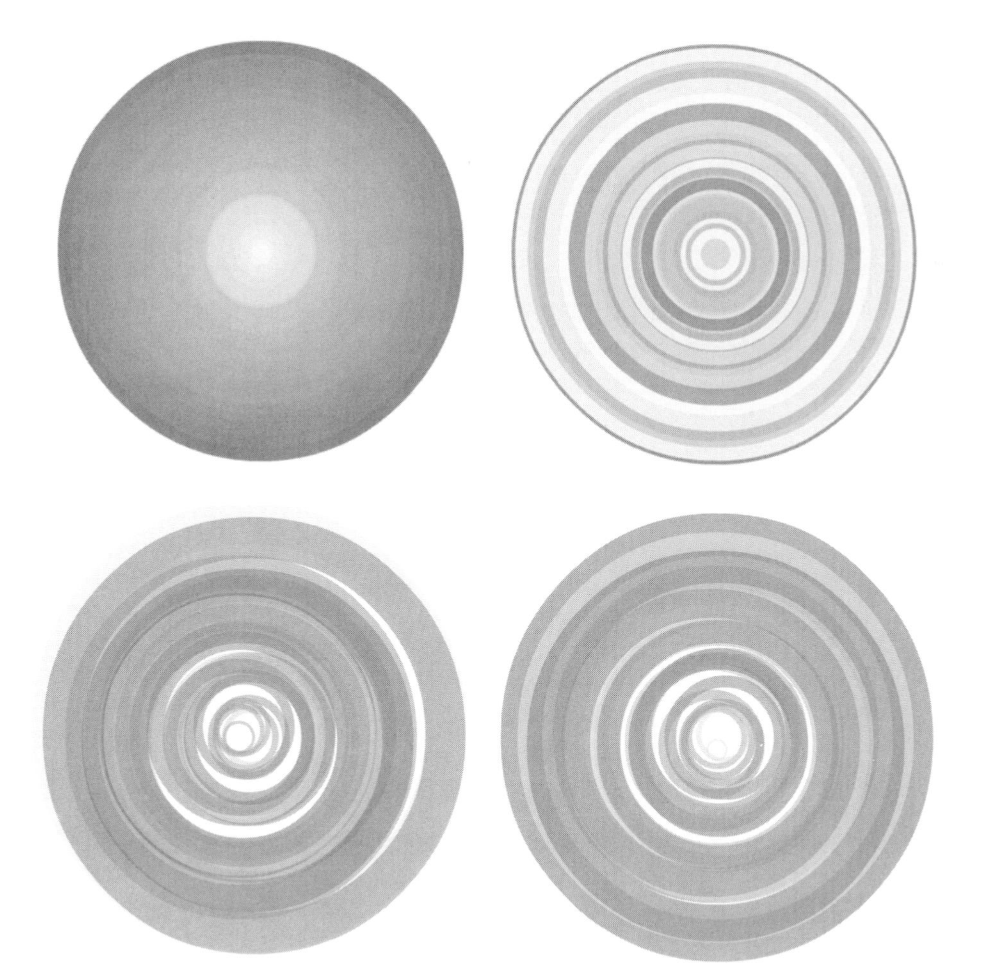

Figure 6.8

Two duplicates of the Pond Ripples component. The ripple on the right has Color Mixing Chaos set at 100%.

Figure 6.9

The Pond Ripples component can take on many different appearances. These ripples have a small value set for Centerpoint Offset and a bit of transparency.

The Concentric Path Component

The Concentric Path component shown in Figure 6.10 draws a random walking, concentric path. Starting from the outside, a single line works its way inward by following prescribed paths of a given radius. At random intervals, it drops one ring towards the center and, based on settings within the component, either chooses to continue going in the same direction or switches and heads back the other way. Once the line finally drops into the center, a new one begins. Each path takes a different route to the center. The result is a geometric construction similar to a maze or the artistic work of the ancient Mimbres people of North America.

Figure 6.10

The default appearance of the Concentric Path component

Component Basics

The following parameters control the appearance and behavior of the Concentric Path component.

Number Of Rings Controls the number of unique ring levels the path will follow on its journey towards the center.

Erase Old Paths After Controls the frequency with which old paths will be erased. Each time the drawn line of the Concentric Path reaches the center, it begins again at the outside radius. Paths eventually begin to overlap each other and also require more and more CPU resources, so the Erase Old Paths After value can be used to wipe the old paths away after so many have been drawn.

Draw Only Once Setting this Boolean value to True forces the component to draw only one path.

Outer Radius, Inner Radius These values control the outside and inside radii of the Concentric Path. Double the outer number to figure the total size in pixels. The Inner Radius should not be greater than the Outer Radius.

Resolution The Concentric Path is drawn using a large number of straight lines. The Resolution is a value that controls how closely together the straight lines are placed. The smaller the values, the higher the resolution of the path. Extremely large values begin to show the straight lines at higher radii. This can also be used as an interesting effect.

Line Thickness, Line Color The first parameter controls the width in pixels of the drawn line; a value of 0 creates a hairline path. The second describes the color and opacity of the line; all paths of the Concentric Path use the same color.

Chance Of Drop A percentage that determines how often the path drops to the next ring. High values create paths that quickly reach the center. Low values create paths that tend to circle the origin before dropping in.

Chance Of Switch You use this percentage to be used in combination with the Chance Of Drop value. This value determines how likely it is that the path will switch directions (clockwise or counterclockwise) after it drops. High values create paths that switch back and forth quite a bit. Low values create paths that tend to spiral towards the center.

Random Wandering This value adds a nice little arbitrary walk to the path as it is drawn. A value of 0 creates a perfectly round path, while higher values tend to create a path that looks hand drawn.

XYZ Rotation Using this setting, in degrees, the Concentric Path can be instructed to rotate about any of its axes. If the component seems to rotate too fast, try using decimal values (0.01). Positive values will rotate the path clockwise, while negative values will rotate the path counterclockwise.

Inspirational Examples

This first illustration (Figure 6.11) shows a typical rendering process of the Concentric Path component as it draws itself from nothing to several dozen paths. Note how each path takes a unique course to the center. For purposes of detail, the instance used in this example was given a large Outer Radius (250 pixels) and a higher Number Of Rings (50). All other values were kept at default.

This next example (Figure 6.12) shows how you might combine several Concentric Path components to create a larger, more colorful path. This image was created using six instances, all centered at the same point. The purpose of using several unique instances of the Concentric Path component is to allow them to overlap in ways that are simply not possible with only one instance. In this example, all paths shared the same radii and number of rings. The result is a mesmerizing display of swirling paths.

The final example using the concentric components in their unmodified form (Figure 6.13) takes advantage of the XYZ Rotation settings. Since it's not quite possible to display a moving image within the confines of this printed page, several consecutive screen shots were combined and blurred to demonstrate the wildly oscillating nature of the rotating Concentric Path.

Figure 6.11

The intricate construction process of the Concentric Path can be seen in these timed screen captures.

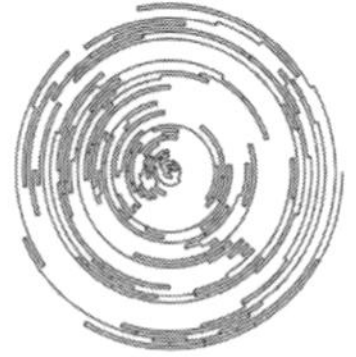

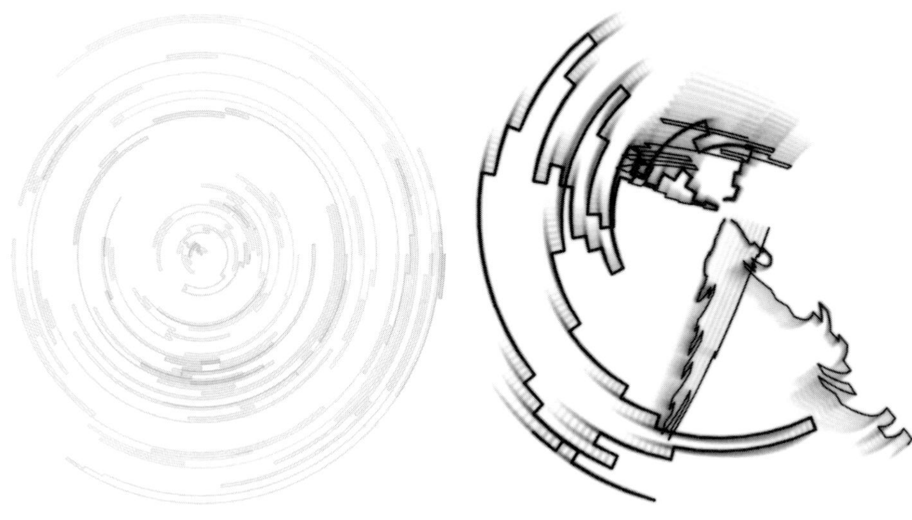

Figure 6.12

By overlaying two or more Concentric Path components, you can create complex color patterns.

Figure 6.13

Setting small values for XYZ Rotation creates a concentric path that appears to spin about its center.

The Pebbles Component

The Pebbles component creates a computationally arranged field of simple graphic objects, as shown in Figure 6.14. The Pebbles component is perhaps the simplest of all these animation components. In that sense, though, its general-purpose nature makes it a powerful tool for creating many diverse effects with minimal effort.

We have all had visions of vast fields; whether they be fields of flowers or of stars, large collections of self-similar objects are a common occurrence in nature. The Pebbles component was created with this in mind. By dragging a single instance of this component onto the stage, you can instantly generate an entire universe of self-similar movie clips.

Component Basics

In addition to the general parameters listed in the first section of this chapter, the following parameters control the appearance and behavior of the Pebbles component.

Region Width, Region Height The width and height of the area in which to place pebbles, measured in pixels.

Pebble Size, Pebble Size Variation The average size of each pebble created, measured in pixels. The variation between pebbles is measured as a percent of the Pebble Size. For example, a Pebble Size of 10 with a Pebble Size Variation of 50 would produce pebbles ranging from 5 to 15 pixels.

Rotation Speed This value adjusts the speed with which the pebbles rotate. Each pebble has a built-in rotational property that allows it to orbit a single point. Higher values will produce faster rotation. Negative values will produce rotation in the opposite direction, generally counterclockwise.

Rotation Variation This percentage sets the rotational variability between individual pebbles. The larger the number is, the more extreme the differences in rotation speed between pebbles.

Show Build Process The placement of individual pebbles within the field can be animated. Setting this Boolean value to True shows each pebble as it is created. Setting it to False instantaneously shows the entire pebble field.

Inspirational Examples

For this example, we used a single Pebbles component to fill a finite space with very small pebbles of varying color intensity. To create the example, we dragged a single instance of the component to the top-left corner of the stage of the movie. A Region Width of 800 and a Region Height of 600 (the same dimensions as the movie document) was specified so that the entire screen would be filled with stars. Pebble Size was set very low at 5 pixels. Pebble Size Variation was set very high at 80%, to create a sky of diversely sized stars. The variation in color was achieved by loading the Color Points array with exactly two colors, white and black (0xFFFFFF, 0x000000). Snap To Colors was set at False so that stars could be any of the grays in between.

The result (Figure 6.15) is one of my favorite examples. It reminds me of a starry sky in New Mexico on an especially clear night. The best thing about this component is that each time it is run, a totally unique sky of stars will be produced. This means that every user who visits your site will see an entirely unique field of stars.

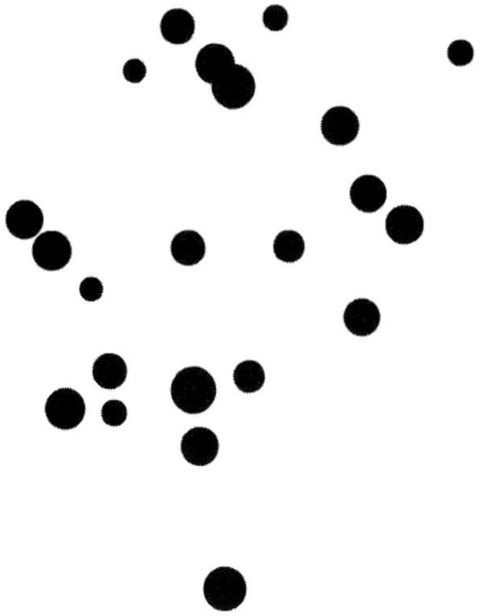

Figure 6.14

The default appearance of the Pebbles component

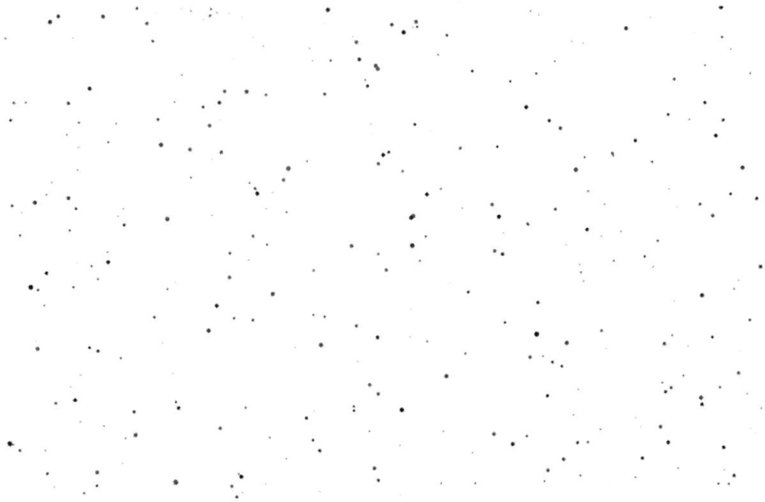

Figure 6.15

The Pebbles Component can generate a simple star field.

The Seeds Component

The Seeds component generates a seed pattern in a natural, radiating configuration, as shown in Figure 6.16.

In nature, the relative rotation of 137.5 degrees occurs frequently. You can see the production of this strange alignment in pinecones, sunflowers, strawberries, the pineapple, and thousands of other botanical specimens. Are you getting hungry?

The Seeds component uses this naturally occurring phenomenon to generate a computational structure of intriguing geometric form. To extend the power of the component, we've added a breathing animation behavior, demonstrated in Figure 6.17, to the individual seeds.

Component Basics

Figure 6.16
The default appearance of the Seeds Component

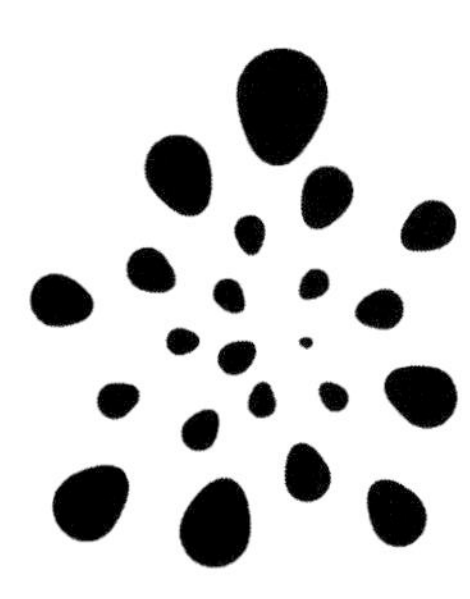

In addition to the number and color parameters listed in the first section of this chapter, the following parameters control the appearance and behavior of the Seeds component.

Outer Radius, Inner Radius The outside and inside radii of the seed arrangement. All seeds will be placed between the outer and inner radii.

Outside Seed Scale, Inside Seed Scale These set the scale of the seeds at the outside and inside of the arrangement. Individual seeds are exponentially scaled within a range of sizes defined at both the outside and inside of the arrangement.

Color Mixing Chaos This percentage determines to what extent the colors in the Color Points array will be mixed when applied to the seeds.

Breathing Intensity This value controls the depth of breaths each seed takes. Larger values produce more exaggerated breaths. A value of 0 produces seeds that do not breathe at all.

Breathing Variation This percentage is used to mix up the times that seeds take their breaths. A value of 0 creates a seed arrangement with seeds that breathe simultaneously, while higher values create a seed arrangement with seeds that breathe further and further out of sync.

Figure 6.17
This illustration shows a sequence of the Seed breathing cycle. Note the subtle, asynchronous variations in individual seed size between frames.

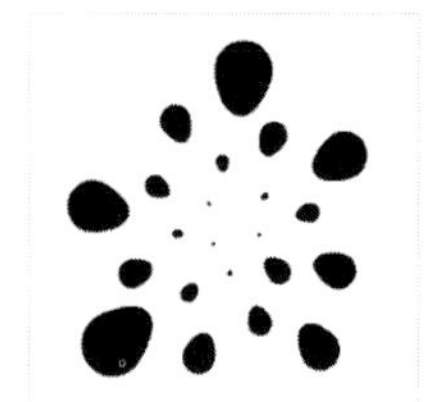
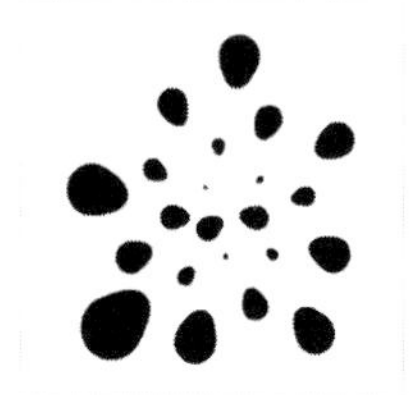
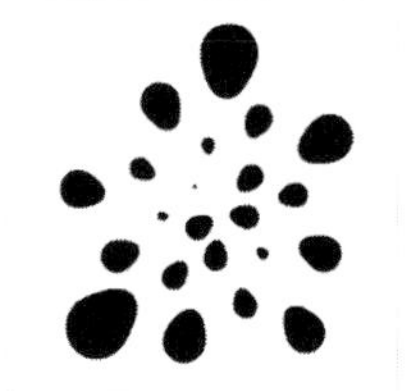
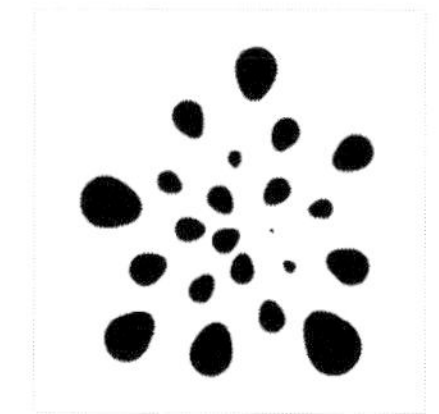

Show Build Process This Boolean value determines if the construction of the seed arrangement is shown as it happens or after it has completed. If this value is set to True, the seeds are placed one at a time, starting from the outside edge. If it is set to False, the seed arrangement is instantaneously constructed and shown all at once.

Inspirational Examples

A great example of the seed arrangement is shown in Figure 6.18. Here, the radius has been increased to 250 pixels, producing a seed arrangement approximately 500 pixels wide and tall. The Number Of Seeds was also increased to fill the larger size. Three colors of unique brightness were added to the Color Point array. Color Mixing Chaos has been set at zero, and Snap To Colors was left at false. The net result of these last two component parameters is a seed arrangement with a smooth transition of brightness from the inside out.

Figure 6.19 uses the clever trick of setting the inner and outer radii very close to each other. The result is a ring of seeds.

One slight deviation using the Seeds component takes advantage of foreground / background dynamics. Instead of using the seeds as objects to be observed, we can use the seeds to block out an object behind them. In Figure 6.20, our seeds are white, the same color as the background. A single black disc has been drawn on a layer below the seeds. The resulting animation is a spongelike form, whose porous perimeter pulsates with the breathing cycle of the seeds. In development, watching this particular form hypnotized me for what seemed like hours.

Figure 6.18

The Seeds Component with some color and a large number of seeds

Figure 6.19

The seeds in this example have been compacted around the edge of the component by setting the values of the Inner Radius and Outer Radius very close to each other.

Figure 6.20

An unusual shape has been created by the Seeds component using seeds the same color as the background, placed over a black disc. The seeds in this example are perfect spheres.

Customizing the Artwork Used by Animation Components

Now that we've introduced the animation components, let's get started using them. The goal of this section is to get you comfortable using the components in creative ways through simple modification of the artwork used by the component.

Each one of these animation components, with the exception of the Concentric Path, uses a basic geometric shape to build itself up. These shapes are located in their own movie clips, so that you can easily edit them without interfering with the complex programming behind the component.

Modified Seeds

Let's start off with one of my favorites, the Seeds component. As we learned earlier in the chapter, the Seeds component uses the golden ratio to lay down multiple instances of a single graphic object, the SeedShape.

Start a new movie and drag an instance of the Seeds component out onto the stage. Now open the movie's library. Notice how the SeedsComponent movie clip has been added along with a folder called `Component Elements`. Inside that folder are two more folders called `Designer Elements` and `Developer Elements` (see Figure 6.21). This is where all the assets required to make the Seeds component are located. Of particular interest to us are the assets located in the `Designer Elements` folder. Open it and edit the SeedShape movie clip.

The SeedShape is a very simple movie clip. Within the first and only frame exists a graphic shape, shown in Figure 6.22, roughly translated to be a seed.

Now here's the secret: this shape can be anything! We can draw a thousand different forms here and come up with some pretty spectacular results. We can even add a *tween*, or multiple frames of animation. Really, the SeedShape movie clip can be any valid Flash movie object—even another animation component, as we will see later in the chapter.

There are a couple things to keep in mind when editing these shapes. Note how the shape is centered with the registration mark. This is not required, but it is important if you want your seeds to be placed where you expect them to be through the settings in the Seeds component parameters.

Also, notice how the seed roughly fits within the green guidelines. Those green lines have been pulled into the stage to mark a 100×100 pixel area. Again, it is not required that the shape fit within this area, but if you want the numeric settings for size in the component parameters to remain consistent, the shapes should be approximately 100×100 pixels.

Modified Pond Ripples

The Pond Ripples component offers some interesting opportunities for customization because of the concentric nature of its composition. Similar to the Seeds component, the Pond Ripples component uses a movie clip called PondShape as the basic graphic building block of the final arrangement. Modifying the graphic shape on the first frame of the PondShape movie clip allows us to completely change the effects this component is capable of.

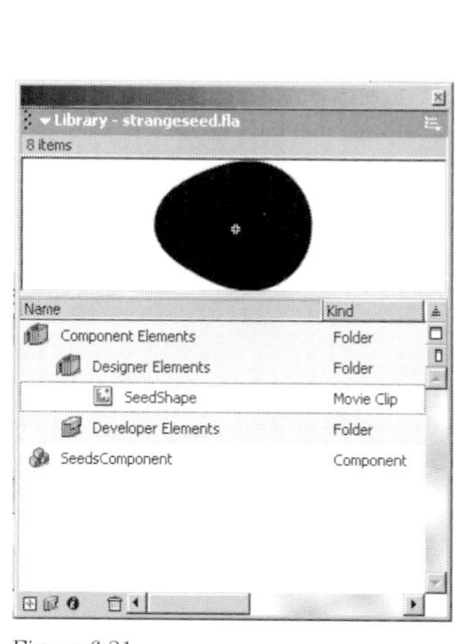

Figure 6.21

After you have dragged the Seeds component into your movie, your library will contain all the elements required to build the seed arrangement.

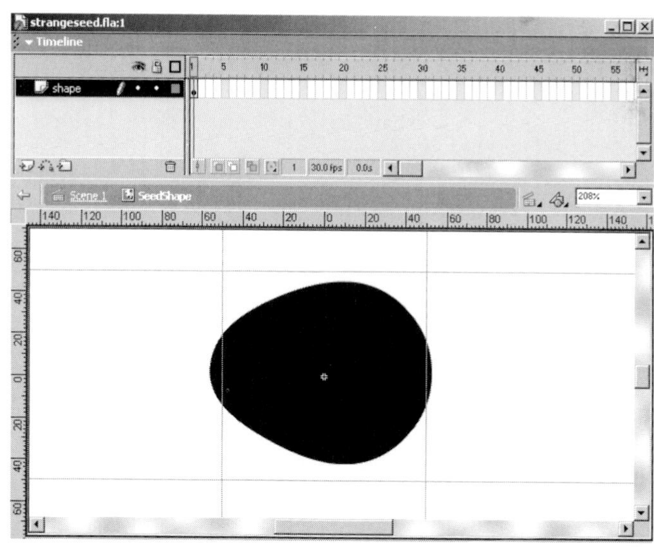

Figure 6.22

Editing the SeedShape movie clip

Here's a great example of just how wild these animation effects can become with a few home-brewed shapes. Using the hand-drawn shape shown in Figure 6.23 as the pond shape, I produced the animation in Figure 6.24.

Note the orientation of the PondShape in the resulting Pond Ripple arrangement. An Alpha setting of 15 creates a nice effect, especially in the center, where there is a high amount of overlap. When breathing, this component-driven, computational specimen seems to take on a life of its own, pulsating to an internal, almost self-determined interval. This, in fact, cannot actually be true, but this should be the goal of the computational designer.

Another example that takes advantage of the breathing animation is built from the Pond-Shape movie clip shown in Figure 6.25, creating the effect in Figure 6.26. This structure looks amazing when viewed in motion because the spindles and gears pulse in and out as it breathes, giving the whole structure a kind of "broken timepiece" effect.

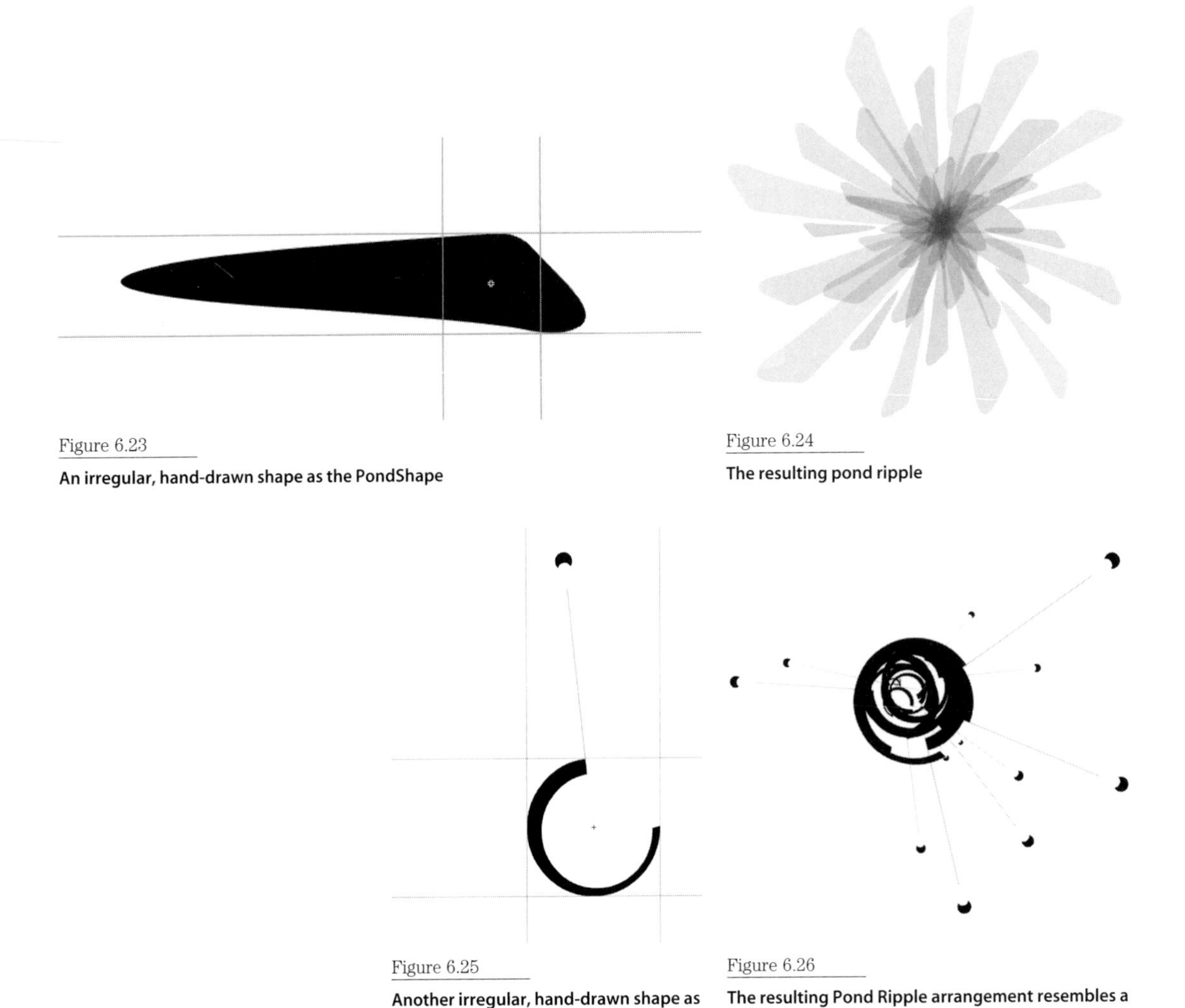

Figure 6.23

An irregular, hand-drawn shape as the PondShape

Figure 6.24

The resulting pond ripple

Figure 6.25

Another irregular, hand-drawn shape as the PondShape

Figure 6.26

The resulting Pond Ripple arrangement resembles a broken timepiece.

Figure 6.27

Using the same shape modification techniques as in the previous section, the Parallel Bars component can render moving fields of text.

Modified Parallel Bars

We certainly aren't limited to only drawing abstract shapes. Figure 6.27 shows some great examples that use the Parallel Bars component to move around some stylized text, in an array of diverse colors. Keep in mind that when using text as an animated object, you must break apart the text to its graphic equivalent, or embed the font outline.

Modified Pebbles

It's hard to describe just how fun it is to throw some hand-drawn shapes into a computational system. With minimal effort, a complex landscape of form and function (admittedly, mostly form) can be brought to life.

The field of modified Pebbles in Figure 6.28 is a great example of how to have fun. The basic shape used to create this pattern resembles a wheat chaff (Figure 6.29).

Of course, do not forget that all of this, as I try to show in Figure 6.30, is gracefully animated!

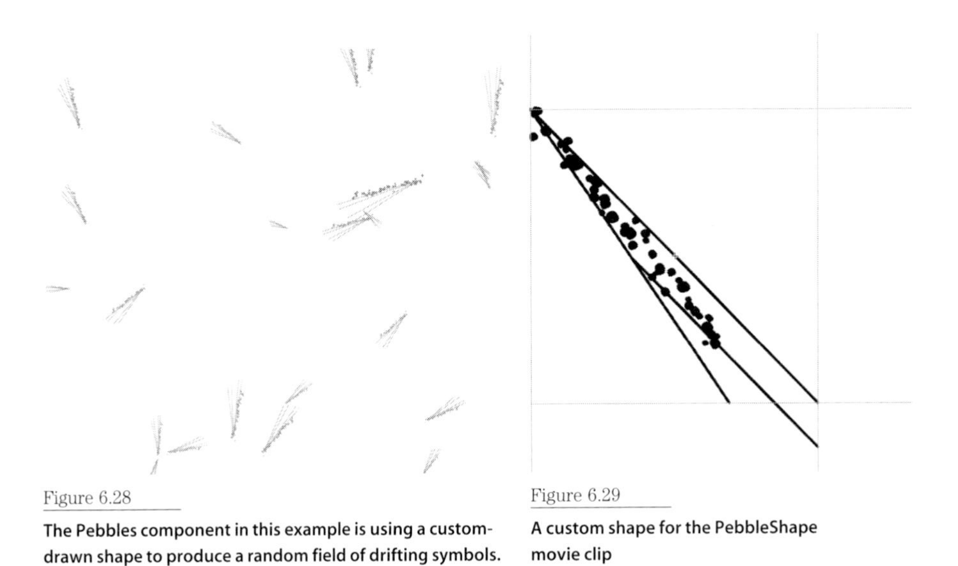

Figure 6.28

The Pebbles component in this example is using a custom-drawn shape to produce a random field of drifting symbols.

Figure 6.29

A custom shape for the PebbleShape movie clip

Figure 6.30

Some additional inspirational Pebble arrangements using custom shapes

Understanding the Limits of Flash Animation

Before we continue further, let us take a moment to reflect on the trouble we might be getting ourselves into. Flash is an amazing platform from which to develop graphic-intensive applications. That being said, however, serious limits exist governing what is and what is not possible with Flash. This is important to keep in mind, especially when working with animation components, as every one of these components is leveraging computational resources to get the job done.

Here are some short tales of woe and slow.

Too Many Moving Objects

Flash allows us to move graphics with a great amount of power and flexibility. It is fun to move things around in a virtual space, and it is the principal reason why I get excited about computer graphics. There are limits to how many things can be moving at the same time. In my years of working with Flash, I have found that about 30 simultaneously viewable moving objects is a comfortable number for almost all computers. In extreme situations, up to 100 simple or small objects can be successfully moved around with no slowdown.

Workarounds:

- Shut down (stop) objects when they are not moving.
- Decrease the size and line complexity of the moving objects.
- Move objects to where they need to go faster (bigger steps).
- Remove objects no longer important to the scene.

Too Many Instances

Sometimes there are simply too many static graphic objects on stage. It is difficult to put a number on the amount of unmoving graphic objects that can safely be on stage, but for most computers, it is about 500. This is important to keep in mind, especially when working with our animation components, as they are actually composed of many small objects.

Workarounds:

- If duplicating a large number of instances, make sure they are defined as symbols.
- Simplify objects that are instantiated multiple times.
- Install more RAM!

Too Much Transparency

Flash supports transparency well—very well, in fact. However, it does require quite a bit more processing power to handle an object with a transparent fill than an object with a solid fill. Astonishingly, the processing power required for transparent fills doubles with each overlapping layer. So for scenes where a large number of transparent objects are passing over each other, processing speed will be drastically affected.

Workarounds:

- Keep transparent objects from excessively overlapping, if possible.
- Avoid using only “slight alphas” (for example, use 100% alpha instead of 96%).
- Use solid color mixing to simulate transparency if transparency is not really needed (for example, use a gray instead of a transparent white fill over a black background).

Too Much Area Filled with Gradients

Gradients are sweeping areas of averaged color that extend between well-defined points of color. The gradient is a computed fill. This means that every time a gradient requires drawing, the Flash player must stop and compute the values of the color bands for each pixel inside the region. For small objects, this isn't too much of a problem. When the object becomes large, filling a significant portion of the screen, you'll notice an immediate slowdown.

Workarounds:

- Develop your own gradients by creating many objects, each with a solid fill (the approach taken by this chapter).
- Define your gradients with as few color points as possible.
- Be selective about where gradients are used.
- Limit the size of regions filled with gradients.

Too Many Characters

The problem with the text character is that oftentimes, it appears in large groups of characters, forming these wild things called words. The words are then seen getting together with other words, until before you know it, you've got a paragraph. The typical paragraph might have some 300 characters in it. This collection of text characters represents a very dense amount of information, both for the computer drawing the text and for the user reading it. Many new users underestimate the power and complexity of text and, for this reason, slow their programs down by moving it haphazardly all over the stage.

Workarounds:

- Change the quality of the text to low while moving it; set it back to high when still.
- Use clean, efficient font outlines (i.e., no serifs or fancy fonts).
- If possible, do not move text.

Through experience, you begin to understand the limits of your environment. Flash is no exception. If you are new to Flash, keep this short list of cautionary tales in mind, so that you might avoid crashes or slow-moving animations.

Using Multiple Animation Components

By combining components, we have the potential to create animation effects way beyond the original intentions of the components. Let us explore the ways components can be combined.

Overlapping Components

Simply overlaying one component on top of another is an effective way of producing some interesting results.

Oftentimes, we will want to align our components on top of each other to achieve symmetric results, as in Figure 6.31. Here, we have one instance of the Seeds component with a specially modified SeedShape and one instance of the Pond Ripples component with a high amount of transparency. The components have been placed on unique layers within the movie. We do this because it eases the editing process, allowing quick access to either component through the selection of its layer.

A few variations of this same theme produced some very interesting results. All of the images in Figure 6.32 are snapshots of the same composition. The composition is a simple movie containing four instances of the Pond Ripple component and one instance of Seeds component.

Figure 6.31

A combination of the Pond Ripple and Seeds components produced this complementary design.

Common Multiples

Another method for increasing the visual interest of the animation components is to lay them out side by side. Due to the unique randomization properties of these components, each one will be slightly different. The juxtaposition of common multiples is a great way to induce contrast and comparison by the observer.

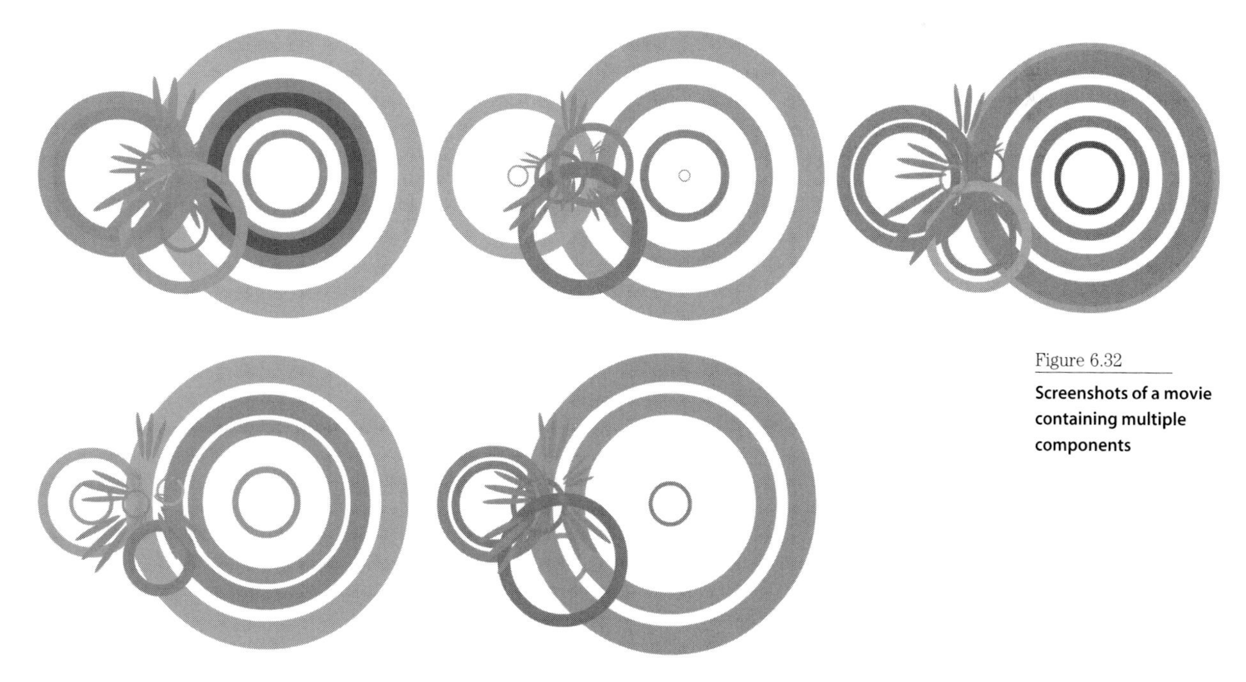

Figure 6.32

Screenshots of a movie containing multiple components

Figure 6.33
Multiple screenshots of the Parallel Bars component with a custom BarShape using the word *hope*

Figure 6.33 shows some common multiples of the Parallel Bars component using text as the shape. Some varieties of basic Pond Ripples are shown in Figure 6.34.

Masked

Flash MX amazed many developers with its support for dynamic masks. A dynamic mask is simply a process of using a changing shape as a view into the layers below it. By using an animation component as a dynamic mask for another animation component below it, we can create some fantastic results.

In Figure 6.35, I've used a Seeds component with particularly large seeds as a mask for a high resolution Concentric Path below it.

Similarly, an inspirational complexity created with Pebbles and Parallel Bars is shown in Figure 6.36.

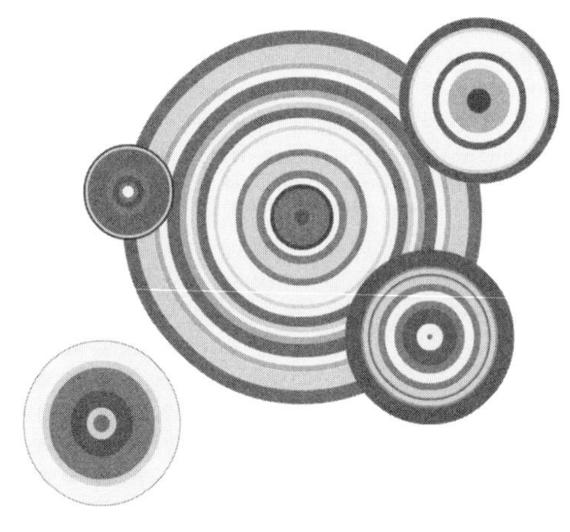

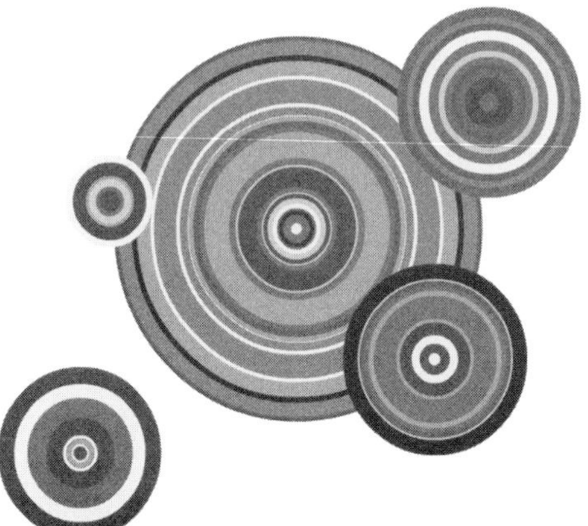

Figure 6.34
Due to the random nature of the Pond Ripples component, the same setup will produce thousands of different arrangements.

Embedded

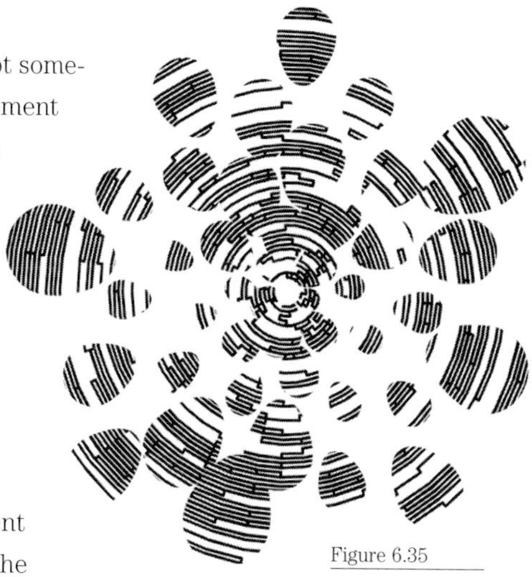

For our final exploration using multiple components, we will attempt something a bit dangerous: embedding a component as a basic building element of another component. Why is this dangerous? First of all, with extreme enough settings, every one of these animation components has the potential of consuming all available resources on just about any computer. So by embedding one component within the other, we are compounding the complexity of our scene.

For the sake of setting a good example, let's abandon caution and get right into it. The images in Figure 6.37 were created by two different instances of the Seeds component. The major difference between the two is the scales used for the seeds.

To make each seed element a concentric path, the graphic element in the SeedShape movie clip was replaced with a single instance of the Concentric Path component. To lighten the computational load a bit, the Concentric Path was set to draw only one path, at a fairly low resolution, and with only seven rings.

Both Seeds instances were set to generate 42 seeds, meaning that 84 Concentric Paths were drawn each time the movie ran. We definitely did not want to draw all these paths at the same time, so the Show Build Process setting was set to True.

Figure 6.35

A Seeds component being used as a mask for the high resolution Concentric Path component below it. The result is an unusual organic-shaped construct.

Figure 6.36

A Parallel Bars component being used as a mask for a Pebbles component below it. This might have made for some great wallpaper in 1973.

Figure 6.37

By embedding a Concentric Path component as the SeedShape for the Seeds component, we produce something greater than the sum of its parts.

Conclusion

Creating animations with components is fun and relatively painless. In just a short amount of time, you can achieve spectacular effects with a very minimal set of components. In this chapter, we worked with only five very basic animation components. There are hundreds in existence; many of the best are at Eyeland Studio. Keep an explorer's attitude when working in Flash and you will surely discover some amazing things!

Chapter 7: Text Effect Components

Starting with Flash 4, text effects became a very popular add-in to many projects, mainly due to new software. Swish, for example, is a program completely separate from Flash that creates an SWF animation of a text effect. You can then import the SWF into Flash as a series of frames.

Soon after that, step-by-step instructions were created by fellow Flash developers to demonstrate the ActionScript way of creating such text effects. But Flash 4 was too primitive to use ActionScripted text effects in an easy-to-use, modular fashion. When Flash 5 arrived, designers had more hope to build a completely modularized component that would be simple to plug in to any project. However, Flash 5 lacked control of text fields through ActionScript.

Finally, with the release of Flash MX, portable text effects are now possible. Using the new technologies of Flash MX, we can drag components to the stage and edit them only slightly to create a full-blown, quite complex text effect. The most amazing thing about this set of components is that each employs complicated mathematics and programming techniques, yet neither needs to be known to the user. In this chapter you will learn the various topics that surround text effects.

- **Why use component text effects?**
- **The Text Effect component set**
- **Shared fonts in Flash MX**

Why Use Component Text Effects?

Programmed effects have nearly always been preferred over graphical animations. Two reasons are that effects made with programming take up very little file size, and they are easier to customize. The former reason is apparent; the footprint of programming code on a file's size is nearly nonexistent. The effects made with the components in this book produce files that are only 3 KB in size, although file size can increase slightly depending on the fonts used. The latter reason may not be so obvious right now, but after you see how easy it is to use the components, you will understand. Prerendered animations, on the other hand, add a considerable amount of file size and are quite unforgiving when it comes to modification.

The most common concern about programmed animations is the drain they can cause on the CPU. This is true; executing many lines of code can bring a computer to its knees faster than even the most intensive graphics. Fortunately, this only partly applies to the types of animations we will be dealing with. Text effects are kind of the middle ground when it comes to comparing CPU cycles for programmed and rendered animations. Firstly, text effects are so simple that programming their movement and interaction is not the most demanding thing on a computer. Secondly, since text effects use so many objects (each letter in a set of text), a prerendered animation can cause a major lag in the computer's responsiveness. So, when it comes to text effects, the CPU issue is somewhat nullified.

In the end, do not be afraid to use these text effects. They have been developed to be CPU-friendly, and they have very little, if any, effect on file size.

The Text Effect Component Set

Three text effect components are featured in this chapter: Flush, Spin, and Scramble. Each of the components are easy to use and provide impressive results. All three have been packaged into an MXP file to make them easier to work with, especially since they contain multiple effects. Go into the Chapter 7 folder on the CD and open the file `TextEffectSet.mxp` to install the components.

Once you install the component set, you will see all the components you have installed through the Extension Manager so far, as shown in Figure 7.1. The extension you just installed is named TextEffect Component Set, although more extensions may be listed, depending on what you have installed previously. The next time you open Flash, a new division in the Components panel is added under the name TextEffect-Set, as shown in Figure 7.2. From here you can either drag or double-click a component to add an instance to the stage.

Figure 7.1
Components installed through the Extension Manager

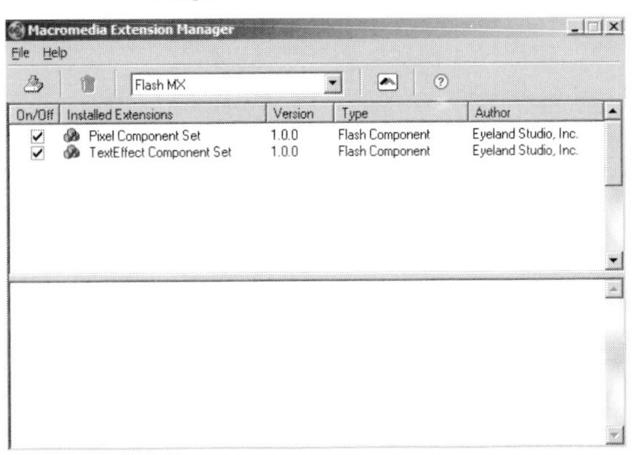

After you have dragged a few components to the stage, you will see the folder structure that has been created, as in Figure 7.3. One main folder contains the component movie clips, and a few subfolders hold the components' assets. The terrific thing about these components is that they require no alteration or external graphics, so in general you can leave all the component-related symbols alone.

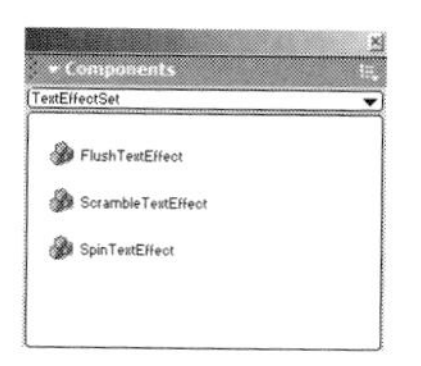

Figure 7.2

Use the Components panel to add the text effects to your movie.

The FlushTextEffect Component

Open a fresh Flash movie and drag the FlushTextEffect component to the stage. The first thing you will notice is that text is in the component already, as shown in Figure 7.4. This is actually a live preview that displays the set of text to be animated, and it will change when you change the component's parameters. Do not mess with the parameters just yet; we are only experimenting for now.

Test the movie by pressing Command/Ctrl+Enter. The movie starts with a blank screen, and then small pieces of the text gradually come into form until the entire set of text is visible. Then, shortly after the text has been fully uncovered, the animation reverses itself and the text dissolves back to blankness. Really, the effect is quite simple. Many small rectangles having the same color as the background are fitted to cover the text exactly. Next, they start to shrink to point size, slowly uncovering the text that lies beneath, as shown in Figure 7.5.

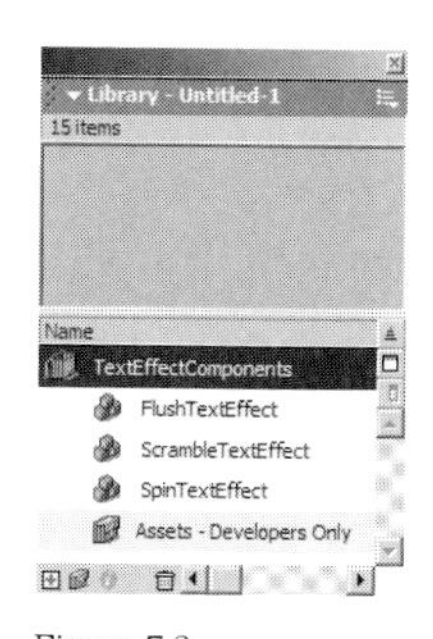

Figure 7.3

Folder structure created by the components

You will notice that the text continuously animates in and out in a loop. This is because only one set of text is entered in its parameters. One of the most powerful features of this component is that you can enter any number of text sets into an array; the component will cycle through the sets, performing the animation on each. The parameters also allow you to customize what the component should do once it has cycled through all the text sets; it can either go back to the beginning and start over or simply quit and remove itself from the stage.

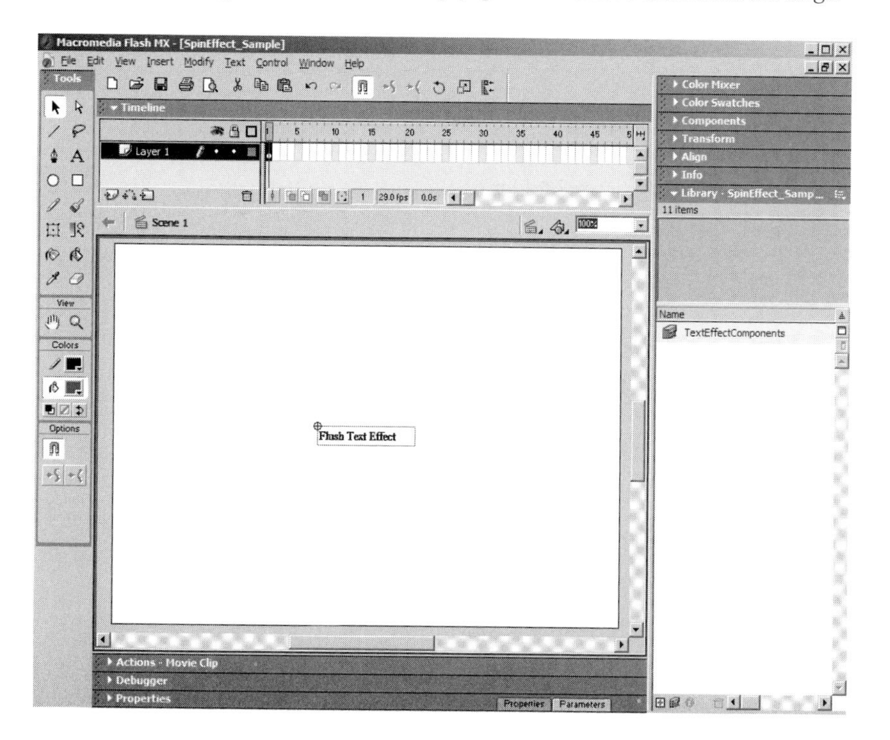

Figure 7.4

The live preview shows what the text will look like when fully animated.

Table 7.1

Parameters for the FlushTextEffect Component

PARAMETER NAME	DESCRIPTION
Text Messages	Array that holds all the sets of text you want the component to cycle through. These messages are HTML-enabled, so you can use Flash-compliant HTML tags, such as bold, italics, and line break.
Text Size	Size of the text in each set.
Text Font	Font of each set of text. This value is case-sensitive, so be sure to enter the exact font name.
Text Color	Color of the text in each set.
Text Alignment	Alignment of the text in each set.
Flush Density X	Number of rectangles created along the x-axis of the text.
Flush Density Y	Number of rectangles created along the y-axis of the text.
Flush Start Difference	Controls how many frames must pass before all rectangles animate. Each rectangle waits a random number of frames between 1 and the value of this parameter before it animates either in or out.
Flush Color	Color of the rectangles that flush over the text.
Loop	True or false value that determines if the sets of text should play continuously in a loop or not.
Uncovered Frame Delay	Number of frames that the sets of text remain uncovered before the rectangles begin to animate and cover the text.

Table 7.1 is an exhaustive list of the parameters you can customize in the FlushTextEffect component.

There are just a few things we should discuss when looking at these parameters. Firstly, the text font parameter says we can use HTML in our messages, but what exactly is Flash-compliant HTML? The only tags supported by Flash are `<a>`, `<b>`, `<font color>`, `<font face>`, `<font size>`, `<i>`, `<p>`, `<br>`, and `<u>`. Any other tags will produce unreliable results.

Also, the values for Flush Density X and Flush Density Y should be used in strict moderation. Using large values for these parameters will slow down the user's computer due to the number of rectangles being animated. To calculate the number of rectangles, simply multiply together the values you enter. So, if each density is 10, then 100 rectangles are being animated. Obviously, these numbers will grow very large with even small increases in the individual densities. Fortunately, this is one of those cases where greater numbers do not necessarily result in a better effect. Even with very small values for the densities, you can pull off a unique effect.

To demonstrate a few common uses of the FlushTextEffect component, I've included some samples for experimentation. You'll find the first, `FlushEffect01_Sample.fla`, in the Chapter 7 folder on the CD. This sample is similar to the default effect, except that I've added sets of text and changed the font and font size. Also notice that I've used the HTML tag for italics for this book's title, as shown in Figure 7.6.

The next, `FlushEffect02_Sample.fla`, demonstrates that small flush densities can give a very clean look to the effect, which also runs smoother because it contains fewer rectangles. I've reduced each flush density to only 4, which is 16 rectangles total, and yet the effect is still very effective. Also, I used the line break tag to create sets of text that flow into two lines, as shown in Figure 7.7. Be sure to keep in mind that the component is not restricted to only one line of text.

In the file `FlushEffect03_Sample.fla`, I have used the exact same parameter settings as in the previous file, with the exception that the density values have been increased. Each flush density is now 15, which results in 225 rectangles. If you test this movie, you can see that smaller bits of the text become visible (as shown in Figure 7.8), and it appears to be smooth. However, if you had any other animations or actions playing elsewhere in the movie, you would see a noticeable drag in their performance. On top of that, the effect is not much better compared to the previous file, so in general the CPU lag is not worth it.

With these examples, you should start to see how you can use this text effect in your own files. You can also experiment with using the effect to flash bytes of text in a banner or to display instructions to a viewer. However, always keep in mind that the component can truly bog down someone's computer if not used in moderation. Using many instances of this component on the stage is not a good idea.

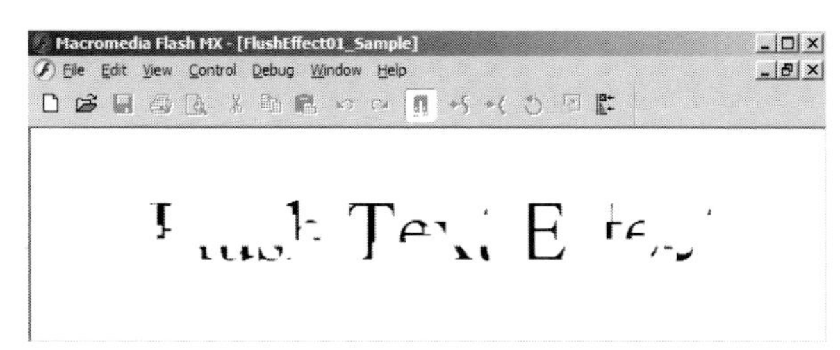

Figure 7.5

The Flush Text effect in midaction. The text is uncovered slowly by a series of animated rectangles.

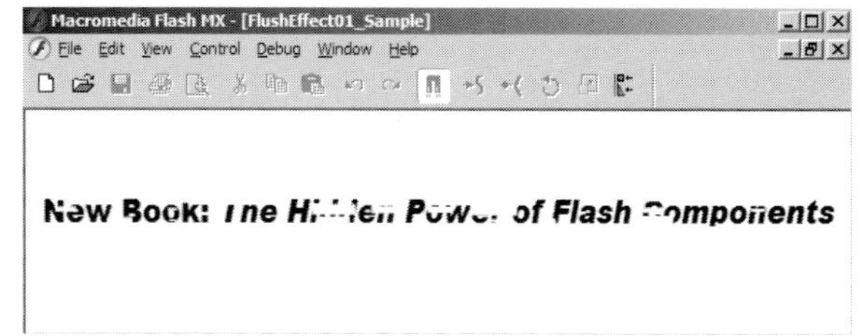

Figure 7.6

Add multiple sets of text for the component to loop through.

Figure 7.7

Text can flow into two or more lines through the use of the line break tag <br>.

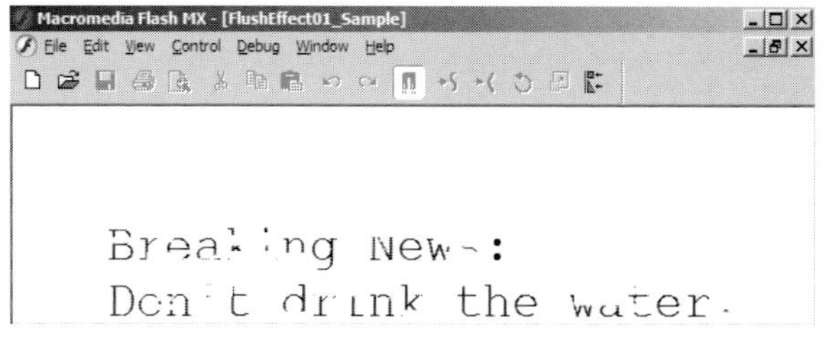

Figure 7.8

The increased flush densities do not necessarily result in a better effect.

Shared Fonts in Flash MX

Before we can discuss the other two components in the text effects set, we must first talk about a new technology in Flash called *shared fonts*. Shared fonts are used through ActionScript, and you can think of them as analogous to embedding font outlines into a text field. During your time as a Flash developer, you have most likely encountered the problem of disappearing text. It happens in the authoring environment when you create a text field that is either the Dynamic or Input type. When you are using such a text field on the stage and you rotate the field, the text disappears. This is because you are using a *device font*, a font that is assumed to be on the viewer's computer. The limitation of device fonts is that the text field must be perfectly horizontal, or else the text will not render in the movie's SWF. Flash's help files tell you that the solution is to embed the font you want to use into the text field, which literally exports the font with the rest of the movie. Once you've done this, you can rotate and size the text field in any way you want since Flash can simply use the embedded font.

The Chapter 7 folder on the CD contains a file named `Textfield_Testing.fla` that demonstrates the need for embedding fonts. On the stage, I've created four input text fields with the Flash MX text components, two of which are rotated counterclockwise by 45 degrees (as shown in Figure 7.9). Also, the bottom two text fields have embedded fonts.

When you test this file, you see that the top-right text field does not render, as shown in Figure 7.10. The top-right field does not use an embedded font.

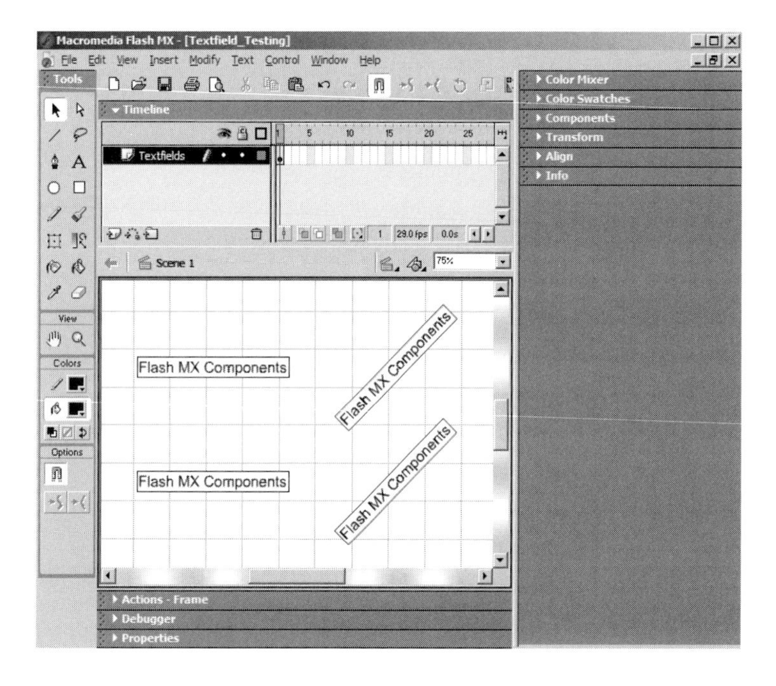

Figure 7.9

The stage in the `Textfield_Testing.fla` file. The bottom two text fields use an embedded font.

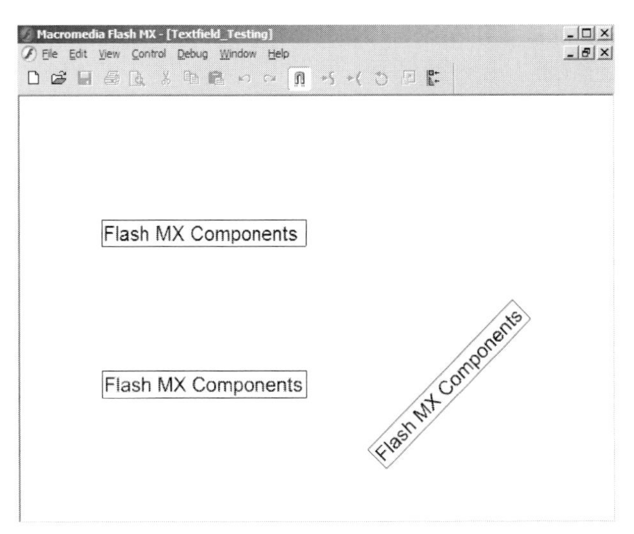

Figure 7.10

When the movie is published, one text field disappears.

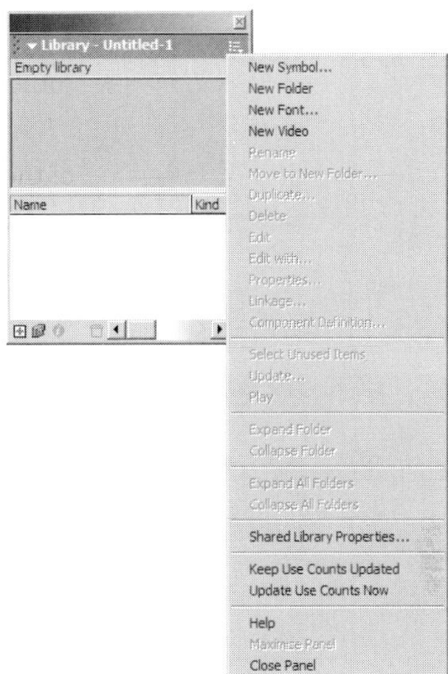

Figure 7.11

Open the library's menu to create a new shared font.

Outside of disappearing text, the ability to embed a font is very important. If you are using an input text for users to enter their e-mail addresses, or something of that sort, you may want to use a custom font that users most likely do not have on their computers. If you were to use the text field without embedding the font, then the font would change to the default Arial font when a viewer used the file. However, by embedding the font, viewers can see the custom font even if they do not have it on their computers.

As you can see, the concept of font embedding is quite useful. With Flash MX's new commands that give greater control of text fields, there should be an analogous way of embedding fonts through ActionScript. This is where shared fonts come into play. A shared font is simply a library symbol representing a specific font on your computer. To export the font with the movie, you give the symbol a linkage name, and that name is used to embed a font into a dynamically created text field. We need to know how to dynamically embed fonts because the next two components must be able to rotate a text field.

Creating a Shared Font

Creating a shared font is very simple. Start up a new movie in Flash and open its library. Click the small white graphic in the top-right corner of the menu to open a drop-down menu, as shown in Figure 7.11. Then, click on New Font to create a shared font.

You use the dialog box that pops up to set the attributes of the font: symbol name, font name, and style. The symbol name is not crucially important because it is only the identifier that appears in the library, but you should try to use something descriptive. For the font name, use the drop-down menu, which lists every font on your computer. Set the style attributes to make the text either bold or italic, if you want. Click OK in the dialog box, right-click the newly created font symbol, and click Linkage. Here you give the symbol a linkage name so that it will be exported with the movie. The only restriction on this name is that it cannot be the same name as the font, as that will cause some problems later on. Use a simple, descriptive name for the linkage, and remember it because you'll enter that name into the components' parameters.

The ScrambleTextEffect Component

The scramble text effect needs the concept of a shared font in order to work properly because it rotates the individual letters of a set of text quite a bit. Open a new Flash movie and drag an instance of the ScrambleTextEffect component from the Components panel. Once again, you will notice that some text appears in the component already, because of the component's live preview. Before we try anything else, let's get the effect working with its default settings. This takes a little bit more work than the FlushTextEffect component. Start by creating a new shared font, with the font of your choice, and give it the linkage name "scramble_font." Although we could use any linkage name, we'll use this name because it is the default value in the component's parameters.

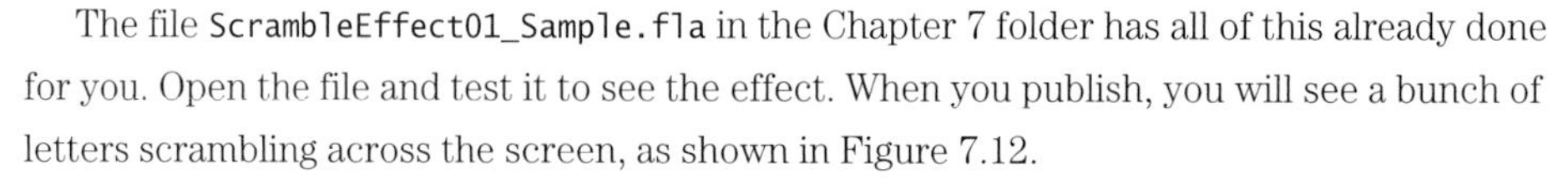

The file `ScrambleEffect01_Sample.fla` in the Chapter 7 folder has all of this already done for you. Open the file and test it to see the effect. When you publish, you will see a bunch of letters scrambling across the screen, as shown in Figure 7.12.

Once the letters have come to a stop, they will start to rotate around the screen in what seems a chaotic fashion. However, after a few moments, the letters fall into their final place, and the set of text comes into form. After this, the process repeats ad infinitum.

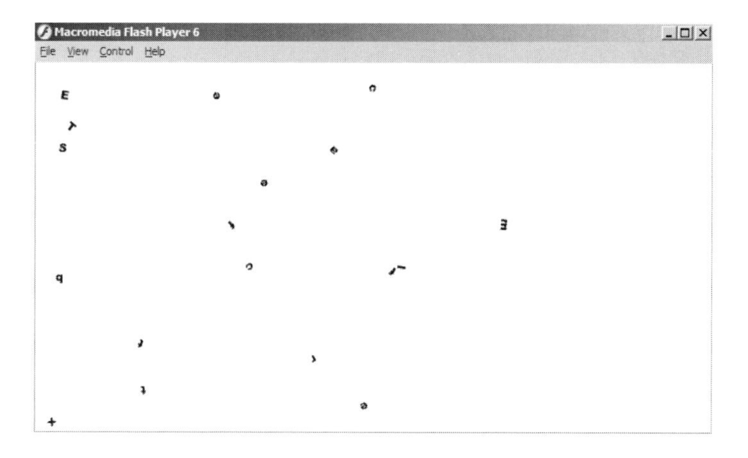

Figure 7.12

The text effect scrambles the letters of a message across the screen and then rotates each letter to its final place.

Table 7.2

Parameters for the ScrambleTextEffect Component

PARAMETER NAME	DESCRIPTION
Text Messages	Array that holds all the sets of text that you want the component to cycle through. The only HTML tag enabled in these messages is the line break tag .
Text Size	Size of the text in each set.
Font Linkage	Linkage name of the shared font you created in your library.
Text Color	Color of the text in each set.
Text Kerning	Number of pixels between each letter in the set of text.
Frame Delay	Once the text is fully animated in, this parameter determines the number of frames that must pass before the next set of text begins to animate in.
Stage Width	Width of the stage you are using in your movie.
Stage Height	Height of the stage you are using in your movie.
Loop	True or false value that determines if the sets of text should be played continuously in a loop or not.

Like the flush text effect, this component can handle many sets of text. Also, there are fewer parameters to customize for this component, and they are much simpler. Table 7.2 shows a complete list of parameters for the ScrambleTextEffect component.

At first it may seem weird that the component asks for the dimensions of the movie's stage, but the two parameters are actually very important. If you look at the effect in action again, you will see that the letters are scattered across the screen randomly. The parameters that hold the width and height of the stage are used to ensure that the letters stay within the boundaries of the stage, so that the letters remain visible to the user.

One important change to take note of is that, unlike the flush component, we cannot use all Flash-compliant HTML tags. In fact, we can only use one: the line break tag. Because each set of text has to be broken down to its letters, it would be overly complicated to parse a string for any HTML tags and apply the style to each individual letter. Considering the fact that this component is supposed to be dead easy to work with, I've taken every measure to make sure the component stays true to that. In Figure 7.13, you can see that the line break tag was used to create three lines of text. Open the `ScrambleEffect02_Sample.fla` file in the Chapter 7 folder to see an example of the line break being used.

If you experiment with the effect long enough, you will notice that the text does not always show up exactly where the live preview predicted it would. Although the top-left corner of the text will be exactly at the top-left corner of the live preview, the text seems to extend further out than the live preview showed. This is due to the kerning of the text. It is near impossible to detect the exact width of a letter in an arbitrary font directly in Flash MX since a small buffer is always added around text in a text field, which adds a few pixels to the font's width. To fix this problem, I've added the kerning parameter. The value for the parameter can be either 0, positive, or negative. Although you may want some extra buffering between each letter, most of the time you will probably want to remove the space to make the letters fit together more tightly, as shown in Figure 7.14. You can accomplish this by using a small negative number such as –2 or –3. The Chapter 7 folder contains a file named `ScrambleEffect03_Sample.fla` that shows how this is done.

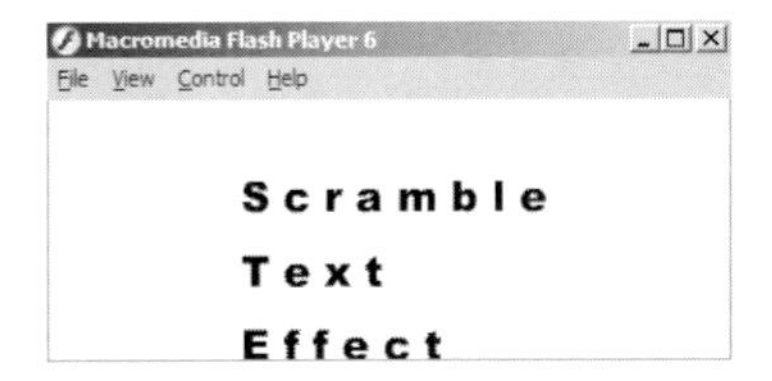

Figure 7.13

Even though most HTML tags have been disabled in the ScrambleTextEffect component, you can still use the line break tag to create text that flows into two or more lines.

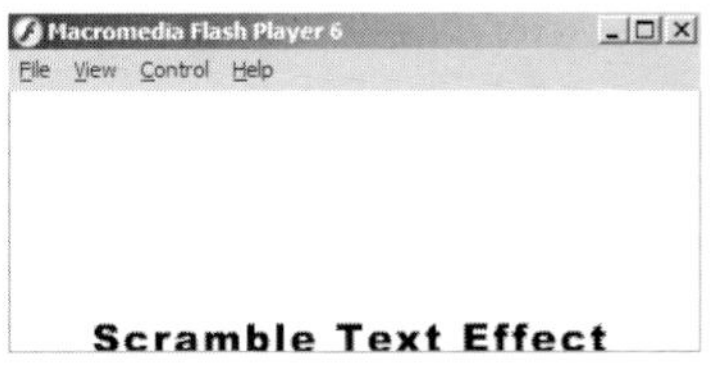

Figure 7.14

Use a negative kerning value to make the letters of the text set fit closer together.

One last thing to keep fresh in your mind is that the font changes you make in the component's parameters are not reflected in the live preview of the component. This may seem like a glitch at first, but it is actually quite obvious and could be no other way. Since you are providing a font through a shared font symbol, there is no way for the component to have access to that symbol from the live preview. So, remember that the amount of space the text takes up on the stage can be slightly altered by which font you choose.

The SpinTextEffect Component

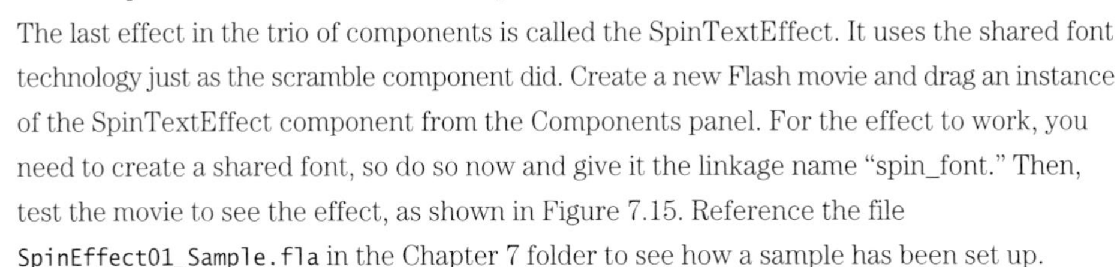

The last effect in the trio of components is called the SpinTextEffect. It uses the shared font technology just as the scramble component did. Create a new Flash movie and drag an instance of the SpinTextEffect component from the Components panel. For the effect to work, you need to create a shared font, so do so now and give it the linkage name "spin_font." Then, test the movie to see the effect, as shown in Figure 7.15. Reference the file `SpinEffect01_Sample.fla` in the Chapter 7 folder to see how a sample has been set up.

When you publish, you will see all of the individual letters of the text set flying in from the foreground. Each letter spins around the x-axis as it flies through 3D space to the 2D surface of the stage. Once a letter reaches the stage, it finishes its spin and then comes to a rest in its final position.

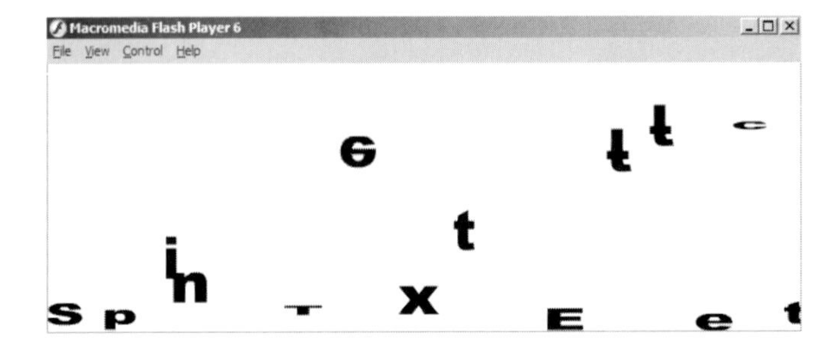

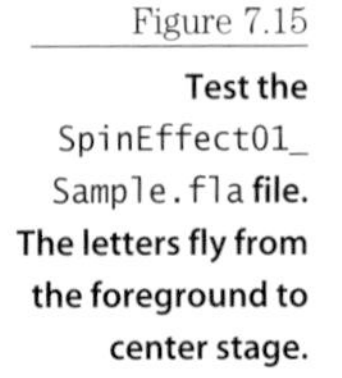
Figure 7.15

Test the `SpinEffect01_Sample.fla` file. The letters fly from the foreground to center stage.

Table 7.3

Parameters for the SpinTextEffect Component

PARAMETER NAME	DESCRIPTION
Text Messages	Array that holds all the sets of text that you want the component to cycle through. The only HTML tag enabled in these messages is the line break tag .
Text Size	Size of the text in each set.
Font Linkage	Linkage name of the shared font you created in your library.
Text Color	Color of the text in each set.
Text Kerning	Number of pixels between each letter in the set of text.
Spin Radius	Radius of the circle each letter spins around as they fly from the foreground to the 2D flat stage.
Frame Delay	Once the text is fully animated in, this parameter determines the number of frames that must pass before the next set of text begins to animate in.
Loop	True or false value that determines if the sets of text should be played continuously in a loop or not.

Just like the previous two components, this component can handle many sets of text. Despite the greater complexity of this component compared to the others, the SpinTextEffect component has few parameters. Table 7.3 provides a full list of parameters.

We have already encountered all but one of the above parameters, so there should be very little confusion so far, although the Spin Radius parameter does not make a whole lot of sense. To understand that parameter, you must understand the paths the letters are traveling from their starting position to their final destination.

Imagine for a moment that your computer screen is not flat, but instead renders everything in 3D space. In this case, all of the letters start behind you, moving forward towards the stage of the Flash movie. As they move towards the stage, they each oscillate up and down and back and forth, around the x-axis. This distance from the x-axis that the letters travel as they move up, down, forward, and backward is controlled by the Spin Radius parameter. Values between 0 and 50 are generally the best-looking, although no particular value produces a better result than any other.

In the file `SpinEffect02_Sample.fla`, the text effect contains a couple of small changes. To show that the kerning problem of the ScrambleTextEffect component is still present in this component, I've lowered the kerning value from 0 to –2. Also, I've lowered the spin radius of the letters from 20 to 5. These two changes actually produce quite a different effect, mainly due to the spin radius, as you can see in Figure 7.16.

If you read the parameter descriptions carefully, you might have noticed that the sets of text in this component follow the same rules as the text in the Scramble-TextEffect component as far as HTML is concerned. No tags other than the line break tag are allowed. Open the file `SpinEffect03_Sample.fla` to see the line break being used, as well as a larger spin radius value, as shown in Figure 7.17.

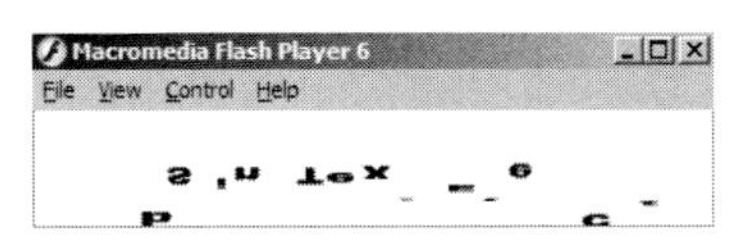

Figure 7.16

Use a small value for the spin radius to produce different effects. This also constrains the component to a smaller area, if you want.

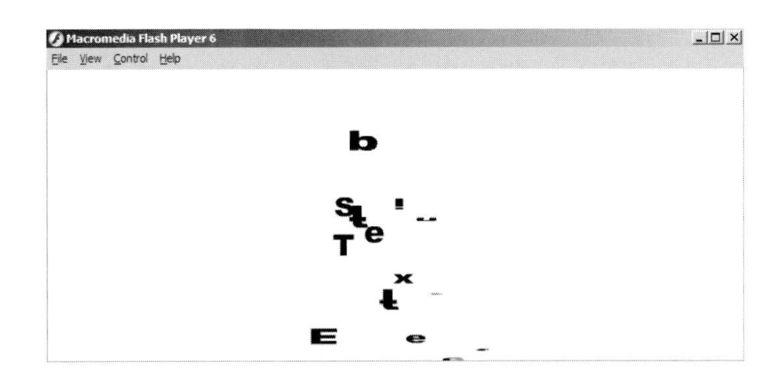

Figure 7.17

The line break tag is the only HTML tag you can use with the Spin-TextEffect component.

With all the components discussed in this chapter, you may feel that you have quite a bit of information to memorize. Fortunately, the ScrambleTextEffect and SpinTextEffect components act nearly identical outside of their animations—meaning the same quirks that were involved in the live preview of ScrambleTextEffect, such as font and letter spacing, are still present in SpinTextEffect.

The FlushTextEffect Component and Shared Fonts

Now that we have covered all of the components in the text effects set, we can backtrack a little to see how to apply the knowledge of shared fonts to the FlushTextEffect component. As I mentioned earlier, one drawback of the FlushTextEffect component is that if you enter a font in the component's parameters that is not on a user's computer, then the text will be rendered in the default font of Arial. As we saw earlier, embedding a font into a text field fixes this problem for Dynamic and Input text fields. However, when it comes to components and ActionScripted control of text fields, we have to make use of shared fonts.

This is the solution to the problem in FlushTextEffect. Although the parameter in FlushTextEffect asks for the name of the font you want use, it can also accept the linkage name of the shared font. So, to use a custom font, you simply create a shared font like we have done already, give it a linkage name, and input that name into the component's parameters—nothing different from before. By following those steps, you can use any font on your computer without worrying if your viewers have the font.

Conclusion

Out of all the components featured in this entire book, the text effects described in this chapter fully capture the sense of components as a whole. The painstaking job of creating incredibly intricate effects is reduced to the mediocrity of drag and drop. Although simple to use, these components have presented quite a bit of information to you. You have learned how to use the three text effects provided in this chapter and how to use the new shared fonts available in Flash MX.

Chapter 8: Video and Audio Components

One of the most useful features of Flash is being able to import and play video and music files, especially since the Flash player is more common than any media player on the Internet. Fortunately, any beginner can import a media file into Flash, publish the movie, and view the media through Flash. Unfortunately, there is much more to controlling media types in Flash than simply importing files.

In this chapter, we'll work with the Audio Player and Video Player components. Although these are very complex—perhaps the most intricate in the entire book—they have very few parameters, which are very basic. However, because of the density of the components, we must take extra care when editing their graphics. I'll take the most time going over how to "skin" the components: replacing the player's default graphics with your own.

The components in this chapter will greatly simplify your projects whenever you need a media interface. They offer advanced functionality with very little work outside of graphic skinning. You will learn how to create the media files that will be controlled by the players and how to customize the various parts of the player. When you are done with this chapter, you won't be afraid to add a soundtrack or video presentation to your site.

- **An audio player component**
- **A video player component**
- **ActionScript control of the players**

The Audio Player

I've set up a sample use of the Audio Player component in the `Audio Player Component` folder, which resides in the Chapter 8 folder on the CD. The folder contains `AudioPlayer.fla`, `AudioPlayer.swf`, and another folder named `songs`. (There are two other files named `AS_Controller_AudioPlayer.fla` and `AS_Controller_AudioPlayer.swf`, which I'll cover later in the chapter.) When you want to use this component on your own, you simply open `AudioPlayer.fla`, shown in Figure 8.1, and save to your local disk so that you can use it with your project.

If you also copy the `songs` folder to the same directory as the audio player, you can test the file and hear the audio files provided on the CD. Take note of the various features and functionalities of the player (shown in Figure 8.2). Beyond the basic commands such as stop, play, and pause, you can pan the audio to the left and right speakers, slide the track marker to jump to a point in the audio, scroll through a list of available songs, and double-click any

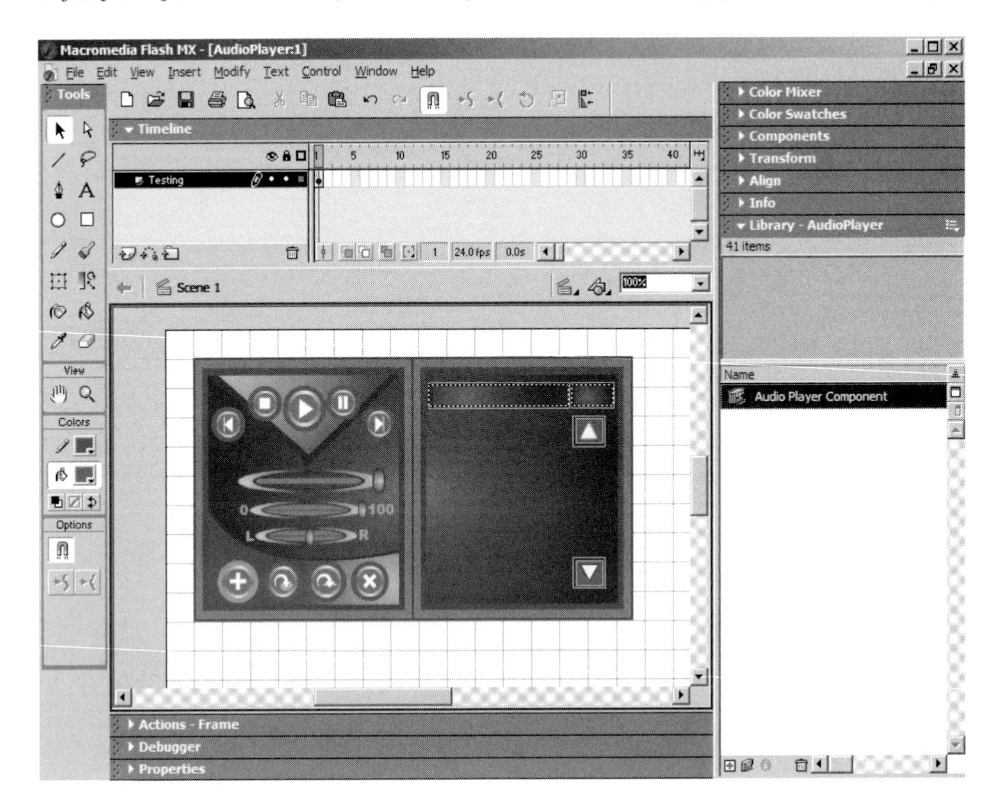

Figure 8.1

The open `Audio-Player.fla` **file**

song to play it. If you mess with the player long enough, you'll notice that your settings for the volume and pan stay the same each time you reopen the player. Indeed, the player saves your setting information each time you use it. There is also a display for the song title and length of time the song has been playing.

A special feature of this audio player lies in the four icons below the volume and pan controls. They allow you to add certain songs to a favorites list, load your favorites list, load the original song list, and clear your favorites. The favorites list allows a user to compile a list of preferred songs. This list is saved to the user's computer. Upon return to your site, the user can load this list of favorites again. Most importantly, the list gives the user a feel of personalization to your player, which is usually a surprise to those who are familiar with other media players.

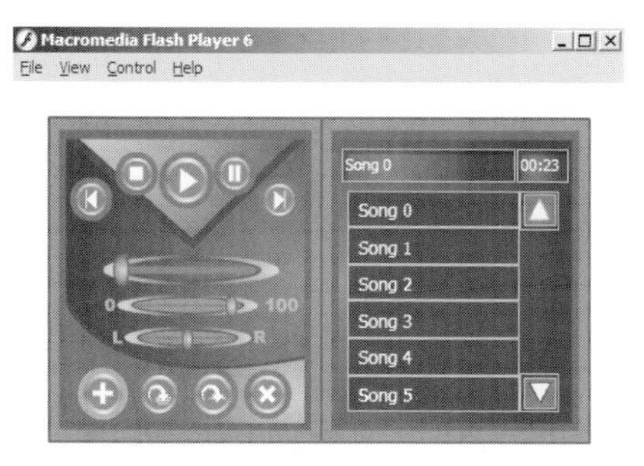

Figure 8.2

Test the movie to experiment with the various functions.

Going back to the authoring environment, we see that there is only one folder in the library, named `Audio Player Component`. This folder contains all of the assets of the component. Directly in this folder are the component movie clip, the symbol you drag to the stage to use the component, and two folders: one for designers and one for developers. The folder for designers holds all of the graphics and is probably the only folder you will want to delve into; the folder for developers holds core resources such as code. Look at Figure 8.3 to become familiar with the structure of the folders.

Before we take a gander into the hordes of movie clips and buttons that are contained in these folders, delete the component currently on the stage and drag a new instance of the component onto the stage. Once you have it on the stage, open the Component Parameters panel by pressing Option/Alt+F7 and note the features of the component you can change immediately. Descriptions for each parameter are listed here:

Figure 8.3

The library of the AudioPlayer component holds assets for developers and designers.

Song Names An array that determines the names of each song. These are the names that show up in the playlist and in the title display when the song is playing.

Song URLs An array that holds the URLs to each media file that is to be played in the audio player.

Shuffle? A Boolean value that determines if the playlist should be shuffled randomly so that the songs do not play sequentially.

Num Visible Songs A parameter that specifies the number of song items that are visible at any one time before you have to scroll through the items. Indirectly, it sets the size of the playlist because its size is based on the number of items that are displayed at once.

Playlist Position An x- and y-coordinate that determines where the top-left corner of the playlist should be positioned.

FPS The frames per second setting you are using for your movie. To find this value, press Command/Ctrl+J in the authoring environment and look in the field named Frame Rate. This parameter is very important as it is used to calculate the number of seconds the song lasts.

The songs featured in the sample of the AudioPlayer component are provided courtesy of SoundRangers. SoundRangers provides sound effects and music optimized for Flash and interactive media. Their online laboratory hosts thousands of original, royalty-free sounds instantly downloadable in both WAV and AIF format. They can be found on the Web at `www.soundrangers.com`.

Unlike most components, none of these parameters directly affect the appearance of the component. The only parameter that comes close to affecting the component's exterior is the playlist's position, although it's quite a technical aspect of the process. Observe that the entries in the Song Names array and the Song URLs array correspond to each other, meaning the first name in the Song Names array is the title of the song at the URL in the first entry of the Song URLs array. The values in these two arrays are what create the playlist, so add as few or as many as you want.

Creating Audio Files

Customizing the parameters of this component has been a breeze. The next big job is creating the media files that will be linked up with the component. You might wonder why you do not merely import all the media you want to use for the player and use it from directly inside Flash, but it becomes painfully obvious when you look in the `songs` folder, where some sample songs have been prepared. Separately, each song averages 350 KB, and the collection all together is over 3.5 MB. If you were to import all the songs into Flash at once, your users would face a massive download and would wonder why they shouldn't just download a professional media player.

The process for creating the media files is very simple, but it's also very repetitive and tedious. The only type of media file the audio player can handle is SWF, which means we must import the songs into a Flash movie and publish its SWF. Start by opening a new Flash movie and save it as `song0.fla`. Press Command/Ctrl+R to open the Import dialog box and select the song you want to bring in; this must be either an MP3 or WAV file. Once the song is fully imported, it will appear in the library; however, click the first frame of the main stage and select the song from the frame's Properties panel to use it. When placing a sound on a frame, you have two options for synchronizing the sound with the Timeline: event and stream. The event setting starts to play the song when the Timeline reaches the frame with the sound, and the song plays independently from the stage in its entirety. This means that if an event sound starts, it will fully play even if the Timeline is stopped. The other type of sound is stream, and it synchronizes with the Timeline's frame rate. The sound plays if the playhead is on a frame the sound occupies and if the Timeline is playing; if the Timeline stops, then so does the streamed sound. This is the type of synchronization that we want for the audio file, as shown in Figure 8.4.

Considering all of this, we can see that the sound we added to the first frame must be a streamed sound. In addition to this, we must also create enough frames to accommodate the full sound. Unfortunately, there is no precise way of creating the frames the song needs, so you have to scroll to the end of the Timeline, right-click a frame, click Insert Frame, and repeat until you see the end of the song. Although you have to make sure you have enough frames for the song, you must also make sure you don't have too many frames (see Figure 8.5).

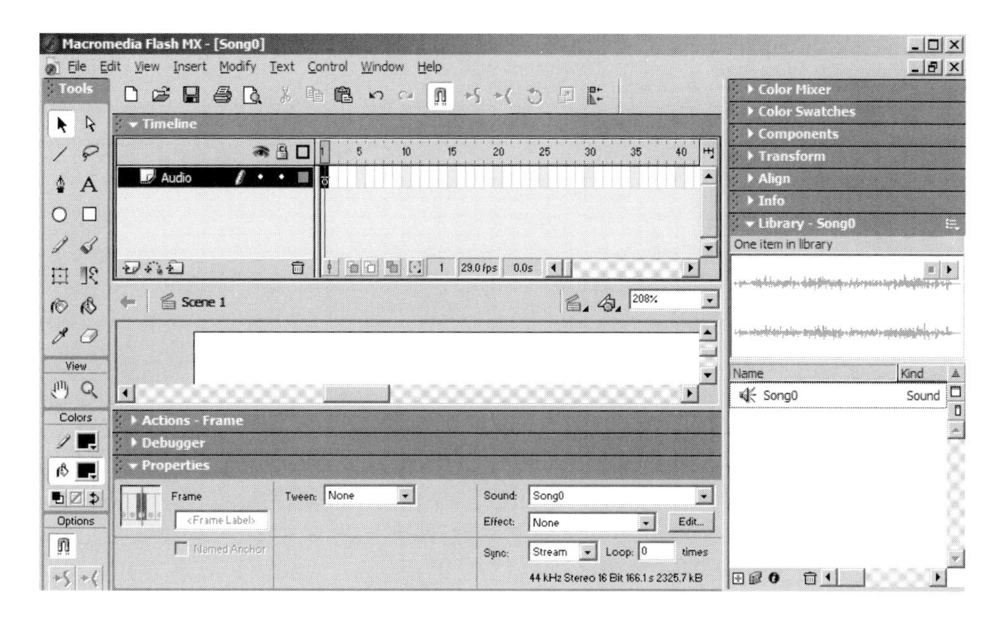

Figure 8.4

The first frame of the movie with a streamed sound

Finally, click File to publish the movie, or press Shift+F12. You have now created your first media file to use with the component. The bad news is that you have umpteen more files to create going through this same progression.

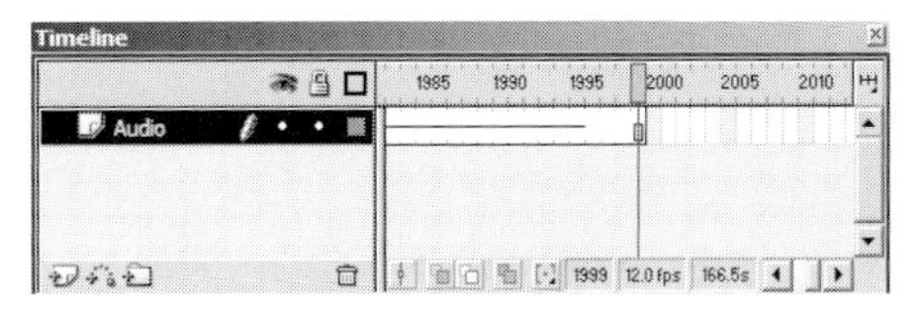

Figure 8.5
Make sure there are enough frames to accommodate the sound, but not too many frames.

After you have gone through the laborious task of creating all the media files, you must enter their file paths into the component parameters. Since we placed our songs in the `songs` folder, typical entries in the Song URLs array would look like `songs/song0.swf`, `songs/song1.swf`, `songs/song2.swf`, and so on, depending on the number of songs you are using.

Skinning the Audio Player Component

Now comes time for by far the lengthiest expedition for this component: reskinning the component. We will venture into each individual button and movie clip that makes up the entire component in order to understand how to add in other graphics. Take heed that we will only undertake the folder that holds assets for the designer; the developers' folder is quite a dangerous place and beyond the extent of this chapter.

Start by opening the folder `AudioPlayer Assets - Designers Only` and looking at how the graphics are divided into logical categories, as shown in Figure 8.6: control buttons, favorites buttons, graphics for the pan and volume sliders, graphics for the playlist, and graphics for the track slider.

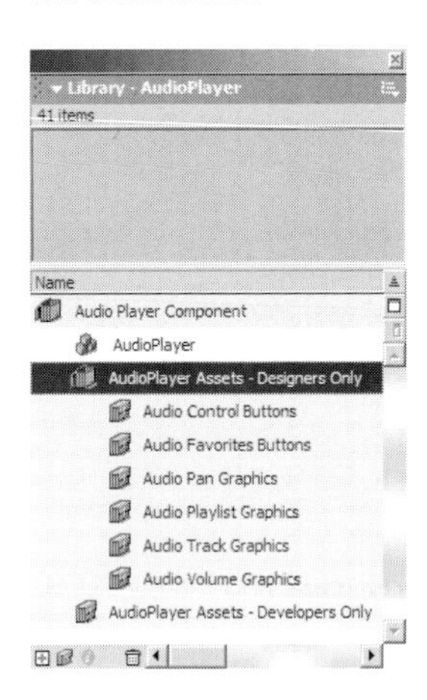

Figure 8.6
Folder hierarchy for the player's graphics

The most important thing to remember when editing the graphics of a component is to not change the dimensions, tint, or alpha of any button or movie clip directly. That is, make sure to only edit the vector graphic of a symbol. If you click a graphic and the Properties panel tells you that it is an instance of a symbol in the library, then you should not do anything to the graphic. Edit only the graphics that say Shape in the Properties panel. Look carefully at Figures 8.7 and 8.8 to see how you can use the Properties panel to determine if you can edit a graphic or not. The best strategy for editing these symbols is to just double-click the symbol in the library; that way, you can ensure that you will edit the vector graphics inside it.

In the first folder, `Audio Control Buttons`, you will find the buttons for controlling the audio that let you play, stop, pause, and go back and forth between tracks, as shown in Figure 8.9. If you want to change the placement of these buttons, then you must go back to the AudioPlayer movie clip and move the buttons to where you would like. Take extra care that you do not change the instance name of the button, which is done through the Properties panel. If you do not want the user to have access to a particular button, simply delete it or drag it off to the sides so that the user cannot see it. Note that you will not be able to replace any button you delete.

The next folder, `Audio Favorites Buttons`, contains graphics for the buttons related to favorites (see Figure 8.10). Although icons are used, you can also use text to be less ambiguous.

Figure 8.9

Control buttons for the audio

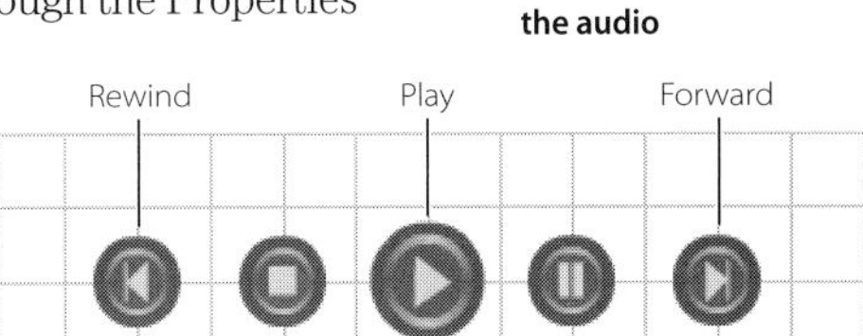

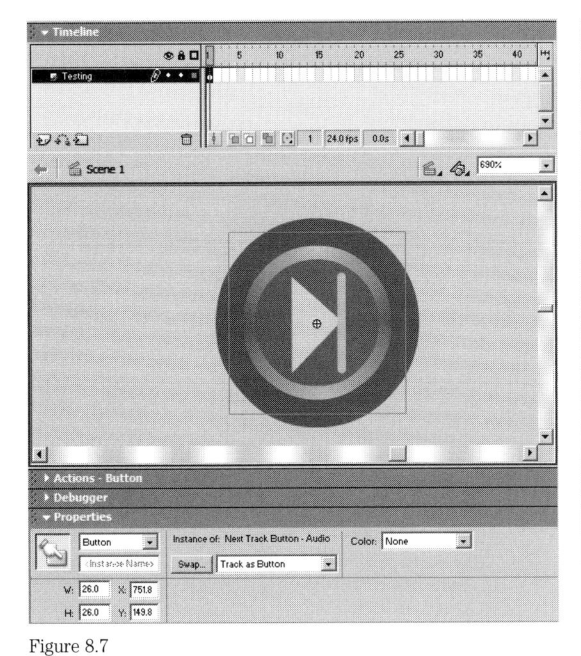

Figure 8.7

Do not transform a graphic directly if the Properties panel says it is a library symbol.

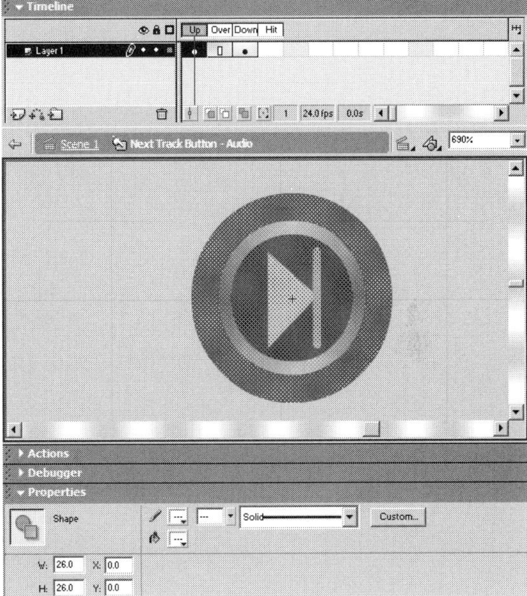

Figure 8.8

Edit only the vector graphics (the Shape objects) inside of a symbol.

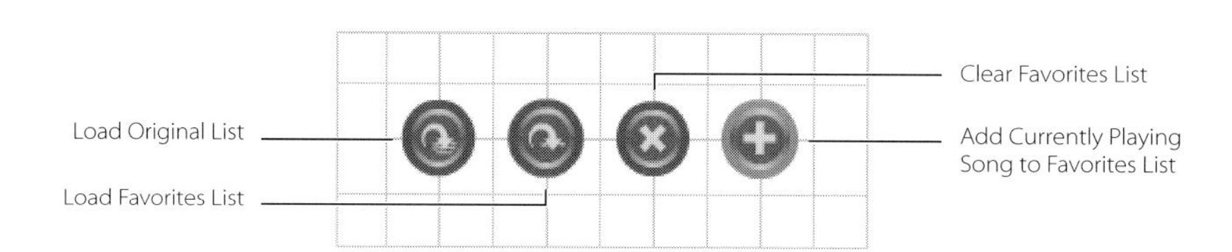

Figure 8.10
Buttons for managing a list of favorites

The folders `Audio Pan Graphics` and `Audio Volume Graphics` are very similar. Inside each is a movie clip for a background and a movie clip for a slider. The slider is the graphic that the user clicks and drags, and the background is the graphic that the slider glides over. Unlike the previous graphics, these graphics have some requirements and some strange inconsistencies.

To ensure that the sliders stay over the backgrounds, you must center the graphics in the sliders. Select your graphic entirely, press Command/Ctrl+K to open the Align panel, and click the Align Horizontal Center and Align Vertical Center buttons to guarantee the graphic is centered. These buttons are shown in Figure 8.11.

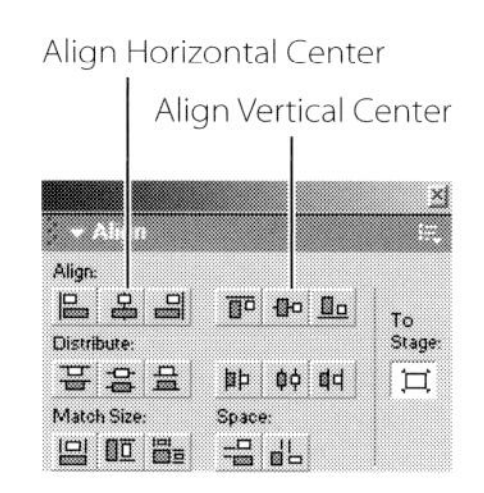

Figure 8.11
Use the Align panel to center your graphic.

For the background graphics, you must check many things. First, the far-left edge of the graphic must be placed at the origin (the center of the movie clip). In addition to this, you must also give the graphic an integer width.

Since Flash is a vector-based animation program, it can hypothetically handle curves and points to any degree of accuracy. However, certain functions in Flash, such as `startDrag`, will snap to the nearest integer, and if your background does not have an integer width, the slider will not snap to the background correctly.

Failing to comply with the integer-width condition sometimes results in being able to set the volume to –1% or being able to go up to 99% but no higher.

Finally, the background and the slider must be positioned at a "lattice point" on Flash's stage, which is a point with an integer x- and y-coordinate. These graphics are shown in Figure 8.12.

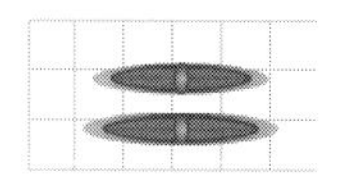

Figure 8.12
Sliders and backgrounds for the volume and pan controls

The next folder, `Audio Playlist Graphics`, holds all the graphics that make up the player's playlist. This includes a scroll up button, a scroll down button, and a generic item graphic that the user double-clicks to play the song. There are no strict requirements for the scroll buttons, except that they should be centered with respect to the button's center. Most importantly about these buttons, do not worry about their position in the component; the internal code of the component will reposition the scroll buttons so that they fit perfectly at the top and bottom of the playlist.

When editing the graphics of the playlist item, you must keep a few things fresh in your mind. The top-left corner of the item must always be at 0 along the x- and y-axes (the center of the movie clip). It is imperative to meet this condition because it is used exclusively when rendering the playlist. Feel free to change the font size, font, color, and dimensions of the text field. After you have made your graphic, be sure there are no stray graphics hanging out of the area that contains the item. Such wandering graphics will alter the appearance of the playlist in an unwanted way. The graphics for a playlist item and the scrolling buttons are shown in Figure 8.13.

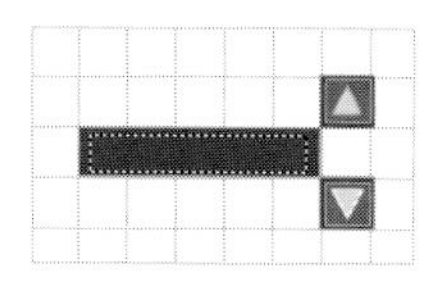

Figure 8.13

Graphics of the playlist item and scroll buttons

The last folder, `Audio Track Graphics`, contains the most complicated set of graphics. These graphics allow the user to click and drag a slider to jump to any specified point in a song, but they do so much more than that. As the song plays, the slider moves along the background, graphically showing the progress of the song. As the slider moves from left to right, a bar graphic fills the space between the left-side point where the slider started and where the slider is currently, showing how much of the song has been played. An extra bar shows how much of the audio has been streamed. This bar fills up as the song is downloading, and once it reaches the far-right side of the background, the song is fully downloaded and begins to play.

These four graphic elements work in tandem to give a graphical representation of the song's progress, as shown in Figure 8.14. Similar to previous graphics, these graphics have certain requirements. The slider must be centered about its origin, and the slider's background must have an integer value for its width and x- and y-position on the stage. The bars for the audio progress and audio streaming must also have integer widths, but their positions must coincide exactly with the background; their depth orderings on layers is up to you.

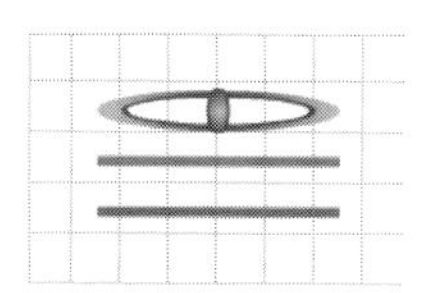

Figure 8.14

Individual graphics that make up the graphical rendering of the audio's progress. All four parts provide the user with helpful information about the audio, such as streaming and playing progress.

Arranging Component Elements

If you have made it this far, then you have learned to skin the various graphical elements of the audio player. Before you're done with this player, however, you need to take note of a few other things. Since all of your graphics are inside each symbol in the library, you may want to rearrange the way the various buttons and movie clips are inside the component. When you move the parts of the component around, be very careful and take close measurements. You must be careful because you do not want to change the instance names of any buttons or movie clips on the stage or accidentally delete anything. You must take precise measurements because it may take a few tries to get the playlist in the exact position—you do this by entering numbers into the Component Parameters panel. Also, if you ever want to find the height of the playlist when it is rendered, simply multiply the height of the playlist item by the value of the number of visible items (you entered this in the Component Parameters panel). That value may become useful when arranging parts in the component.

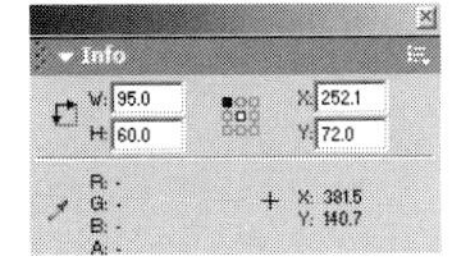

Figure 8.15

Use the Info panel to get the numeric values you will enter into the component's parameters.

To get the information needed for the Component Parameters panel, you can use a temporary filler graphic and the Info panel. Follow these steps:

1. Double-click the AudioPlayer component symbol in the library; do not right-click the symbol on the main stage and go to Edit In Place, as that will alter the coordinate system of the component.
2. Create a solid color rectangle with Flash's Rectangle tool, having the width of the playlist item you created and the height equal to the value calculated before (number of visible playlist items multiplied by their individual height).
3. Place this vector graphic in the exact position you would like inside the component.
4. Open the Info panel by pressing Command/Ctrl+I, as shown in Figure 8.15. If the rectangle is still selected, this panel will give information about the graphic, such as width, height, and position relative to either the graphic's center or the graphic's upper-left corner. It is the latter attribute that you are interested in. Note the position of the graphic's upper-left corner, because you will enter that information into the component's parameters.
5. Return to the Timeline where the component exists, open its Component Parameters panel, and enter the values for Playlist Position.

The player renders the player instantly when it appears on the stage, so you can even leave that filler graphic for reference because it will be covered up.

Organizing Component Assets

To make positioning the different parts of the audio player a little easier, I've placed the parts on different layers and grouped them into folders, as shown in Figure 8.16.

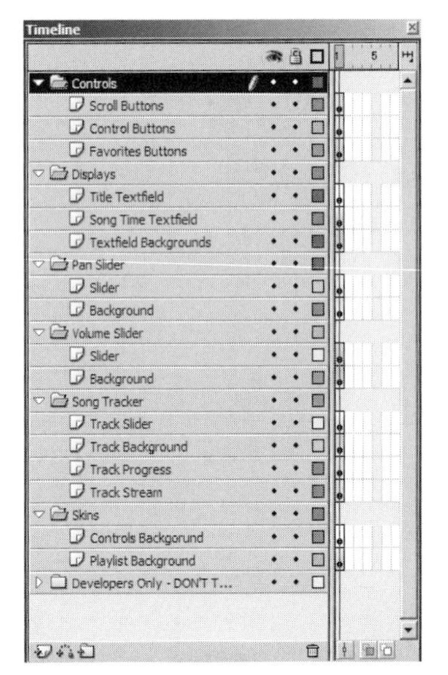

Figure 8.16

The folder hierarchy of the layers in the AudioPlayer component

It is beneficial to your development process to preserve this folder hierarchy. Taking someone else's work and adding your own graphics can become messy very fast. Having a sloppy Timeline and stage only hinders your progress. Within each folder, you can order the layers any way you want, and you can even order the folders in any way—just try not to mix folders, keep all the graphics for the volume slider in one folder, and keep all the graphics for the pan slider in another.

The Video Player

Video is something new to Flash MX, believe it or not. In past versions of Flash, you had to find a program that exported videos into a sequence of pictures that would then be exported into Flash. Some programs even exported your video as an SWF file that was simply many frames containing a sequence of pictures that gave the illusion of being video. Now, in Flash MX, we can import videos in formats such as QuickTime, AVI, MPEG, DV, and MOV and play them back as SWF files.

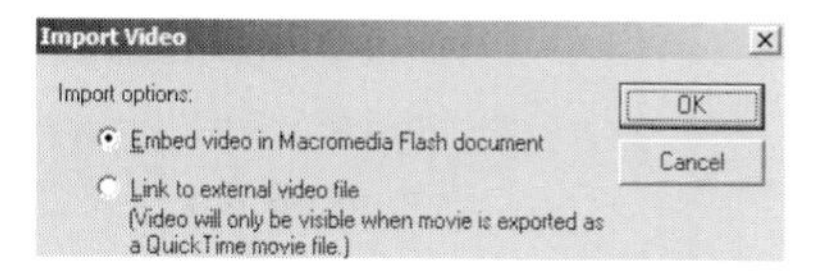

Figure 8.17

The initial dialog box when importing a QuickTime video

Importing Videos

Open a new Flash movie and save it as `video0.fla`. Go to File → Import to bring up the dialog box that lists the video you want to import. Once you select the video, a few things might happen depending on the file type of the video.

If you choose to import a QuickTime file, you will see an initial dialog box asking if you want to embed the file in Flash or link to an external video file, as shown in Figure 8.17. The first option is the one you want; it inserts the video into Flash so that you can play it back as an SWF. The second option allows you to add Flash elements to a QuickTime movie and export it as a QuickTime movie. That's not our goal here. Select the Embed radio button and click OK; the Import Video Settings dialog box will open, as shown in Figure 8.18.

If you choose to import a Windows Media file type, such as MOV, MPEG, DV, or AVI, you skip the Import Video dialog box and go straight the Import Video Settings dialog box, shown in Figure 8.18.

The Import Video Settings dialog box holds many options that you should carefully consider.

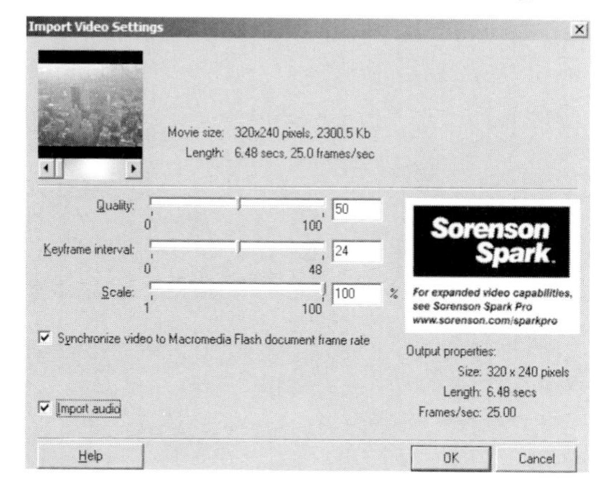

Figure 8.18

Set options that pertain to your video here. You'll encounter this dialog box any time you import a video, no matter the file type.

Quality This option, in the form of a slider from 0 to 100, affects the quality of the video. For each unit you decrease the video's quality, you are also decreasing the video's file size, so some experimentation may be in order to find the perfect balance between file size and quality. The videos used for this chapter averaged about 5 MB and were exported at qualities between 50 and 90; their average file size is now 550 KB.

Keyframe Interval You should set this option to the frame rate in your movie, which is importing the video.

Scale You use this option to reduce the size of the video you are importing. Scale affects the size of the video when exported as an SWF, so you may want to conduct tests with it if you do not need the full size of the video. For example, one video I tested was over 10 MB when published as an SWF at 100% quality and scale. However, when I reduced the scale to 50%, the file size shrank to 3.5 MB. Take note that any sizing you do in Flash will not affect the file's size—meaning, if you import a movie at 100% size and use the Free Transform tool to make the video only 20 pixels by 20 on the stage, the file size will stay the same, as if it were full size. So, be sure to take this option into account when you do not need the full size of the video.

Synchronize Video To Macromedia Flash Document Frame Rate This check box controls the relationship between the video's frame rate and Flash's frame rate. Checking this box will put the two rates in a 1-to-1 ratio so that the video will play in Flash exactly as it does when played back in any other media player. Unchecking this box opens a drop-down list box with additional ratios, shown in Figure 8.19.

Number Of Video Frames To Encode Per Number Of Macromedia Flash Frames The drop-down list box shown in Figure 8.19 holds seven options that represent the most commonly used ratios. Consider the left number (which I'll call LN) and the right number (RN). Selecting one of these ratios means that LN frames of the video will play for every RN frames that play in Flash. If you calculate the numeric ratio by dividing LN by RN, then the closer the ratio is to 0, the jerkier the video will be. The closer the ratio is to 1, the smoother the video will be. Considering this, 1:1 is the same as synchronizing the video to Flash's frame rate, and 1:8 is the jerkiest of the settings. You can take off quite a few extra kilobytes of the file's size by choosing a ratio that is close to zero.

Figure 8.19

Selecting a frame rate ratio

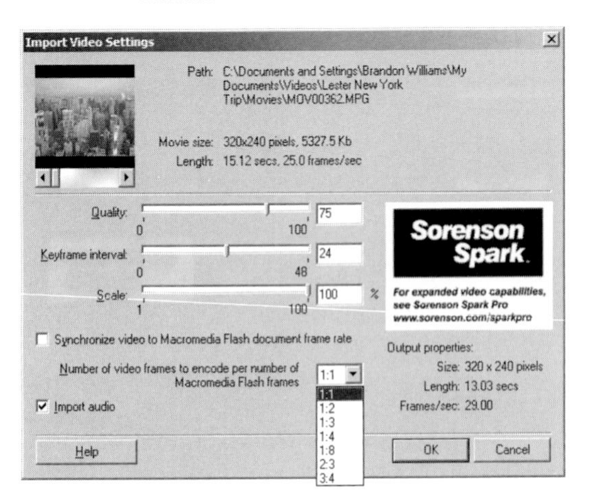

Import Audio You have the choice of importing the video's audio. You might think that not having any audio would greatly reduce the file's size, but it does not have any affect. Uncheck this item only if you do not want to use any sound, without considering file size.

After customizing all of these settings, you can click OK and the video will be imported into your Flash file. There is only one constraint for the video once it is fully imported: the video's top-left corner must lie exactly on the movie's origin. This is critical when the component loads the video in and positions it. You can do this by opening the Info Panel using Command/Ctrl+I and setting the numerical values of the video's x- and y-position.

Now, press Shift+F12 to publish the file as an SWF. Repeat this process as many times as you need to create SWF files of all your videos.

> Note that it is not necessary to set the movie stage dimensions because when a movie is loaded its stage is not rendered.

Customizing Component Parameters

Once you have created all the media files, you can open the `VideoPlayer.fla` file, which is in the Chapter 8 folder on the CD, and save it to your local disk. The first thing you will want to do is customize the component's parameters, which are very similar to the audio player's:

Video Names An array that determines the names of each video. These names show up in the playlist and in the title display when the song is playing.

Video URLs An array that holds the URLs to each media file that is to be played in the audio player.

Video Position An x- and y-coordinate that determines where the center of the video should be positioned.

Shuffle? A Boolean value that determines if the playlist should be shuffled randomly so that the videos do not play sequentially.

Num Visible Videos A parameter that specifies the number of video items that are visible at any one time before you have to scroll through the items. Indirectly, it sets the size of the playlist because its size is based on the number of items that are displayed at one time.

Playlist Position An x- and y-coordinate that determines where the top-left corner of the playlist should be positioned.

FPS The frames per second setting you are using for your movie. To find this value, press Command/Ctrl+J in the authoring environment and look in the Frame Rate field. This parameter is very important because it is used to calculate the number of seconds the video lasts.

The only new parameter is an ordered pair of coordinates that are used to position the video. Later on, we will learn a very easy way to calculate the numeric values coordinate to enter into the Component Parameters panel.

Before we continue to customize the player by skinning it and whatnot, take a moment to publish the file and play around with the features. The video player, shown in Figure 8.20, is very similar to the audio player; in fact, the only additions to the controls are two buttons with double arrows on them. These buttons rewind and fast-forward the videos.

Skinning the Video Player Component

The next step in customizing this component is to skin it. If you look in the library, you will see that it is set up in much the same way as the audio player, with a few extra symbols and a few less folders. The two new buttons, Rewind and Fast-Forward, have been added to the `Video Control Buttons` folder.

The good news about skinning the graphic elements in this player is that it is the exact same as it was in the audio player. For the control buttons such as Play, Stop, Pause, etc., there are no requirements; you can put anything you want in them.

The graphics in the `Video Playlist Graphics` folder also have the same conditions that must be upheld. The playlist item must have its upper-left corner at the origin of the movie clip. The scroll up and scroll down buttons must also have their contents positioned such that the top-left corner is at each button's origin.

The `Video Track Graphics` folder contains all the elements that collect together to provide the user with a graphical representation of the video's status. A slider enables the user to jump to arbitrary points in the video, the slider moves over a background area, and two movie clips track the progress of the video and the video's downloading status.

Finally, the `Video Volume Graphics` folder holds the graphics that make up the volume slider.

When positioning the parts of the video player, you must keep in mind all the same rules and conditions of the audio player. However, we now have one more element to consider: the position of the video. The component parameter asked for the x- and y-coordinate of the center of where the videos appear. You might wonder why it does not ask for the position of the top-left corner, as most other parameters have in the past. Well, one consistent thing we want for this video player is for all the videos to show up in the same position, regardless of size. The only thing that should differentiate a 320×240 video from an 800×600 video playing in our player is the size. To ensure that all videos load into the same position, we must provide the x- and y-coordinate of where we want the center.

Figure 8.20

Test the movie to experiment with the various functions.

For the audio player, we made use of a filler graphic to pinpoint where the playlist should be positioned. We can use this same technique for finding the position of the video. Follow these steps:

1. Double-click the VideoPlayer component symbol in the library to edit it locally.
2. Create a solid color rectangle with Flash's Rectangle tool and give it the dimensions of a typical movie in your playlist.
3. Position the rectangle in the component at the point where you would like all of your videos to appear.
4. Open the Info panel by pressing Command/Ctrl+I and then record the information in the panel.
5. Close out the component and enter that data into the component's parameters.

You can either keep the filler graphic in place or remove it; it does not matter since the videos will be loaded on top of it.

ActionScript Control of the Players

Sometimes you'll want to take control of the player out of the hands of the user and manage the player through ActionScript. For example, if you are using the audio player for background music on your site, and you want the music to turn off when the user gets to a certain area of your site, what are you to do? Trust the user to turn it off and concentrate on an important part of your site's experience? Not likely. This is why certain controls have been added to both the audio and video players to give you the last word in controlling them.

We will use the audio player as an example by using the player we created earlier, but this time we'll add some outside buttons that will play, stop, and pause the player. An exact copy of the `AudioPlayer.fla` has been created and named `AS_Controller_AudioPlayer.fla`, which can be found in the Chapter 8 folder on the CD. With this file, you will start by giving your audio player the instance name audio_player. To do this, click the audio player and press Command/Ctrl+F3 to open the Properties panel. The Component text field currently says < Instance Name >. Click in the text field to clear that out and type **audio_player**, as shown in Figure 8.21.

Now, create three buttons that will be used to control the audio in the player and arranging them along the bottom of the audio player, as you can see in Figure 8.22.

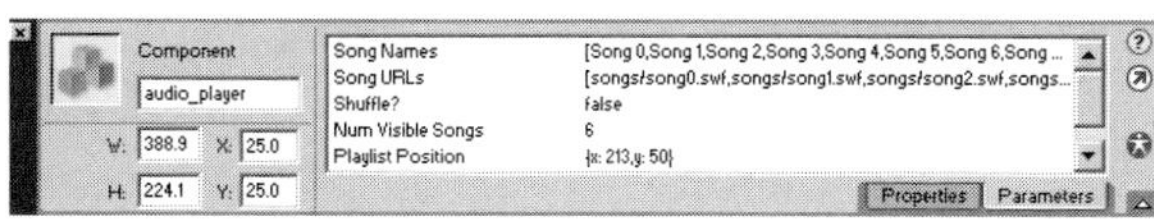

Figure 8.21

Give the AudioPlayer component an instance name.

Now we must add actions to the buttons that will control the audio player. Although you might recoil from just the mention of ActionScript, it is actually quite uncomplicated. You are familiar with the basic functions that are attached to every movie clip such as `stop ( )`, `play ( )`, and `gotoAndStop (`*`frame`*`)`. What it means for these functions to be attached to the movie clip is that if you have a movie clip with the instance name my_movie, then you can use the following ActionScript to play the contents in the movie: `my_movie.play ( )`. This same structure is preserved in the AudioPlayer component—meaning, if you want to stop the audio in the player, you only have to write the ActionScript: `audio_player.stop ( )`. In a sense, you are pressing the Stop button with ActionScript. There are other functions you are can use too; some of the most basic are described in Table 8.1.

Table 8.1

Functions for Controlling the AudioPlayer Component through ActionScript

FUNCTION NAME	DESCRIPTION
`stop`	Stops the audio from playing and resets the playhead to the beginning of the song.
`play`	Plays the current song if the player is not already.
`pause`	Stops the audio from playing, but the playhead stays still.
`next_track`	Plays the next track in the playlist.
`previous_track`	Plays the previous track in the playlist.

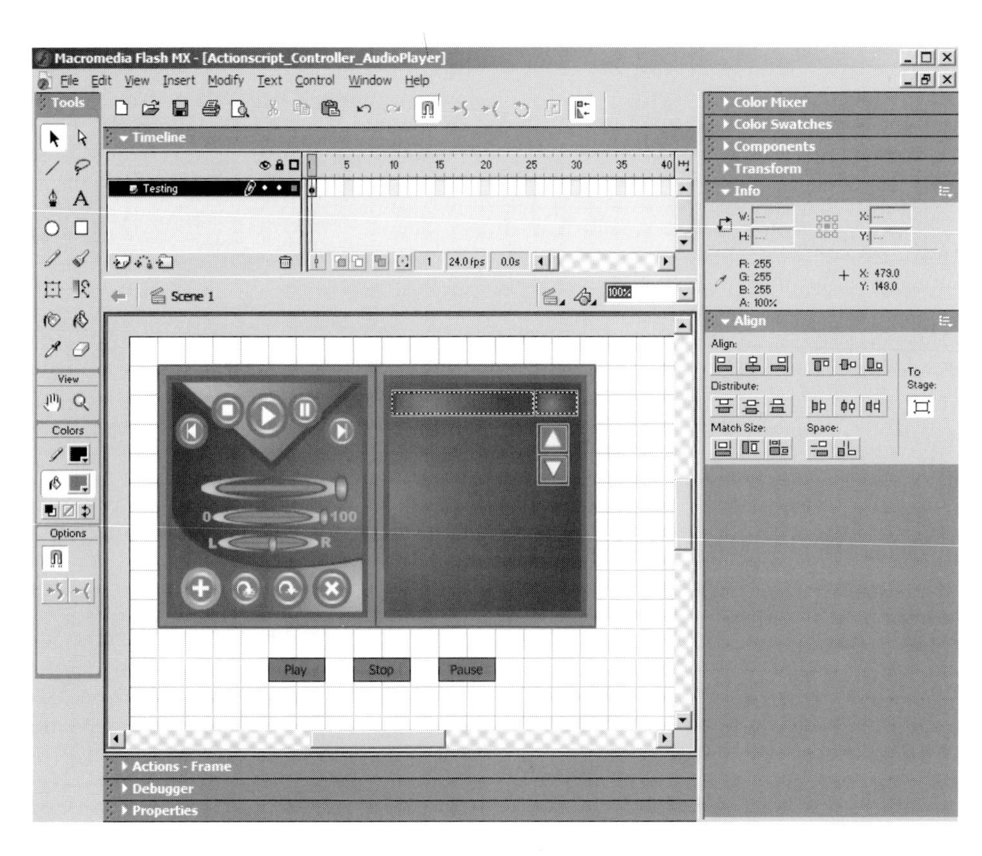

Figure 8.22

Create play, stop, and pause buttons that will be used to control the audio player.

Bearing in mind all this new information, we can now write the ActionScript for the buttons we created (those scripts are shown in Listings 8.1, 8.2, and 8.3). To apply ActionScript to a button, click the button that resides on the stage and press F9. A blank text window will appear where you can type your ActionScript. The first part of the code specifies what the user needs to do to execute the button. Since we want the button's actions to be executed when the user presses the button, we wrap all of its actions with `on (press)` (see Figure 8.23). The action in the `press` button event is simply a call to one of the functions listed in Table 8.1, which is attached to the component.

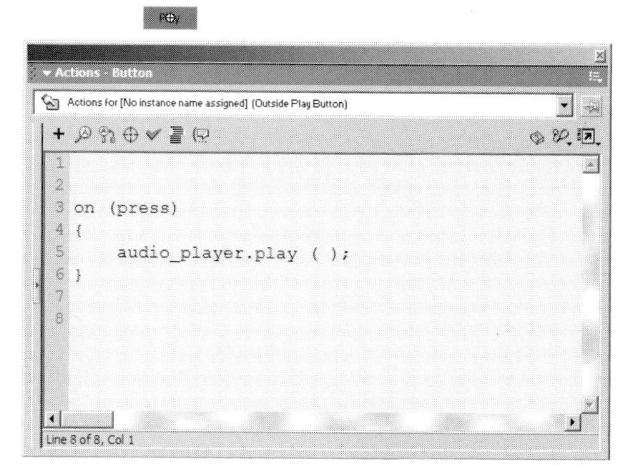

Figure 8.23

Actions placed on the external Play button

Listing 8.1

Code for the Play Button

```
on (press)
{
   audio_player.play ( );
}
```

Listing 8.2

Code for the Stop Button

```
on (press)
{
   audio_player.stop ( );
}
```

Listing 8.3

Code for the Pause Button

```
on (press)
{
   audio_player.pause ( );
}
```

Now test the movie and see how you can control the audio player with buttons that are completely separate from the player. Although the ActionScript in this sample was placed on buttons, it can be placed anywhere, such as frame actions. Remember this to use the component to its full potential.

The video player also has similar functions attached to it (see Table 8.2). You can use them in the exact same way as in the sample of the audio player.

Table 8.2

Functions for Controlling the VideoPlayer Component through ActionScript

FUNCTION NAME	DESCRIPTION
`stop`	Stops the audio from playing and resets the playhead to the beginning of the song.
`play`	Plays the current song if the player is not already.
`pause`	Stops the audio from playing, but the playhead stays still.
`next_track`	Plays the next track in the playlist.
`previous_track`	Plays the previous track in the playlist.
`fast_forward`	Starts the video fast-forwarding.
`rewind`	Starts the video rewinding
`stop_fast_forward`	Stops the video from fast-forwarding, if it is indeed fast-forwarding. Keep in mind that the player will continue to fast-forward until this function is called.
`stop_rewind`	Stops the video from rewinding, if it is indeed rewinding. Keep in mind that the player will continue to rewind until this function is called.

Conclusion

In this chapter, you have learned how to fully utilize Flash MX's video and audio powers with the use of components. By themselves, these components are massive projects. You would never want to re-create them every time you need a player, or even make them once, because they are quite complex. Outside of the remedial editing of the component's parameters, you have gained two important tools: skinning a component's graphic elements without messing up the component's functionality and controlling a component through ActionScript.

Chapter 9: Game Components

When Macromedia Flash began to include programming, developers naturally started to use Flash for web games. With Flash, developers could deliver games with better animation and faster download times then Flash's cousin, Macromedia Director's Shockwave.

However, the nature of programming in Flash can make it difficult to customize games. ActionScript is often appended to a series of Flash objects such as movie clips and buttons, making it difficult to keep track of variables and other resources used in the game. Fortunately, components can greatly simplify the process of customizing Flash games.

In this chapter, we will look at two games and see how the components were used to organize the games and make them easy to customize.

- **Editing a quiz component**
- **Working with external text files**
- **Customizing the images**
- **Editing a concentration component**
- **Replacing the images**

Editing a Quiz Component

Open the `quiz.fla` file in the Chapter 9 folder on the CD (see Figure 9.1). Save the file to your local computer so that you can save your edits as you follow along. Locate the file named `quiz.txt` and copy it to the same folder on your local computer that you saved the `quiz.fla` file.

> The components in this chapter are from `www.gamesinaflash.com` and are for educational purposes only. To use these games on your websites, you must license them from Eyeland Studio, Inc. (`www.eyeland.com` or `www.gamesinaflash.com`).

Go ahead and test the movie to see how the quiz game works. If you play the game, you will see that the quiz game works like standard quiz games. You are presented with a question in a white box, and you need to click on the button next to the correct answer, as shown in Figure 9.2. If you get the answer right, the game pauses for a few seconds and then moves on to the next question. If you get the answer wrong, the game pauses to show you the correct answer and then moves on to the next question after a few seconds.

Close the test movie window after you've observed how the quiz game works with its current or default settings. Now let's look at the Quiz component and the options the component provides for customizing the game. Make sure that you are on frame 1 in the scene named

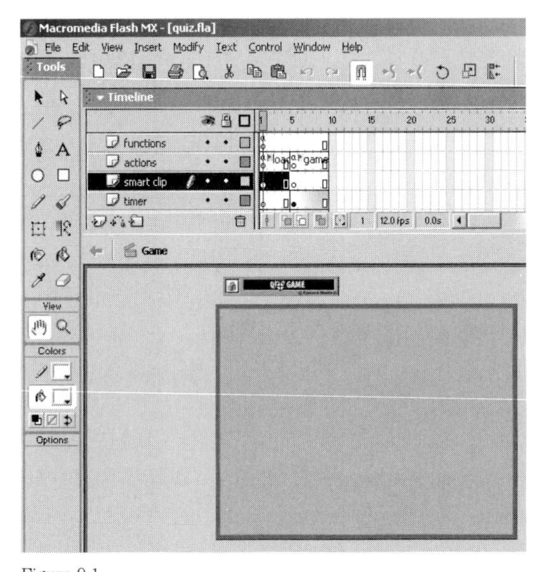

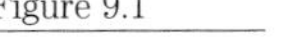

Figure 9.1

The open `quiz.fla` file

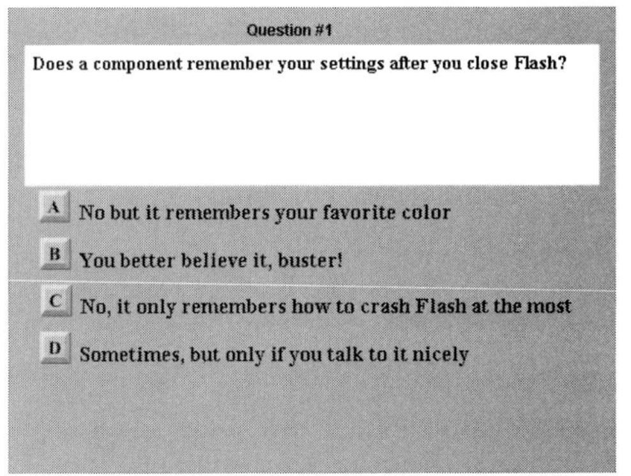

Figure 9.2

Test the Quiz game to observe how it functions with the current or default settings.

Game, and then select the Quiz component and open the Component Parameters panel. Click the Next button to view the first page of parameters (Figure 9.3).

Here is a list describing the Quiz component parameters:

File Name The File Name parameter is where you specify the name of the text file that contains the quiz questions and answers (the parameter is not case-sensitive). The text file needs to be located in the same directory as the `.swf` file for the quiz game. The game uses the text and answers in the text file to generate the game.

Game Time The Game Time parameter specifies how much time the player has to answer all the questions. The game is over when time runs out. A value of 0 in the Game Time parameter results in no time limit. That is, the player will have an infinite amount of time to play the quiz game. If you have a value greater than 0, then the component displays a Time Remaining field that shows the time counting down from the value you specified in this parameter. If the value for the Game Time parameter is 0, then the Time Remaining field is not displayed.

Question Time The Question Time parameter specifies how much time the player has to answer each individual question. If time runs out, the game moves on to the next question. A value of 0 in the Question Time parameter results in no time limit for each question. That is, the player will have an infinite amount of time to answer each question. If you have a value greater than 0, then the component displays a Question Time field that shows the time counting down from the value you specified in this parameter. If the value for the Question Time parameter is 0, then the Question Time field is not displayed.

Figure 9.3

The Component Parameters panel for the Quiz component

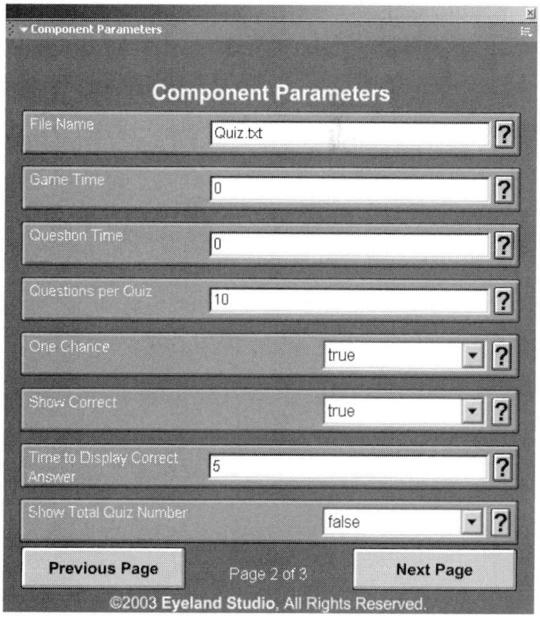

Questions Per Quiz The Questions Per Quiz parameter specifies how many questions there are in the quiz game. The Quiz component randomly displays the questions from the text file that you specify in the File Name parameter. If you have more questions in the text file than you specify in the Questions Per Quiz parameter, then the component randomly selects the number of questions you specified from the available questions in the text file. For example, if you specify 10 questions in the Questions Per Quiz parameter and you have 25 questions in your text file, then the component will randomly select 10 questions from the 25 questions.

One Chance The One Chance parameter specifies whether or not you want the player to have more than one chance to get the correct answer. If the One Chance parameter is set to True, then the player has only one chance to get the answer right. If the player gets the answer wrong when the One Chance parameter is set to True, then the game moves on to the next question. If the One Chance parameter is set to False, players can guess until they have answered the questions correctly.

Show Correct The Show Correct parameter works in conjunction with the One Chance parameter. If the One Chance parameter is set to True and the Show Correct parameter is set to True, then the component displays the correct answer when the player gets the question wrong. If the One Chance parameter is set to True and the Show Correct parameter is set to False, then the component does not display the correct answer when the player gets the question wrong.

Time To Display Correct Answer The Time To Display Correct Answer parameter works in conjunction with the two previous parameters (One Chance and Show Correct). If both of the two previous parameters are set to True, the Time To Display Correct Answer parameter specifies how long the correct answer is displayed when the player gets the answer wrong. The correct answer is displayed for the duration of the value set in this parameter, and then it moves on to the next question.

Show Total Quiz Number The Show Total Quiz Number parameter controls whether or not a text readout is displayed. The text readout displays the number of the question that is currently being displayed and how many total questions there are. For example, if you are currently answering question 3 out of 10 questions, the readout will display "Question #3 out of 10." Setting this value to False removes this readout.

Correct Sound, Wrong Sound, Waiting Sound, and Question Time Expired These parameters specify the identifier or "linkage" names for sound files that will be played in certain circumstances:

PARAMETER	SOUND PLAYED WHEN...
Correct Sound	The player answers the question correctly.
Wrong Sound	The player selects the wrong answer for the question.
Waiting Sound	The game is waiting for you to answer a question.
Question Time Expired	Time is expired for the question.

If you leave a field blank, no sound is played in that situation. The sound will also not play if you enter the wrong value for the identifier in a field or if you forget to set the identifier for a particular sound effect.

The Waiting Sound should be a looping sound; it is designed to give the player a auditory clue that time is passing. The Question Time Expired sound is only played if you have entered a value other than 0 for the Question Time parameter.

The first parameter in the custom UI for the Quiz component already references the `quiz.txt` file. This is a variable because you may need to name the text file something other than `quiz`. For example, if you use this component for several quizzes on your site, you might want to use a different text file for the different quizzes. If so, they can't all be named `quiz.txt`. For now, however, let's leave the value for the File Name parameter as Quiz.txt.

Figure 9.4

Setting the Game Time and Question Time parameters

Component Parameters

Parameter	Value
File Name	Quiz.txt
Game Time	100
Question Time	10
Questions per Quiz	10
One Chance	true

Change the value of the Game Time parameter to 100 and change the value of the Question Time parameter to 10 (see Figure 9.4). When you are done, close the Component Parameters panel and test the movie.

Now when you play the game, you will notice there are two timers on the top left and top right of the game. The timer on the top left is labeled Time Remaining, and it counts down from 100. The timer on the top right is labeled Question Time, and it counts down from 10 for each question. If you do not answer each question within 10 seconds, you will see the message "Too Late" appear on the screen for a moment before the game moves on to the next question (Figure 9.5). After you have tested the movie to see the results of the changes, close the test movie window.

As you can see by this simple example, the Quiz component's parameters allow you to adjust the timing and pacing of the quiz game. You can set the quiz game to quiz the player on 100 questions or on only two. You can set the quiz to have a time limit of 3 minutes or give the player unlimited time to play the game. You can adjust the game so that the player has to answer correctly before moving on to the next question, or you can force the game to move on to the next question whether or not the player has selected a correct answer.

Figure 9.5

The game flashes a "Too Late" message when time has run out.

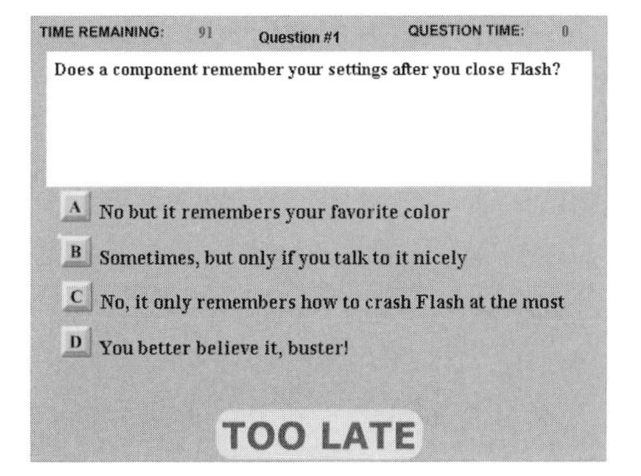

You can edit and adjust the parameters and test the results until the game functions as you prefer. Editing the values in the component's parameters is significantly easier than rooting around for the actual variables in the game's code in order to accomplish the same thing.

You can also edit the graphics and the audio in the same way we have discussed in previous chapters. For example, you don't need to settle for the yellow buttons used for selecting the questions. You can edit the movie clips that contain the artwork and leave their instance names intact.

For example, go to frame 5 on the main Timeline and select the movie clip that contains the button labeled A. Open the Properties panel and notice that the movie clip has the instance name "answer1" (see Figure 9.6). You can edit this movie clip and change the graphics or the font to any image or font you want. The important thing is that you make sure that the movie clip named "answer1" is still on the stage when you play the movie, because the Quiz component needs that movie clip to function properly.

Customizing the Images

Of course, the main content for any quiz game is the set of questions. The questions are in the `quiz.txt` file. The questions can be in any text file, but they do need to be set up in a specific format. Let's look at the `quiz.txt` file. You can open `quiz.txt` in any text editor, such as Notepad (see Figure 9.7).

Let's look at the first line in the text file:

```
&question1=What book will teach you how to utilize cool resources
called components?&
```

First notice that the line begins and ends with the ampersand (&) symbol. Flash uses the ampersand symbol to tell each entry apart from one another. It is important that you have an ampersand symbol at the beginning and end of each entry.

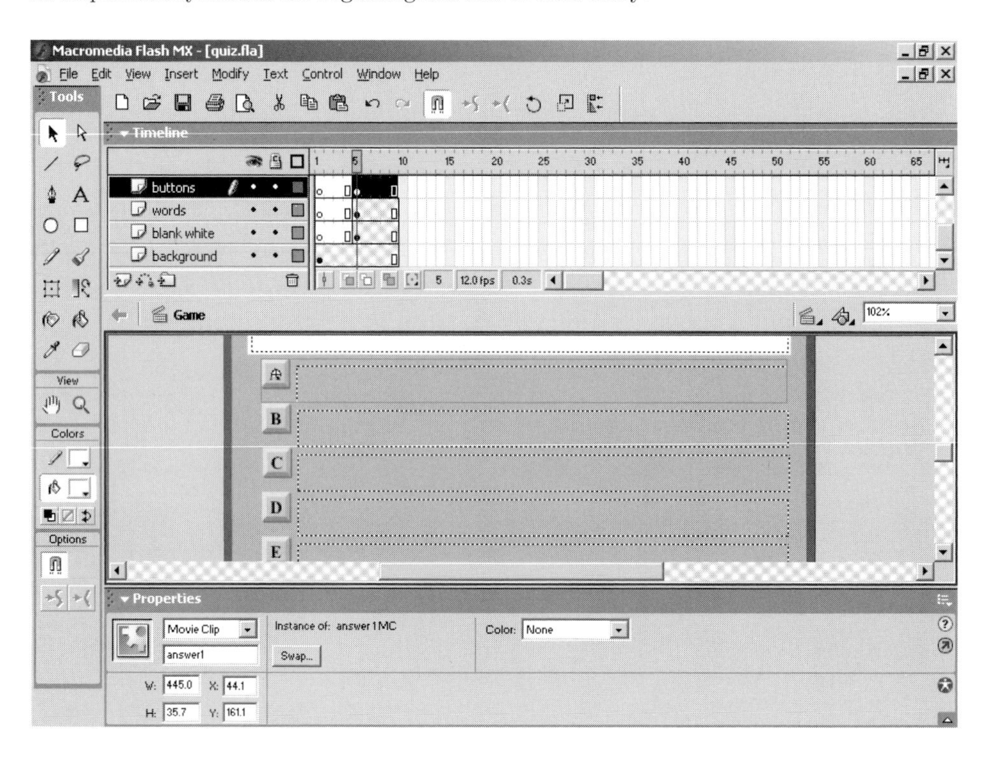

Figure 9.6

You can edit the movie clips to change the graphics, but be sure to leave the instance names for the movie clips as they are.

Next notice that the first line is broken into two parts separated by the equal (=) symbol. On the left side is the variable name (*question1*), and on the right side is the question (`What book will teach you how to utilize cool resources called components?`). Notice that quotation marks are not necessary for the question. If you entered the same sort of variable in Flash, you'd need quotation marks, but Flash parses the *question1* variable correctly without the quotation marks in the text file.

Now let's look at the next four lines in the text file:

```
&answer1_1=The Hidden Power of Flash Components&
&answer1_2=The Scarlet Pimpernel&
&answer1_3=The Catcher in the Rye&
&answer1_4=The Cat in the Hat&
```

These lines are structured the same as the first line. Each line is encased within ampersand symbols. There is a variable name on the left of the equal sign and an answer on the right of the equal sign. Notice that the variable names are sequential. The first is named *answer1_1*, the second is *answer1_2*, and so on.

Notice that all of the *answer1* variables go with *question1*. If you look at the other questions and answers, you'll note that each question is numbered, and the answers to that question have the same number.

The Quiz component allows you to have as many as five answers for each question or as few as two. You do not need to have the same number of questions for each question; one question may have three answers and another have four. In this case, if we want to add an answer, it would look something like this:

```
&answer1_5=Of Mice and Men&
```

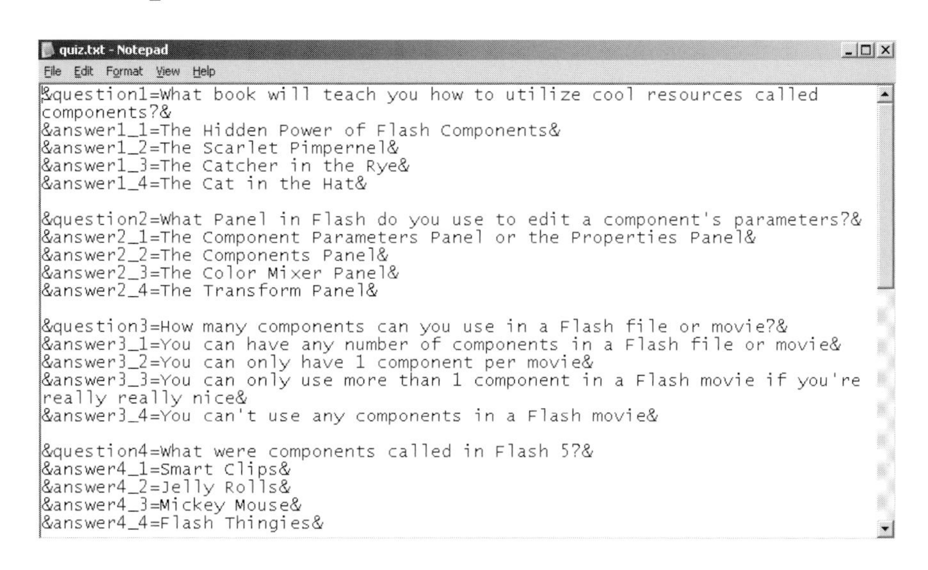

```
quiz.txt - Notepad
File Edit Format View Help
&question1=What book will teach you how to utilize cool resources called
components?&
&answer1_1=The Hidden Power of Flash Components&
&answer1_2=The Scarlet Pimpernel&
&answer1_3=The Catcher in the Rye&
&answer1_4=The Cat in the Hat&

&question2=What Panel in Flash do you use to edit a component's parameters?&
&answer2_1=The Component Parameters Panel or the Properties Panel&
&answer2_2=The Components Panel&
&answer2_3=The Color Mixer Panel&
&answer2_4=The Transform Panel&

&question3=How many components can you use in a Flash file or movie?&
&answer3_1=You can have any number of components in a Flash file or movie&
&answer3_2=You can only have 1 component per movie&
&answer3_3=You can only use more than 1 component in a Flash movie if you're
really really nice&
&answer3_4=You can't use any components in a Flash movie&

&question4=What were components called in Flash 5?&
&answer4_1=Smart Clips&
&answer4_2=Jelly Rolls&
&answer4_3=Mickey Mouse&
&answer4_4=Flash Thingies&
```

Figure 9.7

The `quiz.txt` file conforms to a specific structure in order to work properly with the Quiz component in Flash.

The Quiz component knows that this is the fifth answer to question 1 by how the variable name is structured. So the game will display five responses. You might wonder, however, how the game knows which answer is correct. The first answer in the text file is always the correct answer. So for each question, you simply need to enter the correct answer as the first answer. When the component generates the game, it randomly positions the answers to the question. Therefore *answer1_1* might appear as answer D instead of answer A.

As you can see, the format for the `quiz.txt` file is easy to grasp and easy to manage. You can experiment with it by deleting a few of the fourth answers for the questions. Let's add a ninth and a tenth question. Add the following to the end of the `quiz.txt` file (but before the line `&endOfFile=1&`):

```
&question9=Can components be made to work with external text files?&
&answer9_1=But of course, don't be ridiculous!&
&answer9_2=Nope&
&answer9_3=Forget about it&
&answer9_4=No and stop asking me all these silly questions, buster!&

&question10=Are components too cool for school?&
&answer10_1=Oh yeah, baby!&
&answer10_2=No, I think Brussels Sprouts are cooler.&
&answer10_3=What was the question again?&
&answer10_4=Whatever, ya geek.&
```

Notice that to add new questions, we simply name the variables sequentially. For example, in the original `quiz.txt` file, the last question variable was *question8*. Therefore, we start by creating a variable named *question9* and then add answer variables that correspond to the *question9* variable. There's nothing to it.

Editing a Concentration Component

Quiz games are well and good, but now let's look at a game that is more graphic-dependent. One of the classic games of all time is concentration or memory. Concentration is one of those game that everyone knows how to play. While it's not the most exciting game in the world, it has a lot of practical applications because you can place just about any set of images in a concentration game. Let's look at a component for creating concentration games.

Close the `quiz.fla` file and open the `concentration.fla` file from the Chapter 9 folder on the CD. Go to the first frame on the Game scene and notice the instance of the Concentration Game component above the upper-left corner of the stage (see Figure 9.8).

You should notice the images to the left of the stage. You will be working with them shortly, but first let's look at the parameters in the Concentration Game component. Select the component and open the Component Parameters panel. Click on the Next Page button to go to the second page (see Figure 9.9).

Here is a list of the component's parameters:

Game Time The Game Time parameter specifies how much time the player has to make all the matches. It is otherwise the same as the Game Time parameter described earlier in the section "Editing a Quiz Component."

Number Of Available Pieces The Number Of Available Pieces parameter specifies the potential number of pairs the game has to draw from. This parameter is a little difficult to understand, so let's use an example. Let's say you have specified 4 rows and 5 columns. This means that there will be 10 matching pairs because 5 times 4 equals 20, and 20 divided by 2 equals 10. However, let's say you've created 15 object pairs. This means that you have up to 15 object pairs from which the game could randomly choose 10.

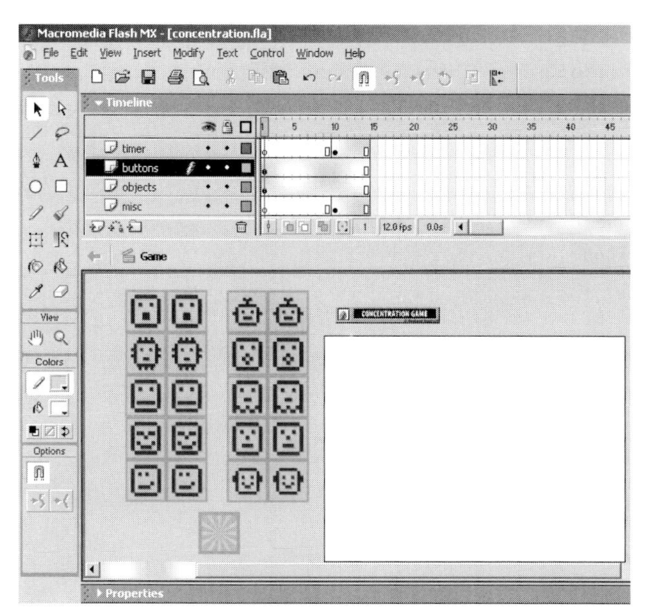

Figure 9.8

Open the `concentration.fla` file and go to the first frame on the Game scene.

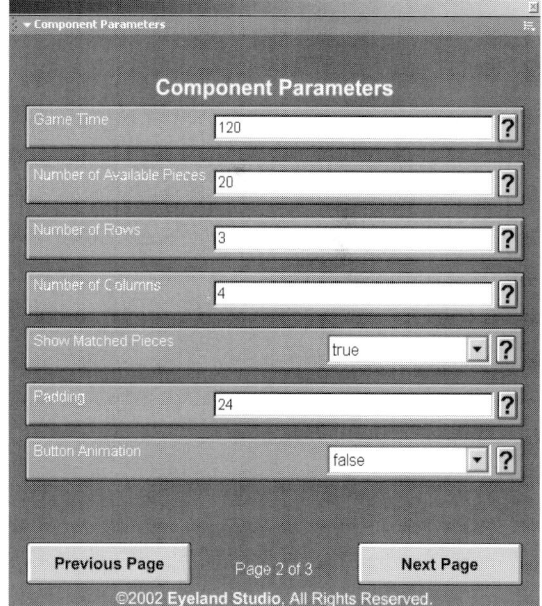

Figure 9.9

The Component Parameters panel for the Concentration Game component

In the example above, you would want to enter 30 (15 times 2) for the Number Of Available Pieces parameter. The concentration game engine would then know that there are up to 15 possible objects that it can use for the 10 available matches for the game. Thus this parameter allows you to create a slightly more variable and interesting game because the game will not always use the exact same objects each time.

Number Of Rows, Number Of Columns These establish the number of rows and columns for the objects and buttons. The number of rows times the number of columns must equal an even number. For example, 3 rows and 3 columns will not work because the nature of the game is that the player must match two objects, and, of course, 3 time 3 equals 9. This means there would be one extra piece, making it impossible for a player to win.

Show Matched Pieces The Show Matched Pieces parameter establishes whether or not the objects will disappear when they are matched. There are only two options: True or False. True leaves the pieces visible when the player matches them, and False makes them invisible when the player matches them.

Padding The Padding parameter establishes the distance between each of the objects. For example, a value of 10 spaces each of the objects and their corresponding buttons approximately 10 pixels apart. A value of 0 forces the objects and their corresponding objects and buttons to abut one another.

If you want to hide an image below the objects/buttons like in the classic Concentration game, use a Padding value of 0 and set the Show Matched Pieces parameter to False. This forces the objects and buttons to cover any image you have in the background. When the player makes a match, the objects will disappear and reveal the background image through the vacant spaces.

Button Animation The Button Animation parameter establishes whether or not the button will play some animation when revealing the objects underneath. There are only two options: True or False. True displays any animation in the Button movie clip when you click it. You will need to set the Button movie clip with an animation after the first frame. The animation must end with nothing showing so that the object can be seen. A value of False causes the object to be displayed immediately after you click on the button.

Object Base Name The Object Base Name parameter refers to the instance names used on the objects. You should assign each object an instance name. For example, the 10 objects that come with this game are named: "object1," "object2," and so on. The basis for these instance names is "object" with a number appended at the end. If, for any reason, you want to change the instance names to something else, you'll need to change the reference in the Object Base Name parameter. For example, if you want to change the name of your objects or game pieces to "image1," "image2," and so on, then you need to enter the word **image** in the Object Base Name parameter. See the "Replacing the Images" section later in this chapter for more information on working with the object.

Button Base Name The Button Base Name parameter refers to the instance name used on the button. The *button* is the image that covers each of the objects. The button artwork is contained within a button that is, in turn, contained within a movie clip. That movie clip should have an instance name assigned to it. The default name for this movie clip is Button. If, for any reason, you want to change the instance name to something else, you'll need to change the reference in the Button Base Name parameter. For example, if you want to change the instance name of your button to Cardback, you'll need to enter **Cardback** in the Button Base Name parameter.

X Placement, Y Placement These parameters establish the x- and y- coordinates (respectively) for the upper-left corner of the grid of the objects. If both are both set to 0, the grid will start at the upper-left corner of the stage. For the X Placement parameter, negative numbers move the starting point to the left, and positive numbers move it to the right. Usually, you will want to use a number that is greater than or equal to 0, because negative numbers will result in all or part of some of the objects being off the stage or visible area. For the Y Placement parameter, negative numbers move the starting point up, and positive numbers move it down. Usually, you will want to use a number that's greater than or equal to 0, because negative numbers will result in all or part of some of the objects being off the stage or visible area.

Object Sound Base Name The Object Sound Base Name parameter refers to the identifier set in the Linkage Properties dialog box. This parameter allows you to set a base name for the identifiers so that you can set a sound for each of the pieces in the game. The default for the Object Sound Base Name parameter is "sound." In the library, you'll find an Audio library containing many sound files with identifier names such as "sound1," "sound2," and so on. The audio file that has the linkage name "sound1" corresponds to "object1a" and "object1b." The audio file that has the linkage name "sound2" corresponds to "objet2a" and "object2b" and so on. You can leave this parameter blank if you do not want matching sounds for the game pieces.

CorrectSound, WrongSound These parameters specify the "identifier" for the audio effect that you enter in the Symbol Linkage Properties dialog box. You should not enter the actual filename here. For example, if you want to use an audio file called `correctsound.wav` for the sound effect that plays when the player makes a correct match, you do *not* enter `correctsound.wav` in the CorrectSound parameter. Instead, you assign an identifier to the `correctsound.wav` file from the Symbol Linkage Properties dialog box. This *identifier* is what you enter in the CorrectSound parameter. Leave the CorrectSound and/or WrongSound parameters blank if you do not want an audio file to play when the player makes a match.

Now let's modify a few parameters and start to customize the game a little. Follow these steps:

1. Set the Game Time parameter to 0.
2. Change the Number Of Rows parameter to 4 and the Number Of Columns to 5.
3. Set the Show Matched Pieces parameter to False.
4. Set the Padding parameter to 0. Figure 9.10 shows these parameter settings.
5. Click on the Next Page button to go to the third page of the custom UI for the Concentration Game component's parameters.
6. Change the value for the X Placement and Y Placement parameters to 0 (see Figure 9.11).
7. Close the Component Parameters panel.

Replacing the Images

Before we test the movie, let's talk about what we've done in the component's parameters. First, we removed the time limit so that people playing the game have an infinite amount of time to make the matches. Next, we changed the rows to 4 and the columns to 5. This means there will be 20 game pieces or objects on the stage. Setting the padding to 0 will display all the pieces directly next to one another. Then we set the pieces so that they will be arrayed out starting at the upper-left corner of the stage.

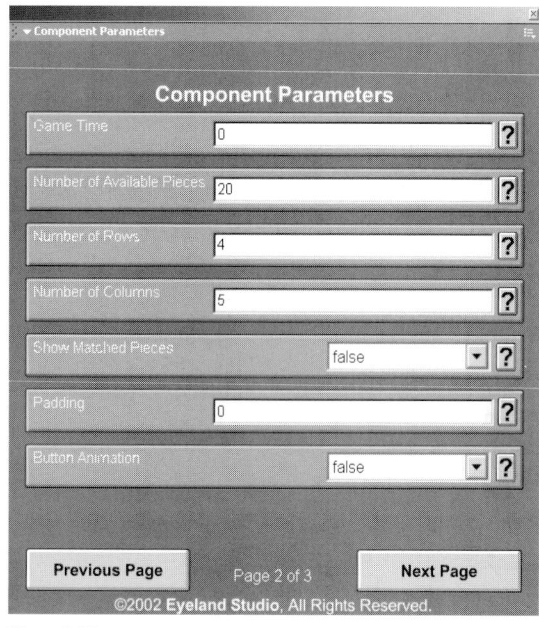

Figure 9.10

Editing the parameters for the Concentration Game component

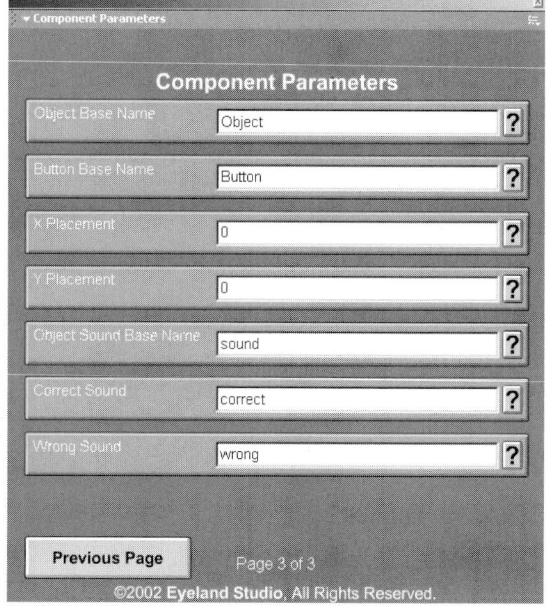

Figure 9.11

Editing the X Placement and Y Placement parameters

Let's say we want only the game pieces visible. That means we need to change the stage size so that it will only display the game pieces and nothing else. The game pieces or objects are all 75 pixels square. Therefore, to determine our stage size, we multiply 5 times 75 for the width and 4 times 75 for the height. Follow these steps:

1. Select Document from the Modify menu to open the Document Properties dialog box.
2. Change the Width to 375 and the Height to 300.
3. Click OK to close the Document Properties dialog box.

Now the stage size matches the size all of the game pieces. In other words, the game pieces will cover the entire stage.

One other change that we made to the Concentration Game component's parameters was setting the Show Matching Pieces parameter to False. This means that when players match pieces, those game pieces will go away. Let's place a picture below the game pieces so that when the player matches the pieces, an image will appear underneath.

1. Create a new layer named "background" and place that layer below all the other layers.
2. Place a keyframe on frame 10 on the new background layer.
3. Open the library, open the folder named `Bitmaps`, and drag the `clown.jpg` onto the keyframe on frame 10 of the new background layer.
4. Center the `clown.jpg` image on the stage, as shown in Figure 9.12.

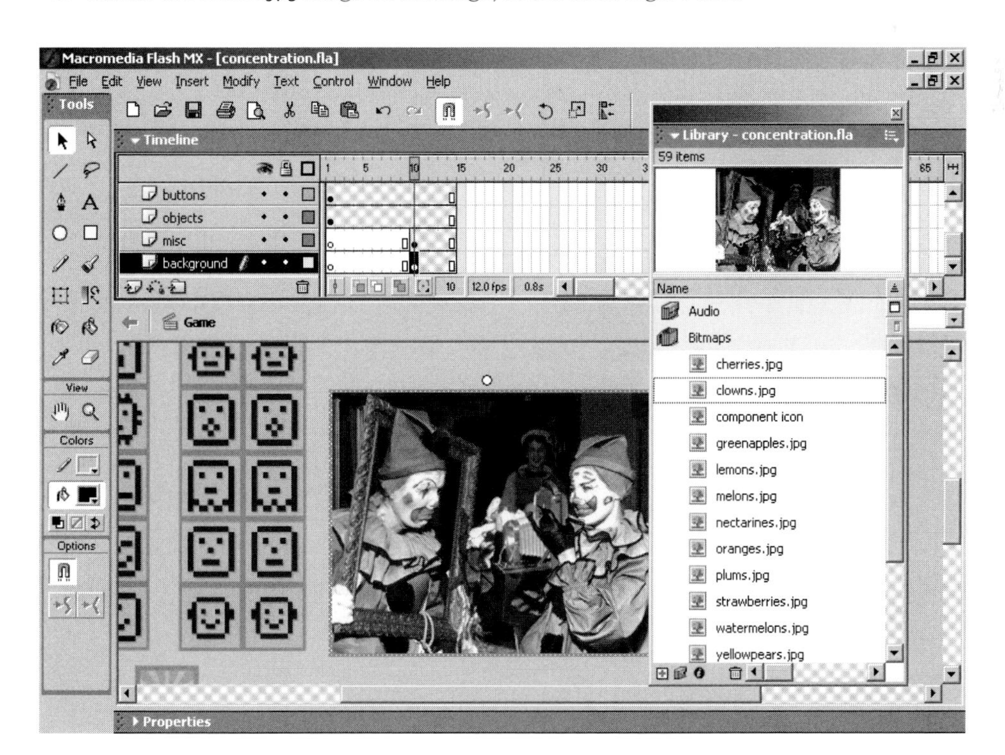

Figure 9.12

Placing the `clown.jpg` image on the stage

Now let's change the imagery that you need to match in the game. Notice the images to the left of the stage. These are the images that the player must match. They aren't very interesting, so let's change them.

1. Select the image in the top-left corner.
2. Open the Properties panel and notice that it has the instance name "object1a" (see Figure 9.13). The game will not work properly if the objects are not named with this syntax. However, you can edit these movie clips and put whatever artwork you want in them.
3. Double-click the object1a movie clip in the library to open it on the stage.
4. Open the folder named `Pics` in the library.
5. Delete the artwork in the object1 movie clip and drag the movie clip named "pic1" onto the stage.
6. Center the movie clip on the stage.
7. Return to the main Timeline and notice that the new artwork is in both the movie clip with the instance name "object1a" and the movie clip with the instance name "object1b" (see Figure 9.14).
8. Repeat this process for all the other objects on the stage. For example, replace the artwork in the object2 movie clip with the "pic2" movie clip and so on. When you are finished, the objects on the stage should look like Figure 9.15.

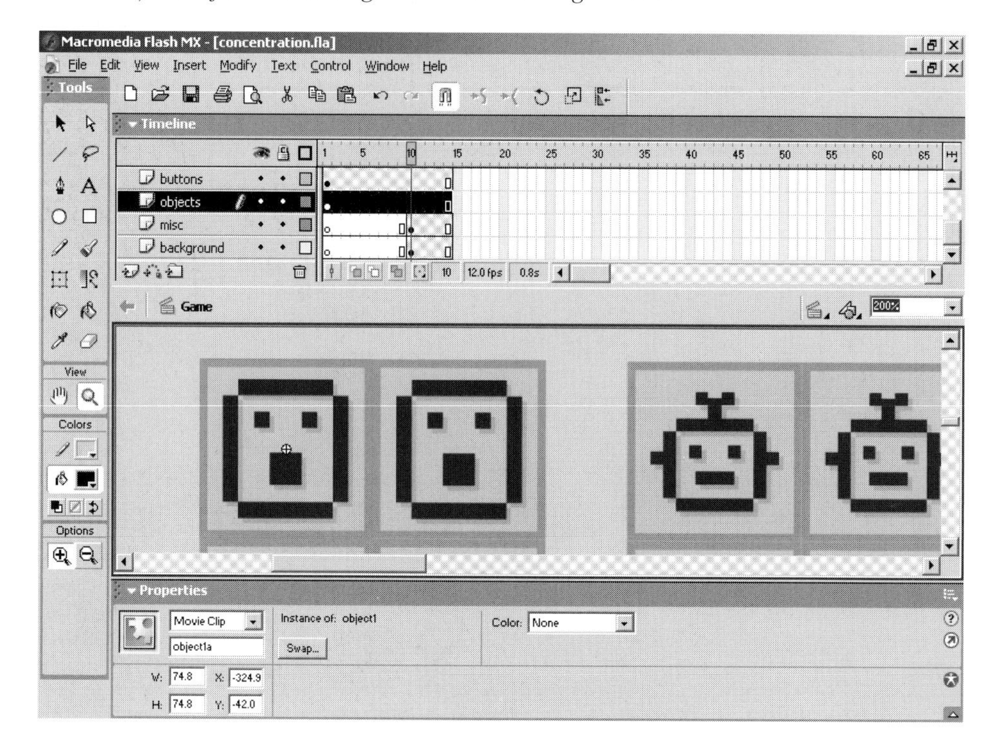

Figure 9.13
The first object in the upper-right corner has the instance name "object1a."

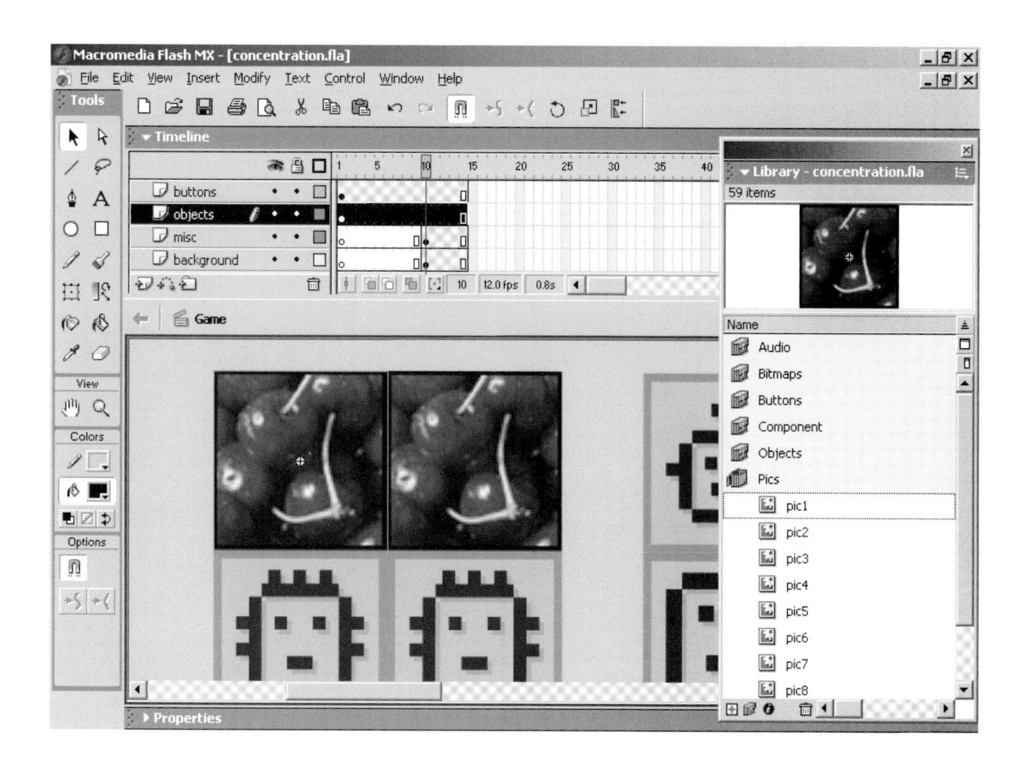

Figure 9.14

Edit the object1 movie clip and replace the original artwork with the pic1 movie clip.

Figure 9.15

Replace the artwork in all of the objects with the corresponding movie clips in the Pic library.

Now you're ready to test the movie. Notice that when you match the pieces, the image shows through the background, as in Figure 9.16. Also notice that the game uses all the game pieces you placed into the object movie clips.

Figure 9.16
The background image shows through when the player makes a match.

Conclusion

This chapter showed you how easy it is to customize the Quiz and Concentration Game components. The components take care of the functionality, leaving you with the relatively simple tasks of adding questions or placing any artwork you want to use with the games. All of the tedious programmatic issues are taken care of. Component-based games give Flash game designers a great competitive advantage. The components allow you to focus on content issues like artwork and audio. With components, you can make better games in much less time.

Of course, the examples in this chapter only scratch the surface of the sort of games that can be created with components. See `www.eyeland.com` or `www.gamesinaflash.com` for more component-based games.

Chapter 10: Creating Components

The components discussed so far touch on nearly every possible type, from user interfaces and text effects to animations and games. However, what do you do when you come up with a new component idea that you would like to see in action? Now the spotlight is on you; it is time to use your imagination to think of some original ideas, or to just reexamine projects you have created in the past and see what elements could be "componentized."

Knowing how to make a component will be a substantially useful tool to have under your belt. You will see that anything worth building once is in fact not worth building twice. When you have taken time to create an element, you should consider creating a generalized version, in the form of a component.

In this chapter, we explore something quite different from the previous. You will become familiar with the workflow involved in creating a component and learn how to use nearly every feature Flash offers in component creation. This chapter is abstract and complicated all at once, and it's by far the most advanced work that you'll encounter in the entire book, so pay close attention.

- **The component creation process**
- **Modules of a component**
- **The architecture of a professional component**
- **Code of a component**

The Process of Component Creation

When you sit down to create a component, you must put quite a bit of thought and brainstorming into the process. Think of all the different aspects of the component you want the user to have control of, and of course having an inkling of an idea of how you will program the functionality of the component won't hurt.

Above all, make the component as easy to use as possible. The point of taking the time to create components is to make working with a particular element a breeze with as little extra effort as possible. Do as much as possible to keep the user from having to do anything themselves. For example, don't have your component call on the user to provide a certain graphic if you can create this graphic through the use of Flash's drawing methods. Take the extra effort to keep the user from having to providing anything. All of the additional efforts you put into the component during the development process will truly pay off when you use the component for the first time.

The motivation for components may or may not be something new to you. If you're a developer, you have probably at one time or another needed to modularize certain aspects of a project, meaning you divided large tasks into smaller tasks, quite possibly the most important concept in large-scale projects. Likewise, your component should be abstracted to be independent from outside elements—in a sense, a self-supported subprogram that operates separately from your movie.

Designing a Simple Component

To drive the modularity concept home, we will create a very simple component that does not necessarily take advantage of everything a component has to offer, but it does show the basic structure of a component. This component is very simple so that you can ease into the process. It merely draws a bunch of random squares on the screen, but it will contain quite a few parameters to customize how the squares are drawn; however, that is part of the brainstorming process.

GOOD PROGRAMMING APPLIES TO COMPONENTS

Never hard-code any values. If you find yourself using a number or string that is not obvious—for example, using the number 1.67 in some mathematics calculation—then you should set a variable (or, as it applies to components, define a parameter) to hold your numerical value. This is why we use `Math.PI` and `Math.E` for the values of widely used constants instead of hard-coding 3.14 and 2.81 everywhere. This principle of general programming is also important to practice while creating components, except instead of creating a new variable for the value, you use a parameter in the component.

We are going to give the user control of seven different parameters to customize this component:

- Obviously, one parameter will control the number of squares drawn on the stage.
- Another parameter will let the user assign each square a random color or a predefined color. For the latter case, we will include two parameters to control the fill and border color of the squares.
- There will also be a parameter to set the thickness of the borders of each rendered square.
- To determine the dimensions of each square, a parameter will specify the maximum and minimum dimensions of each square, and the rendered squares will have a random width between the two values.
- Finally, to spread the squares across the stage randomly, we need the dimensions of the stage, which is what the last parameter will track.

Randomizing Colors

Now that we know the parameters we are going to use, we should think about how to accomplish the task of drawing the squares on the stage. There are quite a few small code snippets that will help us in this large task.

Remember, we are just brainstorming the code for now. We'll enter it into ActionScript later in the chapter.

First, how can we calculate a random number between any two numbers? This will mainly be used to calculate a random dimension for the squares between the two predefined dimensions given by the user. If the minimum and maximum numbers are a and b, we can get a random number c between them with the following code:

```
c = Math.random ( ) * (b - a) + a;
```

Also, we need to calculate a random color to apply to the squares when the user chooses to color each rendered square differently. As you probably know, a hexadecimal number of the form RRGGBB—where RR, GG, and BB are two-digit hexadecimals—represents a color with red, green, and blue parts. For example, FF0000 is a full red, 00FF00 is a full green, and 0000FF is a full blue. Obviously, 000000 is black and FFFFFF is white. There are decimal numbers that correspond to hexadecimal numbers, but they do not correspond to colors in such an obvious way. For instance, the decimal representation of FF0000 is 16711680.

Fortunately, Flash's ActionScript can handle hexadecimal numbers so that we don't have to worry about making conversions. To specify that a number is being used as a hexadecimal, you must append the prefix 0x to the number. So, the hexadecimal number FF00FF becomes `0xFF00FF` in ActionScript. With this knowledge, we can write the following code to calculate a random color in the entire spectrum:

```
random_color = Math.floor (Math.random ( ) * 0xFFFFFF);
```

Drawing Squares

Finally, a useful piece of code to have at hand is one for drawing an arbitrarily sized square with arbitrary colors for its border and fill. Let's assume we have two variables already declared, *min_dim* and *max_dim*, which hold the range of the square's possible dimensions. To start off, we'll calculate a random dimension for the square and two random colors for the square's border and fill:

```
dim = Math.random ( ) * (max_dim - min_dim) + min_dim;
border_color = Math.floor (Math.random ( ) * 0xFFFFFF);
fill_color   = Math.floor (Math.random ( ) * 0xFFFFFF);
```

With these preliminary values calculated, we can now draw the square using Flash MX's new drawing methods. The drawing methods are functions attached to every movie clip that allow you to draw certain geometric primitives, such as lines and filled objects that are defined by a set of points. A square is made up of four vertices and has equal-length sides. We start the drawing process by setting the line style of the movie clip we are drawing in; for simplicity, we'll draw to the `_root`. We will also start with a 1-pixel border for the square, but later in the component, we will use the value specified by the user. The `lineStyle` method takes three arguments: the first for the line's thickness, the second for the color of the line, and the last for the alpha, or transparency, of the line.

```
_root.lineStyle (1.0, border_color, 100.0);
```

Next, we start the filling procedure with the `beginFill` method. It takes two arguments: the first for the fill's color and the second for the fill's alpha. All vertices set with the `lineTo` method after `beginFill` has been called will create a fill of the polygon defined by the `lineTo` points. When you are done creating the fill, you must call `endFill` to properly stop drawing; failing to call this method will result in total disaster for your ActionScripted drawings.

```
_root.beginFill (this.fill_color, 100.0);
```

Finally, we specify the vertices of the square, thus drawing a filled square on the stage. Note that for this small demonstration, we are going to draw the square with its top-left vertex at (0,0), its top-right vertex at (*dim*,0), its bottom-right vertex at (*dim*,*dim*), and its bottom-left vertex at (0,*dim*). When we go into the actual code for the component, all the vertices will be shifted by certain values since the squares should be positioned randomly across the screen.

```
_root.moveTo (0.0, 0.0);      // upper-left corner
_root.lineTo (dim, 0.0);      // upper-right corner
_root.lineTo (dim, dim);      // bottom-right corner
_root.lineTo (0.0, dim);      // bottom-left corner
_root.endFill ( );            // stop the fill drawing
```

All of this code combined draws a square on the stage. Listing 10.1 shows the code in full for your reference.

Listing 10.1

Drawing a Square on the Stage

```
dim = Math.random ( ) * (max_dim - min_dim) + min_dim;
border_color = Math.floor (Math.random ( ) * 0xFFFFFF);
fill_color   = Math.floor (Math.random ( ) * 0xFFFFFF);
_root.lineStyle (1.0, border_color, 100.0);
_root.beginFill (this.fill_color, 100.0);
_root.moveTo (0.0, 0.0);      // upper-left corner
_root.lineTo (dim, 0.0);      // upper-right corner
_root.lineTo (dim, dim);      // bottom-right corner
_root.lineTo (0.0, dim);      // bottom-left corner
_root.endFill ( );            // stop the fill drawing
```

Basic Component Creation: The RandomSquares Component

Once we have brainstormed the component's formation, we can dive into its development. We start by creating a new Flash movie named `RandomSquaresComponent.fla`, which will hold the component and all of its assets. By this point in the book, you know that a component is simply a movie clip with added functionality by means of customizing its parameters. Therefore, we must first create a movie clip that will be the graphical representation of our component. This is a very important notion; our component is abstracted into two separate parts: the code, which handles functionality, and the graphics, which provide the user interface. So, create a new movie clip by pressing Command/Ctrl+F8 and name it RandomSquares. This will be the movie clip users drag to the stage when they want to use that particular element.

To be as organized as possible, a folder structure has been created for the component in the library of the component file. A folder named `RandomSquares Component` has been created, in the root of the library, where the component and its assets are kept. The component sits immediately in this folder along with another folder that will hold all of the component's assets—that is, any other symbols the component needs to function properly.

Defining Parameters

Right now, nothing differentiates the common movie clip from our supposed component. The crucial step where the movie clip crosses into the component domain is done by right-clicking the movie clip in the library and selecting Component Definition. In the dialog box that opens (see Figure 10.1), you add the parameters that users can edit.

To add and remove parameters, use the plus and minus buttons at the top. The first column of the parameters box is the name that appears to users when they edit the parameters in the Component Parameters panel. The name should be a very short, descriptive phrase about the component.

The second column is the name of the variable that will hold the parameter's information. This value is automatically placed in the movie clip at the very start of the movie. The third column is the default value of the parameter.

The last column of the RandomSquares component is a choice of nine data types that the parameter can use, as shown in Figure 10.2. Data types are very important for parameters; hence the large selection. Always know what data type a parameter will hold and stick by that choice. Table 10.1 is a description of each data type.

Table 10.1

Flash MX Data Types

DATA TYPE	DESCRIPTION
Default	This data type should never be used for Flash MX components. I discuss the Default data type in Chapter 12, where we'll see how to make Flash 5–compliant components.
Array	Allows you to use an array in the component. In the Component Parameters panel, the user can add and remove elements from the array. Elements are stored as strings.
Object	Allows you to use an object in the component. You can use the Component Definition dialog box to add properties to the object, which can be set by the user in the Component Parameters panel. Use this parameter whenever you have a large number of parameters that pertain to essentially the same thing. For example, your parameters call for the user to specify the width, height and color of a square that will be drawn on the screen, then all three of those parameters could be put in an Object.
List	Allows you to use a combo box interface for a set of choices. You add the choices to the list in the Component Definition dialog box, and the user chooses from the list in the Component Parameters panel.
String	A simple string data type.
Number	A simple number data type.
Boolean	A list in which the only choices are True and False.
Font Name	Produces a combo box with all the fonts on the user's computer to choose from. The user can either choose a font on their system, or type in a string. The latter option is important when using Shared Fonts, as we will see later.
Color	Produces a color palette from which the user chooses a specific color.

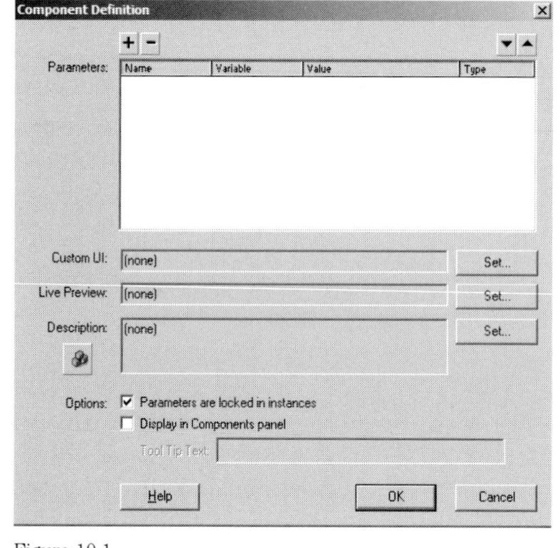

Figure 10.1

Open the Component Definition dialog box to define its parameters.

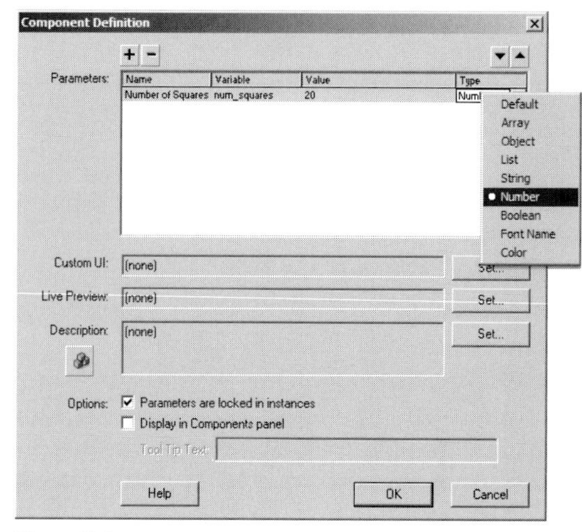

Figure 10.2

You can choose from many data types for your parameters.

Since we have already planned out the parameters that we want to use, we can simply add each one to the Component Definition dialog box. Once a parameter is added, be sure to set the parameter's data type before you set its initial value; when a data type is selected, the value column of the parameter is cleared. Figure 10.3 shows how the parameters were entered for the RandomSquares component.

The general steps you take to add a parameter to a component are outlined here:

1. Right-click the component in the library and select Component Definition.
2. Click the plus sign in the upper-left corner of the Component Definition dialog box to add a parameter to the Parameters data grid.
3. Click the text "varName" and type a very short phrase to describe the purpose of the parameter. This is what users will see when they open the Parameters panel.
4. Click in the blank area in the Variable column and type the name of the variable that will hold the parameter's value. This is the name of the variable that you will use in your code for the component.
5. Click the drop-down menu under the Type column and select the data type for the parameter.
6. At this point, you might have to do different things depending on which data type you selected:
   a. If you select Array, double-click the brackets under the Value column. This will bring up an interface where you can add and remove elements to the array for the default value of the array.
   b. If you select Object, double-click the curly braces under the Value column. This will bring up an interface where you can add and remove properties to the object and set their default values.
   c. If you select List, double-click the text <empty> under the Value column. This will bring up the same interface as Array, and you add and remove list items the same way. However, remember that items you add to this list are simply the possible values for the parameter, from which the user will choose.
   d. If you select Number or String, simply click the 0 (Number) or text defaultValue (String) and enter the default value for the parameter.
   e. If you select Boolean, click the drop-down menu under the Value column and select the default Boolean value (True or False) for the parameter.

Figure 10.3

The Component Definition dialog box with all the parameters added

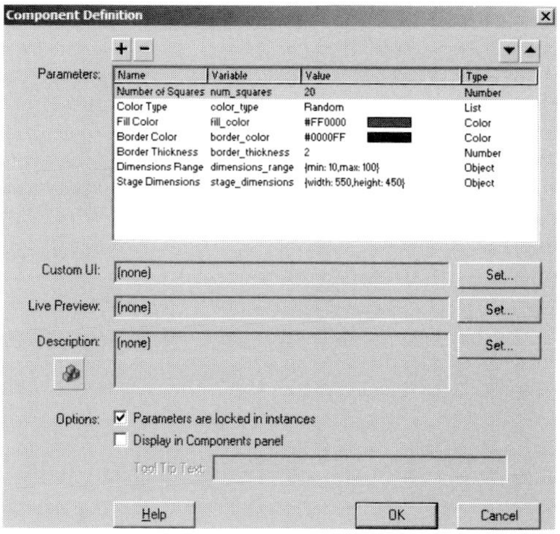

f. If you select Font, click the drop-down menu under the Value column and select the default font for the parameter.

g. If you select Color, click the color palette under the Value column and select the default color for the parameter.

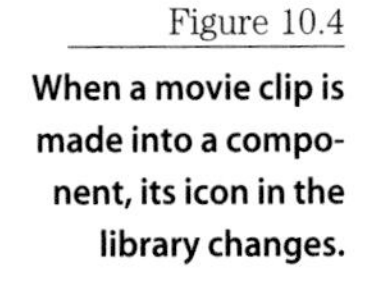

Figure 10.4

When a movie clip is made into a component, its icon in the library changes.

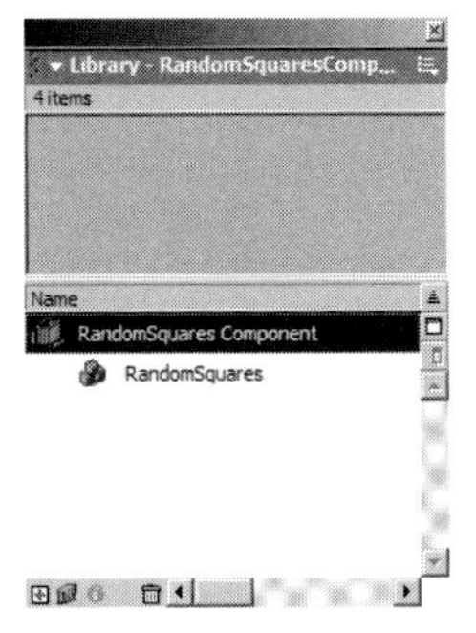

To utilize many different data types at once, the parameters that hold the minimum and maximum possible dimensions of the squares and the parameters that hold the width and height of the stage have been coupled into just two object variables. That is, one object has two properties, "min" and "max," which correspond to the minimum and maximum dimensions, and another object has the two properties "width" and "height," which correspond to the width and height of the stage.

The Color Type parameter is a list that holds two values: Random and Constant. This parameter controls whether the colors of the squares should be random.

When you close the Component Definition dialog box, your movie clip will appear a little differently in the library, as shown in Figure 10.4. The movie clip's icon has changed to an image of orange, green, and blue blocks to signify that the movie clip is serving as a component.

How a Component and Its Parameters Are Related

Oddly enough, just with these few mediocre tasks taken care of, and no actual functionality programmed, you can see how any component works in the first place. Using the debugging features of Flash, you can see that any movie clip to which you've added parameters is automatically given an `onClipEvent` function, which declares all the variables associated with the parameters (as shown in Figure 10.5).

To check this yourself, drag an instance of the component to the stage and test the movie in debugging mode by pressing Command+Shift+Enter/Ctrl+Shift+Enter. You will see a drop-down window in the debugging panel that displays every movie clip and button in the movie. Click on your component's movie clip in this menu, and you will see all `onClipEvent` actions that are placed on the movie clip. This is how the component gets the information of its parameters when the movie is published. Note that the actions you see in the debugging panel are not physically there in the authoring environment. They are added by Flash when the SWF is created.

It is also curious to note that the component uses a strange "initialize" `onClipEvent`, which is not discussed in any of Flash's documentation. This "initialize" is a legitimate movie event to use with `onClipEvent`, and it fires before the load movie event.

Creating the Component's Code

From our work so far, users can drag the component to the stage and edit all of its parameters. After that, these parameters are added as variables to the movie clip's Timeline. Now all that is left to complete our component is to use those newly added variables to produce a horde of random squares across the screen. This means we start coding the functionality of the component; this coding is always 99 percent of the work that goes into creating a component. Start by double-clicking the RandomSquares movie clip in the library and renaming the layer on which you'll place the actions to "Actions." Next, open the Actions panel on the first frame of the Actions layer, and you can begin with the fun.

Although it may not seem like an obvious thing to do, you must first set the component's x- and y-position to zero. This aligns the component's stage with that of the main stage. This is important because the main stage's width and height determine the viable area in which the squares can be rendered. Type the following code in the actions for the first frame in the Actions layer.

```
// align the component's stage with the main stage
this._x = 0.0;
this._y = 0.0;
```

Remember that the keyword `this` refers to the movie clip of the component.

Next you need a `for` loop to produce the number of squares the user specified in the parameters. Once in the `for` loop, you will need to calculate a random position, dimension, and color of the square being rendered. From our brainstorming and planning session, we already know how to do this; the only difference is using the variables from the parameters. The code that accomplishes this, shown in Listing 10.2, looks very similar to what we did before; take note of the conditional statement used to check whether the user wants random colors or not.

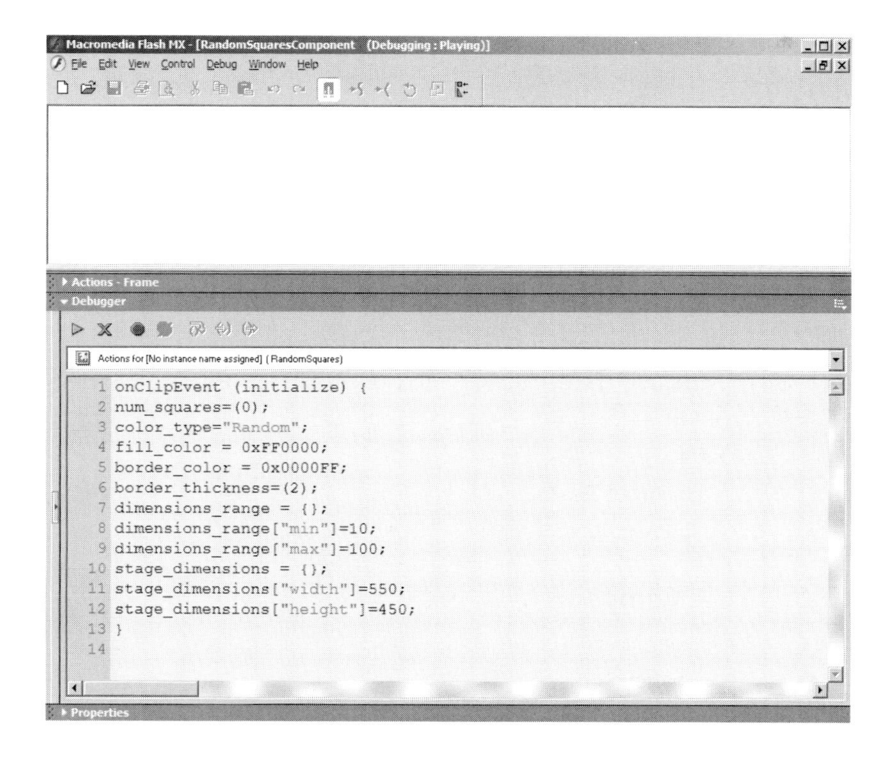

Figure 10.5

By making a movie clip a component, Flash automatically creates an `onClipEvent` function, which is used to initialize the variables associated with the component's parameters.

After the attributes of the square have been calculated, you are only left to render the square. Once again, our brainstorming has nearly completely taken care of this task. Using the variables from the parameters, and shifting the vertices of the rendered square by the variables x and y, you get the set of actions marked in Listing 10.2 by the "start the drawing process" comment.

Listing 10.2

Calculating the Position, Dimension, and Color of the Square

```
// loop through the number of squares to create random squares
for (var j = 0; j < this.num_squares; j++)
{
   // calculate random position for the upper-left corner of the square
   var x = Math.random ( ) * this.stage_dimensions.width;
   var y = Math.random ( ) * this.stage_dimensions.height;

   // calculate a random dimension for the square
   var dim = Math.random ( ) * (this.dimensions_range.max -
             this.dimensions_range.min) + this.dimensions_range.min;

   // check if we should calculate a random color
   if (this.color_type == "Random")
   {
      // calculate random colors for the fill and border
      this.fill_color   = Math.round (Math.random ( ) * 0xFFFFFF);
      this.border_color = Math.round (Math.random ( ) * 0xFFFFFF);
   }

   // start the drawing process so we can draw the square
   this.lineStyle (this.border_thickness, this.border_color, 100.0);
   this.beginFill (this.fill_color, 100.0);
   {
      // set the vertices of the square to draw it
      this.moveTo (x,       y);
      this.lineTo (x + dim, y);
      this.lineTo (x + dim, y + dim);
      this.lineTo (x,       y + dim);
   }
   this.endFill ( );
}
```

Believe it or not, your first component is done!

In the Chapter 10 folder on the companion CD, we've added one extra thing to the `RandomSquaresComponent.fla` file. A movie clip with the text "Random Squares" inside has been added in the component's movie clip so that users can easily see where the component is on the screen. If the label were not there, then only a small white dot would appear in the component's place, reflecting that the component contains no visible graphics. In order to stay organized, the label movie clip is placed in the `Assets` folder. The label is used as a movie clip so that you can make it invisible once the component starts up. In the first frame of the label movie clip, we've added the following action to remove the label from sight:

```
this._visible = false;
```

Take a minute to bask in all of this component's excellence. Look at Figure 10.6 to see what the component produces. Don't worry if you find this component a little elementary, or even quite simply useless; the next component, which exploits most of what components have to offer, is much cooler.

Figure 10.6

The RandomSquares component generates... just what it says.

Advanced Component Creation: The Particles Component

You are now going to focus your energy on creating an advanced component that pulls out all the bells and whistles. Before you can really put your hands to work in creating the component, you must go through a few waves of brainstorming. This is especially important in advanced components, because changes in mid-development will result in a sloppily built component.

The new component we are going to construct will be much more advanced, as it will contain most everything a professional component should include. The component we will create is called the Particles component, and it will simply create a bunch of particles and move them randomly around the screen, as shown in Figure 10.7.

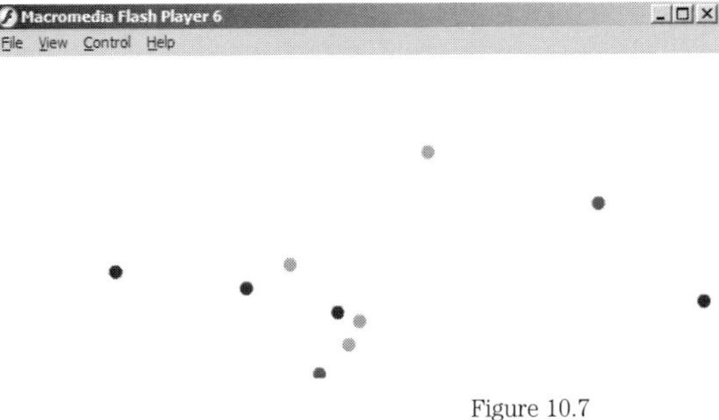

Figure 10.7

Randomly scattering particles on the screen

To create a continuous stream of particles, a new particle will be placed on the screen after a certain number of frames have passed, and a particle will be removed when it travels off the stage. This component will be a lot more functional than the last, because we will provide custom methods attached to the component movie clip that will allow the user of the component to start and stop the streams of particles. You can edit those methods using ActionScript, for example on a button, which will then control the stream of the particles. I'll further develop the concept of interacting with components through ActionScript as we progress through the chapter.

As we saw previously, the brainstorming step really helped us out. We planned out the parameters we wanted the user to be able to change, and we coded a few short procedures that were used in the code for the component. Since this component is more sophisticated, it has more parameters to edit:

Frame Delay The first parameter the user can edit determines the number of frames that must pass before a new particle is added to the stage; the smaller the value, the faster the particles are added.

Particle Graphics Linkage Next, an array is used so that the user can provide their own graphics for the particles. The user will create movie clips to hold their graphics for the particles, give each movie clip a distinct linkage name, and then enter those names into the component. The component will in turn use those graphics for the particle animations by choosing a linkage name at random from the array and attaching an instance of the particle to the stage.

Particle Creation The third parameter is a list that determines the behavior of the particles when a new one is created. If you choose Convergent, then the particles will initially start in a specified area; if you choose Divergent, then the particles will start in a random place on the screen.

Convergence Radius, Convergence X, and Convergence Y These are all related, yet they are not all set in an Object data type. The reason for this will become clear in Chapter 11 when we build a custom UI for the component. These parameters define the area the particles should initially start when the Convergent setting is used. Together they define a disk with its center and radius determined by the parameters. When a new particle is created, it will start at a random point contained in that disk.

Maximum Acceleration This parameter specifies the maximum rate of change at which any particle can speed up or slow down. In a sense, it controls the overall speed of the particle system.

Stage Width, Stage Height These next two parameters are no strangers to you; they record the width and height of the stage you are using for your movie. These values are important because they are used to determine when a particle has traveled outside of the stage so that it can be removed.

Creation Handler, Deletion Handler Finally, the last two parameters are event handlers. This special type of function may be something new to you. *Event handlers* are simply functions that are called when a certain event occurs in the Flash movie; arguments may or may not be passed in the function call. They allow you to add extra customization and functionality to the component by using code of your own. In the context of this component, the Handler functions are called when a particle is created and removed, respectively. A movie clip reference to the particle that is being created or deleted is passed to the function.

If any of these parameters seem mysterious or confusing, do not fret; after we've created the component, we'll see a few small demos that show how to take advantage of each of the parameters.

Building the Component's Modules

Now, considering all the parameters we are adding to the component and the original idea of the component, let's develop a few tangible parts of the component that can be pieced together later on for the final production.

One of the first things you might be clueless about is how to move the particles randomly about the screen. To solve this problem, we will pull from a few elementary concepts from physics. Velocity is the rate of change at which an object moves—in our case, two separate movements: one along the x-axis and one along the y-axis. The unit of measurement we will be using for velocity is pixels per frame; so, for example, a particle can move at 5 pixels per frame, which means that 5 pixels will be added to the object's position every frame. In addition to velocity, an object can have acceleration, which is the rate of change of the object's velocity. This quantity is also split into two components, one along the x-axis and one along the y-axis. The unit of measurement for acceleration will not help in understanding acceleration because it is quite awkward at first, but in our movie it is pixels per frame squared. The "squared" part is due to the fact that acceleration is the rate of change of a rate of change. All you need to know is that if an object has an acceleration of 2 pixels per frame squared, then the object's velocity is increased by 2 every frame.

Using this information, we can formulate a way of creating a random, fluid movement. The idea is to start with an object that has 0 velocity in the x- and y-directions. Then, every frame a random acceleration will be calculated for the object, which will result in the velocity of the object changing by random values. Finally, when the velocity is added to the object's position, the result is a nice, fluid movement. This concept can be demonstrated with a simple example. Create a new Flash movie, add a movie clip to the stage with a simple graphic inside, and give the movie clip the name "thing." Then, add the actions of Listing 10.3 to the first frame on the main stage.

Listing 10.3

Giving an Object Random, Fluid Movement

```
// set the onEnterFrame handler of the object to handle its movement
thing.onEnterFrame = function ( )
{
   // calculate a random acceleration between 1 and -1
   var acceleration_x = Math.random ( ) * 2.0 - 1.0;
   var acceleration_y = Math.random ( ) * 2.0 - 1.0;

   // increment the object's velocity by its acceleration
   this.velocity_x += acceleration_x;
   this.velocity_y += acceleration_y;

   // increment the object's position by its velocity
   this._x += this.velocity_x;
   this._y += this.velocity_y;
}
```

With these actions in place, you can test the movie and see your movie clip wander about the screen aimlessly. An example of this effect in motion can be found in the `RandomFluid-Movement.fla` file in the Chapter 10 file on the CD.

With one of the more complicated tasks taken care of, we can turn to some simpler areas that need to be discussed. The Frame Delay parameter asks for the number of frames that the component should let pass by before a new particle is added to the system. Obviously, we must have a way to track the number of frames that pass after the movie starts, so we should create a frame counter variable that will be incremented every frame; we'll call this variable *`frame_counter`*. Next, to detect when a particular number of frames have passed, which will be a variable called *`frame_delay`*, we will use the modulus operator, which is the percent sign (`%`) in ActionScript. When the line `a % b`, for two integers a and b, is executed, the modulus operation returns the remainder left when dividing a by b. For our component, *`frame_delay`* number of frames will have passed when *`frame_delay`* divides evenly into *`frame_counter`*—that is, the modulus of the two values is zero. By means of this information, we can now write the code in Listing 10.4, which will trace the message "10 frames have passed" in the output window for every 10 frames that pass.

Listing 10.4

Detecting When a Certain Number of Frames Have Passed

```
// number of frames that must pass
frame_delay = 10;
// number of frames that have passed since the movie started
frame_counter = 0;
// onEnterFrame event for the _root that will trace the message
_root.onEnterFrame = function ( )
{
   // keep track of the current frame count
   this.frame_counter++;
   // check if enough frames have passed to trace the message
   if ((this.frame_counter % this.frame_delay) == 0)
   {
      // trace the message that 10 frames have passed
      trace ("10 frames have passed");
   }
}
```

Once we have determined when to create a new particle, we then have to figure out a way to randomly place the particle on the stage. For the simple case when the divergent behavior is chosen, we can merely choose a random number between 0 and the stage's width for the particle's x-position, and a number between 0 and the stage's height for its y-position. However, for the convergent case, we must find a way to calculate a random position in a circle with arbitrary radius and center. Although only elementary trigonometry is used to do this calculation, a full explanation is beyond the scope of this book. So, here is a sample of how to calculate such a point:

```
// radius of the disk
r = 50.0;
// center of the disk
cx = 100.0;
cy = 100.0;
// choose a random angle and radius to plot in the disk
var radius = Math.random ( ) * r;
var angle = Math.random ( ) * 2.0 * Math.PI;
// calculate the random point in the disk
var random_x = radius * Math.cos (angle);
var random_y = radius * Math.sin (angle);
```

Outside of the actual structure and architecture of the component's code, the only small programming tasks that stand in our way are getting a random element of an array and how to remove a specific element from an array. The former task will be used to pick a random linkage name from the array provided by the user, while the latter will be used when a particle is removed from the stage (this will become clear when we write the actual code for the component). Both of these objectives are very simple and can be done with basic ActionScripting:

```
// just an arbitrary array to operate on
var _array = new Array (0, 1, 2, 3, 4, 5);
// trace a random element from the array
trace (_array[Math.floor (Math.random ( ) * _array.length)]);
// remove the third element from the array
_array.splice (3, 1);
```

With our newly found information, we can start discussing the architecture of a typical, professional component.

The Architecture of a Professional Component

As I said, the processes and concepts in this part of the chapter are by far the most complicated in the entire book. However, they are included here because the ideas they represent form the very basis of the component movement.

The component we will be developing gets its functionality from what is called a *class*. A class is best thought of as a blueprint of an object from which instances can be created. Any attributes associated with the class can be represented with variables and are called *properties* of the class; any functions associated with the class can be attached as functions and are called *methods* of the class. Using this abstract definition of a class, we can formulate a simple example: a `Ball` class. The `Ball` class has properties such as color and size, and it might have methods that change the color of the ball or change its size.

To define a class, we use a regular function. The keyword `this` is used to set properties in the class. For example, we could declare a `Ball` class like this:

```
Ball = function (color, width)
{
   this.color = color;
   this.width = width;
}
```

Methods are attached to the class through the use of the `prototype` object. Essentially, any property or function that you want to be a part of the blueprint of the class, you set in the class's prototype. For example, a `change_color` method can be implemented in the `Ball` class like this:

```
Ball.prototype.change_color = function (new_color)
{
   this.new_color = color;
}
```

With this very simple class defined, we can create instances of the class through the use of the `new` keyword:

```
my_ball = new Ball ("red", 100);
```

You might notice some similarities between creating an instance of the `Ball` class and creating an instance of ActionScript objects such as `Array`. In fact, they are the exact same; the `Array` object is merely a class that handles the functionality of an array. Of course, such functionality cannot be written in ActionScript and is probably handled through C++, but that still does not take away from the fact that the array's functionality has been encapsulated as a class.

The one drawback to the class we have just written is its lack of graphical representation. If we wanted to link the simple `Ball` class with a graphic, we would probably have to write a method for the class to render a circle to the screen. This is where components prevail. Components provide the very fundamental link between graphics and code, and once the two are connected, the component movie clip will act as an instance of the ActionScript class that handles the functionality of the component.

To start, create a new Flash movie named `ParticlesComponent.fla` and add a movie clip to the library; this will be the graphical representation of the component. Like before, we'll turn this plain movie clip into a component by adding some parameters to it. We have already planned the parameters we are going to use (at the start of the "Advanced Component Creation: The Particles Component" section); Table 10.2 and Figure 10.8 present the specifics on how the parameters are added to the component's definition.

At this point, take an extra step and open the component movie clip's Linkage Properties dialog box to give it a linkage name, as shown in Figure 10.9. The name given will be used to establish the connection of the code with the component movie clip.

Table 10.2

Parameters for the Particles Component

PARAMETER NAME	VARIABLE NAME	DEFAULT VALUE	DATA TYPE
Frame Delay	`frame_delay`	`5`	Number
Particle Graphics	`Graphics_linkage`	`[particle0, particle1, particle2]`	Array
Particle Creation	`particle_creation_type`	`Convergent`	List
Convergence Radius	`convergence_radius`	`25`	Number
Convergence X	`convergence_x`	`275`	Number
Convergence Y	`convergence_y`	`200`	Number
Maximum Acceleration	`max_acceleration`	`2`	Number
Stage Width	`stage_width`	`550`	Number
Stage Height	`stage_height`	`400`	Number
Creation Handler	`creation_handler`	`creation_handler`	String
Deletion Handler	`deletion_handler`	`deletion_handler`	String

Now we are in a position to associate an ActionScript class with the movie clip of the component. Remember that for now we are only interested in the architecture of the component and not any specific implementation of the code we are mentioning. The code for the component will be covered in due time, but for now let's look at the best possible way to create a component.

The first part of setting up the relationship at hand is to write the ActionScript class that handles all of the functionality of the component. However, we are not yet worried about the implementation of the class since that code can be hundreds of lines. For now, we create a simple filler class with no properties or methods so that the code and component relationship can be set up:

```
ParticlesClass = function ( )
{
}
```

Next we associate this class with the component in two steps: (1) we register the class with the movie clip of the component, and (2) we impose the structure of the movie clip on all particles.

```
// register the class with the component
Object.registerClass ("ParticlesComponent", ParticlesClass);

// inherit the class from the MovieClip class
ParticlesClass.prototype = new MovieClip ( );
```

Figure 10.8

Component definition for the Particles component

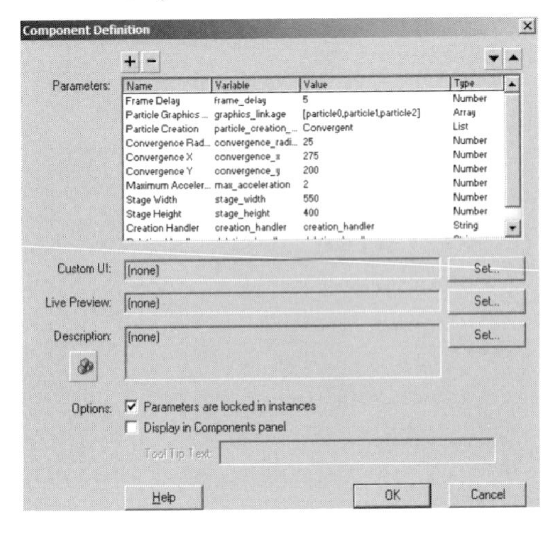

The call to the `registerClass` function takes two arguments: the first is a string for the linkage name of the component, and the second is the function of the constructor of the component's class. The `registerClass` function essentially strips everything from the movie clip, including its movie clip properties such as `_x` and `_y`, and then gives the movie clip all of the class's properties and methods. So, in a sense, the movie clip has become an instance of the component's class; this is what we wanted. However, a side effect of the call to `registerClass` is that the movie clip that represents the component has had all of its functionality removed; there are no longer the `removeMovieClip`, `swapDepths`, or any method attached to the movie clip. To offset this consequence, we must inherit the ActionScript class we wrote from the `MovieClip` class; this means that all the properties and methods of the `MovieClip` class will be added to the properties and methods of the component's class. To do this, we set the `prototype` object of `ParticlesClass` equal to an instance of the `MovieClip` class.

Now, let us assume that the full `ParticlesClass` has been written and implemented. Every time we drag an instance of the component to the stage, it is like we are creating an instance of the class. However, behind the scenes we are also redeclaring the entire class for every instance of the component on the stage. This is an obvious drain on the computer's memory. Macromedia provides two commands that you can place at the top and bottom of a block of code, and any code in between the two commands is only executed once at the very start of the movie. These commands are `#initclip` and `#endinitclip`; using them, our code becomes Listing 10.5.

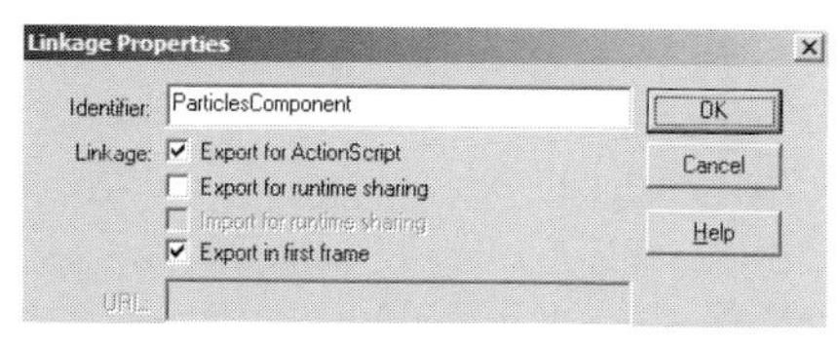

Figure 10.9

Give the component a linkage name.

Listing 10.5

Setting Up the Relationship between the Component's Code and the Component's Movie Clip

```
#initclip
ParticlesClass = function ( )
{
}
// register the class with the component
Object.registerClass ("ParticlesComponent", ParticlesClass);
// inherit the class from the MovieClip class
ParticlesClass.prototype = new MovieClip ( );
#endinitclip
```

Quite a bit of information has been presented to you so far, so here are a few things to keep in mind that may have slipped by with all the bits of data flying everywhere. Because the component movie clip is inherited from the component class, you can attach event handlers to the ActionScript class and those handlers will become the movie clip's handlers. For example, if we added an `onEnterFrame` method to `ParticlesClass`, then the actions in the method would be called every frame the component is on the stage. Same goes for `onMouseDown`, `onMouseUp`, and every other handler that the `MovieClip` class allows. In addition to this, every method you attach to the component class can be called from the component movie clip. Assume you have an instance of the component on the stage, and you have given it the instance name "component." Also assume that the component's class has a method named `some_method`. Then, you can call the method of the class as if it were attached directly to the movie clip:

```
component.some_method ( );
```

With this code in place, we are now ready to fill in the missing pieces of the class's implementation.

Assembling the Component's Code

The final step to creating this component is to implement all of the component's functionality that we planned in the brainstorming process. To understand how the actions in the `ParticlesClass` class can control the component, we simply draw from previously developed ideas. The two-step inheritance discussed earlier brings the class and the component into an intimate relationship; in fact, they are made into a single thing. So, when you set a property in the class via the `this` keyword, you are also setting a variable directly in the component movie clip. Therefore, the keyword `this` refers directly to the Timeline of the component; any time you want to set the position of the component movie clip, use `this._x` and `this._y`, or if you want to attach a movie clip to the component's Timeline, use `this.attachMovie`.

All of this insightful data greatly simplifies the programming side of the component. The first set of actions executed when a component is being initialized on the stage is the `ParticlesClass` constructor (see Listing 10.6). In this function, we simply need to initialize all the variables we are going to use later on: a variable to keep track of the frame count, a variable used to keep depths of attached movies separate, and an array that holds a reference to the movie clip of every particle currently on the stage. In addition to these properties, we need to align the component's stage with that of the main stage so we can determine when a particle has fallen out of sight.

Listing 10.6

Constructor for ParticlesClass

```
// class that will handle the functionality of the Particles component
ParticlesClass = function ( )
{
   // frame counter used by the component to determine
   // when to create a new particle
   this.frame_counter = 0;

   // depth variable used to keep the depths of attached movie
   // clips separate
   this.depth = 0;

   // array of particles that are currently on the stage
   this.current_particles = new Array ( );

   // align the component's stage to the main stage
   this._x = 0.0;
```

```
    this._y = 0.0;

    // assign the onEnterFrame event handler for the component
    this.onEnterFrame = this.Particles_onEnterFrame;
}
```

The last line where the onEnterFrame handler for the class is set may be a little confusing. In general, you should never directly attach an onEnterFrame method to a component class because it offers very little flexibility; the same applies to all event handlers. Instead, you create methods that take care of what you want for the event handler, and then simply set up a pointer to the differently named method. So, in the above case, we are pointing the onEnterFrame handler to the Particles_onEnterFrame handler. If we want to change the onEnterFrame handler to another function, we simply point it to another method in the class.

Basic Methods

Next, we will discuss every method that the component will use. First up is the Particles_onEnterFrame method, shown in Listing 10.7. In order to stay as organized and modular as possible, the Particles_onEnterFrame method only calls two other methods: one for checking when a new particle should be created and one for animating all the particles on the stage.

Listing 10.7

Possible Event Handler for the Particles Component

```
// method assigned as an onEnterFrame handler that handles
// the animations of particles
ParticlesClass.prototype.Particles_onEnterFrame = function ( )
{
    // check if a new particle should be created
    this.check_for_new_particle ( );

    // animate all the particles on the screen
    this.animate_particles ( );
}
```

The first thing the check_for_new_particle method (Listing 10.8) does is check if enough frames have passed for a new particle to be introduced to the system. If enough frames have passed, then we call a method that is in charge of initializing a new particle. Lastly, the method increments the frame counter.

Listing 10.8

Checking Whether a New Particle Should Be Created

```
ParticlesClass.prototype.check_for_new_particle = function ( )
{
   // check if enough frames have passed to create a new particle
   if ((this.frame_counter % this.frame_delay) == 0)
   {
      // create a new particle
      this.create_particle ( );
   }

   // increment the frame counter
   this.frame_counter++;
}
```

Continuing with the flow of work, we go on to the `create_particle` method (Listing 10.9).

Listing 10.9

Adding Another Particle to the System

```
ParticlesClass.prototype.create_particle = function ( )
{
   // get a random particle linkage to attach
   var linkage = this.graphics_linkage[
      Math.floor (Math.random ( ) * this.graphics_linkage.length)];

   // attach a new particle to the stage
   var _mc = this.attachMovie
            (linkage, "particle" + this.depth, this.depth);

   // check how the particle should be positioned initially
   if (this.particle_creation_type == "Convergent")
   {
      // calculate a random angle and radius for the particle to be
      // displaced from the center of convergence
      var angle  = Math.random ( ) * 2.0 * Math.PI;
      var radius = Math.random ( ) * this.convergence_radius;

      // position the particle randomly in the disk
      _mc._x = this.convergence_x + radius * Math.cos (angle);
      _mc._y = this.convergence_y + radius * Math.sin (angle);
   }
   else
```

```
        {
            // position the particle randomly on the stage
            _mc._x = Math.random ( ) * this.stage_width;
            _mc._y = Math.random ( ) * this.stage_height;
        }

        // push the movie clip reference to the array that keeps track of
        // the particles on the stage
        this.current_particles.push (_mc);

        // call the creation handler
        this._parent[this.creation_handler] (_mc);

        // increment the depth variable to keep the depths separate
        this.depth++;
    }
```

The `create_particle` method takes care of quite a few things at once, so I'll break it down to one bite at a time. The first thing it does is get a random linkage name from the array defined by the user and attaches an instance of the movie clip to the component's stage.

Take note that the `depth` property of the class is used to give each attached movie a distinct name and depth. Also, a slight shorthand is being used; the `attachMovie` method of the `MovieClip` class returns a reference to the newly created movie clip. So, by assigning that reference to `_mc`, we have a more compact way of referencing the attached particle.

Next, we must set the particles' initial position. This depends on two things: whether the particles' behavior was set to convergent or divergent by the user. If convergent is chosen, then we calculate a random point in the disk defined by the component's parameters. Luckily, we have already figured out how to do such a thing. But, if divergent is chosen, then we are left with the remedial task of calculating a random point on the screen.

The last lines of the method carry out a few miscellaneous tasks. First, the reference to the movie clip is pushed to the end of the `current_particles` array. We use this array in the `animate_particles` method to efficiently loop through all the particles on the stage and animate them across the stage. Next, the creation handler is called. Take note that the handler provided by the user should live on the stage that is parent to the component. Hence the funny-looking syntax used to call the function. Lastly, the `depth` property is incremented to make sure all movie clips have distinct names and depths.

Now we move to the most complicated method in the entire class. The `animate_particles` method (Listing 10.10) loops through all particles on the stage and applies the random, fluid motion, which we discussed previously, to each particle.

Listing 10.10

Animating All Particles on the Stage

```
ParticlesClass.prototype.animate_particles = function ( )
{
   // loop through the particles on the stage
   for (var j = 0; j < this.current_particles.length; j++)
   {
      // get a reference to the movie clip of the particle
      var _mc = this.current_particles[j];
   // calculate a random acceleration for the particle
      var acceleration_x = Math.random ( ) * 2.0 *
         this.max_acceleration - this.max_acceleration;
      var acceleration_y = Math.random ( ) * 2.0 *
         this.max_acceleration - this.max_acceleration;

      // increment the particle's velocity by its acceleration
      _mc.velocity_x += acceleration_x;
      _mc.velocity_y += acceleration_y;

      // increment the particle's position by its velocity
      _mc._x += _mc.velocity_x;
      _mc._y += _mc.velocity_y;
      // check if the particle has gone off the stage
      if ((_mc._x > this.stage_width)  || (_mc._x < 0.0) ||
         (_mc._y > this.stage_height) || (_mc._y < 0.0))
      {
         // call the deletion handler
         this._parent[this.deletion_handler] (_mc);

         // remove the particle from the array that keeps track
         // of particles on the stage
         this.current_particles.splice (j, 1);

         // remove the particle from the stage
         _mc.removeMovieClip ( );
      }
   }
}
```

To start out with, we perform a `for` loop that iterates through each element in the `current_particles` array. Then, just to make our code short and readable, we create a temporary variable that holds the reference to a particular movie clip in the `current_particles` array.

Next, we calculate a random acceleration for the object, apply it to the object's velocity, and finally apply the object's velocity to its position. This is all very similar to the code developed in the brainstorming.

But we cannot stop here; there is an extra step. To keep the user's computer from bogging down with hundreds of particles, we have to remove any particles that fall off the sides of the screen. To detect these particles, we can write out one large conditional statement that checks the particle's position against the width and height of the stage the user defined. If we detect that a particle has fallen off the stage, we need to call the deletion handler, remove the particle's movie clip from the `current_particles` array, and then remove the particle movie clip from the stage. As you can see, we apply the technique used earlier to remove an element from an array.

Control Methods

With all of the code so far, we have created a fully functional component. However, the component does not have all of the features we want it to have. To create a well-designed component, you must give the user control both when they are customizing the component and when the component is already in action in the movie SWF. You provide the latter type of interaction by attaching methods to the component so the user can change some of the component's parameters on-the-fly through the use of ActionScript.

For example, what would the user do if they wanted to be able to stop and start the stream of particles? For this capability, we add on a few "setter" methods—that is, methods whose sole purpose is to give the user the ability to customize the component through ActionScript. For example, the two methods `stop_stream` and `start_stream` (Listing 10.11) enable the user to stop and start streams of particles by simple function calls. Take note that the `onEnterFrame` handler is set to `animate_particles` when the `stop_stream` method is called. This is because when the stream of particles is stopped, we still want the particles that remain on the stage to animate away.

Listing 10.11

Methods to Stop and Start the Stream of Particles

```
// stops the stream of particles
ParticlesClass.prototype.stop_stream = function ( )
{
   this.onEnterFrame = this.animate_particles;
}
// starts the stream of particles
ParticlesClass.prototype.start_stream = function ( )
{
   this.onEnterFrame = this.Particles_onEnterFrame;
}
```

The next three methods (Listing 10.12) are used to change the frame delay of the particles, their convergence radius, and their convergence center.

Listing 10.12

Methods to Change Certain Parameters of the Component

```
// changes the frame delay of the component
ParticlesClass.prototype.change_frame_delay = function (delay)
{
   this.frame_delay = delay;
}
// changes the convergence point of the particle stream
ParticlesClass.prototype.change_convergence_point = function (x, y)
{
   this.convergence_x = x;
   this.convergence_y = y;
}
// changes the convergence radius for the particle stream
ParticlesClass.prototype.change_convergence_radius = function (radius)
{
   this.convergence_radius = radius;
}
```

These additional methods empower the user of the component with the facility to create a far more interesting use of the particles effect. To drive this point home, we will create a sample application using some of these additional methods. The application will have two buttons at the bottom for starting and stopping the stream of particles and another button with a text field for setting the frame delay of the component. Also, we'll write a deletion event handler for the component to play a small animation at the point where the particle falls off the edge of the screen. And finally, an `onEnterFrame` handler will be written for the `_root` to have the particles constantly stream from wherever the mouse is on the stage.

In the file `ParticlesComponent_Sample.fla` in the Chapter 10 folder on the CD, you can see such an application already created. On the main stage, you will see that all the controls give the user control of some the component's parameters, as shown in Figure 10.10.

Drag an instance of the component to the stage and set its initial parameters. Next, click the instance of the component and open its Component Properties panel to set its instance name; we will use the name "particles." Remember that the instance name is very important; it enables us to take control of the component through ActionScript. For the graphics of the particles, I have created three movie clips, each with a small, colored dot in the middle, as shown in Figure 10.11. Give each movie clip a linkage name. For simplicity, I have used "particle0," "particle1," and "particle2."

Next, we'll write the ActionScript for the buttons on the stage. The actions to stop and start the stream of particles are simple. Open the Actions window for each button by right-clicking the instance and selecting Actions from the pop-up menu. The buttons will either call the `start_stream` or `stop_stream` method of the component, which can be done with the following code:

```
on (press)
{
   particles.start_stream ( );
}
on (press)
{
   particles.stop_stream ( );
}
```

The text field that holds the frame delay of the component has the instance name "delay." So, the actions for the Set Delay button are:

```
on (press)
{
   particles.change_frame_delay (delay.text);
}
```

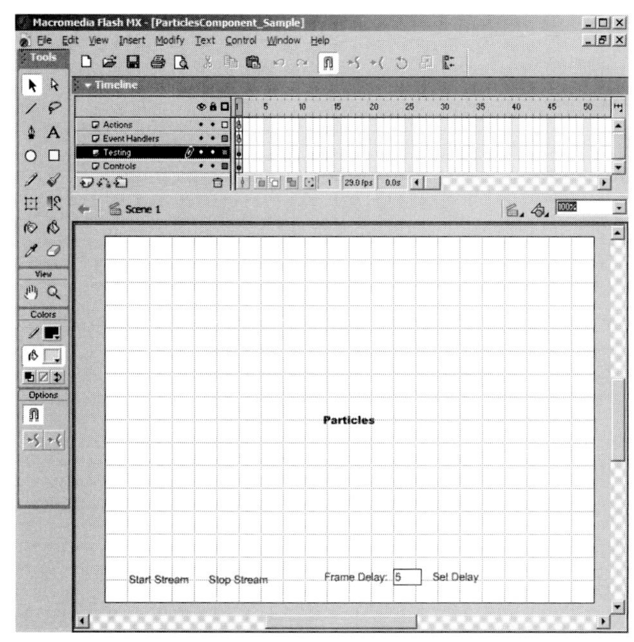

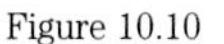
Figure 10.10

Open the sample file to view the controls for the component.

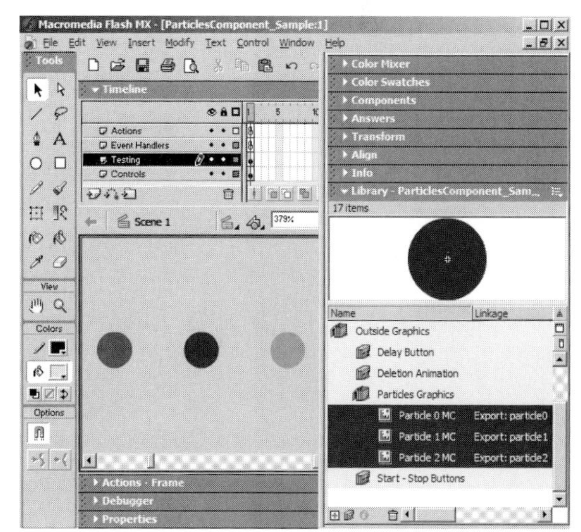

Figure 10.11

Create graphics for the particles used in the component.

The `onEnterFrame` handler of the `_root` makes use of the `change_convergence_point` method to force the particles to stream from the user's mouse.

```
_root.onEnterFrame = function ( )
{
   this.particles.change_convergence_point (this._xmouse, this._ymouse);
}
```

Finally, we need to write the deletion handler that will play an animation at the point the particle is removed from the stage, shown in Listing 10.13. I've added a small animation with the linkage name "deletion_animation" that is simply a small square that fades out. Also, for memory purposes, I've added an action to the last frame that removes the movie clip from the stage when the animation is done playing. So, with the movie clip already made, all we need to do is attach it to the stage and position it over the particle movie clip. Take note that I've used the `depth` property in the same way as in the component to give attached animations distinct names and depths.

Listing 10.13

Function Called When a Particle Is Removed from the Stage

```
deletion_handler = function (particle_mc)
{
   // increment the depth variable to keep the depths and names
   // of attached movies distinct
   this.depth++;

   // attach a deletion animation to the screen
   var _mc = this.attachMovie
      ("deletion_animation", "animation" + this.depth, this.depth);

   // position the animation to be on top of where the particle used to be
   _mc._x = particle_mc._x;
   _mc._y = particle_mc._y;
}
```

You are now done with a drastic customization to the original Particles component! Figure 10.12 shows a capture of the particles streaming from the mouse. Look in the file `ParticlesComponent_Sample.fla` file to see the changes we have made.

Conclusion

By this point in the book, you have learned two of the most important things that surround Flash MX components: how to use them and how to make them. There are still special topics that can be covered for making a component, a few of which I'll discuss in the next chapter, but for the most part, you can now create any component you can imagine. You should be rushing off to your past projects in search of possible new components to experiment with. However, make sure you have absorbed the immense amount of information that I've just put in front of you. A component is worth as much as the foundation it was built upon; the last thing you need is a shaky foundation on which your entire project is based.

If you are not pleased with the unprofessional look of the default user interface that Macromedia forces on you, look forward to the next chapter, where we discuss how to create custom UIs, how to create live previews, and how to package components into MXP files for that added touch of professionalism.

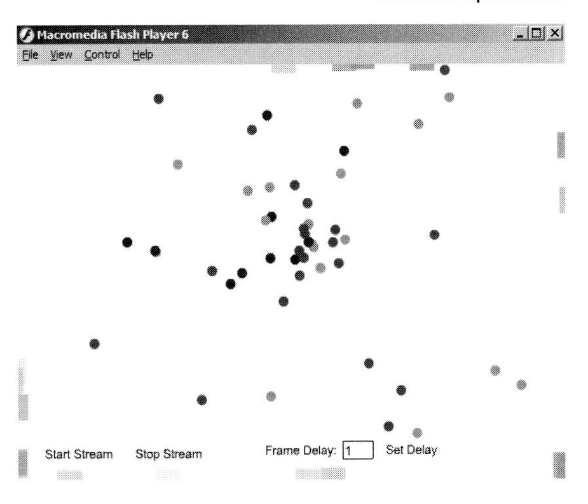

Figure 10.12

With a small customization to the component, you can make the particles continuously stream from wherever the mouse is positioned.

Chapter 11: Component Extras

Now that you've made a component of your own, you might start to see a few things that you'd like to customize. For example, the user interface Macromedia provides to change the parameters of a component is quite drab and counterproductive. Fortunately, Flash allows you to create an SWF that you can use to replace the default UI.

In this chapter, we'll explore of few of the extras that you can use with an already existing component—things that will give it a professional flair. These include custom user interfaces, custom component icons, live previews, and component packaging for Macromedia's Extension Manager. The idea is to make using components as intuitive as possible, and to take away a few of the confusing aspects of working with components.

This chapter wraps up most of the knowledge you will need for component creation. Although all features we discuss here are purely optional, you should carefully consider adding some elements to any component you create. Anything you can do to ease working with your component will be very useful in the long run.

- **Understanding custom user interfaces**
- **Designing a custom UI**
- **Creating a custom icon**
- **Component live previews**
- **Packaging components for release**

Understanding the Role of a Custom UI

The components that you have encountered in this book have come with fancy-looking custom UIs for their parameters. For example, when you open the Component Parameters panel, you are presented with short, descriptive labels for all of the parameters, as well as "tool tip" paragraphs of information about each specific parameter. These tool tips provide insight into what you can and cannot do with the parameters and guide your decision for choosing their values.

While it is obvious that a custom UI can provide more information about the parameters of a component, a custom UI can also check for errors in the values the user inputs. Suppose you created a component that asks for the dimensions of the user's stage. Obviously, the values of the two parameters should be numbers, but they also should not have negative values.

As another example, recall the text effect components discussed in Chapter 7—specifically, the FlushTextEffect component. We discussed the topic of shared fonts to understand how to use a custom font with the various effects instead of relying on device fonts. If you wanted to use a custom font, you had to enter the linkage name of the shared font into the component's parameter, whereas if you wanted to use a device font, you simply had to enter the font's name on the computer.

Now, suppose for a moment that you want to use a device font with the component, but you accidentally misspell the name of the font. That small mistake will completely break the component. Wouldn't it be nice if the UI prompted you, informing you that you are not specifying a device font, and a shared font will be used instead? This can be done with a custom UI.

You can now see that a custom UI can both ease the component customizing process and make a powerful error-checking tool. We'll use these techniques to build a custom UI for the RandomSquares component that I introduced in Chapter 10.

Designing a Custom UI

The first thing you should do when sitting down to create a custom UI for one of your components is refamiliarize yourself with the component's parameters and their data types. In Figure 11.1, you can see the definition of the RandomSquares component. It contains two number data types, two object data types, two color data types, and a list.

We'll represent each of these quantities, with the exception of the list, as a simple text field for the user to enter values into. We can implement the list as a combo box, which happens to be in the set of components that Macromedia provides with Flash MX. Fortunately, the ComboBox component is very easy to use, as you will see.

Creating the Interface

Once you have planned out exactly how you will allow the user to change the values of the parameters, you can start to create the interface. The interface consists of two parts: the parameters, which we've already discussed, and a variable on the `_root` named *`xch`*, which is of `Object` data type. The variable *`xch`* is what makes the UI work in the first place. Any variables that are set inside the *`xch`* object will be passed to the component as the value for its parameters continuously while the UI is open.

Creating an `Object` variable and setting variables inside is a very easy task. In Flash MX, `Object` is an ActionScript class, which simply creates an empty container that you can fill up with variables of any data type, even another `Object` if you see fit. For example, you can create an *`xch`* object, with variables *`stage_width`* and *`stage_height`* inside, with the following code:

```
_root.xch = new Object ( );
_root.xch.stage_width = 550.0;
_root.xch.stage_height = 400.0;
```

With this knowledge, go into the Chapter 11 folder on the CD and drag a copy of the file `RandomSquares_UI.fla` to somewhere on your hard drive. You will also need to grab a copy of the `RandomSquaresComponent.fla` file because it has one small addition to the version we discussed in Chapter 10. Make sure that both FLA files are in the same directory, and then open the `RandomSquaresComponent.fla` file. To see the UI that will be created for the component, right-click the instance of the component and click Component Parameters. The window that appears is simply a holder for the SWF of the UI. The sizing of the window is a little quirky, and you will usually need to resize the UI so that you can read all of the text inside. Figure 11.2 shows the custom UI created for the component.

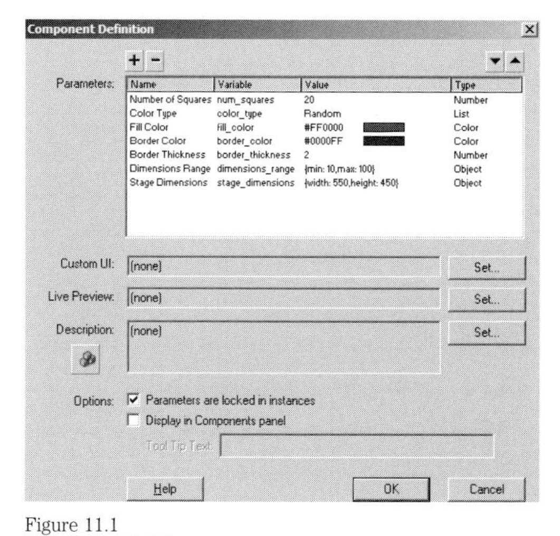

Figure 11.1

The Component Definition dialog box for the RandomSquares component

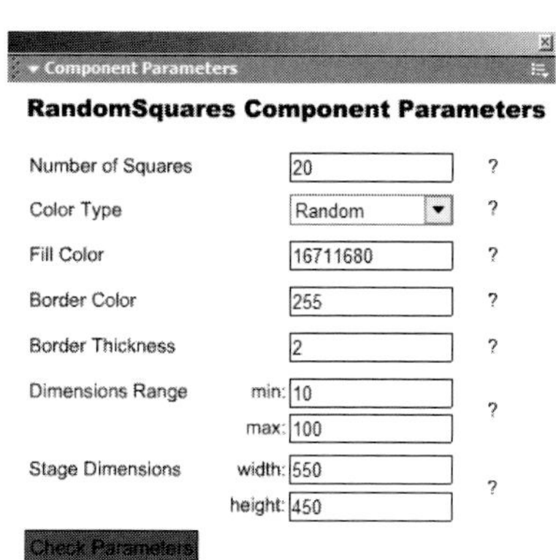

Figure 11.2

The custom UI for the component

As you can see, the UI is simply a line of text fields and one combo box, in which the user enters the parameters of the component. On the right side of each input field is a question mark; if you roll over this question mark, a small tool tip appears, giving a short description of the component. There is also a button at the bottom of the UI that checks if all the values you have entered comply with any requirements of the component. If you were to enter an invalid value—such as a string for the number of squares—the component would draw and click the error-checking button and then open an output window informing you of the error. You can see an example of this in Figure 11.3.

Now, close `RandomSquaresComponent.fla` and open the file `RandomSquares_UI.fla`. Once you open this file, you will see four layers: three of the layers—Initialization, onEnterFrame, and Parameters Check—handle the functionality of the UI through ActionScript, and the last layer, Parameters, holds all the graphics for the UI. Each of the input fields along the right side of the screen has been given an instance name corresponding to the variable name of the parameter it is associated with. This means that the text field that accepts input for the number of squares the component will create has an instance name "num_squares." To access the value of the text field, you simply reference the `text` property of the text field like this: `num_squares.text`. Creating these labels and text fields is repetitive; simply create static text for the label of the parameter, create a input text field for the user to edit, and finally give the text field an instance name.

The combo box is a slightly different story. Open the Components panel by pressing Command/Ctrl+F7 and select Flash UI Components from the drop-down menu, as shown in Figure 11.4. Note that the drop-down menu displays all component sets you have installed, so you may have more or fewer items to choose from.

Figure 11.3

Click the Check Parameters button to view a readout of any errors in the values you are using.

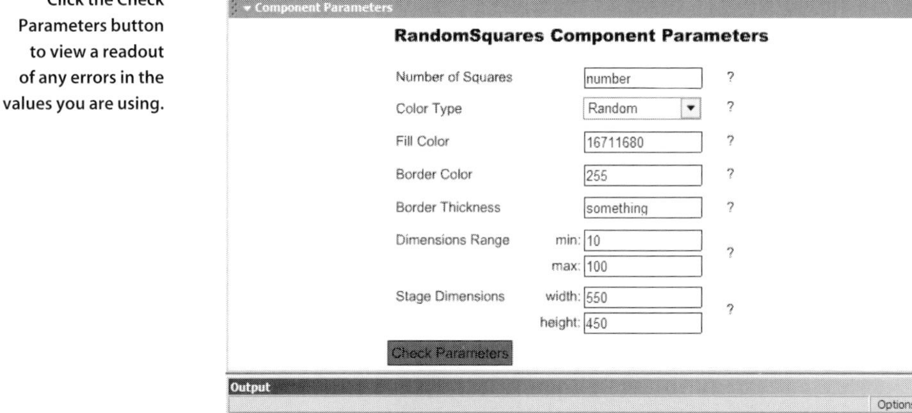

The component we are interested in is the ComboBox component. There is already an instance of the component on the stage, but since using the combo box takes a little more effort than any of the other parameter interfaces, let's learn by creating a new one. Go ahead and delete that existing instance and drag a new one to the stage. Once you have an instance on the stage, position it next to the label for the component and give it the instance name **color_type_cb**. For this component, the combo box is associated with the Color Type parameter, which determines if the squares should be either randomly colored or colored the same. The two possible values are Random and Constant; these are the values that the user will choose from in the combo box. To add the items to the combo box, open the Component Parameters panel and double-click the brackets next to the parameter named Labels (see Figure 11.5).

For now, the last graphic to make is the error-checking button at the bottom. There is nothing special about this graphic; it's just a simple button. The main aspect of the button is its actions, which we'll code later.

Figure 11.4

Selecting the Flash UI Components set in the Components panel

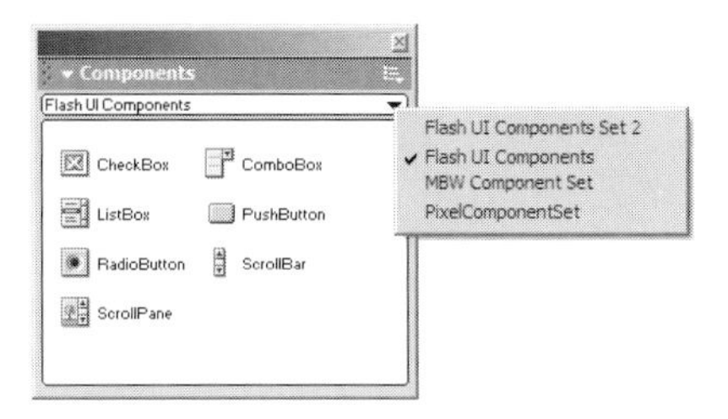

Associating Actions with Graphics

With the graphics of the UI created, you are now only left with the actions, which will handle many things for the UI. The first thing you need to do is create an `Object` named *xch* if one does not already exist. You place these actions in the layer named Initialization. The layer also contains additional actions, which set up the component by setting the text fields and combo box with the values of the parameters from the last time the user had the UI opened. Because of this, the actions need to be executed only once when the UI is first opened; therefore, the actions are placed in the `onLoad` event. The `onLoad` event is a function, which when set on a movie's Timeline is called the instant the movie clip appears in the Timeline.

In Listing 11.1, you'll find the complete code used in the movie, which is found in the Initialization layer. Note that the code first creates the *xch* object if one does not already exist, and next displays the values of the parameters as they were when the UI was opened.

Figure 11.5

Add the options for the drop-down menu through the Component Parameters panel.

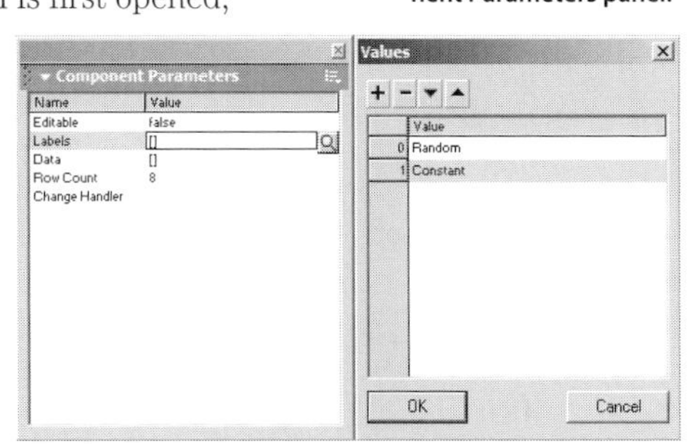

Listing 11.1

The onLoad Event for the UI

```
// onLoad event that sets the values of the parameters to
// what the user had last time the UI was open
_root.onLoad = function ( )
{
   // check if the xch object already exists
   if (_root.xch == undefined)
```

continued

continues

```
    {
       // create the xch object
       _root.xch = new Object ( );
    }

    // set the text fields to the parameters in the xch object
    this.num_squares.text = this.xch.num_squares;
    if (this.xch.color_type == "Random") {
       this.color_type_cb.setSelectedIndex (0);
    }
    else {
       this.color_type_cb.setSelectedIndex (1);
    }
    this.fill_color.text = this.xch.fill_color;
    this.border_color.text = this.xch.border_color;
    this.border_thickness.text = this.xch.border_thickness;
    this.dimensions_range_max.text = this.xch.dimensions_range.max;
    this.dimensions_range_min.text = this.xch.dimensions_range.min;
    this.stage_dimensions_width.text = this.xch.stage_dimensions.width;
    this.stage_dimensions_height.text = this.xch.stage_dimensions.height;
}
```

Most of the code is straightforward, except for the lines with the conditional statements concerning the call to the `setSelectedIndex` function. The combo box component has many methods attached to it for handling its functionality through ActionScript, one of them being `setSelectedIndex`. The method takes one argument, a number corresponding to an item in the combo box, and then sets the selected item for the combo box.The number 0 corresponds to the first entry, Random, and the number 1 corresponds to the second entry, Constant. This is why you need to use an `if` statement to set the selected item depending on the value of the Color Type parameter.

After the initialization of the values in the text fields and combo box, you need to write the code that will continuously take the values set by the user and place them in the ***xch*** object. If you create an `onEnterFrame` function in the `_root`, then that function will be called every frame the movie is opened. That event handler will be used to update the values in the ***xch*** object with those that the user has entered. The code to do this is in Listing 11.2.

Listing 11.2

Updating the xch Object Values with the User's Values

```
// onEnterFrame event that takes all of the user's input and
// sets it in the xch object
_root.onEnterFrame = function ( )
{
```

```
    this.xch.num_squares = Number (this.num_squares.text);
    this.xch.color_type = this.color_type_cb.getSelectedItem ( ).label;
    this.xch.fill_color = parseInt (this.fill_color.text);
    this.xch.border_color = parseInt (this.border_color.text);
    this.xch.border_thickness = Number (this.border_thickness.text);
    this.xch.dimensions_range.max = Number (this.dimensions_range_max.text);
    this.xch.dimensions_range.min = Number (this.dimensions_range_min.text);
    this.xch.stage_dimensions.width = Number
(this.stage_dimensions_width.text);
    this.xch.stage_dimensions.height = Number
(this.stage_dimensions_height.text);
}
```

Finally, we write the code for the error-checking button. The actions for this button are quite long, but also simple. The idea is to do a separate `if` statement for each parameter that you want to provide error checking for; if you find something wrong with the value that the user entered, then you will do something to notify the user about the error.

Determining whether there is an error can be done in many ways. Since the component we are using has mostly numeric values, we only need to check if a value is of the number data type. You can do this using a few ActionScript functions. Suppose you have a variable named *foo*; you can use the code in Listing 11.3 to determine if the variable is a number.

Listing 11.3

Determining Whether a Variable Is a Number

```
if (Number (foo).toString ( ) == "NaN")
{
    // the variable is not a number
}
else
{
    // the variable is a number
}
```

In the case of your UI, you will check if all of the numeric parameters are entered as numbers, and if any fail to be a number, then you can report it to the user. That is another issue you must decide on: how to inform users that they have entered invalid data. This UI uses a simple `trace` action. Since the SWF of the UI is run directly in the Flash authoring environment, the `trace` actions work just as they normally would. So, if you enter unacceptable values while using the UI for the RandomSquares component, an output window will appear to detail what values you need to change. The code listing for the error checking is too long to repeat here, but if you open the actions on the Parameter Check layer, you will see the `onRelease` button handler that has been written for it.

So far you have done quite a bit of work, but you are not home free yet. The final step is to set the custom UI for the component. Open the `RandomSquaresComponent.fla` file. In the library, right-click the component and select Component Definition. In the middle of the dialog box is a text field labeled RandomSquares_UI.swf (embedded). This is because the UI has already been embedded into the FLA. However, before the UI was embedded it read (none). When that is the case you have to set the Custom UI yourself. To do this click the Set button on the right. The dialog box that appears here has a few options, but you are only interested in two settings. As Figure 11.6 shows, you want to set the Type radio button to embedding the custom UI movie, and the Display radio button to displaying in the Components Parameters panel. You also need to specify the file path to the SWF of the custom UI, which can be either absolute or relative to the directory the component is in.

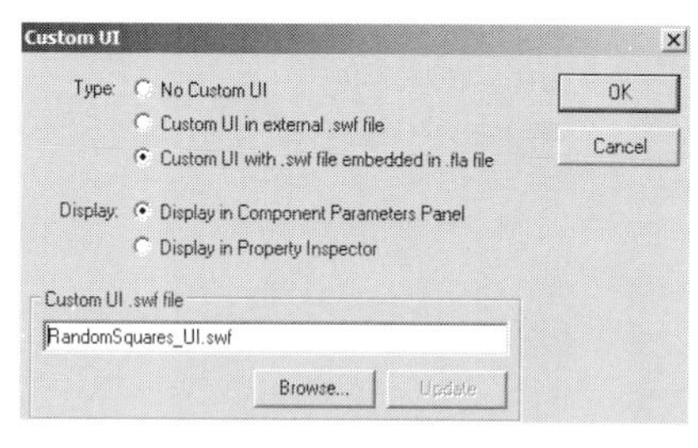

Figure 11.6

You can embed the UI movie into the component and make the UI display only in the Component Parameters panel.

Next, click OK in both dialog boxes and test your UI by opening the Component Parameters panel. A practical feature of the UI is that once you have embedded it into a component, you no longer need the SWF. That does not mean you should delete the FLA and SWF files of the UI, but you can relocate an FLA that uses the component to anywhere on your computer without worrying about taking the UI along with it.

You are now done with the custom UI! You may have noticed that there is a very formulaic approach to creating a custom UI:

1. Create and position the graphics and text fields that allow the user to change the parameters of the component.
2. Write the code that initializes the UI by taking the current parameters in the component and setting the interface elements' initial values; you should do all this in an `onLoad` event handler.
3. Write the code that continuously takes the user's values and sets them in the *`xch`* object every frame; you should do all this in an `onEnterFrame` handler.
4. Finally, create a button for error checking, if you feel your UI needs one.

Creating a Custom Icon

Custom icons give you the ability to engrave your logo or your company's logo into all of your components. The icons become visible in the library, replacing the default block pyramid icon. Figure 11.7 shows how custom icons appear in the library.

To create the custom icon, follow these steps:

1. Use your favorite graphics program to create a bitmap image 25 pixels by 20 pixels with a white or transparent background. The actual graphic for the icon can occupy only an

area of the picture 18 pixels by 18 pixels, and you must place it on the right side of the picture so that there is a 1-pixel buffer space between the graphics and the edge of the image. For example, the icon made for the RandomSquares component looks like Figure 11.8 when zoomed in Microsoft Paint.

2. Once you have created the icon, save it as a bitmap file.
3. Import the picture into Flash. To associate the icon with the component, create a folder named `FCustomIcons` in the same directory as the component, and move the bitmap to the folder.
4. Give the bitmap symbol in the library the exact same name as the component. To ensure that the two symbols have the same name, double-click the name of the component symbol, copy its value, and paste it into the name of the bitmap symbol.
5. Edit the component by double-clicking its symbol in the library. You must place the bitmap in the component to fully associate the image with the component. Take care to keep the icon from becoming visible to the user. You can do this by creating a new layer named Custom Icon, placing the icon in the layer, and making the layer a guide layer.

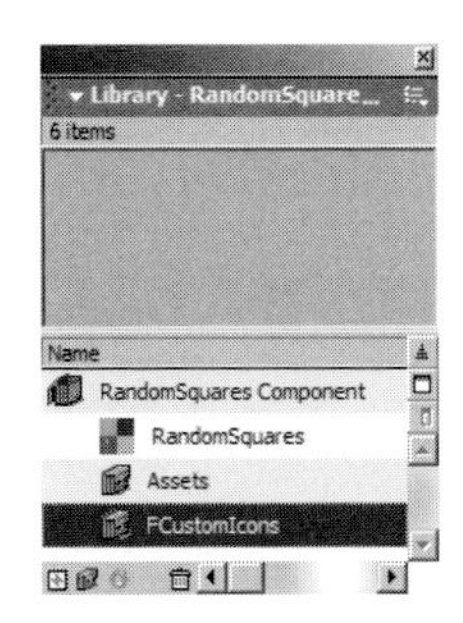

Figure 11.7

A custom icon replaces the default for the component.

At this point, if you were to close the library, go back to the main Timeline, and reopen the library, you should see the icon in place of the default. If it does not happen right away, you may have to close and reopen Flash MX. The steps to add a custom icon are very short and easy; you just have to take extreme care when you create the graphic.

Component Live Previews

In Chapter 4, you encountered the topic of live previews with the PixelButton component set. A *live preview* is simply a Flash movie that plays in place of the component movie clip on the stage, and only in the authoring environment. Live previews show you how your changes to the component's parameters affect the look of the component. Live previews are purely optional because they are meant only to aid you in using a component, so they can be turned off by clicking the Control menu and deselecting the Enable Live Preview option. The reason you might turn them off is because live previews can sometimes cause Flash or your computer to run slowly, since you may be running many SWFs at once.

The process to create a live preview is similar to that of creating a custom UI, but with fewer steps. The most important aspect of the procedure is to create a Flash movie that will take the values the user has entered for the component's parameters and render something useful to the stage from that information. No matter what frame rate the Flash movie is set to, Flash will force it to run at only one frame per second during a live preview so as not to take up too much of the computer's resources.

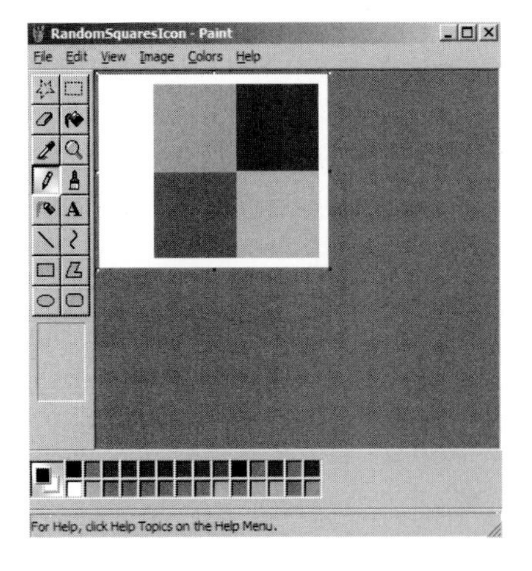

Figure 11.8

Be careful when positioning the graphic of the icon within the bitmap image.

The live preview movie consists primarily of two things: an `Object` variable named *`xch`* and a function named `onUpdate`. The *`xch`* object serves the same purpose as before; it simply holds the values of each parameter of the component. The only difference is that you cannot change the values of the parameters. The `onUpdate` function is called every frame by Flash and should be used to create a graphical representation of the component from the values of the parameters. For example, the PixelButton component from Chapter 4 colored the buttons differently depending on what colors you chose in the parameters. The size of the stage of the live preview movie should be exactly the size of the component with its default parameter values.

Once you have made the live preview movie, you should publish its SWF and open the FLA that holds your component. There is only one more thing you have to do to your component before you can plug in the live preview. Create a movie clip of an invisible rectangle with the exact dimensions of the stage used in the live preview, and then position the rectangle such that its top-right corner is at the center of the component. This movie clip defines the default dimensions of the component, and it is imperative for the live preview to work properly.

Finally, you can set the component's live preview to the SWF you created. Open the library, right-click the component, and select Component Definition. In the middle of the Component Definition dialog box, click the Set button to the right of the Live Preview box, as shown in Figure 11.9. In the Live Preview dialog box that opens, simply set the text field to the file path of the SWF you want to use and make sure that the live preview is embedded into the component.

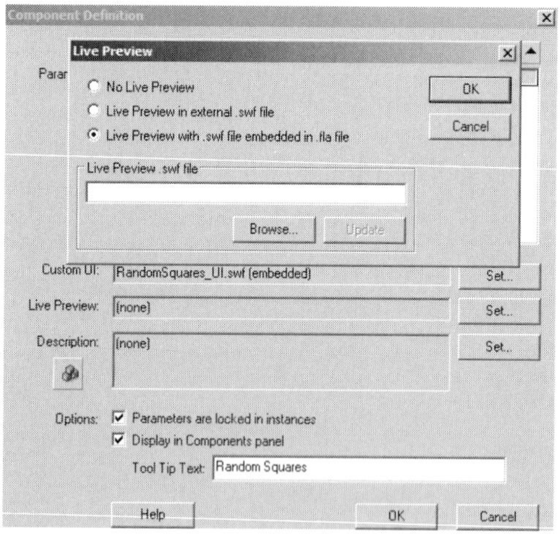

Figure 11.9
Add the live preview SWF to the component through the Component Definition dialog box.

That is the basic outline of how to create a live preview. Unfortunately, live previews are generally quite complicated, and the worst part is that most users will turn off the live preview option. Only consider creating a live preview if it is a very simple component to do so, and if the rendering of the live preview uses only the simplest commands. Usually, if users sense their authoring environment is being slowed down by something unnecessary, they will simply disable it.

Packaging Components for Mass Release

Packaging a component is one of the most useful features of components, especially when you want to distribute it to others, perhaps within your company. The process involves creating an XML file, although with a different extension, which is then used by the

Macromedia Extension Manager to create an MXP file. When a user opens the MXP file, it will install a component or components into the Components panel. You will need to make a small change to the component you want to include with the MXP package.

The XML file you need to create has a specific format to it, and it is not even of XML file type. The Extension Manager processes MXI files to create MXP files. Fortunately, you do not need to know anything about XML or anything related to it to create an MXI file. In the Chapter 11 folder on the CD, you will find a file named `MXI_Template.mxi`, which is a simple template for you to enter your own information into. Drag a copy of the file to your computer so that you can edit it. If you do not have any software in which to edit XML files, you can open a simple text editor and drag the file into the editor, as shown in Figure 11.10.

Once you are looking at the XML code, the first thing you need to change is the line that currently looks like this:

```
name = "Component Set Name"
```

The attribute `name` specifies the name of the component or set of components, which is displayed only in the Extension Manager. In the context of the RandomSquares component, you should set this value to `Random Squares Component`.

The next value you will edit is a node that allows you to put your name on the component. The author's name shows up in the last column of the Extension Manager, and it is important if you are going to distribute your component over the Internet. To set the author name, find the following line and edit it as you see fit.

```
<author name = "Author Name"/>
```

```
MXI_Template - Notepad
File Edit Format View Help
<macromedia-extension

        name            = "Component Set Name"
        version         = "1.0.0"
        type            = "flash component"
        requires-restart = "true">

        <products>
                <product name = "Flash" version = "6" required = "true"/>
        </products>

        <author name = "Author Name"/>

        <description>
                <![CDATA[Description of the component that shows up in the Extension Manager
        </description>

        <ui-access>
                <![CDATA[After installing the component you can find it in the Components Pa
        </ui-access>

        <files>
                <file   source = "ComponentSet.fla"
                        destination = "$flash/Components"
                        shared="false" />
        </files>

</macromedia-extension>
Ln 18, Col 13
```

Figure 11.10

You can edit the XML file by dragging it into a simple text editor such as Notepad.

The lines underneath the author's name allow you to provide a short description of what your component does, which is shown in the Extension Manager when a user clicks on your component. To change the default description, edit the string between the quotation marks of the following line:

```
<![CDATA[Description of the component that shows up in the Extension
➥ Manager.]]>
```

Finally, you must specify which components are being added to the Components panel. You do this by providing the file path to the FLA that contains your component or components. Then every component in the FLA is packaged into the MXP file. The divisions in the drop-down menu of the Components panel are determined by the name of the FLA that holds your components. Specify the component FLA by editing the line that currently looks like this:

```
<file source = "ComponentSet.fla"
```

You are now finished editing the MXI file. Before you can create the MXP file, you must open the `RandomSquaresComponent.fla` file to make one small change. In the library, right-click the component and select Component Definition. At the bottom of the dialog box, click the check box labeled Display In Components Panel and type the name of your component into the Tool Tip Text field, as shown in Figure 11.11.

Checking the option makes the component appear in the Components panel when installed by an MXP, and the text field specifies the tool tip text that appears when you hover over a component in the Components panel. Once you have made these changes, save the FLA and close Flash. Be sure that all windows of Flash are closed before you continue.

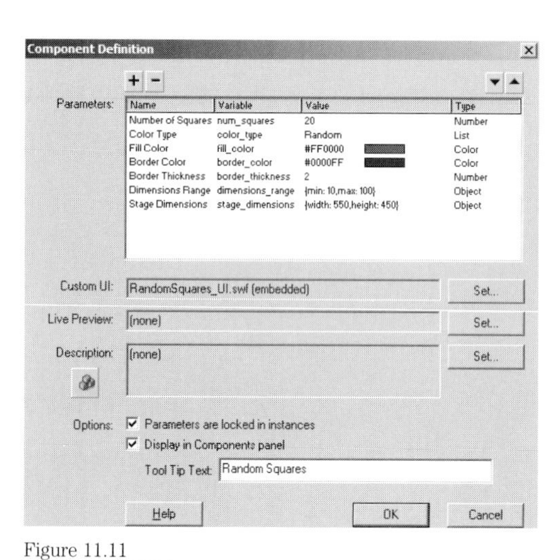

Figure 11.11

Make sure to allow the component to be displayed in the Component panel.

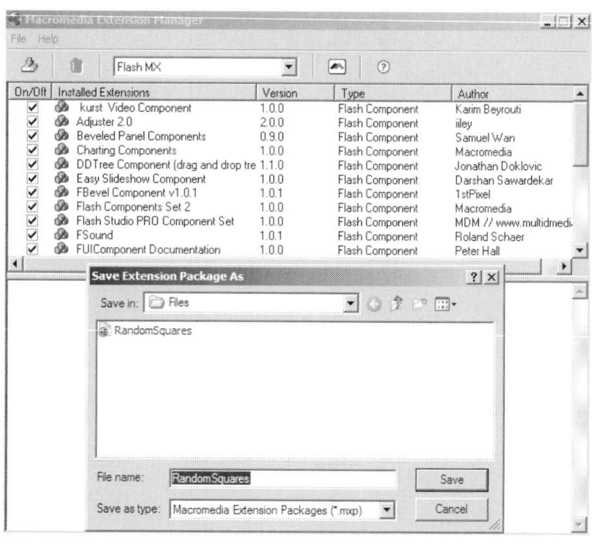

Figure 11.12

Create the MXP file by double-clicking the MXI file and selecting the name of the MXP package.

Now you can double-click the MXI file to open the Extension Manager, in which you will be prompted to choose a name for the MXP file that will be compiled from the MXI file, as shown in Figure 11.12.

It is the MXP file, and not the MXI file, that you will distribute to whomever you want to have your component. So choose a name and click OK, and the Extension Manager will create the MXP file for you. If you wish to test your work, double-click the MXP file and install your component. It should appear in the Components panel just as in Figure 11.13.

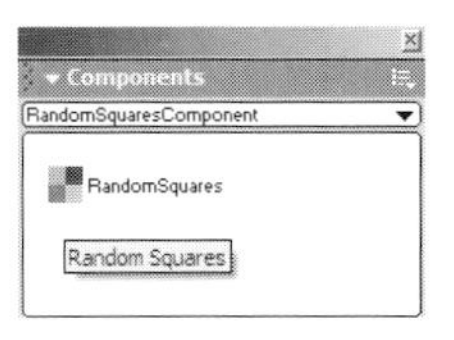

Figure 11.13

After you open the MXP file of the component, it should appear in the Components panel.

Obviously, your work is done in packaging your component. Be sure to keep in mind that you can put as many components into an FLA as you want and package them all in an MXP file. It simply means that there will be more components in a particular division in the Components panel. It is not uncommon for a company to build a large component library over the years and distribute MXP files of all resources to the company's employees.

Conclusion

In this chapter, you have learned the small extra touches that will separate your components from the mediocre ones. These include custom UIs, custom icons, live previews, and packaging your component sets into MXP files, all of which are intended to make your components more usable and approachable to others. At this point, you may feel you can do anything with your knowledge of components. But keep reading, for in our final chapter, we will discuss the common pitfalls encountered when creating components and other troubleshooting tips.

Chapter 12: Troubleshooting Components

By now you have learned nearly everything you need to know to take the full benefit from components, both by using and creating them. However, you might have noticed an inconsistency: components enhance your projects in a nonhassle way, but making them is far from being simple and hassle-free. This chapter eases the development process of components by exploring a few of the well-known pitfalls. These drawbacks include preloading problems associated with components, the quirks and inconsistencies of Flash that could make your component creation process a nightmare, and more.

Also discussed is the topic of Flash 5 compatibility. Most components in Flash MX can be made as smart clips in Flash 5, although more work is involved. If you have enough patience to make Flash 5–compatible components, you will have an advantage, considering the extensive penetration of the Flash 5 player. Flash 5–compatible components can be made in Flash MX, with all the benefits of the MX authoring environment.

On the whole, this chapter attempts to reduce your all-night sessions of hair-pulling, eye-gouging, debugging hysteria. Refer to this chapter for the small problems that break your component when you are absolutely certain that your code and design is flawless.

- **Preloading components**
- **Building conscientious components**
- **Common mistakes with MXP files**
- **Reducing errors when creating components**
- **Building components that are compatible with Flash 5**

Preloading Components

One of the most costly aspects of using components is preloading. As you saw in Chapter 10, components rely heavily on a structure that is organized by linkage names of the component's movie clip; you give the component a linkage name so you can associate the code for the component, which handles its functionality, with a movie clip, which is the graphical representation of the component. When you enter the linkage name for the component, you encounter a dialog box like Figure 12.1.

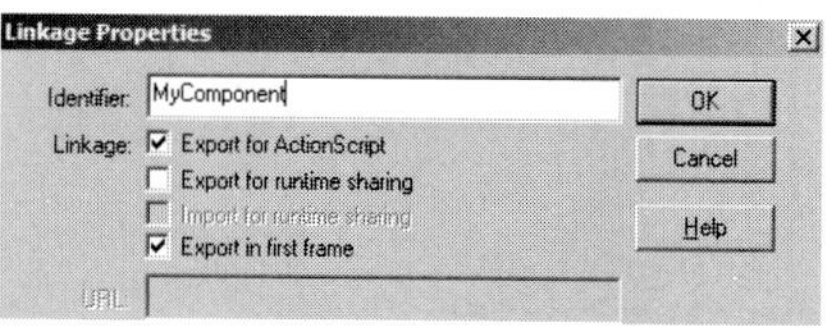

Figure 12.1
Linkage properties for a component

The last check box, Export In First Frame, is the key to the organization of the component structure. It forces the component movie clip and everything inside it to load before anything can happen in the movie; the term *anything* includes preloaders, animations, and actions. This means that the user will not see your preloader, or even know that the movie is loading at all, until the component is downloaded. Why would Macromedia impose this strange restriction? It makes sense when you consider the complicated relationship between the code and graphics of the component. Before Flash can set up the relationship we explored in Chapter 10, everything pertaining to the component must be downloaded.

Figure 12.2
Components in the library add kilobytes to your movie even if they are not on the stage.

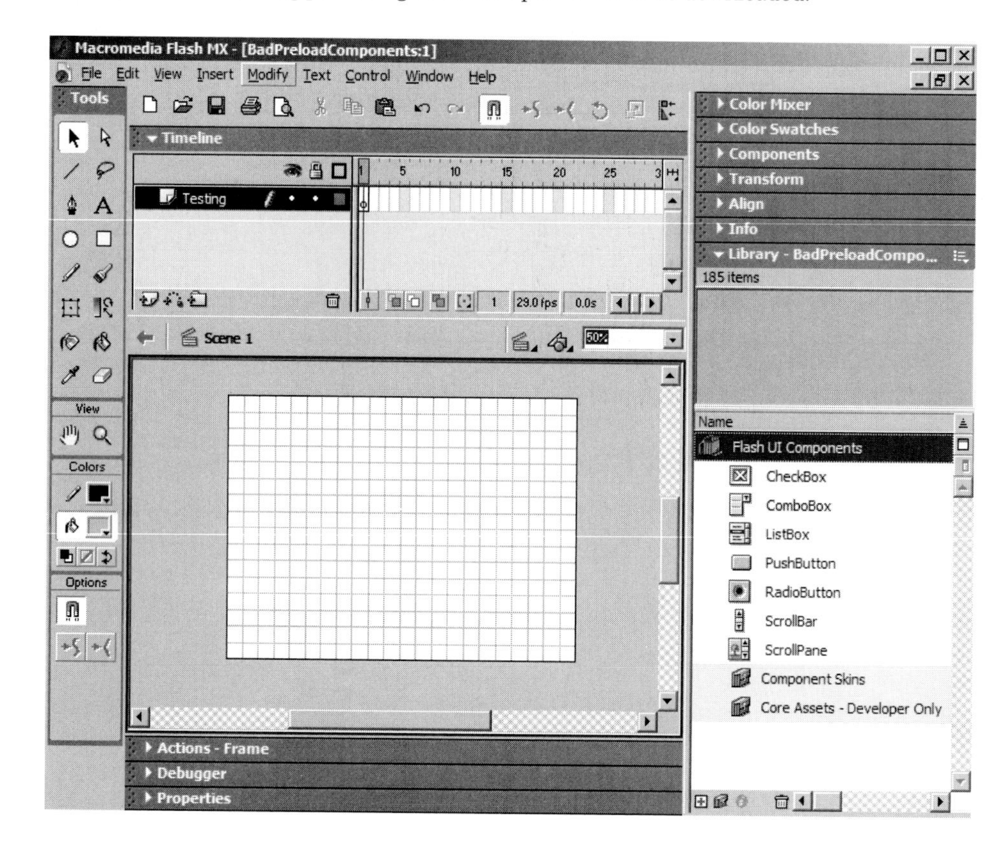

The Wrong Way

To see this problem in action, we can make use of the bandwidth profile in Flash's authoring environment. In the Chapter 12 folder on the CD, you will find the file `BadPreloadComponents.fla`, where all the components from the Flash UI Component Set, which comes with Flash MX, have been added to the movie's library. After you have opened the file, you will notice that none of the components are actually on the stage (see Figure 12.2).

Since each of these components has linkage names, they are exported with the rest of the movie when published to an SWF file, which explains the added kilobytes to the file even though they are not on the stage. The crux of the problem is exposed when we test the file in the authoring environment (press Command/Ctrl+Enter) and take a look at the bandwidth profiler (Command/Ctrl+B). The bar chart that appears at the top of Flash displays the number of kilobytes in each frame of the movie, which added together are the file size of the movie. This information tells us how much must be downloaded before a particular frame can be played; if any frame needs a lot of memory, we may want to cut it down for streaming purposes. Looking at the bandwidth profiler for this file (see Figure 12.3), we see something startling. The user must download nearly 100 KB before even a preloader will appear!

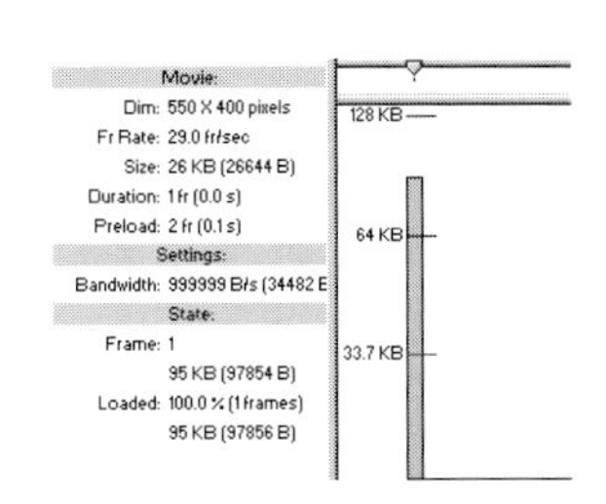

Figure 12.3

The user who views this file will need to download nearly 100 KB before the movie begins to play.

The Right Way

Seeing as how components are so useful, you might feel compelled to use many components in tandem to create a project. If so, a serious drawback comes about when using components: Do you take the full benefit of components and leave the user without a preloader, hoping that they wait long enough for everything to load? Or do you resort back to creating elements from scratch, but allow the user to once again find solace in the preloader? Luckily, there are a few tricks you can use to reduce the ghastly 100 KB to something more manageable.

Since a movie clip must have a linkage name to work with `attachMovie`, we keep from exporting the symbol. So, we are left with only one alternative: uncheck Export In First Frame in the Linkage Properties dialog box. The only problem with unchecking this option is that the symbol must be on the stage at some point in the movie in order for it to be exported at all. As a result, if you start unchecking the option in all of your components and their assets, you will end up with a broken component.

To see how to get the components back up and running even when the Export In First Frame option is unchecked, let's go back to the sample with all the UI components that came with Flash. Open `GoodPreloadComponents.fla` from the Chapter 12 folder on the CD. Three scenes have been created to organize the main parts of the file: Preloader, Pre-Assets, and Main. One holds the preloader, one holds all the assets that have had their Export In First

Frame option unchecked, and one holds the components as you want the user to see them. The intermediate scene, which simply holds assets and does nothing else, guarantees that the component and its assets are loaded before the components start to initialize and execute actions. It is also useful to have this scene if you are using a component only through `attachMovie`, in which case you would not have any instances on the stage.

In the Preloader scene, a very simple preloader, which is only there for reference, has been constructed. It simply takes care of displaying the percentage of the movie downloaded and plays the movie when finished downloading.

The Pre-Assets scene is the place we dump all of the assets for each component we are using. There is a very systematic way to do this, so don't rush into dragging a bunch of symbols from the library to the stage. Follow these steps:

1. Open the Pre-Assets library and make sure it is not docked with any other panels. Size the panel so that it is quite tall and wide enough to see the Linkage column, as in Figure 12.4.
2. Thoroughly scour each folder and their subfolders, looking for any symbol with a linkage name. If a symbol has a linkage name, the text Export:*LinkageName* will show up in the Linkage column, where *LinkageName* can be any string.

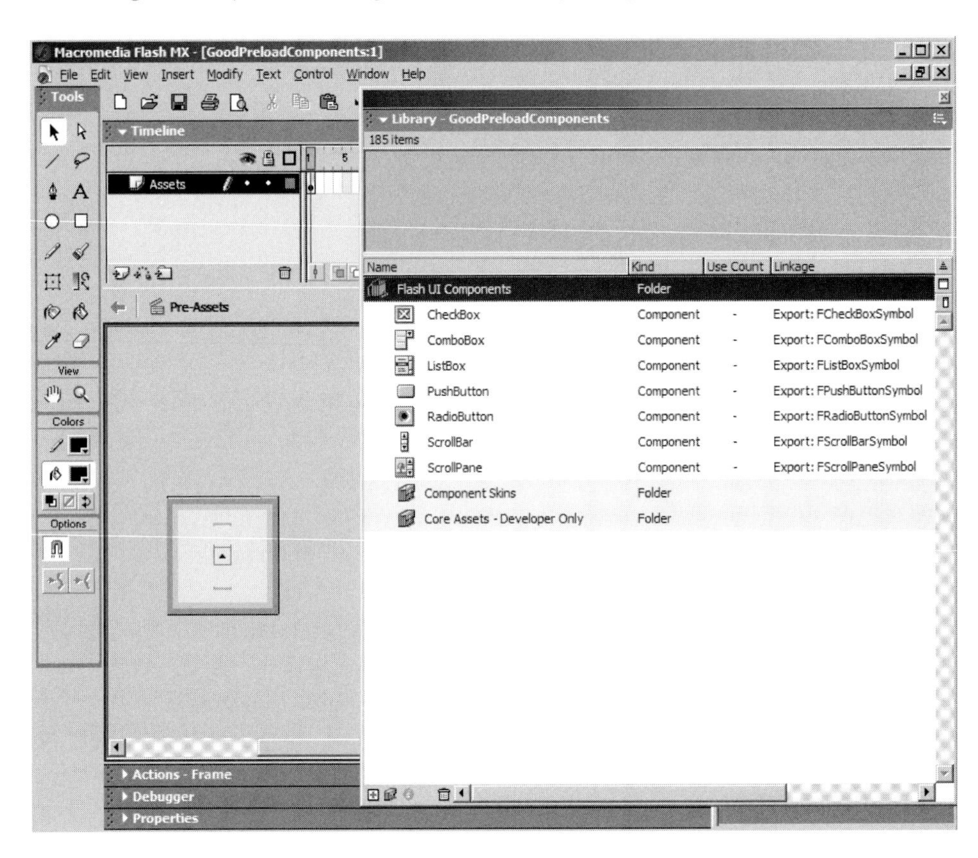

Figure 12.4

Open the library big enough to view many symbols at once and have the Linkage column in full view.

3. When you find such a symbol, open its Linkage Properties dialog box and uncheck Export In First Frame.
4. Drag that symbol to the stage.

Again, make sure you do all of this in the Pre-Assets scene, as it should all occur before any use of these components. Also, be sure to follow the above steps exactly; this is the only way to make sure you drag each symbol that was unchecked onto the stage. Any slip-up of unchecking a symbol and not dragging that symbol to the stage will ultimately render the component unusable.

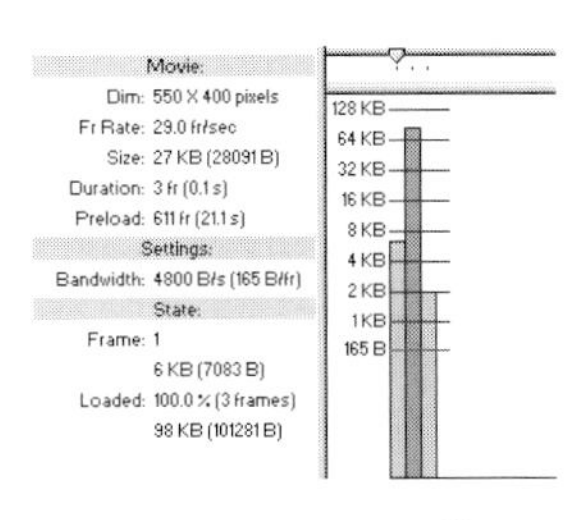

Figure 12.5

The bandwidth profile reports that only 6 KB needs to download for the movie to start playing.

The steps described were followed precisely to produce the `GoodPreloadComponents.fla` file. As a result, the bandwidth profiler reports the data shown in Figure 12.5 for the new file.

We have reduced the amount of data the user must download before the movie starts by over 1,500 percent to only 6 kilobytes, some of which is due to the preloader. The set of components is now in the most user-friendly way possible, and you've seen that one of the more serious drawbacks to using components has an elementary fix. Be sure to use this technique when using components to lessen their heavy blow on the preloader.

Building Conscientious Components

We've come to the conclusion that any project can use many components at once, and we should therefore be mindful of the preloading aspect. However, a completely conscientious component—one that is "aware" of what is going on elsewhere in the Flash movie—will do more than simply improve the preloading; it will be able to handle whatever the user throws at it, whatever the rest of the movie is doing, and all of this in an efficient manner.

Tracking a Component's Mode

With the preloading problem fixed, the next most important thing to keep in mind when creating a component is efficiency—its effectiveness at taking care of a task. Always remember that the user of your component will have many components in their projects, so you cannot tie up the CPU with many calculations. Your component is hardly ever going to be the only one in use; if you lose track of this, you will end up bringing the computer to its knees.

If your component is quite large and complicated, it is a good idea to have a ***`mode`*** variable that keeps track of the current mode of the component from a selection of many modes. For example, the audio and video components covered in Chapter 8 had modes for when the media played, stopped, paused, streamed, and so on. By keeping track of the mode of a component, you can make sure that you are performing calculations specific to some mode and not executing surplus actions that will not do anything, but nonetheless take up CPU cycles.

Tracking a Component's Mode by Strings

There are many ways to implement a mode system in your components, but we'll discuss two popular customs here. The first is using strings to determine a stage. Simply declare the variable **`mode`** in your component's ActionScript class and assign a string to it describing the mode it is in. Keep track of the modes that you allow the component to be in, maybe by making a commented list of the modes at the top of your actions. To change the mode of the component, simply reassign the **`mode`** variable to another string. Then, when you want to determine what mode the component is in, you can do a series of `if` statements:

```
if (this.mode == "Mode0")
{
   // actions for Mode0
}
...
if (this.mode == "ModeN")
{
   // actions for ModeN
}
```

Tracking Mode by Bitwise Operations

Another way to set up a similar system takes advantage of the bitwise operations Flash can perform. To understand bitwise operations, consider the fact that every positive integer can be represented as a string of 0s and 1s, called the *binary representation* of the number. You do not need to know anything about how to convert binary numbers to decimal or vice versa, because the idea is very simple. All you need to know is that each digit is associated with a decimal number that is a power of 2; the first digit is associated with 2, the second with 4, the third with 8, and so on to the nth digit, which is associated with 2^n.

> The more modes there are, the bigger the advantage of this "bitwise ops" method over the "strings" method.

To see how this information helps us, imagine a long string of digits, containing only 0s or 1s, where each digit has a mode linked with it. If the digit for a mode is 0, then the component is not in that mode, but if the digit for a mode is 1, then the component is in that mode. Therefore, instead of keeping track of strings, which use more memory than integers, we can use one binary representation to keep track of many modes once. In fact, if needed, we can have a component be in multiple modes at once.

Before we can use this type of mode tracking, we must first familiarize ourselves with bitwise operators. Each digit of a binary number is called a *bit*, so a *bitwise operation* is something that acts on the individual bits of the number. Given two binary numbers, say X and Y, the operator & is called the bitwise AND, and it performs a logical operation on each pair of bits in X and Y and returns a new binary string. If each bit in a pair is a 1, then the new string has a 1 in the same bit, otherwise there is a 0 in the bit. As an example, consider the following two binary numbers and the binary number that results from the action of &:

```
  1001101010
& 1100101000
  1000101000
```

Another bitwise operation is |, which is called the bitwise OR. Consider the action of the operation on two binary numbers X and Y. Taking each pair of bits in X and Y, we assign the resultant binary number a 0 if the pair consists of two 0s, and a 1 otherwise. For example, here is the previous example using | instead of &:

```
  1001101010
| 1100101000
  1101101010
```

Finally, the bitwise operation ^ is called the bitwise XOR, where XOR stands for exclusive OR. The ^ operation is the same as |, except for the case when both digits in a pair are 1, in which case the resultant binary number has a 0 in its digit. Here is our example using the ^ operator:

```
  1001101010
^ 1100101000
  0101000010
```

We construct this binary system for controlling the mode of a component by first declaring constants. The constants hold values of powers of 2 that represent each possible mode. For example, the AudioPlayer component discussed in Chapter 8 used the following constants for its modes:

```
this.PLAYER_INITIALIZING      = 2;
this.PLAYER_PLAYING           = 4;
this.PLAYER_STOPPED           = 8;
this.PLAYER_PAUSED            = 16;
this.PLAYER_CHANGING_VOLUME   = 32;
this.PLAYER_CHANGING_PAN      = 64;
this.PLAYER_STREAMING         = 128;
```

Remember that we use the variable ***mode*** to keep track of the current mode of the component. Before, when using strings, we would have to reassign the ***mode*** variable another string, but now we only need to find the bit associated with the mode we want to change to and set its value to 1. To do this, we concatenate the ***mode*** variable with whatever mode you want to change the component to by means of the | operator. In reverse, removing a mode from the ***mode*** variable is done with the ^ operator. Listing 12.1 is an example use of the bitwise operators.

Listing 12.1

Using the | and ^ Operators to Add and Remove Modes to the Component

```
// initial mode of the audio player
this.mode = this.PLAYER_INITIALIZING;
// change the mode to stopped and streaming
this.mode |= this.PLAYER_STOPPED;
this.mode |= this.PLAYER_STREAMING;
// remove the streaming and stopped modes, and set to playing mode
this.mode ^= this.PLAYER_STOPPED;
this.mode ^= this.PLAYER_STREAMING;
this.mode |= this.PLAYER_PLAYING;
```

Since the mode manager has been vastly changed through the use of bitwise operators, the way of checking which mode the component is in has also changed. To determine if the ***mode*** variable has a 1 in the bit associated with a certain mode, you merely concatenate the ***mode*** variable and the mode constant; it will return a 0 if the mode is inactive and return a nonzero positive integer if the mode is active. In other words, the series of `if` statements and string comparisons are replaced with the code in Listing 12.2.

Listing 12.2

Using the & Operator to Test Whether a Mode Is Active

```
if (this.mode & this.PLAYER_INITIALIZING)
{
}
if (this.mode & this.PLAYER_PLAYING)
{
}
if (this.mode & this.PLAYER_STOPPED)
{
}
if (this.mode & this.PLAYER_PAUSED)
{
}
if (this.mode & this.PLAYER_CHANGING_VOLUME)
{
}
if (this.mode & this.PLAYER_CHANGING_PAN)
{
}
if (this.mode & this.PLAYER_STREAMING)
{
}
```

By utilizing this new structure, we can manage many modes at once and mix and match distinct modes with each other. For example, using the binary mode system, the audio player was able to be in multiple modes at once. If the modes had been implemented via strings, I would have had to use many more string values. If you are wondering just how much "many more" is, then suppose your component can be in seven disjoint modes, much like the audio player. In that case, there are 128 ways to combine the modes into new modes. This is obviously very messy to keep track of.

Sizing a Component Interactively

Your component must be able to handle almost anything that happens to it. Flash MX provides some new tools that allow you to integrate components seamlessly. For example, the `Stage` object gives you access to properties of the stage that were unavailable in Flash 5, such as its width and height. If in your HTML page you have a Flash movie filling an entire frameset, table cell, or even the entire web page, then the embedded movie will change dimensions as you resize the browser window. Previously, it was impossible to get the data of how much of Flash's stage was visible, but now it is all public information, available through the `Stage.width` and `Stage.height` properties.

Before using the `Stage.width` and `Stage.height` properties, you must be familiar with the alignment conventions that Flash uses and its scaling modes. The `Stage.align` property is used to set the alignment of the Flash movie. The possible values you can assign to the property are listed in Table 12.1.

The `Stage.scaleMode` property forces the movie to a specified scale mode. Examples of these modes are when you right-click a Flash movie and select either 100% or Select All. The possible values you can assign to the property are listed in Table 12.2.

To see how each of these values affects the alignment and scale of a movie, open the `AlignOptions.fla` file in the Chapter 12 folder on the CD. A border has been drawn around the perimeter of the stage so that we can see where the stage is positioned when using the

Table 12.1

Possible Values for the `align` Property of the `Stage` Object

VALUE	FLASH MOVIE ALIGNMENT
T	The top of the stage is always at the top of the movie.
B	The bottom of the stage is always at the bottom of the movie.
L	The left edge of the stage is always at the far left of the movie.
R	The right edge of the stage is always at the far right of the movie.
TL	The top-left corner of the stage is always at the top-left corner of the movie.
TR	The top-right corner of the stage is always at the top-right corner of the movie.
BL	The bottom-left corner of the stage is always at the bottom-left corner of the movie.
BR	The bottom-right corner of the stage is always at the bottom-right corner of the movie.
[Default]	Any value different from the previous eight aligns the Flash movie such that the center of the stage is always at the center of the movie.

Table 12.2

Possible Values for the `scaleMode` Property of the `Stage` Object

VALUE	FLASH MOVIE SCALING
`exactFit`	The movie's stage (defined in the Document Properties dialog box) fits exactly in the player. This means that the contents of the Flash movie are stretched and distorted in order to fit into the player.
`showAll`	All of the movie's contents are visible and undistorted no matter how the user sizes the player.
`noBorder`	Nothing outside of the movie's stage is visible, but the movie is undistorted.
`noScale`	The movie does not scale at all in this mode.
[Default]	Any value different from the previous values sets the `scaleMode` to `noScale`.

various alignment values. Open the actions for the first frame, and you will see that each alignment value has been assigned to the `Stage.align` property, but all are commented out except for one. Experiment with the values by uncommenting one setting, commenting out all others, and then testing the movie.

Using this knowledge of alignment and scaling with the `Stage.width` and `Stage.height` properties, we can make movie clips that always stay in a certain corner of the movie even when the user goes wild with resizing the player. In the Chapter 12 folder you will find the file `CornerAlign.fla`. Four movie clips have been created in this file, and actions attached to them force them to stay in each of their respective corners no matter how the user resizes the player. It is best for you to see this yourself. Open the file, test it, and resize the Flash player to any crazy dimensions you want. In previous versions of Flash this was unheard of; there was no way to get the dimensions of the visible stage, let alone control the properties of the stage.

The file was entirely made from the actions in the first frame of the Actions layer. The first thing the actions take care of is setting the properties of the stage. Since we want to place movie clips in the corners of the stage, there should be no scaling involved when the user changes the dimensions of the player. Therefore, `Stage.scaleMode` is set to `noScale`. The top-left stage alignment was used, although any of the possible values could have been used. Top-left was chosen because the stage's origin (0,0) will always be at the very top-left corner of the player.

Next, the `onEnterFrame` handlers for each movie clip were set. These are functions attached to the movie clips that are called every frame. The functions take care of positioning the movie clips. The top-left movie clip is simply placed at (0,0), the top-right movie clip is placed at (`Stage.width`,0), the bottom-left movie clip is placed at (0,`Stage.height`), and finally the bottom-right movie clip is placed at (`Stage.width`,`Stage.height`).

Knowing this feature, you can build powerful components—for example, drop-down menus or audio players that snap to the sides of the screens. One component you might want to experiment with to test your knowledge of the Stage object and creating components is a BorderComponent: a component that will tile a graphic around the edges of the player. Since you can determine the edges of the player with the Stage object, all that's left is to position and scale some images around the border.

Making a Component Robust

Outside of making your component handle any situation, you also need to thoroughly test it to make sure there are no bugs. The first determinant of your component's stability is if it works with many instances of the component on the stage. Simply drag a few instances of your components, and even other components, to the stage and make sure your component functions as it should. Testing a component's functionality means experimenting profusely with the component's parameters. Try all combinations of the values, and make sure to try a few extreme cases, the types of values you do not expect a user to ever enter but that might break your component. Take debugging your component very seriously. In most cases, the foundation of your movie rests on the solidity of the components you use. You are in a sense trusting the components you use with the very idea and movement of your project, so you are in trouble if the basis of your system is buggy.

Reducing Errors in Component Creation

Now we will discuss some common mistakes you can make during the development process of components. Be sure to keep these ideas fresh in your mind while creating a component, as they are very annoying to correct when you are done.

By far the most aggravating problem you will encounter is making typos. Although you cannot fully prevent typos, you can try to avoid certain common mistakes. Firstly, the name of component's ActionScript class is more likely to be misspelled than anything else. Since you have to type it so many times, your fingers can become fatigued from doing the same thing. Therefore, it is best to go through each prototyped method you have written and make sure the name of the class is spelled correctly.

The most important step in the component creation process is setting up the relationship between the ActionScript class and component movie clip. You therefore need to double-check that this association has been set up correctly. Open the Linkage Properties dialog box of the component movie clip and check the spelling of the linkage name. Also check that you gave the movie clip a linkage name in the first place. Next, look in the actions of the component to confirm that the inheritance is set up correctly. In general, it should look like this:

```
Object.registerClass ("ComponentLinkage", ComponentClass);
ComponentClass.prototype = new MovieClip ( );
```

Finally, the last place to look for small faults is in the Component Definition dialog box. In it, recheck the names of the variables you are using for the parameters, and make sure those are the identifiers you use in your code. Often you will change and remove parameters from the component, and you must make sure that your code reflects all of those changes.

When Changing Parameters

The last thing you should keep an eye on is very counterintuitive, but it has caused developers the greatest distress. It has to do with the small irregularities in how Flash deals with the parameters of the component. When you drag a component to the stage, its parameters are changed to variables, as we saw in Chapter 10, but those variables stay local. Meaning, the only way to change them is to open the instance's Parameters panel and change those values. This may seem like common sense, but imagine this situation: You have an instance of your component on the stage while in middevelopment because you need it for testing. During this time, you change the component's default values, yet the instance of the component on the stage retains the same values as before. As a general rule, whenever you change the component's definition, you should delete all the instances off the stage, and redrag them to them to where you want.

Another quirk occurs when you change a component's definition while instances of the component are on the stage. If you change the component's definition in certain ways, such as adding a parameter or changing the name of a parameter, then the changes to the definition will not be saved. After closing the Component Definition dialog box and saving, the parameters will resort back to their values from before. Indeed, this is quite a strange happening, and it is probably a bug in Flash MX. So, from now on, delete all instances of a component off the stage if you are going to change its component definition, and replace the instances when you are done, or else the changes will not stay.

Common Mistakes with MXP Files

When working with MXP files, you need to think about a couple of things to deter any weird errors that may come from packaging your components. First and foremost, open the Component Definition dialog box and make sure you have checked the Display In The Components Panel check box. If left unchecked, the component will be installed to the Components directory by the MXP, but it will not show up in the Components panel.

There is also the problem of a component's assets not being included when a user drags an instance to the stage from the Components panel. When a component is added to a movie, only the symbols that are physically in the component are imported into the movie. Therefore, all asset movie clips, buttons, and graphics must physically be in the component to ensure that everything is brought with the component. To do this, you usually create an Assets layer in your component and throw all the symbols you need into the layer. But, to make sure that the assets will not drain the user's memory and that they do not interfere with the component's functionality, you usually make the layer a Guide layer; that way, the assets are actually in the component, but they are not visible to the user.

Flash 5–Compatible Components

Building Flash 5 components is more of an art than building Flash MX components; it takes time and quite a few neat tricks to make it work. At the beginning of the chapter, I said that nearly every MX component could be made to be Flash 5–compatible. This is true, but it is not without a little bit of extra work. Realize that you cannot use any MX-specific commands, such as the drawing methods, and you cannot directly set up the relationship between code and graphics via `registerClass`.

Something new to Flash MX, which should have been added a long time ago, is the ability to save the FLA file in the format of a past version of Flash. This means you can work in the Flash MX authoring environment but save the file as Flash 5, provided that you do not use any MX commands.

Modifying the Component Definition

Let's demonstrate making Flash 5 components by making the Particles component from Chapter 10 to be Flash 5–compatible. Follow these steps:

1. Make a copy of the component's FLA and rename it `ParticlesComponent_Flash5.fla`; for now, keep the file MX.
2. Open the library, and then open the Component Definition dialog box for the Particles component.
3. In Flash MX, you are allowed to add descriptive phrases for each parameter, but Flash 5 does not allow such a thing. In Flash 5, only the variable name column in Flash MX corresponds to the Variable column in Flash 5, so to set the variable identifier for a particular parameter, you must input under the Name column. Take all the text under the Variable column and put it in the corresponding entries under the Name column. Be sure you have deleted all text from under the Variable column. The Component Definition dialog box should now look something like Figure 12.6.
4. After you have fixed the parameters, you need to save the file as Flash 5. The reason you changed the Component Definition dialog box first is because in the process of a file being saved from MX to Flash 5, the Component Definition gets mucked up and is a pain to fix. To save as Flash 5, select File → Save As and select Flash 5 from the Save As Type drop-down menu.
5. As soon as you press the Save button, Flash informs you of all the Flash MX features that will be lost when you save as Flash 5. Continue to save as Flash 5; you will have to do without those features.

At this point, if you look in the Component Definition dialog box again, you will see that all Number and String data types have been changed to Default. Flash 5 components can have only three data types: Array, List, and Default. However, the Default behaves the exact same way as String. Furthermore, if you look in the side panel of any Actions window (see Figure 12.7), you can see the commands that cannot be used—the ones that are highlighted yellow.

Modifying the Component's Class

We now need to modify the code for the component to be Flash 5–compliant. We cannot use the two-part inheritance that associates the component with the code anymore, but we can do our best to approximate it. First, we remove the commands `#initclip` and `#endinitclip` from the top and bottom of the actions, as they cannot be used in Flash 5. Also, delete these two lines from the actions:

```
Object.registerClass ("ParticlesComponent", ParticlesClass);
ParticlesClass.prototype = new MovieClip ( );
```

The good news is that the component's class can be used with only a few changes. The first change we need to make is to set the parameters of the component in the class somehow. You can do this manually by going through each parameter and attaching its respective variable to the class via the prototype object. For our component, you can use the code in Listing 12.3.

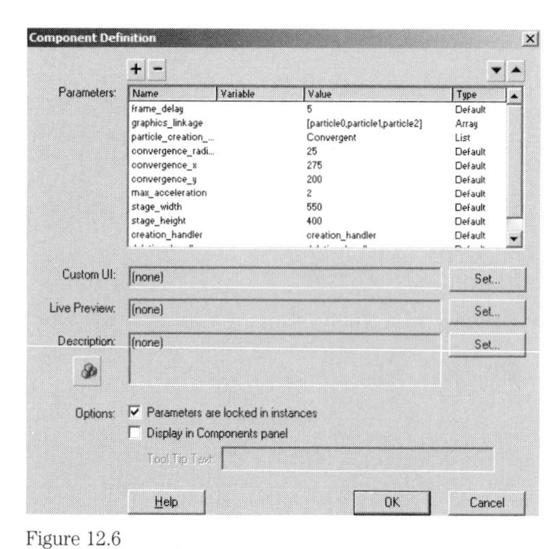

Figure 12.6

The Component Definition dialog box for the Flash 5 component

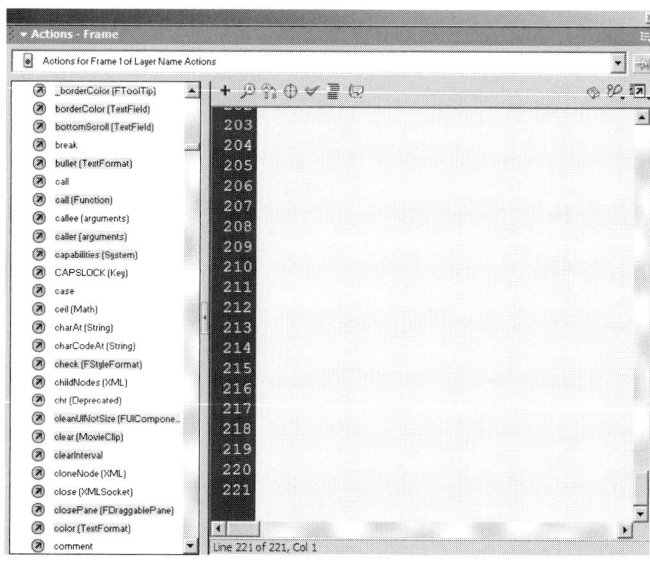

Figure 12.7

Commands that cannot be used in Flash 5 are highlighted yellow.

Listing 12.3

Creating Properties in the Component's Class for All of the Component's Parameters

```
ParticlesClass.prototype.frame_delay = Number (frame_delay);
ParticlesClass.prototype.graphics_linkage = graphics_linkage;
ParticlesClass.prototype.particle_creation_type      =
particle_creation_type;
ParticlesClass.prototype.convergence_radius = Number (convergence_radius);
ParticlesClass.prototype.convergence_x = Number (convergence_x);
ParticlesClass.prototype.convergence_y = Number (convergence_y);
ParticlesClass.prototype.max_acceleration = Number (max_acceleration);
ParticlesClass.prototype.stage_width = Number (stage_width);
ParticlesClass.prototype.stage_height = Number (stage_height);
ParticlesClass.prototype.creation_handler = creation_handler;
ParticlesClass.prototype.deletion_handler = deletion_handler;
```

Notice that we have wrapped the parameters that need to be of Number data type with the `Number` object in order to safely convert its data type. The actions in Listing 12.3 directly create new properties in the class for every parameter in the component.

Previously, we could simply use the keyword `this` to refer to the Timeline of the component, but we no longer have the luxury. Instead, we are going to create an extra property in the class named `timeline`, which will hold a reference to the component's Timeline.

```
ParticlesClass.prototype.timeline = this;
```

Now, we must take on the painstaking task of going through the entire class and finding all references to the component's Timeline, and replacing that reference with the newly added `timeline` property. Fortunately for us, our component needs only about five corrections. The first appears in the class constructor where we referenced `this._x` and `this._y`; it should be changed to this:

```
this.timeline._x = 0.0;
this.timeline._y = 0.0;
```

Next, in the `create_particle` method, we encounter the bit of code that attaches a random particle to the stage. Instead of attaching a movie to `this`, we now need to attach to `this.timeline`. Also, before, we were using the fact that `attachMovie` returns a reference of the newly attached movie clip, but this is not the case in Flash 5. So, we need to get the reference to that attached movie ourselves. It is done with this code:

```
// attach a new particle to the stage
this.timeline.attachMovie (linkage, "particle" + this.depth, this.depth);
var _mc = this.timeline["particle" + this.depth];
```

The only other two places we need to make `timeline` adjustments are where we call the creation and deletion handlers. Instead of referencing the `_parent` of `this` we need to reference the `_parent` of `this.timeline`.

```
this.timeline._parent[this.creation_handler] (_mc);
this.timeline._parent[this.deletion_handler] (_mc);
```

There are more changes to be made to the code, but they will come later. For now, we need to figure out a bigger problem. In the previous file, we had set up such a close relationship between the component movie clip and the component's code that an instance of the component was treated exactly as an instance of the class. But we do not have this extra anymore, so we have to manually create an instance of the class via the `new` keyword. So create another layer in the component named Initialization, and add the following code.

```
component = new ParticlesClass ( );
```

Modifying Functions and Methods

Now, we have all the functionality of the component bundled up into the instance of the class; how do we unleash its power? We need some way of firing the various event handlers of the component, such as onEnterFrame or onMouseDown. The way you could determine things like mouse down, key down, and so on is through the user of onClipEvent. It provides the means to detect all of the event handlers that were provided in Flash MX. And, luckily enough, we have a movie clip that does not have an entirely useful purpose in our component: the label movie clip. We can add movie events to the label movie clip that will fire all the various events that were written in the component's class. In the particular case of our component, we used only one event: onEnterFrame. But typically a component will use many events, so we fire every event from the onClipEvent actions in the label. Listing 12.4 shows how it is done.

Listing 12.4

Using a Movie Clip's onClipEvent Actions to Fire the Events of the Component

```
onClipEvent (load)
{
   _parent.component.onLoad ( );
}
onClipEvent (unload)
{
   _parent.component.onUnload ( );
}
onClipEvent (enterFrame)
{
   _parent.component.onEnterFrame ( );
}
```

```
onClipEvent (mouseDown)
{
   _parent.component.onMouseDown ( );
}
onClipEvent (mouseMove)
{
   _parent.component.onMouseMove ( );
}
onClipEvent (mouseUp)
{
   _parent.component.onMouseUp ( );
}
onClipEvent (keyDown)
{
   _parent.component.onKeyDown ( );
}
onClipEvent (keyUp)
{
   _parent.component.onKeyUp ( );
}
onClipEvent (data)
{
   _parent.component.onData ( );
}
```

This provides Flash MX functionality through Flash 5 commands. The component is almost entirely functional. The only parts of the component that need to be changed are the methods that we added to give the user control over the component through the use of ActionScript. These are methods that stop and start the stream, change the frame delay, and so on. In order to have those methods provide the same type of functionality as they do in MX, the user needs access to them as if they were directly attached to the movie clip. We can accomplish this by creating intermediate functions that are directly attached to the movie clip, and all they do is call the corresponding methods in the component class. Listing 12.5 shows the code that accomplishes this.

Listing 12.5

Functions to Handle ActionScript-Related Functionality That You Have Given to the User

```
stop_stream = function ( )
{
   this.component.stop_stream ( );
}
start_stream = function ( )
```

continued

continues

```
{
   this.component.start_stream ( );
}
change_frame_delay = function (delay)
{
   this.component.change_frame_delay (delay);
}
change_convergence_point = function (x, y)
{
   this.component.change_convergence_point (x, y);
}
change_convergence_radius = function (radius)
{
   this.component.change_convergence_radius (radius);
}
```

With the last line written, you are done converting a Flash MX component to Flash 5. The process was not entirely tedious, and in the end it is definitely worth it. Be warned that sometimes in the middle of the development process, you might hit Ctrl+S to save the file, and Flash will suddenly inform you that you are using a Flash MX element and the file must be saved in the MX format. Don't worry when this happens; simply hit Cancel and do the Save As routine to save the file as Flash 5. Flash will again warn you that all Flash MX–related content will be removed, at which point you can see what MX-specific elements you accidentally used.

Conclusion

Although Chapters 10 and 11 probably got your brain racing for original component ideas and experiments, this chapter really puts the lid on everything. The ideas developed here are very important to keep imprinted on the back of your eyelids. There is nothing worse than having a terrific idea for a component and ending up with broken, unrecognizable code that does nothing but laugh at your failures.

If you are reading these lines, then you have, I hope, read through the entire book. This means you now have no excuse for not creating components full time. Convince yourself that the next time you sit down to create something in Flash, you might as well make it a component. You can build a large library of components, keep them in the Components panel, and have easy, drag-and-drop elements in no time.

Index

Note to the Reader: Throughout this index **boldfaced** page numbers indicate primary discussions of a topic. *Italicized* page numbers indicate illustrations.

A

acceleration, 191
Action parameter
    for Click Action Parameters, 82
    for PixelButton, 58
Action Type parameter, 58, 67–68, *68*
actions
    associating with graphics, 213–216, *216*
    editing, 79–83, *79–81*
Actions parameter, 97
Actions On Press parameter, 51
Actions On Rollout parameter, 51
Actions On Rollover parameter, 51
ActionScript, 2, 80
    for Audio Player, 159–162, *159–161*
    for calling custom functions, 95–105, *96–98*, *103*
    for components, 74–79, *74–77*
    for navigation, 91–95, *91–94*
Advanced ActionScript parameter, 83
advanced mode in custom UI, 37
Advanced Script option, 82, 96
align property, 231–232
alignment of movies, 231–232
AlignOptions.fla file, 231
Alpha parameter, 108
ampersands (&)
    for bitwise AND, 229–230
    for entries, 168
AND operator, 229–230
animate_particles method, 201–202
animation components, 107–108, *109*
    common multiples, 129–130, *129–130*
    Concentric Path, 116–117, *116–118*
    embedded, 131, *132*
    general parameters for, 108
    limitations of, 126–128
    masked, 130, *131*
    modified
        Parallel Bars, 125, *125*
        Pebbles, 125, *126*
        Pond Ripples, 123–124, *124*
        Seeds, 122–123, *123*
    overlapping, 128–129, *129*
    Parallel Bars, 109–113, *109*, *111–113*
    Pebbles, 118–119, *119*
    Pond Ripples, 113–116, *113*, *115*
    Seeds, 120–121, *120–122*
AnimationComponents.mxp file, 108
Array class, 195
Array data type, 25, *25*, 184
arrays, zero-based counting in, 42
Art Today site, 12
AS_Controller_AudioPlayer.fla file, 159
assembling code, 198–199
    basic methods in, 199–203
    control methods in, 203–206, *205*, *207*
Assets folder, 189
associations
    actions and graphics, 213–216, *216*
    checking, 233
attachMovie method, 225–226, 237
audio components, 145
    Audio Player, 146–148, *146–147*
        ActionScript for, 159–162, *159–161*
        asset organization in, 154, *154*
        audio files for, 148–150, *149–150*
        element arrangement in, 153–154, *154*
        skinning, 150–153, *150–153*
Audio Control Buttons folder, 151
Audio Favorites Buttons folder, 151
Audio Pan Graphics folder, 152

Audio Player Component folder, 147
Audio Playlist Graphics folder, 152
Audio Track Graphics folder, 153
Audio Volume Graphics folder, 152
AudioPlayer Assets - Designers Only folder, 150
AudioPlayer.fla file, 146, *146*, 159
AudioPlayer.swf file, 146

B

B field, 60–61
Back_And_Forth value, 22, 27
background graphics, 152
BadPreloadComponents.fla file, 225
Balay, Scott, 9
Ball class, 194–195
Band Spacing parameter, 58, *66*, 67
Bar Thickness parameter, 110
Bar Thickness Variation parameter, 110
beginFill method, 182
Behavior parameter, 40, 46, *46*
binary numbers, 228
bitmap files, 217
bits, 228
bitwise operations, 228–231
Boolean data type, 184
Breathing Intensity parameter
  for Pond Ripples, 114
  for Seeds, 120
Breathing Variation parameter
  for Pond Ripples, 114
  for Seeds, 120
Brightness field, 60–61
Button Animation parameter, 172
Button Base Name parameter, 173
Button Height parameter, 57, 65, 67
Button Text parameter, 57–59, *58*
Button Width parameter, 57, 65, 67
buttons, 55
  color and font parameters for, 56–65, *56–58*, *60–64*
  dimensions of, 65–68, *65–68*
  MXP files for, 68–72, *68–72*

C

calling custom functions, 95–105, *96–98*, *103*
carets (^) for bitwise XOR, 229–230
Center x-Position parameter, 50
Center y-Position parameter, 50
Centerpoint Offset parameter, 114
Centerpoint Offset Variation parameter, 114
Chance Of Drop parameter, 117
Chance Of Switch parameter, 117
change_color method, 194
change_convergence_point method, 204
change_convergence_radius method, 204
change_frame_delay method, 204
Chapter2_A_Modified.fla file, 17, 28
Chapter2_A_Start.fla file, *16*, 17
Chapter3_A_Modified.fla file, 37, 39
Chapter3_A_Start.fla file, 37, *38*
character limitations in animation, 128
check_for_new_particle method, 199–200
Circle Radius parameter, 50
classes for components
  compatibility of, 236–238
  development of, 194–197, *196–197*
Click Action Parameters screen, 80–83, *80–81*, 92, *92*
click actions, editing, 79–83, *79–81*
clipart.com, 74
closing Components Parameters panel, 28, 47
code
  assembling, 198–199
    basic methods in, 199–203
    control methods in, 203–206, *205*, *207*
  for RandomSquares component, 186–189, *187*, *189*
color
  for buttons, 56–65, *56–58*, *60–64*
  random, 181
Color data type, 184
  entering, 111
  working with, 25–26, *26*
Color dialog box, 26
Color Mixing Chaos parameter
  for Pond Ripples, 114–115, *115*
  for Seeds, 120

Color Points list, 112
Color Points parameter, 108
Color Snap parameter, 108
combo boxes, 212–213
ComboBox component, 213
common multiple animation components, 129–130, *129–130*
compatibility of components, 235–240, *236*
Component Definition dialog box, 21–22, *21–22*
  for live previews, 218, *218*
  for parameters
    changing, 234
    defining, 183–186, *184–185*
    for Particles, 235–236, *236*
Component Elements folder, 122
component user interface (UI), *4*, 5
components, 1
  ActionScript with, 74–79, *74–77*
  animation. *See* animation components
  audio. *See* audio components
  buttons, 55
    color and font parameters for, 56–65, *56–58*, *60–64*
    dimensions of, 65–68, *65–68*
    MXP files for, 68–72, *68–72*
  compatibility of, 235–240, *236*
  creating, 179–180
    classes in, 194–197, *196–197*
    code assembly in, 198–206, *205*, *207*
    design in, 180–181
    modules for, 191–194
    random colors in, 181
    RandomSquares, 183–189, *184–187*, *189*
    squares in, 182–183
  description of, 3–4
  editing
    assets, 44, *45*
    click actions in, 79–83, *79–81*
  game. *See* game components
  identifying, 4–5, *4–5*
  interactive sizing of, 231–232
  live previews of, 217–218, *218*
  mode tracking, 227–231
  packaging, 218–221, *219–221*
  power of, 2–3, *2*
  preloading, 224–227, *224–227*
  robust, 233
  sources of, 11–12
  text effect. *See* text effect components
  troubleshooting. *See* troubleshooting components
  user interfaces with
    custom, 37–40, *38–40*
    default, 16–17, *16–17*
  uses for, 5–11, *6–8*, *10*
  video. *See* video components
Components Parameters panel, 18–20, *18–20*
  closing, 28, 47
  resizing, 48–50, *48–49*
Concentration components
  editing, 170–174, *171*
  images for, 174–178, *174–178*
concentration.fla file, 170, *171*
concentration game, 9–11, *10*
Concentric Path component, 116–117, *116–118*
conditional statements, 101–102
constructors, 198
Converge X parameter, 41
Converge Y parameter, 41
Convergence parameter, 41
Convergence Radius parameter, 190, 195
Convergence X parameter, 190, 195
Convergence Y parameter, 190, 195
copying components, 17, *17*
CornerAlign.fla file, 232
Correct Sound parameter for Quiz, 166
CorrectSound parameter in Concentration, 173
create_particle method, 200–201, 237
Creation Handler parameter, 191, 195
custom functions, calling, 95–105, *96–98*, *103*
custom user interfaces, 33
  3D Spin Menu component parameters in, 50–53, *51–53*
  associating actions with graphics in, 213–216, *216*
  Components Parameters panel resizing, 48–50, *48–49*
  using components with, 37–40, *38–40*

creating, 211–213, *211–213*
designing, 210
editing component assets, 44, *44*
feel of, 34–35, *34–35*
good and bad, 35–37, *36–37*
improvements in, 44, 46, *46–47*
purpose of, 210
Spikes component parameters, 40–43, *41–43*

D

data types for components, 20
Array, 25, *25*
Default, 23–24, 184
Font Name and Color, 25, *26*
List, 24
Number and String, 24
working with, 27–31, *27–30*
Default data type, 23–24, 184
default icons, 4, *4*
default user interface, 16–17, *16–17*
definitions
for component compatibility, 235–236, *236*
for parameters, 183–186
deletion_handler method, 206
Deletion Handler parameter, 191, 195
depth property, 201, 206
Designer Elements folder, 122
designing
components, 180–181
custom user interfaces, 210
Developer Elements folder, 122
device fonts, 138
dimensions of buttons, 65–68, *65–68*
Document Properties dialog box, 87–88
dragging components from libraries, 69
Draw Only Once parameter, 116
drawing squares, 182–183
Drop Down Menu component, 76–79, *76–77*
dropdown_press function, 97–98
dropdown_release function, 99–101
Duplicate Symbol dialog box, 43–44, *44*
dynamic masks, 130, *131*

E

Edit Click Action button, 80–81, *80*
Edit Selected option, 31–32
editing
click actions, 79–83, *79–81*
component assets, 44, *44–45*
Concentration components, 170–174, *171*
movie clips, 31–32, *31–32*
Quiz components, 164–168, *164–165*, *167*
element arrangement in Audio Player, 153–154, *154*
else if statements, 101–102
embedded animation components, 131, *132*
embedded fonts, 138–139, *138*
empty.swf file, 104
Enable Collision Detection parameter, 110
Enable Live Preview option, 217
Enable Simple Buttons option, 64
Enable Simple Frame Actions option, 64
endFill method, 182
Ending_Alpha parameter, 24, 27
#endinitclip command, 197, 236
entering color values, 111
equal (=) symbols for variables, 169
Erase Old Paths After parameter, 116
error-checking button, 215
Error opening URL message, 104
event handlers, 191
events for sound synchronizing, 149
Export For ActionScript option, 43
Export In First Frame option, 43, 224
Extension Manager
for components, 69–72, *70–71*
for MXP files, 219–221, *220*
Eyeland Studio, 11

F

Fade Out parameter, 114
fast_forward function, 162
favorites list, 147
File Name parameter, 165
filled area limitations in animation, 128

Flash 5 compatibility, 235–240, *236*
Flash Foundry site, 11
FlashComponents.com site, 12
FlashComponents.net site, 12
Flashkit.com site, 12
Flush Color parameter, 136
Flush Density X parameter, 136
Flush Density Y parameter, 136
Flush Start Difference parameter, 136
FlushEffect01_Sample.fla file, 136
FlushEffect02_Sample.fla file, 137
FlushEffect03_Sample.fla file, 137
FlushTextEffect components, 135–137, *135*, *137*, 144
Font Linkage parameter
  for ScrambleTextEffect, 141
  for SpinTextEffect, 143
Font Name data type, 25–26, *26*, 184
fonts
  for buttons, 56–65, *56–58*, *60–64*
  shared, 138–140, *138–139*, 144
FPS parameter
  for Audio Player, 148
  for Video Player, 157
Frame Delay parameter
  for Particles, 190, 192, 195
  for ScrambleTextEffect, 141
  for SpinTextEffect, 143
frames per second (FPS)
  for Audio Player, 148
  for Video Player, 157
functions for component compatibility, 238–240
FutureSplash, 73

G

G field, 60–61
game components, 163
  Concentration
    editing, 170–174, *171*
    images for, 174–178, *174–178*
  Quiz
    editing, 164–168, *164–165*, *167*
    images for, 168–170, *168–169*
Game Time parameter
  for Concentration, 171
  for Quiz, 165, 167, *167*
Games in a Flash site, 12, 164
global changes for movie clips, 31–32, *31–32*
GoodPreloadComponents.fla file, 225–227
gotoAndPlay action
  for 3D Spin Menu, 51
  for navigation, 93
gotoAndStop action
  for 3D Spin Menu, 51
  ActionScript for, 80–81, *81*
  for navigation, 92–95, *94*
Graphic Linkage parameter, 40–43, *41–42*
graphics
  associating actions with, 213–216, *216*
  in Audio Player, 153
Graphics Linkage parameter, 50, 52, *52–53*

H

height property, 231–232
hexadecimal color system, 112
High Alpha parameter, 41
HSB sliders, 36
Hue field, 60–61

I

icons
  creating, 216–217, *217–218*
  default, 4, *4*
identifiers, 173
if statements, 101–102
images
  for Concentration components, 174–178, *174–178*
  for Quiz components, 168–170, *168–169*
Import Audio option, 156
Import Video Settings dialog box, 155–156, *155–156*
importing videos, 155–157, *155–156*
#initclip command, 197, 236
Inner Bevel Color parameter, 57, 63–64, *63*

Inner Radius parameter
  for Concentric Path, 116
  for Seeds, 120, *121*
Inside Seed Scale parameter, 120
Install Extension option, 70
instances
  in animation, 127
  of components, 17
integers for backgrounds, 152
interactive component sizing, 231–232

J

Jump value, 22, 27

K

Keyframe Interval option, 155
KPT Effects plug-in, 34, *34*

L

layers for stacking components, 113, *113*
Lifetime parameter, 114
Line Color parameter, 116
Line Thickness parameter, 116
lineStyle method, 182
lineTo method, 182
Linkage Properties dialog box, 42–43, *43*
  checking, 233
  for Particles, 195–196, *197*
  for preloading components, 224, *224*, 227
List data type, 24, 184
Live Preview, 63
  for button dimensions, 65–68, *65–68*
  performance with, 59
  working with, 217–218, *218*
Live Preview dialog box, 217, *218*
Load Movie Level parameter
  for 3D Spin Menu, 51
  for Drop Down Menu, 90
  for PixelButton, 58
  purpose of, 77
Load Movie option, 82, 91
Load Movie SWF parameter, 58
Load URL option, 82
loading
  movies, 86, 89–91, *89–90*
  URLs, 83–86, *84–86*
LoadMovie function, 102–103
loop.fla file, 31–32
Loop parameter
  for FlushTextEffect, 136
  for ScrambleTextEffect, 141
  for SpinTextEffect, 143
Low Alpha parameter, 41

M

Macromedia Extension Manager
  for components, 69–72, *70–71*
  for MXP files, 219–221, *220*
Macromedia site, 11
Main Button Border Color parameter, 78
Main Button Color (Default) parameter, 78
Main Button Color (Over) parameter, 78
Main Button Width parameter, 77
Main Text Color (Default) parameter, 78
Main Text Color (Over) parameter, 78
masked animation components, 130, *131*
mass release, packaging components for, 218–221, *219–221*
Maximum Acceleration parameter, 190, 195
Menu Closing Speed parameter, 78
Menu Item Border Color parameter, 78
Menu Item Color (Default) parameter, 78
Menu Item Color (Over) parameter, 78
Menu Item Text parameter, 78
Menu Item Text (Default) parameter, 78
Menu Item Text (Over) parameter, 78
Menu Item Width parameter, 77
Menu Items parameter, 76, 79, 89
Menu Movement parameter, 51
Menu Shadow Color parameter, 79
Menu Shadow Offset X parameter, 79
Menu Shadow Offset Y parameter, 79
Menu Text Indentation parameter, 78
Methinks site, 12

methods
  for classes, 194
  for component compatibility, 238–240
mode tracking, 227–231
modified components
  Parallel Bars, 125, *125*
  Pebbles, 125, *126*
  Pond Ripples, 123–124, *124*
  Seeds, 122–123, *123*
modules, 191–194
Mouse Factor parameter, 51, 53, *53*
Movement Chaos parameter, 110
Movement Frequency parameter, 110
Movement Variation parameter, 110
Movement Velocity parameter, 110
MovieClip class, 196
movies
  editing, 31–32, *31–32*
  loading, 86, 89–91, *89–90*
  setting up, 86–88, *87–88*
music files. *See* audio components
MXI files, 219–221
MXI_Template.mxi file, 219
MXP files
  for buttons, 68–72, *68–72*
  for packages, 219–221
  troubleshooting, 234

N

names of parameters, 20
navigation
  scripts for, 91–95, *91–94*
  Springy Thingy for, 6–9, *6–8*
new keyword, 238
newyork.fla file, 87–91, *88*, *90*
next_track function
  for Audio Player, 160
  for Video Player, 162
nextFrame action, 51
Num Visible Songs parameter, 148
Num Visible Videos parameter, 157
Number data type, 24, 184
Number Of Available Pieces parameter, 171–172
Number Of Columns parameter, 172
Number Of Graphics parameter, 40, 46, *46*
Number Of <items> parameter, 108
Number Of Rings parameter, 116
Number Of Rows parameter, 172
Number Of Seeds parameter, 121
Number Of Video Frames To Encode Per Number Of Macromedia Flash Frames option, 156

O

Object Base Name parameter, 172–173
Object class, 211
Object data type, 184
Object Sound Base Name parameter, 173
Olives site, 9
onClickEvent function, 186, *187*
onClipEvent function, 238–239
One Chance parameter, 166
onEnterFrame function, 214–215, 232
onLoad function, 213–214
onRelease function, 215
onUpdate function, 218
opacity
  for animation components, 108
  sliders for, 34, *35*
OR operator, 229–230
Outer Bevel Color parameter, 63–64, *63–64*
Outer Radius parameter
  for Concentric Path, 116
  for Pond Ripples, 114
  for Seeds, 120, *121*
Outside Seed Scale parameter, 120
overlapping animation components, 128–129, *129*

P

packaging components, 218–221, *219–221*
Padding parameter, 172
Parallel Bars component, 109, *109*
  basics, 109–110
  examples, 110–113, *111–113*
  modified, 125, *125*
parameters, 16–17, *16–17*

defining, 183–186, *184–186*
for Spikes component, 40–43, *41–43*
troubleshooting, 234
Parameters tab, *4*, 5
_parent portion, 95
Particle Creation parameter, 190, 195
Particle Graphics parameter, 195
Particle Graphics Linkage parameter, 190
Particles component, 189–191
assembling code for, 198–206, *205*, *207*
classes for, 194–197, *196–197*
modules for, 191–194
Particles_onEnterFrame function, 199
ParticlesClass, 196–197
ParticlesComponent.fla file, 195
ParticlesComponent_Flash5.fla file, 235
ParticlesComponent_Sample.fla file, 204, 206
pause function
for Audio Player, 160
for Video Player, 162
Pause parameter, 27
Pebble Size parameter, 118
Pebble Size Variation parameter, 118
Pebbles component, 118, *119*
basics, 118–119
examples, 119, *119*
modified, 125, *126*
performance with Live Preview, 59
Perspective Depth parameter, 51
PixelButton component, 56–58, *57*
PixelButton.fla file, 56, *56*
PixelComponentSet.mxp file, 70–71, *71*
PixelFlatRadioButton component, 71
PixelRadioButton component, 71
play action
for 3D Spin Menu, 51
for navigation, 95
play function
for Audio Player, 160
for Video Player, 162
Playlist Position parameter
for Audio Player, 148
for Video Player, 157
Pond Ripples component, 113, *113*
basics, 113-114
examples, 115, *115*
modified, 123–124, *124*
pop-up help fields, 37, *37*
Pre-Assets scene, 226–227
preloading components, 224–227, *224–227*
prevFrame action, 51
previews of components, 217–218, *218*
Previous Page button, 79
previous_track function
for Audio Player, 160
for Video Player, 162
properties, 194
Properties panel, 4–5, *4–5*, 18–19, *19*
prototype object, 194
Publish Settings dialog box, 85, *85*

Q

Quality option, 155
Question Time parameter, 165, 167, *167*
Question Time Expired parameter, 166–167
Questions Per Quiz parameter, 165
Quiz component
editing, 164–168, *164–165*, *167*
images for, 168–170, *168–169*
quiz.fla file, 164, *164*
quiz.txt file, 164, 167–170, *169*

R

R field, 60–61
random colors, 181
random function, 181
Random_Position parameter, 27
Random Wandering parameter, 117
RandomFluidMovement.fla file, 192
RandomSquares component, 183
code for, 186–189, *187*, *189*
parameters for, 183–186, *184–186*
RandomSquares_UI.fla file, 211–212
RandomSquaresComponent.fla file, 183, 211–212, 216, 220
Region Height parameter

for Parallel Bars, 110
for Pebbles, 118
Region Width parameter
for Parallel Bars, 110
for Pebbles, 118
registerClass function, 196, 233, 235
registering classes, 196–197
relative paths, 103
resizing Components Parameters panel, 48–50, *48–49*
Resolution parameter, 116
rewind function, 162
RGB values, 36
Ring Thickness parameter, 114
Ring Thickness Variation parameter, 114
robust components, 233
Rollover Inner Bevel Color parameter, 57
Rollover Outer Bevel Color parameter, 57, 64–65, *64*
_root portion, 92–95
Rotation Speed parameter, 119
Rotation Variation parameter, 119

S

Saturation field, 60–61
scale
of imported videos, 156
of movies, 231–232
Scale option, 156
scaleMode property, 231–232
ScrambleEffect01_Sample.fla file, 140, *140*
ScrambleEffect02_Sample.fla file, 141
ScrambleEffect03_Sample.fla file, 141
ScrambleTextEffect component, 140–142, *140*, *142*
Screen Height parameter, 41
Screen Width parameter, 41
scripts, 2, 80
for Audio Player, 159–162, *159–161*
for calling custom functions, 95–105, *96–98*, *103*
for components, 74–79, *74–77*
for navigation, 91–95, *91–94*
Seeds component, 120, *120*
basics, 120–121, *120–121*
examples, 121, *121*
modified, 122–123, *123*
SeedShape component, 122–123
setSelectedIndex function, 214
shared fonts, 138–140, *138–139*, 144
Show Build Process parameter
for Pebbles, 119
for Pond Ripples, 114
for Seeds, 121
Show Correct parameter, 166
Show Matched Pieces parameter, 172
Show Total Quiz Number parameter, 166
Shuffle? parameter
for Audio Player, 148
for Video Player, 157
Simple ActionScript parameter
for Click Action Parameters, 83
support by, 92
Simple Script option, 82, 92
size
of buttons, 65–68, *65–68*
of components, 231–232
of Components Parameters panel, 48–50, *48–49*
skinning
Audio Player, 150–153, *150–153*
Video Player, 158–159, *158*
sliders
for Audio Player, 152
for HSB, 36
for opacity, 34, *35*
smart clips, 3–4, *4*, 70
Snap To Colors parameter, 108
Song Names parameter, 147
Song URLs parameter, 147
songs folder, 146
SoundRangers site, 148
Spikes Background component
creating, 37–40, *38*
parameters for, 40–43, *41–43*

spikes_sc_UI.swf file, 39–40
Spikes SM Assets folder, 42, *42*
Spin Behavior parameter, 50
Spin Control parameter, 50
Spin Radius parameter, 143
SpinEffect01_Sample.fla file, 142, *142*
SpinEffect02_Sample.fla file, 143
SpinEffect03_Sample.fla file, 143
SpinTextEffect components, 142–144, *142–144*
Spring Inertia parameter, 78
Spring Stiffness parameter, 78
Springy Thingy component, 6–9, *6–8*
squares, drawing, 182–183
Stage class, 231–232
Stage Height parameter
  for Particles, 191, 195
  for ScrambleTextEffect, 141
Stage Width parameter
  for Particles, 191, 195
  for ScrambleTextEffect, 141
Stage_X parameter, 27
Stage_Y parameter, 27
start_stream method, 203, 205
Starting_Alpha parameter, 24, 27
stop action
  for 3D Spin Menu, 51
  for navigation, 95
stop function
  for Audio Player, 160
  for Video Player, 162
stop_fast_forward function, 162
stop_rewind function, 162
stop_stream method, 203, 205
Stray Angle parameter, 41
Stray Convergence parameter, 41
Stray Graphic Linkage parameter, 40–41
Stray Probability parameter, 41
streams for sound synchronizing, 149, *149*
String data type, 24, 184
strings for component mode tracking, 228
Sub Item, 77, 81
.swf files, 39, 149
Synchronize Video To Macromedia Flash Document Frame Rate option, 156

T

take2.fla file, 74–75, *74*, 86–88, *86*
take2_function.fla file, 96, 98
take2_function.swf file, 104
Terrazzo plug-in, 34, *34*
Text Alignment parameter, 136
Text Color parameter
  for FlushTextEffect, 136
  for PixelButton, 57, 60–61
  for ScrambleTextEffect, 141
  for SpinTextEffect, 143
text effect components, 133
  Flush, 135–137, *135*, *137*, 144
  purpose of, 134
  Scramble, 140–142, *140*, *142*
  set of, 134–135, *134–135*
  shared fonts in, 138–140, *138–139*, 144
  Spin, 142–144, *142–144*
Text Font parameter
  for FlushTextEffect, 136
  for PixelButton, 57, 61, *61*
Text Kerning parameter
  for ScrambleTextEffect, 141
  for SpinTextEffect, 143
Text Messages parameter
  for FlushTextEffect, 136
  for ScrambleTextEffect, 141
  for SpinTextEffect, 143
Text Shadow Color parameter, 79
Text Shadow Offset X parameter, 79
Text Shadow Offset Y parameter, 79
Text Size parameter
  for FlushTextEffect, 136
  for PixelButton, 57, 60, *60*
  for ScrambleTextEffect, 141
  for SpinTextEffect, 143
TextEffectSet.mxp file, 134
TextField_Testing.fla file, 138, *138*
this keyword, 187, 194
3D_menu_UI.swf file, 40
3D Spin Menu component, 50–53, *51–53*
Time To Display Correct Answer parameter, 166
Timeline, 149
timeline property, 237

trace actions, 215
tracking, mode, 227–231
Transition parameter, 27
transparency limitations in animation, 127
troubleshooting components, 223
  compatibility, 235–240, *236*
  creation, 233–234
  interactive sizing, 231–232
  mode tracking, 227–231
  MXP files, 234
  parameters, 234
  preloading, 224–227, *224–227*
  robustness, 233
tweens, 123
types for components, 20
  Array, 25, *25*
  Default, 23–24, 184
  Font Name and Color, 25, *26*
  List, 24
  Number and String, 24
  working with, 27–31, *27–30*
typos, 233

U

Uncovered Frame Delay parameter, 136
URL parameter, 58
URL Target parameter, 82, 85
URL To Load parameter, 82
URL Window parameter
  for 3D Spin Menu, 51
  for PixelButton, 58
URLs, loading, 83–86, *84–86*
user interfaces
  for components, 16–17, *16–17*
  custom. *See* custom user interfaces

V

value types, 20
  Array, 25, *25*
  default, 23–24
  Font Name and Color Value, 25–26, *26*
  List, 24
  Number and String, 24
  working with, 27–31, *27–30*
Values dialog box, 25
variables. *See also* parameters
  importance of, 180
  for Object, 211
velocity, 191–192
vertical bars (||) for bitwise OR, 229–230
video components, 145
  Video Player, 155, *155*
    importing videos with, 155–157, *155–156*
    parameters for, 157
    skinning, 158–159, *158*
Video Control Buttons folder, 158
Video Playlist Graphics folder, 158
Video Position parameter, 157
Video Track Graphics folder, 158
Video URLs parameter, 157
Video Volume Graphics folder, 158
VideoNames parameter, 157
VideoPlayer.fla file, 157

W

Waiting Sound parameter, 166–167
white dot character, 103, *103*
width property, 231–232
Williams, Brandon, 9
wizard mode in custom UI, 37
Wrong Sound parameter for Quiz, 166
WrongSound parameter in Concentration, 173

X

X Placement parameter, 173
xch object, 213
xch variable, 211, 218
XML files, 219, *219*
XOR operator, 229–230
XYZ Rotation parameter, 117, *118*

Y

Y Placement parameter, 173

Z

zero-based counting in arrays, 42
Zoom component, 21–22, *21–22*, 28–30, *29–30*
Zoom parameter, 27, *27*
Zoom_Percentage parameter, 23–24, 27–28
Zoom_Speed parameter, 27

ABOUT SYBEX

Sybex has been part of the personal computer revolution from the very beginning. We were founded in 1976 by Dr. Rodnay Zaks, an early innovator of the microprocessor era and the company's president to this day. Dr. Zaks was involved in the ARPAnet and developed the first published industrial application of a microcomputer system: an urban traffic control system.

While lecturing on a variety of technical topics in the mid-1970s, Dr. Zaks realized there wasn't much available in the way of accessible documentation for engineers, programmers, and businesses. Starting with books based on his own lectures, he launched Sybex simultaneously in his adopted home of Berkeley, California, and in his original home of Paris, France.

Over the years, Sybex has been an innovator in many fields of computer publishing, documenting the first word processors in the early 1980s and the rise of the Internet in the early 1990s. In the late 1980s, Sybex began publishing our first desktop publishing and graphics books. As early adopters ourselves, we began desktop publishing our books in-house at the same time.

Now, in our third decade, we publish dozens of books each year on topics related to graphics, web design, digital photography, and digital video. We also continue to explore new technologies and over the last few years have been among the first to publish on topics like Maya and Photoshop Elements.

With each book, our goal remains the same: to provide clear, readable, skill-building information, written by the best authors in the field—experts who know their topics as well as they know their audience.